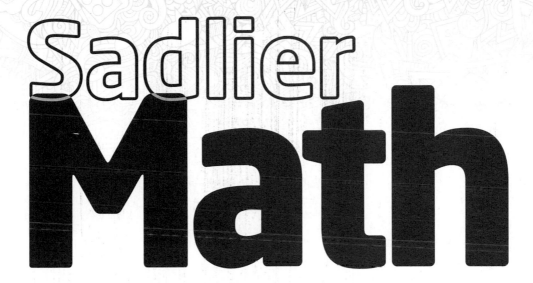

Sadlier Math

Catherine D. LeTourneau

Allan E. Bellman, Ph.D.

Jill A. Perry, Ph.D.

Sadlier School

The Publisher of *Progress in Mathematics*

Program Reviewers

The publisher wishes to thank for their comments and suggestions the following teachers and administrators, who read portions of the series prior to publication.

Cover Series Design: Silver Linings Studios

Photo Credits

Cover: NASA Dryden Flight Research Photo Collection/Helios/Carla Thomas: *bottom*. Shutterstock.com/Lixiang: *top*.

Interior: age fotostock/James Kirkikis: 87; Valery Vvoennyy: 219; ardea.com/Nick Gordon: 26; WaterFrame/imageBROKER: 11. Alamy Stock Photo/marrakeshh: 40; PjrNature: 341; Tim Gainey: 23; Anton Gvozdikov: 276; Richard Maschmeyer: 338; Ian Shaw: 41; Peter Howard Smith: 351; Inga Spence: 95; Danita Delimont/Darrell Gulin: 244; imageBROKER/Frank Sommariva: 43; Panther Media GmbH: 222; Photicon: 363 *right*; Zoonar GmbH/Sergey Galushko: 297. Dreamstime.com/Alisonh29: 121, 139; Picturecorrect: 64; Serhiy Shuilye: 119. Fotolia.com/Cherries: 239; destina: 366 *left*; nikonomad: 21; weerapat1003: 294; BillionPhotos.com: 287. Getty Images/btrenkel: 359; Steve Bronstein: 241; Robbie George: 111; Steve Heap: 195 *bottom*; Dorling Kindersley/Max Gibbs: 363 *left*; Mark Anderson Photography: 97. iStockphoto.com/wsfurlan: 356. Science Source/Mark Garlick: 186 *bottom*; Volker Steger: 298. Shutterstock.com/alexmisu: 67; andik76: 379; cbpix: 303; equinoxvect: 39; Fotofermer: 375 *left*; irin-k: 375 *center right*; MarcelClemens: 1; marchello74: 197; niceregionpics: 302; optimarc: 315; tcareob72: 144; trekandshoot: 369; vvoe: 176; Zorro12: 262; sumroeng chinnapan: 366 *right*; Jenov Jenovallen: 366 *center*; Lucie Lang: 375 *right*; Catalin Petolea: 141; John Swanepoel: 186 *top*; Theerasak Tammachuen: 363 *center*; Charles Taylor: 45; Iryna Tiumentseva: 261; Donovan van Staden: 318; Globe Turner: 349; Mega Pixel: 375 *center left*; Pavel L Photo and Video: 167. Wikimedia Commons/Royal Museums of Fine Arts of Belgium, Brussels: 60. Wikipedia: 317. United States coin images from the United States Mint.

Illustrators

Ken Batelman, David Brooks, Vic Kulihin, Andrew Roberts, Steve Stakiewicz. Shutterstock.com/Agor2012, incredible_movements, miniaria, whanwhan.ai, Zmiter.

For additional online resources, go to SadlierConnect.com.

Welcome to Sadlier Math

Dear Fifth Grader,

Do you know why math is important? Well, we all use math every day.
We use it when we:

- build a stage prop
- calculate attendance
- pick fruit
- compare pH levels
- measure a lobster
- and much more!

Throughout your books are special signs and symbols. When you see them, be sure to stop and look.

Objective This is what you will be studying in the lesson.

Math Words Look at these words. They are important math vocabulary words for the lesson.

Problem Solving Get ready to apply math in real-world contexts.

Write About It This is a question or topic for you to write about.

PRACTICE These are exercises for you to show what you know.

MORE PRACTICE These are exercises for you to build more understanding.

HOMEWORK These are exercises for you to do at home.

We wrote this book just for you!

The Authors

Hi. We are your new math friends. When you see us, pay attention. We have a lot to say!

CONTENTS

Chapter 1 Place Value, Addition and Subtraction

The upper half of your book's front cover shows a biplane. Biplanes have two wings stacked one above the other. A biplane invented by Orville and Wilbur Wright made the world's first successful powered flight in 1903.

Chapter 2 Place Value and Decimals

Chapter 3 Multiplication

Chapter 4 Division

Chapter 5 Number Theory and Fractions

Chapter 6 Fractions: Addition

Biplanes were good choices for early aircraft engines, which were low-powered and couldn't produce much speed. The biplane's greater wing area and light weight allowed it to fly slowly without stalling.

Chapter 7 Fractions: Subtraction

Chapter 8 Fractions: Multiplication

Chapter 9 Fractions: Division

Chapter 10 Decimals: Addition

As the power of aircraft engines increased and greater speeds became possible, biplanes were replaced by single-wing aircraft. A single-wing plane produced less drag and could fly much faster.

Chapter 11 Decimals: Subtraction

Chapter 12 Decimals: Multiplication

The development of the jet engine during World War II led to even faster planes. Today's jet-powered passenger aircraft travel over 500 miles per hour. Some military jets can exceed 2000 miles per hour!

Chapter 13 Decimals: Division

Chapter 14 Measurement

Chapter 15 Geometry

The bottom half of your front cover shows an unmanned, solar-powered aircraft. The aircraft's huge wing was assembled from 6 rectangular sections, each 41 feet long by 8 feet wide.

Chapter 16 Volume

The solar arrays on the wing of the aircraft on your cover allowed it to fly nonstop for more than 24 hours and reach altitudes of nearly 100,000 feet. That's about 3 times as high as a typical passenger jet flies!

Chapter 17 Graphs and Data

PROBLEM SOLVING MATH PRACTICES

You can become a problem-solving super sleuth! Here are some practices and strategies to use this year.

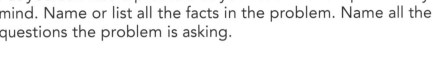

Use these four steps when you solve problems.

Read and Understand

Put yourself into a problem as you read. Make a picture in your mind. Name or list all the facts in the problem. Name all the questions the problem is asking.

Represent the Situation

Show what the problem is about. Use a model, equation, or picture. Be sure to label important information.

Make and Use a Plan

Make a plan for solving the problem. Choose one or more strategies to use. Is this problem like others you have solved? What operations will you use? Estimate before you calculate. Show your work.

Look Back

Be sure you answered everything. Is your answer reasonable? Look back over your work for mistakes. Estimate to check for errors. Be ready to explain how you know your answer is reasonable.

Read the next pages with your teacher and your family. You will find strategies and math practices to help you solve problems.

Work Backward.

Look at the following problem.

Oscar, Trevor, Wyatt, and Roger sell calendars to raise money for the school sports teams. Wyatt sells 4 times as many as Roger. Wyatt sells 2 times as many as Trevor. Oscar sells 18 calendars, which is 3 times as many as Trevor. How many calendars does Roger sell?

To solve this problem, first look for important information. There are three important sentences that relate the numbers of calendars.

Wyatt sells 4 times as many as Roger.
Wyatt sells 2 times as many as Trevor.
Oscar sells 18 calendars, which is 3 times as many as Trevor.

Now look for a starting point.

Oscar sells 18 calendars, which is 3 times as many as Trevor.

From this information, you can find that Trevor sells $18 \div 3 = 6$ calendars.

Wyatt sells 2 times as many as Trevor.
So Wyatt sells $2 \times 6 = 12$ calendars.

Wyatt sells 4 times as many as Roger.

So Roger sells $12 \div 4 = 3$ calendars.

Think
Division "undoes" multiplication.

Ask yourself some key questions to help you.

- What do I know?

- What do I need to know?

- How do I know that I can work backward?

- How can I organize the given information to help me solve the problem?

- How can I check my answer?

Draw a Picture.

Look at the following problem.

Seth makes a polygon by putting 4 regular hexagons together side to side, and then tracing around the boundary. How many sides will the new polygon have?

You can draw a picture to solve the problem.

Use pattern blocks to arrange the 4 regular hexagons side to side.

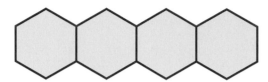

Determine the number of sides in the completed polygon.

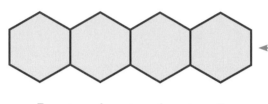

Each end hexagon adds 5 sides to the total, and each inner hexagon adds 4 sides.

$$5 + 4 + 4 + 5 = 18$$

The polygon Seth makes has 18 sides.

Ask yourself some key questions to help you.

- How can a picture help me understand and solve the problem?

- What do I need to draw?

- What labels do I need?

- Can I explain my picture?

Write and Solve an Equation.

Look at the following problem.

A farmer has two fields of corn. The small field has
14 rows of corn plants with 17 plants in each row. The large
field has 126 rows of corn plants with 53 plants
in each row. How many corn plants are there in all?

To solve this problem, you can write an equation
to represent the situation. Then you can solve
the equation.

- Write an expression for the number of plants in each field.

  Small field: rows of plants × number of plants in each row

                            14   ×   17

  Large field: rows of plants × number of plants in each row

                           126   ×   53

- Then write an equation for the total number of plants
  on the farm.

  plants in small field + plants in large field = total plants

        (14×17) + (126×53) =   x

- Now solve the equation.

  $(14 \times 17) + (126 \times 53) = x$

        238   +   6678 $= x$

                  6916 $= x$

There are 6916 corn plants in all.

Ask yourself some key questions to help you.

- What do I know?

- What do I need to know?

- How do I use what is known to write
  an equation?

- How do I show the unknown in
  an equation?

- How do I solve the equation?

Make an Organized List.

Look at the following problem.

Katy has 24 stuffed animals and 3 shelves. She wants to put the same number of stuffed animals on each shelf. How many stuffed animals can Katy put on each shelf?

You can use a factor pair to solve the problem. A factor pair for a number is two factors that you can multiply together to get the number.

The area model shows the number 24 and one of its factors, 3.

$$\begin{array}{c} \quad\quad ? \\ 3\ \boxed{\quad\quad 24 \quad\quad} \end{array}$$

Because $3 \times 8 = 24$,
3 and 8 are a factor pair for 24.

> These are the factor pairs for 24:
> 1 and 24
> 2 and 12
> 3 and 8
> 4 and 6

Katy can put 8 stuffed animals on each shelf.

Ask yourself some key questions to help you.

- How can an organized list help me solve the problem?

- What do I need to list?

- How can I organize my list?

- How can I use the organized list to check my solution?

Use Logical Reasoning.

Look at the following problem.

Carl, Max, Juan, and Ben all run a road race.

Juan finishes 22 minutes before Ben.
Carl finishes 10 minutes before Max.
Ben finishes at 1:22 P.M., 7 minutes after Carl.

What is the finishing order of the runners, from earliest to latest?

You can use logical reasoning and relationships to find the missing information.

Ben finishes at 1:22 P.M., 7 minutes after Carl.
So Carl finishes at 1:15 P.M.

Carl finishes at 1:15 P.M., 10 minutes before Max.
So Max finishes at 1:25 P.M.

Juan finishes 22 minutes before Ben.
Since Ben finishes at 1:22 P.M., Juan finishes at 1:00 P.M.

The times, in order, are 1:00 P.M., 1:15 P.M., 1:22 P.M., and 1:25 P.M.

So the order of the runners is Juan, Carl, Ben, and Max.

Ask yourself some key questions to help you.

- What do I know?

- What do I need to find?

- How can I organize what I know?

- What is my plan for solving the problem?

- How can I explain my reasoning using words?

MP 1: Make sense of problems.

Look at the following problem.

> Giselle makes 3 apple pies, some cherry pies, and some blueberry pies. If she makes 2 blueberry pies, write an expression that represents the total number of pies Giselle makes. Explain your answer.

Ask yourself some key questions to help you.

- How can I say this in my own words?

- What do I know and what do I need to know?

- Is this like any other problems I have solved?

- What is my plan to find what I need to know?

MP 2: Use reasoning.

Look at the following problem.

> The table shows the number of people who went to the school play each day. Show how you can use at least two properties of addition to find the total number of people for all four days.

School Play Attendance	
Day	Number of People
Thursday	35
Friday	40
Saturday	60
Sunday	65

Ask yourself some key questions to help you.

- What relationships do I see?

- Can I describe this using only numbers and symbols?

- Can I work with the numbers without changing what they mean?

- What operations or properties should I use?

MP 3: Justify your reasoning.

Look at the following problem.

Mr. Carter has 3 horses. His heaviest horse weighs 1520 pounds, and his lightest horse weighs 870 pounds. Mr. Carter rounds the weight of each of his 3 horses and adds the rounded numbers. Could an estimated total of 3000 pounds be correct? Explain.

Ask yourself some key questions to help you.

- Why did I solve the problem this way? Was there a better way?

- How can I explain my solution? Can I make my explanation better?

- Does my answer make sense?

- How can I show that my answer is correct?

MP 4: Model with mathematics.

Look at the following problem.

For the school field day, parents bring cases of water bottles. Each case has 24 water bottles. How many water bottles are in 5 cases?

Ask yourself some key questions to help you.

- How would a model help me?

- Can I represent this problem with a diagram? A bar model? An equation? A picture? A number line?

- What does the model show me about the problem?

- What part of the model will lead me to the answer?

MP 5: Use the right tools.

Look at the following problem.

> A total of 1548 children and 2164 adults ride a new roller coaster on the first day it is open. How many people in all ride the roller coaster?

Ask yourself some key questions to help you.

- Do I need a tool to organize or display the problem?

- Can I use a diagram? A number line? A manipulative?

- Which tool is best to use for this problem?

- How does the tool help me to work with the problem?

MP 6: Be precise.

Look at the following problem.

> A rancher puts up four fences. The lengths of the fences are 382 feet, 451 feet, 287 feet, and 195 feet. What is the total length of all four fences?
>
> To find the total length, find 382 feet + 451 feet + 287 feet + 195 feet.

Ask yourself some key questions to help you.

- What exactly is the problem asking me to do?

- Do I need an exact answer or an estimate?

- What units should I use in the problem and the solution?

- How can I use math vocabulary to explain this?

- How can I check my solution?

MP 7: Look for a pattern.

Look at the following problem.

Jalyn arranges toothpicks to make a pattern of hexagons as shown.

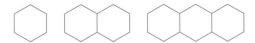

How many toothpicks will she use in the next two designs?

Ask yourself some key questions to help you.

- What is familiar about this problem?

- Is there a rule, property, or formula I can use here?

- How do the parts of the problem go together?

- Can I organize this in a way that makes it fit a pattern?

- What patterns did I find?

MP 8: Generalize.

Look at the following problem.

What pattern do you see when you multiply by a multiple of 10, 100, or 1000?

Find 8 × 30.

$$8 × 30 = 8 × 3 \text{ tens}$$
$$= 24 \text{ tens}$$
$$= 240$$

> Write 8 × 3, or 24, with one zero.

Find 8 × 300.

$$8 × 300 = 8 × 3 \text{ hundreds}$$
$$= 24 \text{ hundreds}$$
$$= 2400$$

> Write 8 × 3, or 24, with two zeros.

Find 8 × 3000.

$$8 × 3000 = 8 × 3 \text{ thousands}$$
$$= 24 \text{ thousands}$$
$$= 24,000$$

> Write 8 × 3, or 24, with three zeros.

Here is the pattern: Multiply the nonzero digits. Count the number of zeros in the factors. Then write the same number of zeros in the product.

Ask yourself some key questions to help you.

- Is this problem like other problems I have solved?

- Can I use a shortcut to skip steps or find the answer?

- Can I repeat this with different numbers?

- How does this connect to other things I know about math?

- Can I use what I know to predict something else?

- Can I extend the pattern?

- Does this always work?

Place Value, Addition and Subtraction

The International Space Station is a large spacecraft that orbits Earth. Astronauts from many countries live and work on the spacecraft to learn more about space.

By the Numbers

♦ The first piece of the International Space Station was launched in 1998.

♦ It has 5 bedrooms, 2 bathrooms, and a gymnasium.

♦ The station weighs almost 1,000,000 pounds.

♦ It orbits 220 miles above Earth and flies approximately 17,500 miles per hour.

Can I Spot the Station?

♦ The station is visible to the naked eye from many worldwide locations.

♦ It is the third brightest object in the sky.

♦ It travels much faster than an airplane.

♦ Every 3 days, the station passes over the same place on Earth.

Place Value to Billions

In January 2016, astronomers announced that they believe they have found evidence of a giant planet orbiting the Sun, at a distance of about 55,935,834,720 miles! The planet has been nicknamed Planet Nine or Planet X. How do you write the number name for this number?

The place value of a digit in a number is its value in that position, or place. You can use a place-value chart to read this number.

Standard Form: 55,935,834,720

In the billions period:

The digit in the ten billions place is 5. Its value is 50,000,000,000.

The digit in the billions place is also 5. Its value is 5,000,000,000.

The value of the 5 in the ten billions place is 10 times the value of the 5 in the billions place.

Billions Period			Millions Period			Thousands Period			Ones Period		
hundreds	tens	ones	hundreds	tens	ones	hundreds	tens	ones	hundreds	tens	ones
	5	5,	9	3	5,	8	3	4,	7	2	0

Commas are used to separate the digits of each period.

In the millions period:

The digit in the hundred millions place is 9. Its value is 900,000,000.

The digit in the ten millions place is 3. Its value is 30,000,000.

The digit in the millions place is 5. Its value is 5,000,000.

▷ The number name for the number 55,935,834,720 is fifty-five billion, nine hundred thirty-five million, eight hundred thirty-four thousand, seven hundred twenty.

PRACTICE

Write the name of the place that is 10 times the given place.

1. thousands

2. ten millions

3. hundred millions

4. ones

5. hundred thousands

6. billions

Write the place of the underlined digit. Then write its value.

7. <u>5</u>,476,807,139

8. 9,4<u>2</u>8,001,230

9. 16,35<u>0</u>,846,780

10. 4<u>9</u>,006

11. <u>8</u>3,460,249,704

12. 604,772,3<u>5</u>5

PRACTICE

Write the number in standard form.

13. three million, five hundred forty thousand, thirty-seven

14. three billion, six hundred six million, seventy-seven thousand, four hundred three

15. nine hundred forty billion

16. seventy-nine billion, one

Write the number name for each number.

17. 1,042,003,051

18. 4,725,000,000

19. 72,200,000,020

Problem Solving

Use the table for Exercises 20–23.

20. Which planet's distance does NOT have an 8 in the ten millions place?

   A. Mercury   **B.** Jupiter
   C. Saturn   **D.** Uranus

21. Which planet's distance has a digit with a value of 600,000?

   A. Mercury   **B.** Jupiter
   C. Venus   **D.** Neptune

Planet	Average Distance from the Sun (mi)
Mercury	35,983,610
Venus	67,232,360
Mars	141,635,300
Jupiter	483,632,200
Saturn	888,188,000
Uranus	1,783,950,000
Neptune	2,798,842,200

22. Which planet's distance has a digit with a value that is 10 times the value of 4,000,000?

   A. Jupiter   **B.** Uranus   **C.** Neptune   **D.** Mars

23. Look at the average distance for Uranus. What is the value of the digit in the thousands place? Explain how you know.

24. Mount Diablo buckwheat was long thought to be extinct. In May of 2015, approximately 1,800,000 plants were discovered in Black Diamond Mines Regional Preserve, CA. Write the number name of this number. What is the value of 8 in this number?

Write About It

25. Emily says that the greatest 10-digit whole number is 9 billion. Do you agree? Explain.

Expanded Form

Objective
- Read and write whole numbers through billions in expanded form.

Math Words
expanded form
place value

The average distance from Neptune to the Sun is about 4,504,299,902 kilometers. How does the value of the digit in the thousands place compare with the value of the digit in the ten thousands place?

The value of each digit in this number can be shown by writing the number in expanded form.

Billions Period			Millions Period			Thousands Period			Ones Period		
hundreds	tens	ones	hundreds	tens	ones	hundreds	tens	ones	hundreds	tens	ones
		4,	5	0	4,	2	9	9,	9	0	2

A place that holds a 0 may be omitted in expanded form.

Each value is shown as a product of the digit and its place value.

The expanded form is the sum of the products.

$(4 \times 1,000,000,000) +$

$(5 \times 100,000,000) + (4 \times 1,000,000) +$

$(2 \times 100,000) + (9 \times 10,000) + (9 \times 1000) +$

$(9 \times 100) + (2 \times 1)$

The value of the 9 in the thousands place is $\frac{1}{10}$ the value of the 9 in the ten thousands place.

PRACTICE

Complete the expanded form of each number.

1. $1487 = (\underline{?} \times 1000) + (\underline{?} \times 100) + (8 \times \underline{?}) + (7 \times \underline{?})$

2. $87,020 = (\underline{?} \times 10,000) + (\underline{?} \times 1000) + (2 \times \underline{?})$

3. $180,764 = (1 \times \underline{?}) + (8 \times \underline{?}) + (\underline{?} \times 100) + (6 \times \underline{?}) + (\underline{?} \times 1)$

4. $32,530,008 = (3 \times \underline{?}) + (2 \times \underline{?}) + (\underline{?} \times 100,000) + (3 \times \underline{?}) + (8 \times \underline{?})$

5. $4,700,930,020 = (4 \times \underline{?}) + (\underline{?} \times 100,000,000) + (9 \times \underline{?}) + (\underline{?} \times 10,000) + (2 \times \underline{?})$

Write the name of the place that is $\frac{1}{10}$ of the given place.

6. ten thousands   **7.** millions   **8.** thousands

Write each in standard form.

9. (4 × 1000) + (5 × 100) + (9 × 1)   **10.** 20,000 + 2000 + 900 + 80 + 7

11. 400,000 + 300 + 5   **12.** 3,000,000 + 9000 + 40 + 8

13. (6 × 10,000,000) + (3 × 1,000,000) + (4 × 100,000) + (5 × 1000) + (7 × 1)

14. (1 × 1,000,000,000) + (2 × 100,000,000) + (5 × 10,000,000) + (3 × 100) + (9 × 1)

Write each in expanded form.

15. 8998   **16.** 15,243   **17.** 672,115   **18.** 700,946

19. 2,200,002   **20.** 13,004,205   **21.** 604,003,200   **22.** 2,005,940,000

Problem Solving

23. The circumference of Earth can be measured as the distance around Earth at the equator. Nami read that the circumference of Earth is about one hundred thirty-one million, four hundred eight thousand, six hundred forty feet. Write this number in expanded form and in standard form.

24. Use the number 35,540,266 to complete each statement.

The digit 6 in the _?_ place has a value that is 10 times the value of the digit 6 in the _?_ place.

The digit 5 in the _?_ place has a value that is $\frac{1}{10}$ the value of the digit 5 in the _?_ place.

Write About It

25. Tan's teacher writes the expanded form of some number on the chalkboard. Tan notices that the number is written as the sum of 4 addends. Without examining each of the addends, Tan concludes that the number must have 4 digits. Do you agree? Explain.

What is the standard form of each number?

1. two million, six hundred eight thousand, ninety-five

   A. 26,895   **B.** 2,680,950   **C.** 2,608,095   **D.** 2,608,950,000

2. 60,000,000 + 400,000 + 1,000 + 500 + 2

   A. 64,152   **B.** 6,401,520   **C.** 60,400,152   **D.** 60,401,502

3. Which of the following are equivalent to the given number? Select all that apply.

   $(7 \times 1{,}000{,}000{,}000) + (3 \times 10{,}000{,}000) + (4 \times 100{,}000) + (8 \times 1)$

   A. 7,030,400,008
   B. 7,300,400,800
   C. seven billion, thirty million, four hundred thousand, eighty
   D. seven million, thirty thousand, four hundred eight
   E. seven billion, thirty million, four hundred thousand, eight

4. Which of the following are equivalent to the given number? Select all that apply.

   three billion, one hundred twenty-five million

   A. 3,125,000
   B. 3,000,125,000
   C. 3,125,000,000
   D. $(3 \times 1{,}000{,}000{,}000) + (1 \times 100{,}000{,}000) + (2 \times 10{,}000{,}000) + (5 \times 1{,}000{,}000)$
   E. $(3 \times 1{,}000{,}000) + (1 \times 100{,}000) + (2 \times 10{,}000) + (5 \times 1000)$

Write the number in expanded form.

5. 3,620,450   6. 5,024,600,401

7. 10,001,100

Billions Period			Millions Period			Thousands Period			Ones Period		
hundreds	tens	ones	hundreds	tens	ones	hundreds	tens	ones	hundreds	tens	ones

Write the number name for each number.

8. 2,505,032   9. 8,900,052,360   10. 168,452,087

Match. Choose the place that is 10 times the given place.

11. hundred thousands

12. ten millions

13. hundred millions

A. millions
B. ten millions
C. hundred millions
D. billions
E. ten billions

Match. Choose the place that is $\frac{1}{10}$ of the given place.

14. millions

15. hundred thousands

16. ten millions

A. thousands
B. ten thousands
C. hundred thousands
D. millions
E. ten millions

Complete the following statements for the number 164,475,025,354.

17. The digit 7 is in the _?_ place and has a value of _?_.

18. The value of the 4 in the billions place is _?_ times the value of the 4 in the hundred millions place.

19. The value of the digit in the hundred thousands place is _?_.

Problem Solving

20. Laurel wrote the expanded form for 9,057,329,019 as
$(9 \times 1,000,000,000) + (57 \times 1,000,000) + (329 \times 100,000) + (19 \times 1)$.
What mistake did Laurel make? What is the correct expanded form of this number?

Maps can be drawn to show the population density of different counties. Population density is the number of people per square mile. Use the map for Exercises 21–22.

21. What is the number name for the population of California in 2015?

22. The population density of San Francisco County in 2010 was about 17,179 people per square mile. Write a sentence comparing the digits in the thousands and tens places of this number.

California 2015
Population:
39,144,818

Powers of 10

Objective
- Multiply and divide whole numbers by powers of 10.

Math Words
power of 10
base
exponent

The Sun is very strong. It hits Earth with an energy that is 10,000 times as much as the whole world uses. This number is a power of 10 and can also be written as 10^4.

Powers of 10 can be written in standard form or by using exponents with the base 10. The exponent tells how many times to use the base 10 as a factor.

For a base of 10 and an exponent of zero, $10^0 = 1$.

Powers of 10
$10^1 = 10 \times 1 = 10$
$10^2 = 10 \times 10 = 100$
$10^3 = 10 \times 10 \times 10 = 1000$
$10^4 = 10 \times 10 \times 10 \times 10 = 10,000$
$10^5 = 10 \times 10 \times 10 \times 10 \times 10 = 100,000$

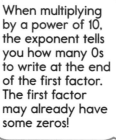

10^5 ← exponent

base

Look for patterns when multiplying a number by powers of 10.

$52 \times 10^1 = 52 \times 10 = 520$

$52 \times 10^2 = 52 \times 100 = 5200$

$52 \times 10^3 = 52 \times 1000 = 52,000$

$52 \times 10^4 = 52 \times 10,000 = 520,000$

$52 \times 10^5 = 52 \times 100,000 = 5,200,000$

When dividing by powers of 10, remove 0s.

For example, $31,000,000,000 \div 10^3 = 31,000,000$.

When multiplying by a power of 10, the exponent tells you how many 0s to write at the end of the first factor. The first factor may already have some zeros!

PRACTICE

Find each missing number or power of 10.

1. $4 \times 10^3 = 4 \times$ _?_

2. $12 \times 10^2 = 12 \times$ _?_

3. $8,000,000,000 \div$ _?_ $= 8,000,000,000 \div 100$

Write each product or quotient.

4. $7 \times 10^3 =$ _?_

5. $9 \times 10^4 =$ _?_

6. $300 \div 10^2 =$ _?_

Find each product or quotient.

7. $41 \times 10^1 = $?

8. $700 \times 10^2 = $?

9. $13{,}000{,}000 \div 10^4 = $?

10. $4000 \div 10^2 = $?

11. $60 \times 10^3 = $?

12. $307 \times 10^4 = $?

13. $20{,}000 \div 10^1 = $?

14. $430 \div 10^1 = $?

15. $108 \times 10^9 = $?

Find each missing number or power of 10.

16. $701 \times 10^? = 7010$

17. $87{,}200 \times 10^4 = $?

18. $80{,}100 \div 10^? = 801$

19. ? $\div 10^3 = 50$

20. ? $\times 10^1 = 8500$

21. $610 \times$? $= 6{,}100{,}000$

Write each number as a number times a power of 10.

22. $14{,}000$

23. $80{,}000{,}000{,}000$

24. $976{,}000$

25. 300

26. $2{,}450{,}000$

27. 890

28. A certain mountain has an elevation of about 3×10^4 feet. How tall is the mountain?

Problem Solving

29. As of June 2016, K2-33b is the youngest planet ever recorded outside the solar system. It is estimated to be only 5 to 10 million years old. Express 5 million and 10 million using powers of ten.

30. Graham is flying to attend an engineering conference. If Graham flies to the conference and back, how far does he travel?

31. Misha finds the product of 17×10^5 and then adds 2. What is the sum?

32. When a certain whole number is multiplied by 10^1, the product has 8 digits. How many digits does the original number have?

Write About It

33. Edgar says the product of 50×10^3 is 5000 because the exponent tells how many zeros are in the product. Do you agree? Explain how you know.

Problem Solving
Use the Four-Step Process

Objective
- Solve problems by using the four-step process.

Math Words
equation
exponent

An animal is classified as a species in the phylum it belongs to. The number of species in a phylum varies widely. The phylum *Pogonophora* has about 150 species. There are about 100 times as many species in the phylum *Annelida*. About how many species are in the phylum *Annelida*?

Read and Understand

Read the problem more than once to find the key information and decide what the question is.

Key Information	Question
About 150 species in *Pogonophora*; about 100 times as many species in *Annelida*	How many species in *Annelida*?

Represent the Situation

Use letters to represent the number of each species.

Let a represent the number of species in Annelida, and p represent the number of species in Pogonophora.

Write an equation.

$a = p \times 100$

Make and Use a Plan

To find the number of species in *Annelida*, solve the equation.

$a = p \times 100$

$a = 150 \times 100$

$ = 150 \times 10^2$

$a = 15{,}000$

Since the exponent is 2, write 2 additional zeros at the end of 150.

Now write a complete sentence to answer the question.

> *There are about 15,000 species in the phylum Annelida.*

Look Back

Check whether the answer makes sense.

The phylum Annelida has more species than Pogonophora. 15,000 > 150, so the answer makes sense.

Phylum Porifera: Sponges

1. The phylum *Porifera* has about 9000 species, which is ten times as many as in the phylum *Nemertea*. How many species are in the phylum *Nemertea?*

2. Most asteroids are about 300 million kilometers from the Sun. The comets in the Oort cloud are about 10,000 times that distance from the Sun. About how many million kilometers from the Sun is the Oort cloud? Hint: Think of *million kilometers* as a unit of distance.

3. In 2012, Americans composted about 19,590,000 tons of yard trimmings. That is about 1,010,000 tons less than the amount composted in 2013. About how many tons of yard trimmings were composted in 2013?

4. In 2013, about 11,540,000 tons of glass were collected as trash. About 3,150,000 tons of glass were reused and the rest went to landfill. About how much glass went to landfill?

5. In 2013, Americans generated about 254 million tons of trash. More than 87 million tons of this material was recycled and composted. Write a question and an answer for the data.

6. Explain how you could use a bar model to solve one of the previous exercises. Include a sample model in your explanation.

7. The owner of a software company claims that profits this year are one thousand times as great as they were 5 years ago. She also says that profits increased by $999,000 over that time. If the profit this year can be represented by a power of 10, how much was the profit 5 years ago?

8. A glacial erratic is a piece of rock that is very different than rocks in the same area. They can be moved by glaciers. Write a sentence that compares the approximate weights of the glacial erratics below. Compare your sentence with those of classmates.

   Big Rock (Canada): 340×10^5 pounds

   Madison Boulder (New Hampshire): twelve million pounds

Write About It

9. Look back at Exercise 2. Explain how using the hint could help make your work more efficient.

Addition Properties and Subtraction Rules

Objective
- Use addition properties and subtraction rules to add and subtract multi-digit numbers.

Math Words
Commutative Property
Associative Property
Identity Property

You can use the properties of addition and the rules of subtraction to add and subtract.

Commutative Property of Addition

Changing the order of addends does not change the sum.

Example: $8 + 7 = 15$ $7 + 8 = 15$

Associative Property of Addition

Regrouping addends does not change the sum.

Example: $(9 + 4) + 6 = 9 + (4 + 6)$
     $13 + 6 = 9 + 10$
     $19 = 19$

Identity Property of Addition

The sum of zero and a number is that number.

Example: $0 + 23 = 23$ $23 + 0 = 23$ | addend + addend = sum |

Rules of Subtraction

When the minuend is equal to the subtrahend, the difference is zero.

Example: $34 - 34 = 0$ | minuend − subtrahend = difference |

When the subtrahend is zero, the difference is equal to the minuend.

Example: $57 - 0 = 57$

When finding an unknown addend, think of subtraction.

Example: $4 + \underline{\ ?\ } = 11$; Since $11 - 7 = 4$, $4 + 7 = 11$.

PRACTICE

Find the unknown number. Tell what property of addition you used.

1. $16 + 19 = \underline{\ ?\ } + 16$

2. $258 + 0 = \underline{\ ?\ }$

3. $23 + (37 + 6) = (23 + \underline{\ ?\ }) + 6$

Find the difference.

4. $67 - 0 = \underline{\ ?\ }$

5. $49 - 49 = \underline{\ ?\ }$

Show two ways to group the addends. Then mark the way that would help you compute faster.

6. $6 + 4 + 7$

7. $10 + 2 + 8$

8. $28 + 2 + 67$

9. $57 + 132 + 8$

10. $30 + 62 + 8$

11. $56 + 74 + 32$

Find the unknown addend.

12. $12 + \underline{\quad?\quad} = 21$

13. $\underline{\quad?\quad} + 33 = 40$

14. $48 + \underline{\quad?\quad} = 48$

15. $71 + \underline{\quad?\quad} = 91$

16. $42 + \underline{\quad?\quad} = 60$

17. $\underline{\quad?\quad} + 50 = 75$

18. $817 + 0 + \underline{\quad?\quad} = 917$

19. $\underline{\quad?\quad} + 75 + 42 + 25 = 150$

Problem Solving

For Exercises 20–23, determine when the statement is true. Explain.

20. Any number plus zero is equal to zero.

21. The difference of a number and itself is zero.

22. If two whole numbers have a sum of 2, their difference is 0.

23. If the difference of two whole numbers is a whole number, the difference is less than their sum.

24. The table shows how many miles Janna runs this week. Explain how you can use mental math to find her total mileage for the week.

Mon.	Tues.	Wed.	Thurs.	Fri.
5	3	6	7	4

25. The sum of three numbers is 24. The difference of any two of the three numbers is 0. What are the numbers?

26. Can the sum and difference of two whole numbers be equal? Explain. Include an example.

Write About It

27. When Carl uses the Associative Property of Addition, he likes to group addends to form sums of 10 or multiples of 10 if possible. Explain why he would do this.

Estimate Sums and Differences

Objective
- Use front-end estimation and rounding to estimate sums and differences of multi-digit numbers.

Math Words
front-end estimation
rounding
estimate

The table shows how many people visited Spruce Park one weekend.

About how many people in all visited the park? About how many more visited on Saturday than on Sunday?

Visitors at Spruce Park	
Friday	4789
Saturday	5332
Sunday	3781

You can use front-end estimation or rounding to make an estimate.

◆ Use front-end estimation to estimate a sum.

Add the front digits. ⟶

$$\begin{array}{r} 4,789 \\ 5,332 \\ +3,781 \\ \hline \text{about } 12,000 \end{array}$$

Write zeros for the other digits.

$$\begin{array}{r} 4,789 \\ 5,332 \\ +3,781 \\ \hline \text{about } 12,000 \end{array}$$

Adjust with the back digits.

$$\begin{array}{r} \text{about } \quad 800 \\ \text{about } \quad 300 \\ \text{about } \quad 800 \\ \hline \text{about } 1900 \end{array}$$

Add the estimates.

$$\begin{array}{r} \text{about } 12,000 \\ +\text{about } \quad 1,900 \\ \hline \text{about } \mathbf{13,900} \end{array}$$

◆ Use rounding to estimate a difference.

$$\begin{array}{rll} 5332 & \rightarrow & 5000 \\ -3781 & \rightarrow & 4000 \\ \hline \text{about} & & 1000 \end{array}$$

Round each number.

Subtract the rounded numbers.

▷ About 13,900 people in all visited the park. About 1000 more people visited on Saturday than on Sunday.

PRACTICE

Use front-end estimation to estimate each sum.

1.
$$\begin{array}{r} 8730 \\ 2582 \\ +6428 \end{array}$$

2.
$$\begin{array}{r} 789 \\ 2345 \\ +5531 \end{array}$$

3.
$$\begin{array}{r} 343 \\ 680 \\ 3729 \\ +1006 \end{array}$$

4.
$$\begin{array}{r} 1468 \\ 864 \\ 5915 \\ +6060 \end{array}$$

Use rounding to estimate each difference.

5.
$$\begin{array}{r} 6410 \\ -2193 \end{array}$$

6.
$$\begin{array}{r} 7641 \\ -5048 \end{array}$$

7.
$$\begin{array}{r} 5875 \\ -5089 \end{array}$$

8.
$$\begin{array}{r} 9323 \\ -3589 \end{array}$$

Estimate each sum or difference.

9.
```
  1 4 7 1
  3 8 5 4
+ 7 2 2 0
```

10.
```
  5 0 0 4
- 1 2 7 8
```

11.
```
    2 9 8
    9 6 5
  5 2 6 2
+ 3 0 4 6
```

12.
```
  7 5 4 3
- 3 9 1 0
```

13.
```
  8 0 7 5
- 3 8 8 8
```

14.
```
  3 5 3 8
  7 0 4 2
+ 8 8 4 4
```

15.
```
  8 0 8 4
- 2 4 2 1
```

16.
```
  9 0 6 5
  4 9 8 7
+ 1 0 8 4
```

Estimate the value of each expression.

17. 830,412 − 277,805 + 66,825

18. 3250 + 16,701 − 9105

19. 4,080,629 − (954,817 + 1,160,207)

20. 48,441 + (90,012 − 59,713)

Problem Solving

21. A furlong is a measure of distance. The length of 7 furlongs is 4620 feet, while the length of 1 mile is 5280 feet. Estimate the length of 1 mile and 7 furlongs in feet.

22. Yosemite Falls in the U.S. has a total drop of 2424 feet. Angel Falls in Venezuela has a drop of 3212 feet. What is the approximate difference in the two drops?

23. Sandy says that 7234 − 189 is about 5000. Do you agree? Explain.

24. Use front-end estimation and rounding to estimate 8904 + 3482. How do the estimates compare?

25. Reginald estimates the sum of five 4-digit numbers using only the front digits. His estimate is 30,000. By how much could his estimate differ from the actual sum? Explain.

Write About It

26. Estimates do not generally give exact amounts. Explain why an estimate may be a better way to express a quantity than an exact amount.

Find Sums and Differences

Objective
- Add and subtract multi-digit numbers.

Math Words

sum
difference

The table shows the attendance for different performances of a play. What is the total attendance? What is the difference between attendances for the Saturday and Sunday performances at 2:00?

You can calculate the exact sum and difference to answer these questions. Be sure to align digits in their places.

Play Attendance	
Friday (8:00)	1815
Saturday (2:00)	1703
Saturday (8:00)	1864
Sunday (2:00)	1629

◆ Find a sum.

Add the ones, tens, hundreds, and thousands. Regroup as needed.

```
     2            1 2          3 1 2         3 1 2
  1 8 1 5      1 8 1 5      1 8 1 5      1 8 1 5
  1 7 0 3      1 7 0 3      1 7 0 3      1 7 0 3
  1 8 6 4      1 8 6 4      1 8 6 4      1 8 6 4
+ 1 6 2 9    + 1 6 2 9    + 1 6 2 9    + 1 6 2 9
        1          1 1        0 1 1      7 0 1 1
```

◆ Find a difference.

Regroup as needed.   Subtract in all places.   Add to check.

```
          9                        9
      6 10 13                  6 10 13                1   1
   1  7  0  3               1  7  0  3            1 6 2 9
 - 1  6  2  9             - 1  6  2  9          +     7 4
                                     7 4          1 7 0 3
```

> The total attendance is 7011. The difference between attendances for the Saturday and Sunday performances at 2:00 is 74.

PRACTICE

Add or subtract.

```
1.   2 6 7 8      2.   3 7 3 6      3.   3 0 6 1      4.   4 0 6 2
     6 4 0 9         - 1 0 1 8             4 0 7         - 2 9 2 9
   + 1 0 7 8                          + 8 7 5 3
```

Align. Then add or subtract.

5. 5400 + 1160 + 3007 + 2040   6. 6543 − 432

Align. Then add or subtract.

7. $6767 - 4444$

8. $2936 + 760 + 500 + 789$

9. $5449 + 2176 + 2347 + 3248$

10. $4848 - 703$

11. $7828 - 4721$

12. $3829 + 1760 + 1857 + 704$

13. $1105 + 1075 + 589 + 2863$

14. $4000 - 784$

15. $746,500 - 28,781$

16. $204,106 + 403 + 7003 + 10,691$

Simplify each expression.

17. $35,235 + 134,468,003 - 82,325$

18. $8,229,614 + 84,257 - 2,000,911$

19. $10^5 + 8034 + 10^2 + 55$

20. $10^6 - 10^3 - 10^5 - 10^4 - 1$

21. Jamal adds two equal 4-digit numbers. Which statements could describe the sum? Choose all that apply.

    A. The sum is a 4-digit number.
    C. The sum is an odd number.

    B. The sum is a 5-digit number.
    D. The sum is an even number.

Problem Solving

22. Sam runs a mile. Omar runs 640 yards. How many more feet did Sam run than Omar? Use the bar diagram to help you.

1 mile = 5280 ft	
640 yd = 1920 ft	?

23. The Riveras have $7560 in their bank account. They write a check for $1375 for vacation and withdraw $300 from an ATM. How much is in the account now?

24. The Browns plant 86 acres with wheat, 475 acres with corn, and 320 acres with rye. How many acres do they plant in all?

25. What is 4 times 10^6 decreased by one hundred thousand, twelve?

26. The Great Barrier Reef includes about 3000 varieties of mollusks, 1625 types of bony fish, and 133 varieties of sharks and rays. How many more types of bony fish are there than varieties of sharks and rays?

Write About It

27. Addition and subtraction are inverse operations. Explain how this concept can help you check computations.

Write the place of the underlined digit. Then write its value.

1. 87,9̲23,401,640

2. 2̲83,100,625,497

3. 1,0̲85,589

Complete the following statements.

4. The value of the hundred thousands place is _?_ times the value of the ten thousands place.

5. The value of the billions place is $\frac{1}{10}$ the value of the _?_ place.

6. In the number 923,240,104, the digit 2 in the ten millions place is _?_ times the value of the 2 in the hundred thousands place.

Write each number in standard form.

7. sixty-two million, five hundred thousand

8. 5,000,000 + 10

9. eighty-eight billion, ten million, fifty

Write the number name and expanded form of each number.

10. 398,100

11. 54,300,431

12. 46,900,308,210

13. Which number has a hundred thousands digit with a value that is $\frac{1}{10}$ the value of its millions digit?

    A. 7,607,288   **B.** 2,604,518,000   **C.** 8,845,293   **D.** 4,425,338,202

Identify the unknown number.

14. $5 \times 10^3 =$ _?_

15. $20 \times 10^2 =$ _?_

16. $8000 \times 10^1 =$ _?_

17. $6000 \div 10^2 =$ _?_

18. $18,000 \div 10^1 =$ _?_

19. $2,000,000 \div 10^3 =$ _?_

20. $162 + 0 =$ _?_

21. $13 + 12 =$ _?_ $+ 13$

22. _?_ $+ 53 = 93$

23. _?_ $+ 32 = 80$

24. $25 +$ _?_ $= 50$

25. $17 + (34 + 8) = (17 +$ _?_ $) + 8$

26. $17 - 0 =$ _?_

27. $62 - 62 =$ _?_

28. $32 - 0 =$ _?_

Use front-end estimation or rounding to estimate each sum or difference.

29.
```
  2 3 0 8
  4 4 1 1
+ 9 7 5 7
```

30.
```
  8 8 4 5
- 1 1 7 5
```

31.
```
  1 0 6
  4 7 8
  2 9 9
+ 7 1 8 7
```

32.
```
  2 5 4 3
- 1 6 8 5
```

33.
```
  8 1 8 9
- 4 7 6 3
```

34.
```
  9 6 4 2
  1 5 1 0
+ 6 2 5 5
```

35.
```
  4 7 6 3
- 2 8 0 7
```

36.
```
  6 0 9 8
  1 1 8 5
+ 3 2 6 4
```

Find each sum or difference.

37.
```
  1 6 4 5
+   4 5 0
```

38.
```
  6 0 0 0
-   8 4 7
```

39.
```
  1 2 9
  3 8 5
+ 8 1 0
```

40.
```
  8 0 5 0
- 6 5 2 8
```

41.
```
  9 5 4 , 0 0 7
-   5 0 , 5 7 5
```

42.
```
  1 5 8 , 1 9 8
    4 6 , 0 8 7
+     2 , 0 6 3
```

43.
```
  9 6 , 0 0 0
- 7 2 , 8 6 9
```

44.
```
  4 5 7 9
  3 5 2 1
+ 6 9 0 7
```

Problem Solving

45. An art teacher needs 1500 boxes of crayons for the upcoming school year. If she already has 862 boxes, how many more does she need?

46. There are 10^3 megabytes in 1 gigabyte. How many megabytes are in 5 gigabytes?

47. Volunteers in Lithuania stacked one million, nine hundred thirty-five coins to form a pyramid. The pyramid was greater than a meter in height. Write this number in standard form. Then write the power of 10 that best approximates this value.

Write About It

48. Taylor estimates the sum shown. Identify the error Taylor made. Then find a more reasonable estimate.

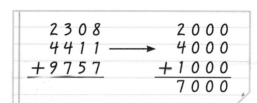

The International Space Station is built from many different parts that are launched at different times and attached together. It is estimated that the space station weighs almost 1 million pounds. The cost of the station is more than 100 billion U.S. dollars.

1. Write 1 million and 100 billion in standard form. Refer to the place-value chart.

Billions Period			Millions Period			Thousands Period			Ones Period		
hundreds	tens	ones	hundreds	tens	ones	hundreds	tens	ones	hundreds	tens	ones

2. How many times as great is the value of the digit 1 in 100 billion as the value of the digit 1 in 1 million? Express your answer as a power of ten. Explain.

3. Suppose that the current weight of the International Space Station is 927,004 pounds. A module that weighs 86,276 pounds detaches from the spacecraft. Estimate the new weight of the spacecraft.

4. Two new modules that weigh 43,139 and 76,803 pounds each are launched from Earth to attach to the spacecraft. Estimate the increase in weight of the spacecraft using front-end estimation.

5. Answer the previous problem by rounding to the nearest hundred. Write your answer in expanded form.

6. Research 5 other number facts about the International Space Station. Try to represent all 4 periods in the place value chart with the greatest place of each number.

The International Space Station can reach speeds exceeding 17,000 miles per hour. Suppose the table shows the number of miles traveled each hour by the spacecraft one morning.

Time	Distance Traveled (miles)
8:00 A.M. to 9:00 A.M.	16,846
9:00 A.M. to 10:00 A.M.	16,729
10:00 A.M. to 11:00 A.M.	17,004

7. Approximately how many total miles did the spacecraft travel between 8:00 A.M. and 11:00 A.M.? Use rounding and a product to approximate to the nearest thousand.

8. Suppose an error was made in the table and the spacecraft actually flew 17,004 miles between 8:00 A.M. and 9:00 A.M., and 16,846 miles between 10:00 A.M. and 11:00 A.M. Would the estimate change? Explain.

Determine the best answer for each problem.

1. What is the missing number?

   $427 + 0 + \underline{\ ?\ } = 527$

   A. 0 **B.** 100
   C. 427 **D.** 527

2. In a place-value chart, each place is how many times as great as the place to its right?

   A. one-tenth **B.** ten
   C. one hundred **D.** one thousand

3. Round 7536 to the nearest thousand.

   A. 7000
   B. 7500
   C. 7600
   D. 8000

4. Order the numbers 308, 297, and 315 from least to greatest.

   A. 315, 308, 297
   B. 308, 315, 297
   C. 297, 315, 308
   D. 297, 308, 315

5. What is the period of the underlined digits?

   238,<u>618</u>,233,805

   A. thousands **B.** millions
   C. ones **D.** billions

6. Select the expressions that equal 78,000. Select all that apply.

   A. 78×10^3
   B. 7800×10
   C. $780 \div 10$
   D. $7,800,000 \div 10^2$

7. What is the missing number?

   $150 \times 10^2 = 150 \times \underline{\ ?\ }$

   A. 0 **B.** 10
   C. 100 **D.** 1000

8. Which number is one thousand times as great as 5,000,000?

   A. 50,000,000
   B. 500,000,000
   C. 5,000,000,000
   D. 50,000,000,000

9. Select the best estimate.

   $$\begin{array}{r} 10{,}738 \\ -\ \ 6{,}511 \\ \hline \end{array}$$

   A. 3000 **B.** 4000
   C. 5000 **D.** 6000

10. Select the best estimate.

   $$\begin{array}{r} 3658 \\ +2195 \\ \hline \end{array}$$

   A. 4000 **B.** 5000
   C. 6000 **D.** 7000

Place Value and Decimals

Some plants and flowers begin as tiny seeds that are similar in size to a speck of dust. The world's smallest seeds are produced by a special kind of orchid in the tropical rainforest. They can be as little as 0.003 inch long! The seeds are not visible to the naked eye—they can only be seen using a device such as a microscope.

What Other Plants Have Tiny Seeds?

♦ A begonia is a bright flower. A begonia seed measures about 0.01 inch. This is only one hundredth of an inch, but the flower can grow up to 8 feet tall.

♦ A petunia is a colorful funnel-shaped flower. A petunia seed is about 0.02 inch long. This is only one fiftieth of an inch, but it can grow up to 3 feet tall.

♦ A mustard seed is about 0.05 inch long. This is one twentieth of an inch. The mustard plant can grow as high as 30 feet.

How Do They Grow?

♦ Plants with fine seeds have a lower survival rate, so they are typically planted in large quantities.

♦ These plants require special care and are often grown in a greenhouse.

Thousandths

Objective
- Read and write decimals to thousandths using standard form and the number name.

Math Word
thousandth

Sahir is building a model house. The directions state that the window should be 0.750 inch wide. In order to describe this to his friend, Sahir will say the number name of this decimal. What is the number name for 0.750?

Parts of whole numbers, such as tenths, hundredths, and thousandths, can be written using fraction or decimal notation.

$$1 \text{ hundredth} = \frac{1}{100} = 0.01$$

If each hundredth in a whole is split into ten equal parts, there will be ten times as many total parts. Each part is one thousandth of the whole.

$$1 \text{ thousandth} = \frac{1}{1000} = 0.001$$

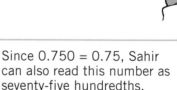

Standard Form	Number Name
0.003	three thousandths
1.065	one and sixty-five thousandths
0.278	two hundred seventy-eight thousandths

Sahir can read 0.750 as seven hundred fifty thousandths.

Since 0.750 = 0.75, Sahir can also read this number as seventy-five hundredths.

PRACTICE

Write as a decimal.

1. $\frac{5}{1000}$

2. $\frac{6}{100}$

3. $\frac{945}{1000}$

4. $1\frac{470}{1000}$

5. $12\frac{1}{10}$

6. two and eleven thousandths

7. twenty-four hundredths

8. eight hundred two thousandths

Write the number name for each decimal.

9. 0.461

10. 1.053

11. 5.159

12. 0.158

13. 0.009

14. 44.090

15. 12.112

16. 0.273

17. 0.419

18. 10.258

Write each number in standard form.

19. seventy-two thousandths

20. two and eight thousandths

21. nine hundred four thousandths

22. five and six tenths

23. eighty-two hundredths

24. one and one thousandth

Write an equivalent decimal.

25. 1.9

26. 0.09

27. 0.23

28. 0.25

29. 0.72

30. 0.80

31. 0.50

32. 0.650

33. 8.300

34. 40.010

35. 5

36. 29.8

37. 12.40

38. 9.90

39. 0.1

40. 15

41. 900

42. 72.340

43. 10.30

44. 6.60

Write the number as a number of thousandths. Write the number name of the decimal.

45. 0.030

46. 0.13

47. 0.01

48. 0.8

49. 0.202

Problem Solving

50. Each rod represents $\frac{1}{10}$. How many thousandths do the blocks represent? Write the standard form and the number name.

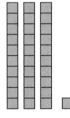

51. A gas station advertises the price of gasoline as \$2.59$\frac{9}{10}$. The fraction represents $\frac{9}{10}$ of a cent. What do you think this number is written in standard form? Justify your answer.

52. Each day, Jamilah rides her bicycle 1.08 km to school, while Lila walks 1.080 km to school. In math class, Lila states that her trip to school is longer than Jamilah's because 80 is greater than 8. Is Lila correct? Explain.

Write About It

53. Since zeros at the end of a decimal number do not change the value of a number, is 40.07 equal to 40.007? Explain your reasoning.

LESSON 2-2 Decimals and Expanded Form

Objective
- Read and write decimals to thousandths using expanded form.

Math Words
expanded form
standard form

A titan beetle can reach a length of 0.541 foot. How can Lily express this length in expanded form?

To write numbers in expanded form, use the place value of each digit. You can show a number using decimal or fraction notation.

Standard Form	Expanded Form (decimal notation)	Expanded Form (fraction notation)
2.003	$2 \times 1 + 3 \times 0.001$	$2 \times 1 + 3 \times \left(\frac{1}{1000}\right)$
0.068	$6 \times 0.01 + 8 \times 0.001$	$6 \times \left(\frac{1}{100}\right) + 8 \times \left(\frac{1}{1000}\right)$
0.888	$8 \times 0.1 + 8 \times 0.01 + 8 \times 0.001$	$8 \times \left(\frac{1}{10}\right) + 8 \times \left(\frac{1}{100}\right) + 8 \times \left(\frac{1}{1000}\right)$

In 0.888, each decimal digit is $\frac{1}{10}$ the value of the digit to its left.

▷ Lily can write 0.541 in expanded form as

$5 \times 0.1 + 4 \times 0.01 + 1 \times 0.001$ or $5 \times \left(\frac{1}{10}\right) + 4 \times \left(\frac{1}{100}\right) + 1 \times \left(\frac{1}{1000}\right)$.

PRACTICE

Write the name of the place that is $\frac{1}{10}$ times the given place.

1. hundredths

2. ones

3. tenths

4. hundreds

5. ten thousands

6. thousands

Write as a decimal.

7. $6 \times \frac{1}{100}$

8. $2 \times \frac{1}{1000}$

9. $1 \times \frac{1}{10}$

10. $4 \times \frac{1}{100}$

11. $9 \times \frac{1}{1000}$

12. $7 \times \frac{1}{10}$

13. $5 \times \frac{1}{100}$

14. $3 \times \frac{1}{1000}$

15. $8 \times \frac{1}{10}$

16. $1 \times \frac{1}{100}$

Write in expanded form.

17. 1.801

18. 2.292

19. 3.567

20. 2.034

21. 7.573

22. 5.951

Write in expanded form.

23. eight thousand and twelve thousandths

24. five and four hundred eight thousandths

25. seven hundred forty-nine thousandths

Write the number name.

26. $4 \times 1 + 1 \times 0.1 + 6 \times 0.01 + 3 \times 0.001$

27. $1 \times 100 + 2 \times 10 + 7 \times 1 + 8 \times 0.001$

Write the standard form and the number name.

28. $2 \times 1000 + 8 \times \left(\frac{1}{10}\right) + 8 \times \left(\frac{1}{1000}\right)$

29. $6 \times 10 + 3 \times \left(\frac{1}{10}\right) + 1 \times \left(\frac{1}{100}\right) + 5 \times \left(\frac{1}{1000}\right)$

30. $3 \times 1 + 1 \times \left(\frac{1}{100}\right) + 4 \times \left(\frac{1}{1000}\right)$

31. $1 \times 10 + 5 \times 1 + 2 \times \left(\frac{1}{10}\right) + 7 \times \left(\frac{1}{100}\right) + 1 \times \left(\frac{1}{1000}\right)$

Problem Solving

32. The fraction $\frac{1}{3}$ is approximately equal to 0.333. Write a sentence that relates the values of each decimal digit in 0.333.

33. As part of a robotics competition, competitors race to build a robot that mimics a given model. Last year's winner finished building her model in 2 minutes. After the competition, it was revealed that she won by $8 \times \left(\frac{1}{100}\right) + 5 \times \left(\frac{1}{1000}\right)$ of an hour. What is this amount of time written in standard form? Was it a close competition? Explain.

Write About It

34. Amy writes a number less than 1 to the thousandths place. The value of the digit in the hundredths place is $\frac{1}{10}$ the value of the digit in the tenths place. She uses only the digits 5 and 7. What could be the number that Amy writes? Explain what you did.

Complete the number name of each number.

1. 6.058 = six and fifty-eight __?__

    A. ones   **B.** tenths   **C.** hundredths   **D.** thousandths

2. 30.1 = thirty and one __?__

    A. one   **B.** tenth   **C.** hundredth   **D.** thousandth

3. 0.420 = forty-two __?__

    A. ones   **B.** tenths   **C.** hundredths   **D.** thousandths

4. 0.420 = four hundred twenty __?__

    A. ones   **B.** tenths   **C.** hundredths   **D.** thousandths

Determine the equivalent expression. Select all that apply.

5. 0.509

    A. $\dfrac{509}{1000}$

    B. fifty-nine thousandths

    C. five hundred nine thousandths

    D. $\dfrac{509}{10,000}$

6. three and twenty-two hundredths

    A. 3.22

    B. $(3 \times 1) + \left(2 \times \dfrac{1}{10}\right) + \left(2 \times \dfrac{1}{100}\right)$

    C. $3\dfrac{22}{100}$

    D. $(3 \times 1) + \left(2 \times \dfrac{1}{1}\right) + \left(2 \times \dfrac{1}{10}\right)$

7. $\dfrac{68}{100}$

    A. sixty-eight tenths

    B. sixty-eight hundredths

    C. $\left(6 \times \dfrac{1}{100}\right) + \left(8 \times \dfrac{1}{1000}\right)$

    D. $\left(6 \times \dfrac{1}{10}\right) + \left(8 \times \dfrac{1}{100}\right)$

8. $\left(7 \times \dfrac{1}{1000}\right)$

    A. 0.007

    B. seven thousandths

    C. seventy hundredths

    D. $\dfrac{7}{1000}$

Complete the fraction form of each number.

9. $0.3 = \dfrac{?}{100}$ **10.** $0.06 = \dfrac{?}{1000}$ **11.** $0.9 = \dfrac{?}{10}$ **12.** $0.75 = \dfrac{?}{1000}$

13. $0.002 = \dfrac{?}{1000}$ **14.** $0.98 = \dfrac{?}{100}$ **15.** $0.5 = \dfrac{?}{1000}$ **16.** $0.4 = \dfrac{?}{10}$

Write each number in expanded form.

17. 4.08   **18.** 8.547   **19.** 0.075

20. 1.9   **21.** 7.002   **22.** 0.83

Write the number name.

23. $3 \times 1 + 6 \times 0.1 + 1 \times 0.01 + 7 \times 0.001$ **24.** $4 \times 100 + 3 \times 1 + 7 \times 0.001$

25. $9 \times 1000 + 9 \times 0.001$ **26.** $4 \times 10 + 4 \times 0.1 + 4 \times 0.001$

Write the standard form and the number name.

27. $6 \times 1000 + 5 \times \left(\frac{1}{100}\right) + 9 \times \left(\frac{1}{1000}\right)$ **28.** $(2 \times 10) + \left(1 \times \frac{1}{10}\right) + \left(1 \times \frac{1}{100}\right) + \left(5 \times \frac{1}{1000}\right)$

29. $3 \times 10 + 5 \times \left(\frac{1}{1000}\right)$ **30.** $7 \times \left(\frac{1}{10}\right) + 9 \times \left(\frac{1}{1000}\right)$

31. How can you use base-ten blocks to show 1.09?

Problem Solving

32. Each rod represents $\frac{1}{10}$. What is the value of the model? Give the standard form, number name, and expanded form.

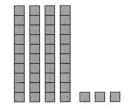

33. How are 9 thousandths and 9 thousands different and similar?

34. Frankie says 40.044 is forty and forty-four hundredths. Sammy says it is forty and forty-four thousandths. Who is correct? Explain.

A teacher writes the number two and six hundred eighty six thousandths in standard form on a whiteboard. Use this information for Exercises 35–36.

35. How does the value of the digit in the tenths place compare to the value of the digit in the thousandths place? Explain your reasoning.

36. Is the digit in the tenths place 10 times greater than the digit in the hundredths place? Explain why or why not.

37. Jo says the number names *twenty and seven thousandths* and *twenty-seven thousandths* represent the same number. Explain her mistake.

Compare and Order Decimals

Objective
- Compare and order decimals using symbols to record the comparison.

Math Words

compare

thousandth

Gymnastics is a sport that is part of the Olympic games. In a recent Olympics, a gymnast scored 15.6 on the floor exercise and 15.066 on the balance beam. In which event did the gymnast have the greater score?

To find the event with the greater score, compare the decimals 15.6 and 15.066.

Compare decimals by comparing the digits in each place-value position. Start at the left and check each place until the digits are different.

Tens	Ones	Tenths	Hundredths	Thousandths
1	5	6	0	0
1	5	0	6	6

← Use zeros as placeholders.

The whole number is the same. 15 = 15

The digits differ in the tenths place. 6 tenths > 0 tenths

You can use a symbol to show the comparison.

15.600 > 15.066

15.600 is greater than 15.066.

< means "is less than."

> means "is greater than."

= means "is equal to."

▷ The gymnast had the greater score on the floor exercise.

PRACTICE

Write an equivalent statement using the opposite symbol, < or >.

1. 4.023 < 4.8

2. 68.251 > 68.090

3. 2.50 > 2.051

Compare. Use <, >, or =.

4. 7.083 _?_ 7.83

5. 3.9 _?_ 3.12

6. 10.80 _?_ 10.80

7. 4.532 _?_ 4.453

8. 20.75 _?_ 21.42

9. 6.78 _?_ 6.721

Write in order from least to greatest and from greatest to least.

10. 1.115; 1.18; 1.12

11. 15.75; 21.42; 11.23

12. 6.78; 6.721; 6.7

Compare. Use <, >, or =.

13. 13.335 ? 13.23

14. 5.45 ? 5.053

15. 0.99 ? 1.070

16. 3.291 ? 13.291

17. 152.1 ? 15.21

18. 0.05 ? 0.005

19. 3.456 ? 34.56

20. 6.8 ? 6.800

21. 12.084 ? 12.2

22. 254,609.703 ? 254,609.933

23. 65,800,100.500 ? 65,100,800.5

Write in order from least to greatest and from greatest to least.

24. 40.06; 46.01; 40.60

25. 0.831; 0.85; 0.819

26. 6.80, 6.08, 6.808

27. 3.700, 3.07, 3.037

28. 12.02, 12.002, 1.2

29. 45, 4.405, 4.5

30. At the gymnastics meet, Cody scores 9.6 on the parallel bars, 10.2 on the rings, and 9.4 on the floor exercise. Order the events from the least to greatest score.

Problem Solving

31. The radii of the first four planets from the Sun are shown. Write a number sentence ordering the radii from smallest to largest. Why can you ignore the powers of 10?

Planet	Radius (km)
Mercury	2.44×10^3
Venus	6.052×10^3
Earth	6.371×10^3
Mars	3.390×10^3

32. Write a number that comes between 23.1 and 23.2. Then write a number that comes between the number you wrote and 23.1. Could this go on forever? Explain.

33. Amanda lives 4.205 miles from the library. Amanda's house is closer to the park than the library. Use the letter *d* to represent a distance. Then write a statement using < or > to compare.

34. A jeweler uses a scale that can weigh diamonds to the nearest hundredth of a carat. He weighs 4 diamonds as 1.29, 1.03, 1.17, and 0.96 carats. If the scale were only accurate to the nearest tenth of a carat, could the jeweler order the diamonds by weight? Explain.

Write About It

35. Rahsaan says that 3.009 is greater than 2.007, since 9 is greater than 7. Do you agree? Explain.

Round Decimals

Objective
- Use place value to round decimal numbers.

Math Words
whole number
rounding
number line

In 1958, a skateboard was made by attaching roller skates to a board. Over the years the designs improved, making the skateboard smoother to ride and faster. One of the fastest downhill skateboard speeds recorded is 80.74 mi/h. What is this speed to the nearest whole number and the nearest tenth?

Rounding decimals is similar to rounding whole numbers.

Locate 80.74 on a number line.

> 80.74 is between the whole numbers 80 and 81 and between the decimals 80.7 and 80.8.

You can round to any place in a number by looking at the digit in the place to the right.

- If the digit is less than 5, round down.
- If the digit is 5 or greater, round up.

Round 80.74 to the nearest:

Whole Number

8<u>0</u>.74 Look at the digit in the tenths place.

81 7 is greater than or equal to 5. Round up.

> The ones digit increases by 1.

Tenth

80.<u>7</u>4 Look at the digit in the hundredths place.

80.7 4 is less than 5. Round down.

> The tenths digit stays the same.

> 80.74 mi/h rounded to the nearest whole number is 81, or 81 mi/h.
> Rounded to the nearest tenth, 80.74 mi/h is 80.7, or 80.7 mi/h.

PRACTICE

Round each to the place of the underlined digit.

1. 3.6<u>8</u>2
2. <u>7</u>.92
3. 2.1<u>9</u>8
4. 2<u>7</u>.46
5. 183.5<u>1</u>7

6. 1.7<u>8</u>3
7. 3.<u>7</u>32
8. 73.1<u>5</u>9
9. 29.8<u>6</u>6
10. 112.5<u>4</u>9

11. Is 5.308 closer to 5.3 or 5.4 on a number line? Explain.

Round each to the nearest *whole number, tenth,* and *hundredth.*

12. 36.375   **13.** 0.847   **14.** 91.194   **15.** 282.651   **16.** 49.028

17. 408,932.109   **18.** 9,174,560.914   **19.** 13,122,074,011.555

Round each to the nearest ten cents and dollar.

20. $13.87   **21.** $156.74   **22.** $1792.29   **23.** $908.44   **24.** $1306.63

25. The world's largest rock crystal ball weighs 106.75 pounds. Write this weight rounded to the nearest tenth.

Match the rounded number with the correct decimal.

26. 88.88 rounded to the nearest tenth

27. 88.088 rounded to the nearest tenth

28. 88.088 rounded to the nearest hundredth

29. 88.888 rounded to the nearest hundredth

A. 88.09
B. 88.1
C. 88.9
D. 88.89

Problem Solving

30. The table shows the weights of some tablets. Tyler's tablet is the one that, when rounded to the nearest tenth, is different from the others. Which is Tyler's tablet?

Tablet	Weight (kg)
A	0.7239
B	0.6954
C	0.7069
D	0.7514

31. What is 3.0845 rounded to the nearest thousandth? Explain how you found your answer.

32. Explain why some numbers can round to the same number when rounded to the nearest whole number, tenth, or hundredth.

33. An engineering firm has 2.581 million dollars in revenue in 2016. Write this revenue in standard form, rounded to the nearest hundred thousand. Explain what you did.

Write About It

34. A number has a 6 in the tenths place. When rounded to the nearest whole number, it rounds to 60. When rounded to the nearest tenth, it rounds to 59.7. Explain how this is possible using an example.

Problem Solving
Use Logical Reasoning

Objective
- Use logical reasoning to solve problems.

Math Words
order
tenths
logical reasoning

The heights of some U.S. presidents are shown. What is the order of the presidents from shortest to tallest?

Read and Understand

What is the question that you need to answer?

What is the order of the presidents by height?

What information does the problem give you?

The names of the presidents, the numbers that show which president each one is, and their heights

What information do you need to answer the question?

The name and height of each of the presidents

Sometimes a problem includes information that is not needed to answer the question. You can ignore that kind of information.

In this problem, you do not need to know what number president each one is.

George Washington
1st President
Height:
1.87 meters

James Madison
4th President
Height:
1.63 meters

Abraham Lincoln
16th President
Height:
1.93 meters

Represent the Situation

Make a table of the presidents and their heights.

Make and Use a Plan

How can I use logical reasoning?

Analyze and organize the facts to devise a plan.

Use the table to compare and order the heights.

- *The ones digits are the same.*
- *Compare the tenths digits.*
- *6 < 8 and 6 < 9, so Madison is shortest.*
- *8 < 9, so Lincoln is tallest.*

President	Height (m)
Washington	1.87
Madison	1.63
Lincoln	1.93

> *The presidents in order from shortest to tallest are Madison (1.63 m), Washington (1.87 m), and Lincoln (1.93 m).*

Look Back

Check whether the answer makes sense.

The question asks for the order of the presidents from shortest to tallest. 1.63 < 1.87 < 1.93, so the answer makes sense.

1. Aubrey is buying flowers to make an arrangement for her living room. She spends $5.89 for 6 lilies, $9.85 for 8 daisies, and $9.89 for 3 sunflowers. For which type of flower does she spend the most money? Explain.

A batting average indicates whether a batter is more likely to get a hit. The greater the average is, the greater the chance of getting a hit. Use the table for Exercises 2–3.

Player	Batting Average
Lena	0.235
Samantha	0.253
Layla	0.233
Brittany	0.250

2. The coach needs to recommend the best batter for the all-star team. Who should she recommend?

3. The coach wants the players to bat in order from the greatest to least likely to get a hit. Explain what line-up the coach uses.

4. Arthur is told that a certain measure must be less than seventeen thousandths of a centimeter. He writes the note shown for the workers. Is Arthur's note correct? If not, correct any errors.

Make sure that each of these has a measure that is > 0.17 cm!

5. Bernie and Ron each draw a line on the chalkboard. When the teacher measures the lines, he finds that Bernie's line is 2.35 meters long, and Ron's line is 2.400 meters long. Who drew the longer line?

6. Beth wants to buy 4 chairs. A store offers a free chair with the purchase of 3 chairs. At this store, one chair costs $125. A different store sells the same chairs for $89.99. What should Beth do? Explain your reasoning.

There were 2435 visitors at the aquarium on Thursday, 2615 visitors on Friday, and 3309 visitors on Saturday. Use the information for Exercises 7–8.

7. How many more visitors were there on Saturday than Friday?

8. How many more visitors were there on Thursday and Friday than on Saturday?

Write About It

9. Explain how logical reasoning can be used to make a plan to solve Exercise 1.

Estimate with Decimals

Objective
- Use front-end estimation and rounding to estimate sums and differences of decimals.

Math Words
front-end estimation
rounding
estimate

Aiden is downloading music. He buys two albums and one single. The table shows the cost of the music.

Music Downloads	
Album #1	$9.59
Album #2	$8.92
Single	$1.45

About how much does Aiden spend altogether? About how much more does one album cost than the other?

- Use front-end estimation to estimate a sum.

Add the front digits.

$$\begin{array}{r} \$9.59 \\ 8.92 \\ + \quad 1.45 \\ \hline \$18.00 \end{array}$$

Write zeros for the other digits.

$$\begin{array}{r} \$9.59 \\ 8.92 \\ + \quad 1.45 \end{array}$$

Adjust with the back digits: 60¢ + 90¢ + 50¢ equals $2.

Add the estimates.

$$\begin{array}{r} \$18.00 \\ + \quad 2.00 \\ \hline \$20 \end{array}$$

- Use rounding to estimate a difference.

Round each number to the nearest whole number.

$$\begin{array}{r} \$9.59 \longrightarrow \$10.00 \\ - \quad 8.92 \longrightarrow 9.00 \\ \hline \text{about} \quad \$1.00 \end{array}$$

Subtract the rounded numbers.

Altogether, Aiden spends about $20 on music. One album he purchases costs about $1 more than the other album.

PRACTICE

Use front-end estimation to estimate each sum.

1. $\begin{array}{r} \$947.60 \\ + \quad 575.09 \end{array}$

2. $\begin{array}{r} 115.2 \\ +609.5 \end{array}$

3. $\begin{array}{r} \$324.54 \\ 276.37 \\ + \quad 436.93 \end{array}$

4. $\begin{array}{r} 64.328 \\ 9.058 \\ + \quad 1.254 \end{array}$

Use rounding to estimate each difference.

5. $\begin{array}{r} 943.86 \\ -137.13 \end{array}$

6. $\begin{array}{r} \$887.56 \\ - \quad 259.60 \end{array}$

7. $\begin{array}{r} \$932.55 \\ - \quad 47.28 \end{array}$

8. $\begin{array}{r} 18.963 \\ - \quad 3.589 \end{array}$

Estimate each sum or difference.

9. $895.25 + $78.24 + $122

10. 72.684 − 8.573

11. 8432.96 + 983.14

12. $532.05 − $485.42

13. 608 − 34.842

14. 13,409.55 + 5087.492

15.
```
  $ 8 3.7 2
−      8.4 4
```

16.
```
  1 5,9 6 5.8
     8,9 8 5.4
+  2,4 5 6.8
```

17.
```
   9 7 6.2 4
− 8 6 4.7 8
```

18.
```
$ 2.2 9
  0.5 8
+ 0.1 1
```

19.
```
  1 6 7.8
−  4 5.3 4 7
```

20.
```
  1 9 2 4.0 8
+   6 8 7.1 7 3
```

21.
```
  2 5,0 9 3.3
  3 0,8 4 0.4 6
+      1 6 2.4
```

22.
```
  3 0 0
− 1 8 9.4 4
```

23. Frankie wants to buy a set of golf clubs that costs $249.99. He receives a paycheck for $184.32. About how much more money does he need to purchase the golf clubs?

Problem Solving

The table shows carbon dioxide (CO_2) emissions data for several countries in a recent year. Use the table for Exercises 24–26.

24. Estimate the total CO_2 emissions of people from these countries. Add the whole numbers, and then adjust using the decimal numbers as back digits.

Country	CO_2 Emissions per Person (tons)
United States	16.39
Qatar	40.46
Denmark	6.78
Canada	13.53

25. Estimate the total CO_2 emissions of people from these countries. Round each value to the nearest whole number.

26. Emily says that one of the countries has about 3 times as much CO_2 emissions per person as another country. Write a sentence that describes her statement and includes the names of the countries.

Write About It

27. Lilly has 7 megabytes (MB) of memory available on her tablet. She wants to download a fitness app that is 2.8 MB, a game that is 2.1 MB, and a math app that is 2.4 MB. Does an estimate ensure that she has enough memory available? Explain.

Write as a decimal in standard form. In the diagram, each square represents one hundredth.

1. $\frac{63}{100}$

2.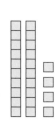

3. two and three hundred seventy thousandths

4. eight-thousandths

5. $(4 \times 1) + \left(5 \times \frac{1}{10}\right) + \left(9 \times \frac{1}{1000}\right)$

6. $9 \times \frac{1}{1000}$

Compare. Use <, >, or =.

7. 6.94 _?_ 6.094

8. 0.386 _?_ 1.021

9. 0.860 _?_ 0.86

10. 5.025 _?_ 5.26

11. 2.084 _?_ 3.085

12. 77.300 _?_ 77.40

Write in order from least to greatest.

13. 8.174; 8.147; 8.074

14. 0.685; 0.687; 0.68

15. 4.3; 4.29; 4.007

16. 0.009; 0.09; 0.9

17. 2.75; 2.5; 2.683

18. 7.04; 7.048; 7.045

19. 12.022; 12.02; 1.222

20. 4.56; 4.065; 4.405

21. 1.040; 1.4; 1.004

Round each number to the nearest whole number, tenth, and hundredth.

22. 5.729

23. 0.254

24. 12.092

25. 8.555

26. 53.492

27. 0.508

28. 108.936

29. 0.777

30. 56.789

Round each number to the place of the underlined digit.

31. $5\underline{3}.95

32. 2.9\underline{6}5

33. $\underline{3}.50

34. 0.\underline{5}48

35. $0.\underline{7}4

36. 8.4\underline{0}2

Round each number to the place of the underlined digit.

37. 12.8<u>4</u>

38. 605.6<u>0</u>5

39. <u>4</u>.571

Estimate each sum or difference.

40. $105.76 + $278.24

41. 84.176 − 15.58

42. 746.48 + 49.2

43. $4962.57 − $32.18

44.
$$\begin{array}{r} \$917.07 \\ -\quad 21.51 \\ \hline \end{array}$$

45.
$$\begin{array}{r} 10,872.8 \\ 2,429.6 \\ +\quad 466.1 \\ \hline \end{array}$$

46.
$$\begin{array}{r} 8.094 \\ -0.617 \\ \hline \end{array}$$

47.
$$\begin{array}{r} \$12.48 \\ 15.74 \\ +\quad 3.96 \\ \hline \end{array}$$

Round each set of numbers to the place of the underlined digit.
Then write the original numbers in order from least to greatest.

48. 0.8<u>4</u>6; 0.8<u>5</u>7; 0.8<u>4</u>2

49. <u>2</u>.843; <u>0</u>.087; <u>1</u>.469

50. 12.<u>7</u>53; 12.<u>6</u>24; 12.<u>9</u>05

51. 12.<u>3</u>44; 12.<u>0</u>4; 12.<u>4</u>03

52. 9.8<u>0</u>2; 9.8<u>1</u>1; 9.8<u>8</u>1

53. 1<u>7</u>.5, 1<u>7</u>.055, 1<u>5</u>.7505

Select the true statement.

54. A. 1.578 > 1.587

B. $2.41 = 2\frac{410}{1000}$

C. To the nearest whole, 19.249 rounds to 20.

55. A. $0.604 = \left(6 \times \frac{1}{10}\right) + \left(4 \times \frac{1}{100}\right)$

B. $\frac{57}{1000} > \frac{57}{100}$

C. The difference $10.08 − $4.86 is about $5.

Problem Solving

Use the map for Exercises 56–58.

56. Compare the distances in the map.

<u> ? </u> < <u> ? </u> < <u> ? </u>

57. Estimate the distance from Tucker's house to the library, then from the library to school, then from school back home. Would the estimate change if the locations were in the reverse order?

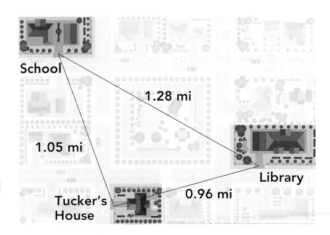

58. Sydney rounds 1.28 miles to 1.3 miles, and 0.96 mile to 1.0 mile. She concludes that the school is 0.3 mile farther from the library than Tucker's house is. Do you agree? Explain.

Some plants begin as very tiny seeds, such as the seeds shown in the table. The table shows the approximate length of each seed.

Mustard seeds

Begonia Seed	Mustard Seed	Petunia Seed
0.01 in.	0.05 in.	0.02 in.

Identify the number name for the length of each seed.

1. begonia

2. mustard

3. petunia

Compare the lengths of the begonia, petunia, and mustard seeds.

4. A ? seed is the longest.

5. A ? seed is the shortest.

6. A ? is shorter than a ? seed but longer than a ? seed.

Round the length of each seed to the nearest tenth of an inch.

7. begonia

8. petunia

9. mustard

10. Would it be more unusual to have a Begonia seed that is 0.1 in. long, or a Petunia seed that is 0.01 in. long? Explain.

Khloe is starting a garden and plants mustard seeds. A mustard seed will grow into mustard greens. Mustard greens are one of the most nutritious leafy vegetables in the world.

11. Khloe builds a rectangular bed for the garden that is 2.86 meters long and 1.82 meters wide. Estimate the amount of fencing needed to surround the bed. Do you know that the estimate is enough fencing?

12. To double-check her measurements, Khloe writes the dimensions of the garden bed in expanded form. Help Khloe complete the expanded form of each dimension.

length: $2.86 = \underline{\ ?\ } \times 1 + \underline{\ ?\ } \times \left(\frac{1}{10}\right) + \underline{\ ?\ } \times \left(\frac{1}{100}\right)$

width: $1.82 = \underline{\ ?\ } \times 1 + \underline{\ ?\ } \times \left(\frac{1}{10}\right) + \underline{\ ?\ } \times \left(\frac{1}{100}\right)$

13. What is another way Khloe could write the dimensions in expanded form? Determine the alternate expanded form of each dimension.

14. Khloe explains to her friends that you plant mustard seeds five tenths of an inch deep, which is the same as the length of the seed. Is Khloe correct? Explain.

The table shows how much money Khloe spends at various nurseries purchasing seeds.

Nursery	Total Spent
Valley Farms	$10.09
Mitchell Gardens	$4.84
Gary's Garden Center	$4.98

15. Compare how much Khloe spends at each nursery. Estimate how much she spends altogether. Explain your reasoning.

16. Measure the length of your favorite fruit seed to the nearest tenth of a centimeter. Compare your value with your classmates for the same fruit and other fruits. Prepare a chart that lists the seeds in order from least to greatest. Discuss whether the same list would apply to the sizes of the fruits themselves.

Determine the best answer for each problem.

1. Round $348.59 to the nearest dollar.

2. Write a fraction in lowest terms that is equivalent to 0.3.

3. Round 8.208 to the nearest hundredth.

A. 8   **B.** 8.2
C. 8.21   **D.** 8.22

4. Order the numbers 1.485, 1.402, and 1.419 from least to greatest.

A. 1.402; 1.419; 1.485
B. 1.419; 1.402; 1.485
C. 1.485; 1.419; 1.402
D. 1.402; 1.485; 1.419

5. What is the missing number?
0.24 × 10 = 0.024 × _?_

A. $\frac{1}{100}$

B. $\frac{1}{10}$

C. 10

D. 100

6. Select the expanded form of 1.076.

A. $(1 \times 1) + \left(7 \times \frac{1}{10}\right) + \left(6 \times \frac{1}{100}\right)$

B. $(1 \times 1) + \left(7 \times \frac{1}{100}\right) + \left(6 \times \frac{1}{1000}\right)$

C. $(1 \times 10) + \left(7 \times \frac{1}{100}\right) + \left(6 \times \frac{1}{1000}\right)$

D. $\left(1 \times \frac{1}{10}\right) + \left(7 \times \frac{1}{100}\right) + \left(6 \times \frac{1}{1000}\right)$

7. What is the missing number?
0.008 × 10 = _?_

8. Round 2.394 to the nearest hundredth.

9. Select the best estimate of the difference.

$$\begin{array}{r} 875.214 \\ -33.504 \\ \hline \end{array}$$

A. 800   **B.** 841
C. 843   **D.** 900

10. Select the best estimate of the sum.

$$\begin{array}{r} 1439.16 \\ 557.09 \\ +1.54 \\ \hline \end{array}$$

A. 900   **B.** 1000
C. 2000   **D.** 3000

Multiplication

An invasive species is any kind of living organism, such as a plant, animal, or bacteria, that is not native to an ecosystem. It could cause harm to the environment, economy, or even humans. Invasive species often prey on native species. They can reproduce quickly and be difficult to eliminate.

Most Damaging Invasive Species in U.S.

- **Constrictors:** These snakes are released into the wild by their pet owners when they become too large to manage.
- **Zebra Mussels:** These mussels cause major clogs in pipes and cling to boat motors and other native mussels.
- **Mongoose:** Originally introduced to protect sugar cane from pests, this animal harmed more wildlife than anticipated, causing the extinction of 12 species from Puerto Rico, the West Indies, and Jamaica.
- **Starlings:** This bird has thrived in the U.S., causing damage to crops and stealing the nesting sites of native birds.

Multiplication Properties

Objective
- Use multiplication properties to compare and evaluate expressions.

Math Words
Commutative Property
Associative Property
Identity Property
Zero Property
Distributive Property

The properties of multiplication, together with the Distributive Property, can help you multiply quickly and correctly.

Commutative Property of Multiplication

Changing the order of factors does not change the product.

Example: $3 \times 4 = 12$ $4 \times 3 = 12$

Associative Property of Multiplication

Changing the grouping of factors does not change the product.

Example: $(2 \times 6) \times 3 = 2 \times (6 \times 3)$

$12 \times 3 = 2 \times 18$

$36 = 36$

Identity Property of Multiplication

The product of 1 and a number is the same as that number.

Example: $8 \times 1 = 8$ $1 \times 8 = 8$

Zero Property of Multiplication

The product of zero and a number is zero.

Example: $12 \times 0 = 0$ $0 \times 12 = 0$

Distributive Property

When the same factor is distributed across two addends, the product does not change.

Example: $6 \times (2 + 5) = (6 \times 2) + (6 \times 5)$

$6 \times 7 = 12 + 30$

$42 = 42$

PRACTICE

Name the property shown.

1. $5 \times (3 \times 1) = (5 \times 3) \times 1$

2. $0 \times 48 = 48 \times 0$

3. $3 \times 25 = 25 \times 3$

4. $10 \times (4 + 3) = (10 \times 4) + (10 \times 3)$

Complete the number sentence to show the given property.

5. Identity Property
$12 \times \underline{\ ?\ } = \underline{\ ?\ }$

6. Distributive Property
$18 \times (15 + 12) = (18 \times \underline{\ ?\ }) + (18 \times \underline{\ ?\ })$

7. Commutative Property
$41 \times \underline{\ ?\ } = \underline{\ ?\ } \times 2$

8. Associative Property
$4 \times (5 \times \underline{\ ?\ }) = (\underline{\ ?\ } \times \underline{\ ?\ }) \times 3$

9. Commutative Property
$\underline{\ ?\ } \times 18 = \underline{\ ?\ } \times 3$

10. Distributive Property
$4 \times (5 + \underline{\ ?\ }) = (\underline{\ ?\ } \times \underline{\ ?\ }) + (4 \times 2)$

11. Zero Property
$9 \times \underline{\ ?\ } = \underline{\ ?\ }$

12. Associative Property
$(7 \times \underline{\ ?\ }) \times 1 = \underline{\ ?\ } \times (5 \times \underline{\ ?\ })$

Problem Solving

13. In New York, Ha and Kelly visit the same number of museums. Ha visits 2 museums during each of her 3 days there. If Kelly visits 3 museums a day, how many days is her trip? How do you know?

14. An engineer can assemble the robots shown in 1 day. Two are considered large robots. Write two expressions that show how many small and large robots the engineer can create in 5 days. How do you know that the expressions are equivalent?

15. Explain how you could use the Distributive Property to multiply 53 by 9.

16. Write an equation that illustrates both the Identity Property of Multiplication and the Zero Property of Multiplication.

Write About It

17. Compare the definitions of the Commutative, Associative, and Identity properties of addition to those of multiplication. Which involve only changing certain words? Explain.

Multiplication Patterns

Objective
- Use patterns to multiply whole numbers by multiples of 10, 100, and 1000.

Math Word
multiple

A data storage company uses computer servers to manage files for hundreds of small businesses. The company has 6 different rooms that each have 200 computer servers. How many servers does the company have?

To solve, multiply 6 by 200. You can use patterns to help you multiply by multiples of 10, 100, and 1000.

Study the patterns for multiplying by a multiple of 10, 100, or 1000.

$80 \times 70 = 5600$	$20 \times 70 = 1400$	$40 \times 50 = 2000$
$800 \times 70 = 56{,}000$	$200 \times 70 = 14{,}000$	$400 \times 50 = 20{,}000$
$8000 \times 70 = 560{,}000$	$2000 \times 70 = 140{,}000$	$4000 \times 50 = 200{,}000$

To multiply a whole number by a multiple of 10, 100, or 1000:

- Write the product of the nonzero digits.
- Count the number of zeros in the factors.
- Write the same number of zeros at the end of the product.

$$500 \times 3 = 1500$$
two zeros

$$\begin{array}{r} 40 \\ \times\,8{,}000 \\ \hline 320{,}000 \end{array}$$ 4 zeros

$6 \times 200 = 1200$, so the company has 1200 servers.

PRACTICE

Find the products.

1. 10×6
100×6
1000×6

2. 10×8
100×8
1000×8

3. 20×3
200×3
2000×3

4. 60×5
600×5
6000×5

5. 30×4
300×4
3000×4

6. 40×9
400×9
4000×9

7. 50×7
500×7
5000×7

8. 80×8
800×8
8000×8

Multiply.

9. $\begin{array}{r} 70 \\ \times\ 6 \\ \hline \end{array}$

10. $\begin{array}{r} 900 \\ \times\ 3 \\ \hline \end{array}$

11. $\begin{array}{r} 4000 \\ \times\ 8 \\ \hline \end{array}$

12. $\begin{array}{r} 5000 \\ \times\ 2 \\ \hline \end{array}$

Multiply.

13.
$$\begin{array}{r} 8 \\ \times 60 \\ \hline \end{array}$$

14.
$$\begin{array}{r} 7 \\ \times 900 \\ \hline \end{array}$$

15.
$$\begin{array}{r} 40 \\ \times 400 \\ \hline \end{array}$$

16.
$$\begin{array}{r} 20 \\ \times 3000 \\ \hline \end{array}$$

17. 4×2000

18. 20×400

19. $6 \times 60{,}000$

20. 2000×30

21. 7×10^2

22. 3×10^3

23. $4 \times 10^4 \times 10$

24. $50 \times 3 \times 10^2$

Complete each problem with the correct numbers by using the properties of multiplication.

25. $2000 \times \underline{\ ?\ } =$
$(\underline{\ ?\ } \times 2) \times 9 =$
$1000 \times (2 \times \underline{\ ?\ }) = \underline{\ ?\ }$

26. $40 \times 600 =$
$\underline{\ ?\ } \times 10 \times 6 \times \underline{\ ?\ } =$
$\underline{\ ?\ } \times 6 \times 10 \times \underline{\ ?\ } =$
$\underline{\ ?\ } \times \underline{\ ?\ } = \underline{\ ?\ }$

Write a numerical expression that matches the phrase.

27. The product of 50 and a multiple of 1000

28. Multiply 277 by 6, then multiply by a power of 10

Problem Solving

6000 sq yd

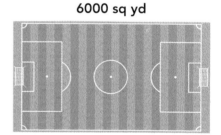

29. There are 9 square feet in 1 square yard. A school builds a sports field as shown. What is the area of the field in square feet?

30. The average household in the U.S. uses about 400 gallons of water in a day. How many gallons of water would the typical household use in a week?

31. Haley rewrites the product of 5000×3. Her work is shown. What property allows her to write the expression as $5 \times 3 \times 1000$ in her second step? Explain.

$5000 \times 3 =$
$5 \times 1000 \times 3 =$
$5 \times 3 \times 1000 =$
$15 \times 1000 =$
15×10^3

Write About It

32. Sarah says the product of $8 \times 200 \times 30$ has three zeros. Her reason is that there are 3 zeros in the factors. Is her reasoning correct?

3-3 Estimate Products

What is the approximate cost of 114 sets of acrylic paint if one set costs $36.74?

Estimate by rounding.

- Round each factor to its greatest place.
- Multiply the rounded factors.

$$\$36.74 \longrightarrow \$40$$
$$\times \quad 114 \longrightarrow \times 100$$

$$\$36.74 \times 114$$
$$\downarrow \qquad \downarrow$$
$$\$40 \times 100 = \$4000$$

> 114 sets of acrylic paint cost about $4000.

Estimate the sum $501 + 498 + 510 + 508 + 485 + 493$ by clustering.

Sometimes a sum has a number of addends that cluster around a certain number. Estimate the sum by multiplying that number by the number of addends.

Estimate:

$$501 + 498 + 510 + 508 + 485 + 493$$
$$\downarrow \quad \downarrow \quad \downarrow \quad \downarrow \quad \downarrow \quad \downarrow$$
$$500 + 500 + 500 + 500 + 500 + 500 = 6 \times 500$$
$$= 3000$$

> An estimate for the sum is 3000.

PRACTICE

Estimate each product by rounding.

1. 88 $\times 51$	**2.** 94 $\times 18$	**3.** 31 $\times 43$	**4.** 127 $\times 46$
5. 392 $\times 78$	**6.** 325 $\times 182$	**7.** 685 $\times 323$	**8.** 176 $\times 521$
9. $\$2.25$ $\times 7$	**10.** $\$4.89$ $\times 29$	**11.** $\$3.27$ $\times 6$	**12.** $\$6.88$ $\times 5$

Estimate each sum by clustering.

13. 25 + 31 + 32 + 31 + 28 + 34 + 31 + 29 + 29

14. 120 + 145 + 95 + 86 + 112

15. 684 + 659 + 739 + 721 + 659 + 744 + 699 + 728 + 641 + 700

Estimate each product by rounding.

16. 22 × 38

17. 81 × 18

18. 68 × 41

19. 217 × 51

20. $5.12 × 81

21. $4.86 × 231

Estimate each expression.

22. 3 × (42 + 44 + 39 + 40 + 37)

23. 691 + 702 + 704 + 696 − 691

24. $2.89 + $3.04 + $3.11 + $2.95 + $19.99

25. 2 × ($15.99 + $16.14 + $15.95 + $15.87 + $16.03 + $16.09)

Problem Solving

26. Write 4 addends with an estimated sum of 240 using clustering.

27. An animator needs to upgrade his computer to a hard drive that has more memory. Each terabyte of storage costs $76.50. The animator estimates that he will need $400. How many terabytes might the animator need? Justify your answer.

28. An architect plans a square fence around a building as shown in the diagram. The fencing costs $38 per foot. He estimates the cost will be $12,000. Is this estimate reasonable? Explain.

323 ft

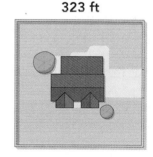

29. A sculptor collects several blocks of granite for his studio. The blocks weigh 22 lb, 18 lb, 24 lb, 16 lb, and 21 lb. About how many pounds of granite does he bring back to this studio?

─Write About It ◇─────

30. Jennie estimates 591 × 37 to be 24,000. How do you think her estimate compares to the actual product? Explain.

Zeros in the Multiplicand

Objective
- Multiply multidigit numbers by 1-digit numbers.

Math Words
multiplicand
multiplier
product

Each of three classes uses 21,708 mL of distilled water in a science experiment. How much distilled water is used altogether by the three classes?

- Estimate by rounding.

    $21,708 \times 3 \longrightarrow 20,000 \times 3 = 60,000$

- Multiply to find the exact value.

Multiply the ones. Regroup.

Multiply the tens. Then add the regrouped tens.

$$
\begin{array}{r}
\overset{2}{} \\
\text{multiplicand} \rightarrow 21,708 \\
\text{multiplier} \rightarrow \times 3 \\
\hline
\text{product} \rightarrow 4
\end{array}
$$

3 × 8 ones = 24 ones = 2 tens 4 ones

$$
\begin{array}{r}
\overset{2}{} \\
21,708 \\
\times 3 \\
\hline
24
\end{array}
$$

Repeat for the hundreds place.

$$
\begin{array}{r}
\overset{2}{}\overset{2}{} \\
21,708 \\
\times 3 \\
\hline
124
\end{array}
$$

Repeat for the thousands place.

$$
\begin{array}{r}
\overset{2}{}\overset{2}{} \\
21,708 \\
\times 3 \\
\hline
5124
\end{array}
$$

Repeat for the ten thousands place.

$$
\begin{array}{r}
\overset{2}{}\overset{2}{} \\
21,708 \\
\times 3 \\
\hline
65,124
\end{array}
$$

The three classes use 65,124 mL of distilled water.

Study these examples.

Use the algorithm.

$$
\begin{array}{r}
\overset{3}{} \\
90,500 \\
\times 6 \\
\hline
543,000
\end{array}
$$

Use the Distributive Property.

$$
\begin{aligned}
6 \times 90,500 &= 6 \times (90,000 + 500) \\
&= 6 \times 90,000 + 6 \times 500 \\
&= 540,000 + 3000 \\
&= 543,000
\end{aligned}
$$

PRACTICE

Use rounding to estimate. Then multiply.

1.
$$
\begin{array}{r}
3302 \\
\times 7 \\
\hline
\end{array}
$$

2.
$$
\begin{array}{r}
6011 \\
\times 8 \\
\hline
\end{array}
$$

3.
$$
\begin{array}{r}
62,090 \\
\times 3 \\
\hline
\end{array}
$$

4.
$$
\begin{array}{r}
\$10,006 \\
\times 4 \\
\hline
\end{array}
$$

5. 2×5209

6. $10,069 \times 5$

7. $60,304 \times 6$

8. $\$50,002 \times 8$

Use rounding to estimate. Then multiply.

9. 2 3 , 0 1 6
    ×   5

10. 6 8 , 5 0 9
    ×   8

11. 4 0 , 0 2 3
    ×   7

12. 5 2 , 0 5 0
    ×   4

13. 8 0 , 4 0 3
    ×   6

14. 8 3 , 6 0 0
    ×   3

15. 9 0 , 0 5 3
    ×   5

16. 4 0 , 0 7 0
    ×   8

17. 8 0 , 0 0 3
    ×   7

18. 8 9 , 0 0 0
    ×   9

19. 4 1 2 , 0 0 9
    ×   5

20. 8 3 9 , 4 0 0
    ×   8

21. 3 4 9 , 0 9 0
    ×   6

22. 7 2 4 , 0 0 8
    ×   9

23. 9 1 1 , 0 6 0
    ×   4

24. $ 4 3 , 0 5 0
    ×   5

Find each product. Use the Distributive Property.

25. 4 × 20,859

26. 8 × 68,806

27. 70,042 × 5

28. 68,006 × 3

29. 8 × $2507

30. 9 × $9050

31. $7080 × 6

32. $5004 × 7

33. 9 × 915,006

34. 4 × 783,500

35. 901,003 × 5

36. $794,000 × 8

Problem Solving

37. A new road being surfaced is 85,003 yards long. An engineer makes a mark at every foot on the road from one end to the other. How many marks will the engineer make on the road? Assume that there is a mark at the end of the road, but not at the start.

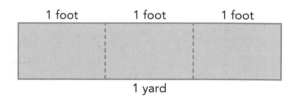

1 foot   1 foot   1 foot

1 yard

38. Suppose you multiply by a one-digit number that is not zero. Will there always be the same number of zeros in the product as there are in the multiplicand? Use an example to justify your answer.

39. To find 69,998 × 5, Kadin multiplies 70,000 by 5 to get 350,000. He then subtracts 2. Explain and correct his error.

Write About It

40. Jesse is multiplying a 5-digit number by 8. The number has a 0 in the hundreds place, a 4 in the tens place, and a 1 in the ones place. Without knowing the number, what can you say about the digit in the hundreds place of the product? How do you know?

Select the best estimate for the product.

1. 43 × 68

   A. 2400   **B.** 2800   **C.** 3000   **D.** 3500

2. $9.50 × 22

   A. $20   **B.** $180   **C.** $200   **D.** $300

3. 6.25 × 325

   A. 1800   **B.** 2100   **C.** 2400   **D.** 2800

4. 186 × 18

   A. 1000   **B.** 2000   **C.** 2800   **D.** 4000

Select the best estimate.

5. About how many centimeters are in 15 inches?

   A. 15 cm   **B.** 30 cm

   C. 45 cm   **D.** 80 cm

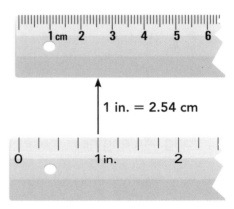

1 in. = 2.54 cm

6. About how many centimeters are in 3007 inches?

   A. 1000 cm   **B.** 1200 cm

   C. 6000 cm   **D.** 9000 cm

Find each product.

7. 6807 × 2   **8.** 7 × 32,005   **9.** 1060 × 3   **10.** 70,606 × 5

11. 6 × 809   **12.** 9 × 4006   **13.** 81,074 × 5   **14.** 5601 × 4

15. 8 × 5083   **16.** 3 × 60,516   **17.** 19,200 × 8   **18.** 67,505 × 4

Estimate each sum.

19. $4.05 + $3.84 + $4.19 + $3.69 + $3.58 + $4.41

20. 768 + 835 + 778 + 793 + 826 + 842 + 839 + 752

21. Almonds cost $9.59 per pound and cashews cost $10.19 per pound. Estimate the total cost of 4.93 pounds of each nut.

Match each number sentence to the property it shows.

22. $0 \times 12 = 0$

23. $6 \times 30 = 30 \times 6$

24. $2 \times (4 \times 3) = (2 \times 4) \times 3$

25. $5 \times (7 + 2) = (5 \times 7) + (5 \times 2)$

A. Associative Property
B. Commutative Property
C. Distributive Property
D. Zero Property

Match. Find each product.

26. 50×3

27. $5 \times 10^3 \times 3$

28. 500×300

29. $5 \times 3 \times 10^2$

A. 150
B. 1500
C. 15,000
D. 150,000

30. 6×900

31. $600 \times 9 \times 10^2$

32. $9 \times 6 \times 1000$

33. 90×6

A. 540
B. 5400
C. 54,000
D. 540,000

Problem Solving

Hannah wants to find the product 18×1007. She writes $(10 + 8) \times 1007$, and then $10 \times 1007 + 8 \times 1007$. Use this information for Exercises 34–35.

34. What property did Hannah use?

35. Find 8×1007. How could you use it to find 18×1007?

Use the canvas for Exercises 36–37.

36. Does a canvas that is 22 inches wide and 27 inches tall have the same area? Explain.

37. Elaine writes $(3 \times 9) \times 22$ and then plans to find the exact area of the canvas using the Associative Property. How can she do this and only multiply by a 1-digit number?

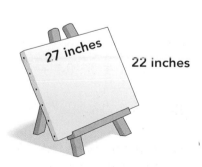

27 inches   22 inches

Multiply by Two-Digit Numbers

Objective
- Multiply a whole number by a 2-digit multiplier.

Math Word
partial product

Lola's computer repair company orders 175 packets of screws. Each packet has 32 screws. How many screws did the company order?

- Estimate by rounding.

  175×32

  $200 \times 30 = 6000$

- Multiply to find the exact value. To multiply by two digits:

Multiply by the ones.	Multiply by the tens.	Add the partial products.
$\begin{array}{r} {\scriptstyle 1\ 1} \\ 175 \\ \times\ 32 \\ \hline 350 \end{array}$ $2 \times 175 \rightarrow 350$	$\begin{array}{r} {\scriptstyle 2\ 1} \\ 175 \\ \times\ 32 \\ \hline 350 \\ 5250 \end{array}$ $30 \times 175 \rightarrow 5250$	$\begin{array}{r} 175 \\ \times\ 32 \\ \hline 350 \\ +5250 \\ \hline 5600 \end{array}$ partial products

> Lola's company ordered 5600 screws. This is close to the estimate of 6000.

Study these examples.

$\begin{array}{r} {\scriptstyle 2} \\ 65 \\ \times 40 \\ \hline 00 \\ +2600 \\ \hline 2600 \end{array}$	$\begin{array}{r} {\scriptstyle 4\ 1} \\ 372 \\ \times\ 16 \\ \hline 2232 \\ +3720 \\ \hline 5952 \end{array}$	$\begin{array}{r} {\scriptstyle 3\ 3} \\ 2044 \\ \times\ 81 \\ \hline 2044 \\ +163520 \\ \hline 165,564 \end{array}$
$0 \times 65 \rightarrow$ $40 \times 65 \rightarrow$	$6 \times 372 \rightarrow$ $10 \times 372 \rightarrow$	$1 \times 2044 \rightarrow$ $80 \times 2044 \rightarrow$

For 65×40, the partial product for the ones is zero. You can choose whether or not to write partial products that are equal to zero.

PRACTICE

Use rounding to estimate. Then multiply.

1. $\begin{array}{r} 62 \\ \times 28 \end{array}$

2. $\begin{array}{r} 54 \\ \times 26 \end{array}$

3. $\begin{array}{r} 43 \\ \times 48 \end{array}$

4. $\begin{array}{r} 62 \\ \times 44 \end{array}$

5. $\begin{array}{r} 206 \\ \times\ 37 \end{array}$

6. $\begin{array}{r} 639 \\ \times\ 58 \end{array}$

7. $\begin{array}{r} 572 \\ \times\ 63 \end{array}$

8. $\begin{array}{r} 450 \\ \times\ 32 \end{array}$

9. $\begin{array}{r} 7009 \\ \times\ 86 \end{array}$

10. $\begin{array}{r} 8506 \\ \times\ 74 \end{array}$

Use rounding to estimate. Then multiply.

11.	44	12.	67	13.	153	14.	396	15.	237
	×16		×30		× 32		× 27		× 82

16.	621	17.	3928	18.	2423	19.	6205	20.	1279
	× 92		× 47		× 74		× 25		× 62

Find each product.

21. 90 × 41	**22.** 83 × 59	**23.** 716 × 89	**24.** 39 × 513
25. 27 × 429	**26.** 625 × 30	**27.** 8044 × 47	**28.** 92 × 5620
29. 3693 × 51	**30.** 6240 × 74	**31.** 23 × 41,127	**32.** 48 × 36,219

Problem Solving

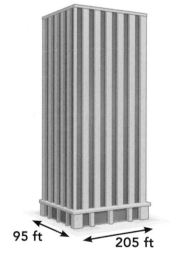

95 ft   205 ft

33. A musical theater sold 187 tickets on Friday and 238 tickets on Saturday. Tickets cost $12. Did the theater reach its goal of $5000 in ticket sales? Explain.

34. In July of 2016, China finished building FAST, the world's largest single-dish radio telescope. Its dish covers an area nearly the size of 30 soccer fields. If a rectangular soccer field is 100 yd by 60 yd, what is the area of the dish?

35. An architect designs the skyscraper shown. The design calls for 76 floors. What will be the total square footage of the building once it is built? Explain.

36. A bakery has muffin trays with 48 molds per tray. The baker bakes 12 trays at a time for one half an hour. If the factory runs 24 hours per day, how many muffins can the bakery bake in a day? Explain.

Write About It

37. Omar multiplies 316 × 81 and gets a product of 2528. Describe and correct his error.

```
        3 1 6
     ×    8 1
        3 1 6
      2 5 2 8
      2 8 4 4
```

Problem Solving
Guess and Test

Objective
- Use the guess and test strategy to solve problems.

Math Word
multiply

A factory ships headphones to stores in cases of 48 headphones and cartons of 12 headphones. Today 6912 headphones are shipped in 360 packages. Describe the shipment.

You can use a guess and test strategy to solve this problem.

To do this, make a table to keep track of your guesses.

Make a first guess. Since there are 360 packages in all, try 60 cases and 300 cartons. Multiply the number of cases by 48. Multiply the number of cartons by 12. Add to get the total.

Number of Cases	Headphones in Cases	Number of Cartons	Headphones in Cartons	Total Shipped
60	2880	300	3600	6480

A case contains more headphones than a carton. So, increase the number of cases and decrease the number of cartons.

This guess gives you a low total, so guess again.

Number of Cases	Headphones in Cases	Number of Cartons	Headphones in Cartons	Total Shipped
80	3840	280	3360	7200

The total for this guess is too high. Try 75 cases and 285 cartons.

Number of Cases	Headphones in Cases	Number of Cartons	Headphones in Cartons	Total Shipped
75	3600	285	3420	7020

The total is getting closer to 6912. Try changing the numbers by 3.

Number of Cases	Headphones in Cases	Number of Cartons	Headphones in Cartons	Total Shipped
72	3456	288	3456	6912

This guess gives the correct total for the number of headphones shipped.

> Today, 72 cases and 288 cartons of headphones are shipped.

This strategy can be used when other strategies fail. It does take more time, and you need to use number sense to adjust your guesses.

David owns a bakery. He wants to bake 246 loaves of bread each day. There are 15 loaves in a batch of rye bread, and 14 loaves in a batch of wheat bread. Use this information for Exercises 1–3.

1. David wants to find how many batches of rye and how many batches of wheat he must bake each day. If you use a guess and test strategy to help him, what guess would you make first? Explain.

2. How many batches of each type must David bake? Describe your next step after your first guess.

3. A special order comes into David's Bakery. He needs to bake 391 loaves of bread on Saturday. He still plans to bake the same number of loaves per batch. How batches of each bread will he need to bake on Saturday?

4. What two whole numbers have a sum of 68 and a product of 1035? Copy and complete the table to find out. Explain how you can use guess and test as a strategy to find the two numbers.

Guess	First Number	Second Number	Sum	Product
1	35	33	68	1155
2	25	?	?	?
3	45	?	?	?

5. Chloe puts her coin collection into an album. She fills 28 pages like the two pages shown with coins, and puts the last 8 coins on the next page. How many coins are in Chloe's collection?

6. A library has 145 shelves of fiction books and 359 shelves of nonfiction books. Each bookshelf holds about 39 books. About how many books are there in all?

7. Joseph says that the value of the digit 9 in 9,065,361 is greater than the value of the digit 9 in 29,000,753 because 29,000,753 is greater than 9,065,361. Is Joseph's reasoning correct? Explain.

8. A number has 3 digits. The tens digit is 5. When the hundreds digit and ones digit are switched, the number increases by 495. What is the number?

Write About It

9. Why is it helpful to use a table when using the guess and test strategy? Relate your answer to finding the solution.

Objective
- Multiply a whole number by a 3-digit number.

Math Word
partial product

Emily is downloading photos from her memory card. She has 189 photos, and each photo uses 335 KB of memory. Estimate the total amount of memory used by the photos. How does your estimate compare to the exact value? Explain the difference.

- Estimate by rounding.

335×189

$300 \times 200 = 60,000$

The product should be close to 60,000.

- Multiply to find the exact value.

To multiply by a three-digit number:

Multiply by the ones.	Multiply by the tens.	Multiply by the hundreds. Add the partial products.

Multiply by the ones.

```
        3 4
      3 3 5
    × 1 8 9
9 × 3 3 5 → 3 0 1 5
```

Multiply by the tens.

```
          2 4
        3 3 5
      × 1 8 9
        3 0 1 5
80 × 335 → 2 6 8 0 0
```

Multiply by the hundreds.
Add the partial products.

```
            3 3 5
          × 1 8 9
            3 0 1 5
            2 6 8 0 0
100 × 335 → + 3 3 5 0 0
            6 3 , 3 1 5
```

▷ Emily's pictures use a total of 63,315 KB of memory.

This is close to, but more than, the estimate of 60,000 KB. This is because the greater factor, 335, was rounded down more than the lesser factor, 189, was rounded up.

PRACTICE

Use rounding to estimate. Then multiply.

1. 541 ×122	**2.** 345 ×211	**3.** 217 ×115	**4.** 431 ×134	**5.** 501 ×272
6. 244 ×152	**7.** 420 ×135	**8.** 305 ×271	**9.** 360 ×417	**10.** 742 ×343
11. 1316 × 287	**12.** 4890 × 121	**13.** 1220 × 390	**14.** 1327 × 441	**15.** 5184 × 748

Use rounding to estimate. Then multiply.

16.
```
   846
 × 163
```

17.
```
   386
 × 274
```

18.
```
   235
 × 555
```

19.
```
   723
 × 461
```

20.
```
   901
 × 822
```

21.
```
  2108
 × 362
```

22.
```
  6382
 × 285
```

23.
```
 12,424
 ×   590
```

24.
```
 27,023
 ×   375
```

25.
```
 39,180
 ×   150
```

26.
```
  3872
 × 163
```

27.
```
  6492
 × 244
```

28.
```
  9532
 × 823
```

29.
```
  1090
 × 977
```

30.
```
  4352
 × 421
```

Find each product.

31. 354 × 120

32. 417 × 131

33. 252 × 204

34. 475 × 218

35. 21,979 × 482

36. 1143 × 236

37. 40,185 × 962

38. 819 × 25,709

39. n × 328 when n = 274

40. n × 853 when n = 418

41. 275 × n when n = 362

42. 415 × n when n = 672

Problem Solving

43. Maria multiplies 318 by 201. Petra multiplies 201 by 318. Their solutions have different partial products. How do the products compare? Explain.

350 sheets

44. A store sells 326 packs of paper on Monday, and 209 packs on Tuesday. How many sheets of paper does the store sell?

45. Without computing, explain why the product 445 × 109 is greater than the product 445 × 108. How much greater?

46. A ticket to a football game costs $149. A season pass for all 16 games costs $2150. Explain whether a season pass is a good deal.

47. On Thursday, 180 tickets for $149 each and 89 season passes for $2150 each were sold. Find the total sales for Thursday.

Write About It

48. How will the product 345 × 569 compare to the product 3450 × 569? Use a property to justify your answer.

3-8 Zeros in the Multiplier

Sullivan paints using pointillism, which is a technique that uses patterns of dots. The painting will have about 225 dots per square inch. If the painting is 208 square inches, how many dots are in the painting?

◆ Estimate by rounding. 225 × 208

$$200 \times 200 = 40{,}000$$

◆ Multiply to find the exact value.

Long Way

$$\begin{array}{r} 2\,2\,5 \\ \times\,2\,0\,8 \\ \hline \end{array}$$

8 × 225 ⟶ 1 8 0 0
0 × 225 ⟶ 0 0 0 0
200 × 225 ⟶ + 4 5 0 0 0
46,800

Short Way

$$\begin{array}{r} 2\,2\,5 \\ \times\,2\,0\,8 \\ \hline \end{array}$$

8 × 225 ⟶ 1 8 0 0
200 × 225 ⟶ + 4 5 0 0 0
46,800

> There are 0 tens in 208, so omit the second partial product.

There are about 46,800 dots in the painting.

PRACTICE

Use rounding to estimate. Then multiply.

1. $\begin{array}{r} 2\,1\,9 \\ \times\,3\,0\,0 \\ \hline \end{array}$

2. $\begin{array}{r} 3\,9\,1 \\ \times\,6\,0\,0 \\ \hline \end{array}$

3. $\begin{array}{r} 5\,0\,8 \\ \times\,7\,9\,0 \\ \hline \end{array}$

4. $\begin{array}{r} 7\,6\,1 \\ \times\,3\,6\,0 \\ \hline \end{array}$

5. $\begin{array}{r} 6\,0\,4 \\ \times\,2\,0\,6 \\ \hline \end{array}$

6. $\begin{array}{r} 4\,5\,7 \\ \times\,3\,2\,0 \\ \hline \end{array}$

7. $\begin{array}{r} 9\,3\,6 \\ \times\,4\,0\,0 \\ \hline \end{array}$

8. $\begin{array}{r} 8\,6\,9 \\ \times\,5\,0\,2 \\ \hline \end{array}$

9. $\begin{array}{r} 9\,4\,7 \\ \times\,7\,3\,0 \\ \hline \end{array}$

10. $\begin{array}{r} 8\,9\,8 \\ \times\,8\,0\,4 \\ \hline \end{array}$

Find each product.

11. 600 × 739

12. 720 × 365

13. 367 × 507

14. 438 × 740

Use rounding to estimate. Then multiply.

15.	302 ×200	16.	521 ×320	17.	757 ×502	18.	435 ×601	19.	605 ×450
20.	633 ×107	21.	842 ×805	22.	610 ×290	23.	2804 × 920	24.	1963 × 209
25.	625 ×108	26.	572 ×550	27.	4004 × 700	28.	6601 × 407	29.	1005 × 840
30.	28,921 × 906	31.	21,075 × 150	32.	30,958 × 605	33.	145,289 × 430	34.	487,203 × 203

Find each product.

35. 625 × 400   **36.** 135 × 250   **37.** 561 × 605   **38.** 1409 × 306

39. 5624 × 300   **40.** 22,302 × 580   **41.** 12,800 × 207   **42.** 564,475 × 320

43. n × 205 when $n = 874$ **44.** a × 521 when $a = 600$

45. 208 × n when $n = 7421$ **46.** 305 × k when $k = 188,272$

Problem Solving

47. Earth is approximately 585 times as far away from Mars as it is from the Moon. If the distance from the Earth to the Moon is 384,400 km, what is its distance to Mars?

48. A realtor sells an office building for $27 per square foot. What is the price of the one-story building?

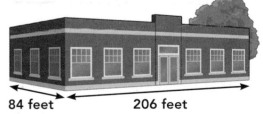
84 feet   206 feet

49. An 8-digit number has exactly 2 digits that are not zeros. David says, "The number is eight million, ten." Change one word so his statement is correct.

50. Compare 4671 × 208 and 4671 × 2080 without computing.

Write About It

51. When multiplying 5028 by 300 using the short way, how many partial products are needed? Explain.

Complete the number sentence using the given property.

1. Commutative Property
$63 \times \underline{?} = 4 \times \underline{?}$

2. Distributive Property
$9 \times (7 + \underline{?}) = (\underline{?} \times \underline{?}) + (9 \times 3)$

3. Identity Property
$100 \times \underline{?} = \underline{?}$

4. Associative Property
$6 \times (2 \times \underline{?}) = (\underline{?} \times \underline{?}) \times 8$

5. Commutative Property
$\underline{?} \times 25 = \underline{?} \times 5$

6. Zero Property
$6 \times \underline{?} = \underline{?}$

7. Distributive Property
$(25 + 12) \times \underline{?} = (\underline{?} \times 3) + (\underline{?} \times 3)$

8. Associative Property
$(18 \times \underline{?}) \times 4 = \underline{?} \times (3 \times \underline{?})$

Find the products.

9.
10×4
100×4
1000×4

10.
30×9
300×9
3000×9

11.
10×8
100×8
1000×8

12.
70×2
700×2
7000×2

13.
40×5
400×5
4000×5

14.
60×7
600×7
6000×7

15.
30×3
300×3
3000×3

16.
80×6
800×6
8000×6

Estimate each product or sum.

17. 31×45

18. $\$8.22 \times 318$

19. 861×23

20. $\$2.50 \times 96$

21. $\$1.99 + \$2.41 + \$2.08 + \$1.75$

22. $56 + 57 + 58 + 59 + 60 + 61 + 62$

Find each product.

23.
$\begin{array}{r} 68 \\ \times 24 \\ \hline \end{array}$

24.
$\begin{array}{r} 229 \\ \times 526 \\ \hline \end{array}$

25.
$\begin{array}{r} 1098 \\ \times \quad 7 \\ \hline \end{array}$

26.
$\begin{array}{r} 124 \\ \times 906 \\ \hline \end{array}$

27.
$\begin{array}{r} 492 \\ \times \quad 67 \\ \hline \end{array}$

28.
$\begin{array}{r} 7419 \\ \times \quad 382 \\ \hline \end{array}$

29.
$\begin{array}{r} 1672 \\ \times \quad 51 \\ \hline \end{array}$

30.
$\begin{array}{r} 7593 \\ \times \quad 209 \\ \hline \end{array}$

31.
$\begin{array}{r} 76,057 \\ \times \quad 3 \\ \hline \end{array}$

32.
$\begin{array}{r} 497 \\ \times 254 \\ \hline \end{array}$

Find each product.

33. 7 4 1 9
× 3 8 2

34. 1 6 7 2
× 5 1

35. 7 5 9 3
× 2 0 9

36. 7 6,0 5 7
× 3

37. 4 9 7
× 2 5 4

38. 3 9 2
× 2 0 5

39. 1 9 2
× 8 2 2

40. 1 5 4
× 3 6 0

41. 2 8 2 2
× 9 7 6

42. 3 1 4 4
× 2 1 0

43. 4 7 2 2
× 8 3 5

44. 5 2 3 2
× 4 2 9

45. 2 7 3 0
× 4 9 1

46. 7 2 9 3
× 3 6 6

47. 8 8 3 6
× 9 3 9

48. 2275 × 36

49. 209 × 4

50. 1654 × 516

51. 761 × 14

52. 254 × 505

53. 78 × 33

54. 842 × 257

55. 7821 × 102

Problem Solving

The bar graph shows the average number of visitors at a science museum each day of the week. Use the bar graph for Exercises 56–58. Assume a year has 52 weeks.

56. Estimate the approximate number of Friday visitors in one year.

57. In the upcoming month of July, there will be 5 Saturdays. How many Saturday visitors should the museum expect this July?

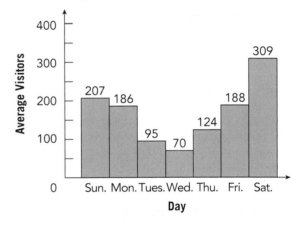

Average Number of Visitors per Day

58. The science museum claims it receives over 25,000 weekend visitors each year. Is this statement true? Explain.

59. On average, an electronics store sells 321 smart phones and 105 tablets each week. How many devices does the store sell in 8 typical weeks?

60. A flight from San Francisco to Houston is 1638 miles. A passenger jet makes 3 of these round-trip journeys each day, 365 days a year. How many miles does the jet accumulate over the course of the year?

61. Think about the product 405 × 398. Without computing, how would the product change if both factors were doubled? Explain.

62. Hayden multiplies 909 × 20 by reasoning that 909 × 10 is 9090, and doubling this gives 180,180. Describe his mistake and write the correct product.

The jellyfish is an invasive species that has stinging tentacles. To improve swimmer safety, some areas have tried to reduce the number of jellyfish by targeting them before they multiply. This is done by scrubbing bulkheads and floating docks where tiny jellyfish polyps grow.

The table shows the number of reported stings at different beaches in a certain town the year before they began targeting jellyfish to reduce the population.

Beach	Number of Reported Stings This Year
Lewis Beach	785
Sunset Beach	836
Harmony Beach	809

1. Estimate the total number of reported stings that occurred this year.

   The town has a total of 39 docks and 62 bulkheads. About 308 jellyfish polyps were scrubbed away from each structure.

2. How many total polyps were removed from docks?

3. How many total polyps were removed from bulkheads?

   Suppose that jellyfish polyps in the area each produce 6 to 9 jellyfish.

4. Scrubbing away polyps from the docks decreased the jellyfish population by at least _?_. It could have decreased the population by as much as _?_ jellyfish.

5. Scrubbing away polyps from the bulkheads decreased the jellyfish population by at least _?_ . It could have decreased the population by as much as _?_ jellyfish.

   The goal for the town is to reduce the number of stings at each beach next year by at least half of those reported at each beach this year.

6. Estimate the maximum number of total stings that can be reported this year for the town to reach its goal.

7. Determine the maximum number of stings that can be reported at each beach for the town to reach its goal.

The table shows the number of reported stings in the following year, after the jellyfish population was targeted.

Beach	Number of Reported Stings Following Year
Lewis Beach	168
Sunset Beach	258
Harmony Beach	209

8. Estimate the total number of reported stings that occurred.

9. About how many times greater was the jellyfish population before the jellyfish were targeted? Explain.

10. Did the town meet its goal? Explain why or why not.

This town's success gained national attention. Other beach towns decided to take the same action, as shown in the table.

Town	Total Polyps Removed	Estimated Jellyfish per Polyp
Cape Bethany	9205	10 to 20
Harris Bay	108	12 to 15
Pine Island	867	9 to 11

11. What is the minimum and maximum number of jellyfish removed by Cape Bethany?

12. What is the minimum and maximum number of jellyfish removed by Harris Bay?

13. What is the minimum and maximum number of jellyfish removed by Pine Island?

14. Suppose a single polyp produces 8 jellyfish one year. The next year, each of those jellyfish produces 5 jellyfish. The year after that, each of those jellyfish produces 13 jellyfish. How many total jellyfish are produced from this single polyp? Write a number sentence and use a property to simplify.

15. Research suggests that in one year, about 1 million polyps were removed from beaches across the country. Assume that each polyp produces about 9 jellyfish per year. How much has this removal reduced the jellyfish population after 1 year? After 2 years? After 3 years?

Determine the best answer for each problem.

1. Which expressions are equivalent to 7 × 500? Select all that apply.

   A. 7 × (5 × 10)
   B. 7 × (5 × 100)
   C. (7 × 5) × 100
   D. (7 × 5) × 10

2. How many inches tall is this statue?

   305 feet

   12 inches = 1 foot

3. Which sentences model the Commutative Property? Select all that apply.

   A. 62 × 57 = 57 × 62
   B. 98 × 0 = 0
   C. 1 × 472 = 472
   D. 905 × 1 = 1 × 905

4. Select the best estimate for the product $3.75 × 621.

   A. $1800
   B. $2100
   C. $2400
   D. $2800

5. Find the product.

   $$\begin{array}{r} 2\,4\,1\,1 \\ \times\ \ \ 3\,0\,4 \\ \hline \end{array}$$

6. There are 365 days in 1 year and 24 hours in 1 day. How many hours are in 1 year?

   A. 8544   B. 8760
   C. 8784   D. 9125

7. In one day, an art museum sold 105 adult tickets and 198 children tickets. Adult tickets are $12 and children tickets are $8. What were the museum's total ticket sales on this day?

   A. $1260   B. $1584
   C. $2844   D. $3216

8. What is the missing number?

   68 × 42 = 2856 × ?

   A. 0   B. 1
   C. 42   D. 68

9. A large aircraft has 2 levels. On each level, there are 48 rows of seats with 10 seats in each row. How many passengers can the aircraft seat?

   A. 480   B. 960
   C. 4800   D. 9600

10. Find the product.

    $$\begin{array}{r} 1\,0,5\,0\,7 \\ \times\ \ \ \ \ \ \ \ 6 \\ \hline \end{array}$$

    A. 16,942   B. 19,102
    C. 60,000   D. 63,042

Division

Irrigation is a method in which water is applied to land to assist in the growth of plants or the production of crops. Farmers use irrigation systems to control the amount of water their crops receive. Homeowners in dry climates, such as in California, often use irrigation systems to water their grass and plants.

Irrigation Techniques

♦ Soil-moisture sensors measure the amount of moisture in the soil and water plants accordingly.

♦ Rain sensors turn off irrigation systems when it is raining. This helps conserve water.

♦ Irrigation systems with technology can use local weather data to determine when and how much to water.

Tips for Responsible Irrigation

♦ Use rotary spray heads instead of mist spray heads. A thicker stream ensures more water reaches the plants or crops and less water evaporates or blows away.

♦ Micro-irrigation systems, which deliver water directly to a plant's root, are more responsible than conventional sprinklers because they use significantly less water.

Division Patterns

Objective
- Use patterns to divide whole numbers by multiples of 10, 100, or 1000.

Math Words
multiple
divisor
dividend
quotient

A printing company uses reams of paper that have 500 sheets each. How many reams are needed for a print job requiring 6000 pieces of paper?

To solve, divide 6000 by 500.
Patterns can help you divide by multiples of 10, 100, or 1000.
Study the division patterns shown.

$8 \div 2 = 4$	$30 \div 6 = 5$	$180 \div 2 = 90$
$80 \div 2 = 40$	$300 \div 60 = 5$	$1800 \div 20 = 90$
$800 \div 2 = 400$	$3000 \div 600 = 5$	$18,000 \div 200 = 90$
$8000 \div 2 = 4000$	$30,000 \div 6000 = 5$	$180,000 \div 2000 = 90$

To divide a whole number by a multiple of 10, 100, or 1000:

- Look for a basic division fact.

- Subtract the number of additional zeros in the divisor from the number of additional zeros in the dividend.

- Write this many additional zeros in the quotient.

Since $60 \div 5 = 12$, $6000 \div 500 = 12$ because 2 zeros − 2 zeros = 0 zeros.

▷ The company needs 12 reams of paper for the print job.

Study these examples.

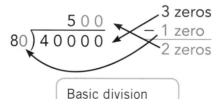

$$500 \div 5 = 100$$

2 zeros − 0 zeros = 2 zeros

Basic division
fact: $5 \div 5 = 1$

$80 \overline{)40000}$ 500

3 zeros
− 1 zero
2 zeros

Basic division
fact: $40 \div 8 = 5$

PRACTICE

Find the quotients. Look for a pattern.

1. $9 \div 3$
$90 \div 3$
$900 \div 3$

2. $48 \div 6$
$480 \div 6$
$4800 \div 6$

3. $30 \div 5$
$300 \div 5$
$3000 \div 5$

4. $120 \div 40$
$1200 \div 40$
$12,000 \div 40$

5. $45 \div 9$
$450 \div 90$
$4500 \div 900$

6. $56,000 \div 7$
$56,000 \div 70$
$56,000 \div 700$

7. $3500 \div 700$
$3500 \div 70$
$3500 \div 7$

8. $72,000 \div 800$
$7200 \div 80$
$720 \div 8$

Divide.

9. $1800 \div 3$ **10.** $6400 \div 8$ **11.** $240 \div 80$ **12.** $420 \div 60$

13. $40\overline{)800}$ **14.** $3\overline{)1200}$ **15.** $50\overline{)4500}$ **16.** $80\overline{)3200}$

17. $30\overline{)120}$ **18.** $50\overline{)2000}$ **19.** $40\overline{)2800}$ **20.** $600\overline{)36,000}$

21. $1600 \div 40$ **22.** $4900 \div 70$ **23.** $4800 \div 8$ **24.** $2700 \div 30$

Use basic facts and patterns to find the value of *n*.

25. $720 \div 9 = n$ **26.** $60 \div 3 = n$ **27.** $560,000 \div n = 8000$

28. $n\overline{)3500}$ quotient 70 **29.** $n\overline{)630,000}$ quotient 900 **30.** $6\overline{)2400}$ quotient n

31. $40\overline{)3600}$ quotient n **32.** $n\overline{)32,000}$ quotient 1600 **33.** $500\overline{)45,000}$ quotient n

Problem Solving

34. A cargo ship can carry about 27,000,000 cubic feet of goods. The goods are carried in 3000 cubic-foot containers that each have a maximum weight as shown. At most, how many pounds of cargo can the ship carry in these containers?

Maximum weight:
5000 lb

An estimate shows that California lost 63 trillion gallons of water in 18 months of drought. This number is written as 63,000,000,000,000. Use this information for Exercises 35–36.

35. Use the division fact $630 \div 18 = 35$ and patterns to estimate how much water was lost on average each month. Explain.

36. Researchers discovered a reservoir of water under California with over 700 trillion gallons of water. However, the water may be as deep as 3000 feet below the surface. If a company can dig 150 feet every two days, how long would it take to reach the water? Explain.

Write About It

37. Hector says that since $45,000 \div 90 \div 50$ is the same as $45,000 \div 50 \div 90$, the Commutative Property is true for division. Describe the mistake Hector is making.

LESSON 4-2

Estimation: Compatible Numbers

Objective
- Use compatible numbers to estimate quotients.

Math Words
estimate
compatible numbers

A ski resort uses 3 identical snowmakers to make 2370 tons of snow. About how many tons of snow does each snowmaker produce?

To find about how many tons, estimate 2370 ÷ 3.

Think about basic facts to find compatible numbers.

Estimate 2370 ÷ 3.

Basic fact: 24 ÷ 3 = 8

Use the compatible numbers to estimate.

2400 ÷ 3 = 800

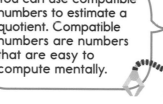

You can use compatible numbers to estimate a quotient. Compatible numbers are numbers that are easy to compute mentally.

▷ Each snowmaker produces about 800 tons of snow.

Study these examples.

It is possible to use different sets of numbers to estimate a quotient.

Estimate: 17,652 ÷ 39

Basic fact:
16 ÷ 4 = 4

16,000 ÷ 40 = 400

17,652 ÷ 39 is about 400.

Estimate: 17,652 ÷ 39

Basic fact:
20 ÷ 4 = 5

20,000 ÷ 40 = 500

17,652 ÷ 39 is about 500.

Both estimates are reasonable.

PRACTICE

Write a basic division fact that would help estimate the quotient.

1. 3951 ÷ 5

2. 7453 ÷ 8

3. 84,796 ÷ 78

Estimate the quotient. Use compatible numbers.

4. 1957 ÷ 4

5. 3319 ÷ 9

6. 2679 ÷ 8

7. 8529 ÷ 92

Estimate each quotient.

8. 4893 ÷ 5

9. 6397 ÷ 8

10. 2740 ÷ 34

11. 4813 ÷ 68

Estimate each quotient.

12. $7945 \div 94$ **13.** $84,796 \div 78$ **14.** $61,958 \div 75$ **15.** $38,958 \div 49$

16. $5921 \div 19$ **17.** $9284 \div 51$ **18.** $36,040 \div 12$ **19.** $15,121 \div 28$

Estimate to compare. Use < or >.

20. $2829 \div 9 \underline{\ ?\ } 4173 \div 8$

21. $5798 \div 2 \underline{\ ?\ } 11,938 \div 6$

22. $2462 \div 46 \underline{\ ?\ } 34,268 \div 84$

23. $68,282 \div 28 \underline{\ ?\ } 86,735 \div 23$

24. $12,636 \div 24 \underline{\ ?\ } 15,296 \div 32$

25. $79,135 \div 19 \underline{\ ?\ } 49,362 \div 9$

Estimate the quotient.

26. $7902 \div a$ when $a = 42$

27. $3791 \div a$ when $a = 84$

28. $42,015 \div a$ when $a = 73$

29. $50,754 \div a$ when $a = 24$

Problem Solving

30. The odometer in Mr. Borso's car shows the miles driven. If he has had the car for 25 months, estimate the number of miles he drives each month.

31. Jane bikes a 24,238-meter trail. She finishes her ride in 1 hour and 22 minutes. About how many meters per minute did she bike? Explain.

32. Courtney divides 3654 by 42. She says the quotient is 902. Is this reasonable? Explain.

33. To estimate $31,281 \div 81$, Esther writes $30,000 \div 100 = 300$. Explain to Esther how to find a better estimate.

34. Gina orders 8-slice frozen pizzas for a local concert. There will be 6364 people attending the concert. If she wants 2 slices available for each person, about how many pizzas should she order?

Write About It

35. When using compatible numbers, how can you determine if the estimate is greater than or less than the actual quotient?

Divide by One-Digit Numbers

Objective
■ Find whole-number quotients with 4-digit dividends and 1-digit divisors.

Math Words
dividend
divisor
quotient

A factory produces 6500 crayons every 5 minutes. If these crayons are put in boxes of 8 crayons, how many boxes can be filled every 5 minutes?

To find how many boxes, divide 6500 by 8.

To divide large dividends, repeat the division steps until the division is completed.

$$\text{divisor} \overline{)\text{dividend}}^{\text{quotient}}$$

```
      8 1 2  R4
8 ) 6 5 0 0
  − 6 4 ↓ |      8 × 8 = 64
      1 0 |      65 − 64 = 1
    −   8 ↓      1 × 8 = 8
        2 0      10 − 8 = 2
      − 1 6      2 × 8 = 16
          4      20 − 16 = 4
```

Check:
(quotient × divisor) + remainder = dividend
(812 × 8) + 4 = 6496 + 4 = 6500 ✓

▷ The crayons can fill 812 boxes with 4 crayons left over.

PRACTICE

Complete each division.

```
        7 8 ?
1. 6 ) 4 7 1 6
   − 4 2 ↓ |
       5 1 |
     − ? ? ↓
         ? 6
       − ? ?
           ?
```

```
        9 ? ?
2. 8 ) 7 6 3 2
   − 7 2 ↓ |
       4 3 |
     − ? ? ↓
         ? 2
       − ? ?
           ?
```

```
        ? ? ?  R?
3. 9 ) 8 2 7 3
   − 8 1 ↓ |
       1 7 |
     − ? ? ↓
         ? 3
       − ? ?
           ?
```

Divide and check.

4. 5) 3 4 0 5   5. 6) 3 8 5 8   6. 7) 4 3 5 1   7. 8) 7 4 5 1

8. 3) 2 1 8 6   9. 5) 3 6 9 5   10. 4) 2 1 3 9   11. 9) 8 3 0 7

12. 9) 1 8 9 9   13. 8) 3 5 3 6   14. 5) 4 2 7 5   15. 7) 2 5 3 4

Divide and check.

16. 6)2 1 1 9　　**17.** 5)3 4 9 7　　**18.** 8)6 7 0 3　　**19.** 9)6 7 8 8

20. 7)5 9 6 0　　**21.** 9)8 5 0 6　　**22.** 3)2 9 5 8　　**23.** 4)3 0 1 6

Find each quotient.

24. 6568 ÷ 8　　**25.** 3979 ÷ 5　　**26.** 5273 ÷ 6　　**27.** 3661 ÷ 7

28. 2724 ÷ 4　　**29.** 3754 ÷ 6　　**30.** 5277 ÷ 3　　**31.** 3771 ÷ 9

32. 1967 ÷ 7　　**33.** 5142 ÷ 8　　**34.** 6825 ÷ 9　　**35.** 9284 ÷ 4

Problem Solving

36. Last weekend, 6372 people attended a 3-day music festival. If an equal number of people attended each day, how many people attended each day?

Use the table for Exercises 37–38.

37. Students track the amount of water their household uses in 7 days. There are 3 people in Amelia's family. If each person uses the same amount of water each day, how much water does each person use daily?

Weekly Water Use	
Student	Water (gallons)
Kevin	4536
Amelia	3822
Shun Chi	4795

38. There are 4 people in Kevin's family and 5 people in Shun Chi's family. Kevin says each person in his family uses 37 gallons less water per day than each person in Shun Chi's family. Is he correct? Explain.

39. Look at the student's answers. Without finding the exact quotients, explain how you know that each quotient is incorrect.

1. 9003 ÷ 4 = 2249 R7
2. 5212 ÷ 6 = 87
3. 3215 ÷ 5 = 642

Write About It

40. Jalyn's brother says that when you divide a 4-digit number by a 1-digit number, the quotient will always be a 3-digit number. Do you agree? Give evidence to support your answer.

Zeros in the Quotient

Objective
- Divide by one-digit divisors to find quotients with zeros.

Math Words
remainder
quotient

A farmer plants a total of 5612 banana plants on 4 acres of land. If he plants the same number of plants on each acre, how many banana plants are on each acre?

To determine how many banana plants are on each acre, find 5612 ÷ 4.

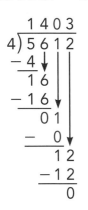

- Divide the thousands.
    5 : 4 = 1 R1
- Divide the hundreds.
    16 ÷ 4 = 4
- Divide the tens.
    1 < 4 Not enough tens
    Write a zero in the tens place.
- Divide the ones.
    12 ÷ 4 = 3

Check:
$$\begin{array}{r} 1\,4\,0\,3 \\ \times\ \ \ \ \ 4 \\ \hline 5\,6\,1\,2\,\checkmark \end{array}$$

> The farmer plants 1403 banana plants on each acre.

PRACTICE

Complete each division.

1. $\begin{array}{r} 1\,?\,3 \\ 7\overline{)7\,2\,1} \\ -7 \\ \hline 0\,2 \\ -\,? \\ \hline ?\,1 \\ -\,?\,? \\ \hline ? \end{array}$

2. $\begin{array}{r} 7\,?\,? \\ 5\overline{)3\,5\,1\,0} \\ -3\,5 \\ \hline 0\,1 \\ -\ ? \\ \hline ?\,0 \\ -\,?\,? \\ \hline ? \end{array}$

3. $\begin{array}{r} ?\,?\,?\ R? \\ 6\overline{)3\,0\,4\,1} \\ -3\,0 \\ \hline 0\,4 \\ -\ ? \\ \hline ?\,1 \\ -\,?\,? \\ \hline ? \end{array}$

Divide and check.

4. $9\overline{)1\,8\,9\,0}$

5. $3\overline{)6\,0\,1\,2}$

6. $8\overline{)2\,4\,0\,6}$

7. $4\overline{)4\,2\,7\,4}$

8. $4\overline{)8\,3\,0}$

9. $6\overline{)6\,4\,8}$

10. $5\overline{)6\,0\,4}$

11. $3\overline{)7\,2\,2}$

Divide and check.

12. 6)662 **13.** 5)535 **14.** 8)828 **15.** 9)927

16. 6)6120 **17.** 8)2565 **18.** 5)1545 **19.** 7)7063

Find each quotient.

20. 1200 ÷ 8 **21.** 1248 ÷ 6 **22.** 1816 ÷ 3 **23.** 2017 ÷ 4

24. 3657 ÷ 6 **25.** 2506 ÷ 5 **26.** 2103 ÷ 7 **27.** 4050 ÷ 9

Problem Solving

28. Jane orders packs of juice boxes as shown for 308 campers. What is the least number of packs of juice she can order for each camper to have 2 juice boxes?

Use the table for Exercises 29–30.

From	To	Distance (km)
Baltimore, MD	Kansas City, MO	1547
Chicago, IL	London, UK	6358

29. Mr. Ritter flew from Chicago, IL to London, UK. His flight was about 9 hours. What was the average speed of the airplane in kilometers per hour? Round to the nearest whole number.

30. Mr. Ritter flies from Baltimore to Kansas City and then back to Baltimore. He spends a total of 3 hours 50 minutes in the air. Ten kilometers is about 6 miles. Estimate the average speed of the airplane in miles per hour. Explain how you found your answer.

Write About It

31. Jaden's sister completes this division. Is her answer correct? Explain why or why not.

```
        1 8 1  R1
  7)7 5 6 8
   −7
    0 5 6
    −5 6
      0 8
      − 7
        1
```

Divisibility and Mental Math

Objective
- Use divisibility rules to mentally determine one-digit factors.

Math Words
divisibility rules
factor
divisible

Josiah buys 84 tomato seedlings at the farmer's market. He wants to plant the seedlings in equal-sized rows. Can he plant the seedlings in three rows? Five rows? Six rows?

Divisibility rules can help you decide if one number is divisible by another number. The chart shows the divisibility rules for 2, 5, 4, 3, 9, and 6.

A number is divisible...	Example
by 2 if its ones digit is divisible by 2.	20, 42, 84, 936, and 1048 are divisible by 2. *Numbers that are divisible by 2 are even.*
by 5 if its ones digit is 0 or 5.	60, 135, 4890, and 53,965 are divisible by 5.
by 4 if its tens and ones digits form a number that is divisible by 4.	6128 → 28 ÷ 4 = 7. 31,816 → 16 ÷ 4 = 4. 6128 and 31,816 are divisible by 4.
by 3 if the sum of its digits is divisible by 3.	27 → 2 + 7 = 9 and 9 ÷ 3 = 3. 3591 → 3 + 5 + 9 + 1 = 18 and 18 ÷ 3 = 6. 27 and 3591 are divisible by 3.
by 9 if the sum of its digits is divisible by 9.	216 → 2 + 1 + 6 = 9 and 9 ÷ 9 = 1. 5058 → 5 + 5 + 8 = 18 and 18 ÷ 9 = 2. 216 and 5058 are divisible by 9.
by 6 if it is divisible by both 2 and 3.	2016 is divisible by 2 and 3. 2016 is divisible by 6.

8 + 4 = 12, and 12 is divisible by 3. So, 84 is divisible by 3.
The ones digit in 84 is 4, so 84 is not divisible by 5.
84 is divisible by both 2 and 3, so 84 is also divisible by 6.

Josiah can plant the tomato seedlings in three or six rows.

PRACTICE

1. Which numbers are divisible by 2?

24; 47; 98; 569; 760; 6135; 79,778; 490,893

2. Which numbers are divisible by 5?

26; 85; 324; 422; 3820; 9416; 20,905; 131,616

Determine which numbers in the list are divisibe by the given number.

3. 64; 90; 745; 872; 4000; 9154; 35,960; 791,620: by 4

4. 69; 87; 136; 159; 3518; 4320; 83,721; 100,512: by 3

5. 84; 93; 204; 396; 1029; 5415; 28,514; 503,640: by 6

6. 69; 87; 136; 159; 3518; 4320; 71,419; 100,512: by 9

Tell whether each number is divisible by 2, 3, 4, 5, 6, or 9.

7. 1425   **8.** 2360   **9.** 4390   **10.** 6570   **11.** 8735   **12.** 9822

13. 13,360   **14.** 19,585   **15.** 23,130   **16.** 240,120   **17.** 335,412   **18.** 350,262

Problem Solving

Alyssa would like to divide the plot shown into identical square plots that are as large as possible. Use the diagram for Exercises 19–20.

171 yards

108 yards

19. Find the size of the plot desired. (Hint: Look for common factors of the side lengths.)

20. How many of these smaller plots will there be? Explain.

21. Yolanda claims that the least number divisible by 2, 3, 4, and 5 is $2 \times 3 \times 4 \times 5 = 120$. Do you agree? Explain.

22. Is a number that is divisible by 3 and 4 also divisible by 6? Explain.

23. Find the missing digit in the 6-digit number 308,4?6. The number is divisible by 3 and 4, and no two digits are the same.

24. Jorge says that if a number is divisible by 2 and 4, it also divisible by 8. Do you agree? Explain.

Write About It

25. Write a divisibility rule for dividing by 10. Justify why it works.

Determine the value of *n*.

1. 800 ÷ 2 = *n*

   A. 4   **B.** 40   **C.** 400   **D.** 4000

2. 5600 ÷ 8 = *n*

   A. 7   **B.** 70   **C.** 700   **D.** 7000

3. 3600 ÷ 60 = *n*

   A. 6   **B.** 60   **C.** 600   **D.** 6000

4. 240 ÷ 80 = *n*

   A. 3   **B.** 30   **C.** 300   **D.** 3000

Choose the best estimate using compatible numbers.

5. 7720 ÷ 8

   A. 7000 ÷ 10   **B.** 7700 ÷ 10   **C.** 7200 ÷ 8   **D.** 8000 ÷ 8

6. 2268 ÷ 81

   A. 2400 ÷ 80   **B.** 2000 ÷ 100   **C.** 2500 ÷ 100   **D.** 1600 ÷ 80

7. 61,915 ÷ 29

   A. 60,000 ÷ 20   **B.** 60,000 ÷ 30   **C.** 70,000 ÷ 20   **D.** 75,000 ÷ 25

8. 73,656 ÷ 72

   A. 72,000 ÷ 80   **B.** 80,000 ÷ 100   **C.** 70,000 ÷ 70   **D.** 70,000 ÷ 100

Select the best estimate of the quotient.

9. 1378 ÷ 2

   A. 60   **B.** 70   **C.** 600   **D.** 700

10. 48,438 ÷ 78

   A. 60   **B.** 80   **C.** 600   **D.** 800

Determine each quotient.

11. $6\overline{)2498}$

    A. 416   **B.** 416 R2   **C.** 426   **D.** 426 R2

12. 832 ÷ 4

    A. 206   **B.** 207   **C.** 207 R2   **D.** 208

13. $7\overline{)4305}$

    A. 614 R5   **B.** 615   **C.** 615 R2   **D.** 715

14. 6052 ÷ 6

    A. 108   **B.** 108 R4   **C.** 1008 R2   **D.** 1008 R4

15. 1184 ÷ 2

    A. 592   **B.** 592 R1   **C.** 692   **D.** 692 R1

Determine whether each number is divisible by 2, 3, 4, 5, 6, or 9. Select all that apply.

16. 1800

    A. 2   **B.** 3   **C.** 4   **D.** 5   **E.** 6   **F.** 9

17. 2400

    A. 2   **B.** 3   **C.** 4   **D.** 5   **E.** 6   **F.** 9

Problem Solving

18. James says that all odd numbers are divisible by 3. Do you agree? Justify your answer.

19. The area of a professional football field is 6400 square yards. Estimate the width of the field.

20. Without dividing, Bryan knows that 8754 ÷ 5 will have a remainder of 4. How does he know that?

21. Give an example of a 5-digit number that is divisible by 2 but not 4.

22. A teacher writes the number 14 billion on the board. Beth divides the number by 10^3 and Mia divides the number by 10^4. Whose quotient will be greater? Explain.

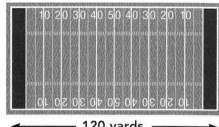

←――――― 120 yards ―――――→

Use Arrays and Area Models to Divide

Objective
- Use arrays and area models to illustrate the process of division.

Math Words

array
area model

To get ready for a sale, a worker at Sports Stuff is filling bags with 12 golf balls from a box of 132 golf balls. How many bags does the worker fill?

Use an array or an area model to divide 132 by 12.

| 10 | 1 | 1 |

◆ Use the array to represent 132 ÷ 12.

- Use tens and ones to model a bag of 12 golf balls. Then use the model of 12 to make an array of 132.

- Each row represents 1 bag. Count to find that the array has 11 rows of 12.

- Check: 11 × 10 = 110, and 11 × 2 = 22. Add to get 110 + 22 = 132.

11 rows

10	1	1
10	1	1
10	1	1
10	1	1
10	1	1
10	1	1
10	1	1
10	1	1
10	1	1
10	1	1
10	1	1

◆ Use an area model to represent 132 ÷ 12.

- Draw a rectangle. Its area is 132, the dividend. Its width is 12, the divisor. To find its length, the quotient, begin by estimating.

- Multiply 12 by 10 and subtract from 132. The difference is 12. Write 12 in a new column.

- Multiply 12 by 1 and subtract from 12. The difference is 0. Add 10 and 1 to get 11.

Think

By what can you multiply 12 to get 132 or less? 10 × 12 = 120, and 120 < 132.

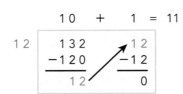

$$10 \quad + \quad 1 \quad = 11$$

$$
12 \quad
\begin{array}{c}
132 \\
-120 \\
\hline
12
\end{array}
\quad
\begin{array}{c}
12 \\
-12 \\
\hline
0
\end{array}
$$

Think

By what can you multiply 12 to get 12 or less? 1 × 12 = 12

The array and the area model each show that the worker fills 11 bags.

PRACTICE

Use an array or an area model to find each quotient.

1. 156 ÷ 13   **2.** 925 ÷ 25   **3.** 2058 ÷ 14

4. 288 ÷ 16   **5.** 676 ÷ 26   **6.** 572 ÷ 11

7. 1247 ÷ 29   **8.** 1360 ÷ 16   **9.** 2250 ÷ 18

Find the missing number in the area model. Write the quotient.

10.

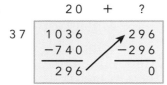

```
          20   +   ?
     37 | 1036    296
        | -740   -296
        |  296      0
```

11.

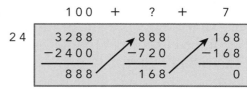

```
          100   +   ?   +   7
     24 | 3288    888    168
        | -2400  -720   -168
        |  888    168      0
```

12.

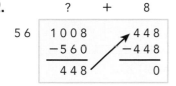

```
          ?    +   8
     56 | 1008    448
        | -560   -448
        |  448      0
```

13.

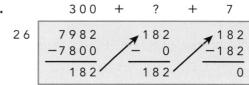

```
          300   +   ?   +   7
     26 | 7982    182    182
        | -7800    0    -182
        |  182    182      0
```

Write the division equation that the area model represents.

14.

```
          60   +   2
     58 | 3596    116
        | -3480  -116
        |  116      0
```

15.

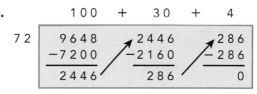

```
          100   +   30   +   4
     72 | 9648    2446    286
        | -7200  -2160   -286
        |  2446   286      0
```

Use an area model to find each quotient.

16. 306 ÷ 18

17. 5278 ÷ 13

18. 2058 ÷ 14

Problem Solving

19. Jaxon draws an array to divide 175 by 35. Describe the model he should use for a row.

20. Mandy is drawing an array to divide 240 by 15. The diagram shows the rows she uses. How many rows of 15 will she need to complete the array?

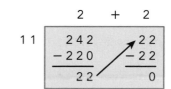

```
|        10        |   | 1 | 1 | 1 | 1 | 1 |
|        10        |   | 1 | 1 | 1 | 1 | 1 |
```

21. Sarah draws this area model to divide 242 by 11. Sarah says that the quotient is 4. What is her error?

```
          2    +   2
     11 | 242     22
        | -220   -22
        |  22       0
```

Write About It

22. Area models and arrays are shown in this lesson. Which strategy would you use to divide 9135 by 87? Explain why this is your choice.

Use Strategies to Divide

Objective
▪ Use strategies based on the relationship between multiplication and division to divide.

Math Words
compatible numbers
partial quotient
multiple

Evan designs a new bracelet with 24 gemstone beads. He has 2952 beads to use. How many bracelets with the new design can Evan make with the beads?

You can use strategies to divide 2952 by 24.

◆ Use the inverse relationship between multiplication and division.

- Write a related multiplication equation. $n \times 24 = 2952$

- Use compatible numbers to estimate the $n \times 20 = 3000$
  value of n. So, n is about 150. $n = 150$

- Use the estimate as the first factor and 24 as the second factor. Compare the product to 2952.

- Adjust the first factor until the product $150 \times 24 = 3600 \longrightarrow$ Too much. Try 130.
  is 2952.
                                                                        $130 \times 24 = 3120 \longrightarrow$ Too much. Try 120.

                                                                        $120 \times 24 = 2880 \longrightarrow$ Too small. Try 123.

                                                                        $123 \times 24 = 2952 \longrightarrow$ Just right. ✓

So, $n = 123$, and $2952 \div 24 = 123$.

◆ Use partial quotients.

The partial quotients method involves subtracting multiples of the divisor from the dividend. First write the problem.

What hundreds number multiplied by 24 gives a product less than or equal to 2952? $24 \times 100 = 2400$, and $2400 < 2952$.

- Use 100 as the partial quotient. Write it above the division bar. Multiply and subtract. The remainder is 552.

What tens number multiplied by 24 gives a product less than or equal to 552? $24 \times 20 = 480$, and $480 < 552$.

- Use 20 as the second partial quotient. Write it above 100. Multiply and subtract. The remainder is 72.

- Use 3 as the third partial quotient. The remainder is 0.

- Add the three partial quotients. $100 + 20 + 3 = 123$

So, the quotient is 123.

```
              3
           2 0
         1 0 0
   24) 2 9 5 2
      - 2 4 0 0
           5 5 2
         - 4 8 0
             7 2
           - 7 2
               0
```

▷ Both methods give the same answer. Evan can make 123 bracelets with the new design.

Use the inverse relationship between multiplication and division to find each quotient.

1. 360 ÷ 15

- Estimate the quotient.
- Multiply. Use your estimate as the first factor and 15 as the second factor.
- Decide how to adjust the first factor.
- Continue until the product is 360.

  360 ÷ 15 = <u>?</u>

2. 1188 ÷ 33

- Estimate the quotient.
- Multiply your estimate by 33.
- Is the estimate too high or too low?
- Adjust and continue until the product is 1188.

  1188 ÷ 33 = <u>?</u>

Use partial quotients to find each quotient.

3. 255 ÷ 15

4. 840 ÷ 35

5. 2244 ÷ 22

6. 5130 ÷ 27

7. 4875 ÷ 75

8. 5929 ÷ 77

9. 6273 ÷ 51

10. 6018 ÷ 59

11. 7744 ÷ 88

12. Write a multiplication fact to help estimate 1152 divided by 48.

Problem Solving

13. The physical education director at the school district office has 576 flying discs. She divides them equally to send to all 16 schools in the district. How many flying discs are sent to each school?

14. Conner uses this area model to find 2890 ÷ 17. He multiplies 17 × 107 to check and gets 1819. What is Conner's error?

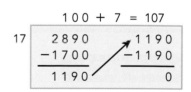

15. Write a related division fact for 8184 ÷ 24 = 341.

16. Write two related multiplication facts for 8184 ÷ 24 = 341.

17. You can swap the multiplicand and the multiplier to get a different multiplication fact. Write a similar statement for a division fact.

Write About It

18. Describe how using partial quotients is similar to and different from using inverse relationships.

Divide by Two-Digit Numbers

Objective
- Use a standard algorithm to divide numbers with up to 4 digits by two-digit divisors.

Math Words
algorithm
quotient

An architect is designing a parking lot for a new stadium. The lot will hold 8925 cars in rows of 75 cars. How many rows of cars are in the parking lot?

Divide 8925 by 75 to find the number of rows.

Use the division algorithm.

Decide where to begin the quotient.

Estimate: $8925 \div 75 \longrightarrow 9000 \div 90 = 100$
Begin the quotient in the hundreds place.

How many times does 75 go into 89 hundreds?
100 times, or 1 hundred

- Write 1 in the quotient in the hundreds place. Find 1×75. Subtract and bring down the 2.

How many times does 75 go into 142 tens?
10 times, or 1 ten

- Write 1 in the quotient in the tens place. Find 1×75. Subtract and bring down the 5.

How many times does 75 go into 675 ones?
9 times, or 9 ones

- Write 9 in the quotient in the ones place. Multiply 9×75. Subtract to get 0.

```
        1 1 9
75) 8 9 2 5
   - 7 5
    1 4 2
   -  7 5
      6 7 5
    - 6 7 5
          0
```

Check:
```
      1 1 9
    ×   7 5
      5 9 5
    8 3 3
    8 9 2 5 ✓
```

▷ The quotient is 119. The parking lot has 119 rows.

PRACTICE

Complete the division by finding the remainder.

1. $961 \div 28 = 34$ R _?_

2. $1994 \div 19 = 104$ R _?_

3. $7368 \div 52 = 141$ R _?_

Divide and check.

4. $29 \overline{)4\,3\,5}$

5. $31 \overline{)7\,4\,4}$

6. $18 \overline{)9\,9\,0}$

7. $73 \overline{)5\,9\,1\,3}$

8. $46 \overline{)3\,1\,2\,8}$

9. $23 \overline{)3\,2\,6\,6}$

10. $94 \overline{)3\,4\,2\,4}$

11. $38 \overline{)8\,8\,7\,0}$

12. $720 \div 15$

13. $2592 \div 72$

14. $1591 \div 43$

15. $2550 \div 15$

Divide and check.

16. 8400 ÷ 35　　　**17.** 5016 ÷ 57　　　**18.** 5130 ÷ 54　　　**19.** 8889 ÷ 44

20. 1372 ÷ 37　　　**21.** 7090 ÷ 65　　　**22.** 9750 ÷ 75　　　**23.** 6652 ÷ 18

24. 8203 ÷ 55　　　**25.** 3190 ÷ 22　　　**26.** 6644 ÷ 18　　　**27.** 9090 ÷ 80

Find the quotient.

28. $714 \div n$ when $n = 42$　　　**29.** $2484 \div n$ when $n = 92$　　　**30.** $9860 \div n$ when $n = 85$

31. Which division problem has a zero remainder?

　　A. 1395 ÷ 4　　　**B.** 6312 ÷ 24　　　**C.** 4872 ÷ 62　　　**D.** 8001 ÷ 25

Problem Solving

32. Cooper has a shortcut for dividing a number by 50. He divides by 10, and then multiplies the result by 5. Does Cooper's shortcut work? Justify your answer.

33. An art class uses 3744 ounces of clay making ceramic pots. Each student makes 12 pots like the one shown. How many students are in the class?

13 ounces

34. Michelle divides 3296 by 16 using the long division shown. But when she checks, she finds that 26 × 16 = 416. What did she do wrong?

35. I am a number between 100 and 110. When I am divided by 18, the quotient has no remainder. What number am I?

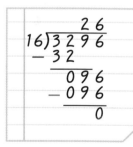

Use the division fact 5136 ÷ 27 = 190 R6 for Exercises 36–37.

36. Write the greatest multiple of 27 that is less than 5136.

37. Write the least multiple of 27 that is greater than 5136.

> Use subtraction and the remainder from the division fact.

Write About It

38. When solving a division problem, why is it important to place the first digit of a quotient correctly? Explain.

Problem Solving
Work Backward

Objective
- Focus on working backward to solve problems.

Math Word
work backward

A truck is carrying berries, vegetables, and nuts.
The vegetables weigh 12 times as much as the berries.
The vegetables weigh 14,000 pounds more than the nuts.
The nuts weigh 4000 pounds. What is the weight of the
berries that the truck is carrying?

You know how much the nuts weigh, so you can work
backward to solve this problem.

Item	Pounds
Berries	?
Vegetables	?
Nuts	4000

Read the problem again to find the key information.

The weight of the vegetables is 12 times the weight of the berries.

The vegetables weigh 14,000 pounds more than the nuts.

The nuts weigh 4000 pounds.

Make and use a plan.

- Find how much the vegetables weigh. Add 14,000 and 4000.

  14,000 + 4000 = 18,000

  The vegetables weigh 18,000 pounds.

- Find how much the berries weigh. Divide 18,000 by 12.

```
          1 5 0 0
    12) 1 8,0 0 0
       − 1 2
          6 0
        − 6 0
           0 0 0
```

When you look back, use your answer to check each fact. If a fact is false, make sure you used the right numbers or operation.

⟩ The weight of the berries is 1500 pounds.

Look back.

Is 18,000 pounds 12 times as much as 1500 pounds? *Yes* ✓

Is 18,000 pounds 14,000 pounds more than 4000 pounds? *Yes* ✓

PRACTICE

1. The inventory at an electronics store shows that there are 16 times as
many resistors as there are fuses. The number of resistors is 4000 less
than the number of capacitors. The number of capacitors is 12,000.
How many fuses are there?

2. When a number is multiplied by 5 four times and 375 is added to the product, the result is 21,000. What is the number?

3. When 130 is subtracted from a number and the difference is divided by 4 four times, the result is 45. What is the number?

4. The Boston Marathon is 46,145 yards long. The marathon is how many yards longer than 26 miles? (1760 yd = 1 mi)

5. Brett rounds a number to the nearest tenth. His result is 23.4. Which of the following numbers could he have started with?

   23.386   23.336   24.462   24.306   24.409

Some friends want to spend their summer vacation of 11 weeks hiking the Appalachian Trail. They can hike 24 miles each day because they can walk 3 miles an hour for 8 hours each day. The trail is 2174 miles. Use this information for Exercises 6–8.

6. How many days will it take the friends to hike the entire Appalachian Trail?

7. Will it be possible for the friends to hike the trail during their summer vacation? Explain why or why not.

8. The friends decide that they can hike 30 miles a day if they walk for 10 hours each day. If they do that, how many days will it take for the friends to hike the trail?

The table shows the ticket prices for various season passes for the basketball season. Prices vary depending on the seating section. Use the table for Exercises 9–10.

Season Passes	
Seating Section	Cost for 1 pass
Section A	$775
Section B	$850
Section C	$1125

9. Amanda buys 4 passes in the same section. She spends $3100. What type of passes does she buy?

10. Maxine buys two Section A passes, one Section B pass, and some Section C passes. She spends $8025 in all. How many Section C passes does she buy?

Write About It

11. How does the work backward strategy compare to guess and test when it comes to solving a division problem?

Order of Operations

Objective
- Use parentheses and brackets in numerical expressions and evaluate expressions using the order of operations.

Math Words

order of operations
simplify

Rosario takes 18 orders for 10 custom mugs on Saturday, and 4 more of the same order on Sunday. When customers received the mugs, each said that 2 mugs were missing from their order. How many mugs were shipped?

You can represent the situation with a product.

$(18 + 4)$	$\times$	$(10 - 2)$
Total number of orders	times	Number of mugs shipped per order

The order of operations is a set of rules that is used to simplify mathematical expressions with more than one operation.

Step 1: Simplify within the parentheses or brackets.
Step 2: Simplify any powers of 10. ← Powers of 10 are written with an exponent.
Step 3: Multiply or divide. Work from left to right.
Step 4: Add or subtract. Work from left to right.

$(18 + 4) \times (10 - 2)$ Simplify within the parentheses.

22×8 Multiply.

176

➤ 176 mugs were shipped.

Study these examples.

$[(49 + 21) \div 7] \times 8 - 13$

$[70 \div 7] \times 8 - 13$

$10 \times 8 - 13$

$80 - 13$

67

$5 \times 4 + 16 \times 2 \div 4 - 6$

$20 + 32 \div 4 - 6$

$20 + 8 - 6$

22

In fractions, simplify numerators and denominators before you divide.

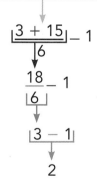

$\dfrac{3 + 15}{6} - 1$

$\dfrac{18}{6} - 1$

$3 - 1$

2

PRACTICE

Copy the problem and underline the calculation you will do first. Then simplify the expression using the order of operations.

1. $8 + 8 \div 4$

2. $4 \times 6 + 3$

3. $10^2 \times 7 - 4$

4. $81 \div (9 - 6)$

Use the order of operations to simplify.

5. $(3 \times 7) + (64 \div 8)$

6. $81 \div 9 - 2 \times 3$

7. $59 - 45 \div 5 \times 3 + 41$

8. $48 \div 6 \times 3 - 5$

9. $10 \times 4 + (49 \div 7) \times 2$

10. $\dfrac{9 \times 4}{6} + 7$

11. $10^3 - 4 \times 200 + \dfrac{19 - 3}{4}$

12. $(35 \div 5) \times 2 + 3 \times 6$

13. $4 + \dfrac{29 - 2}{9} + (16 + 2)$

14. $6 \times 3 \div (17 - 8)$

15. $(24 \div 6) - 3 + (2 \times 6)$

16. $\dfrac{18 - 9}{3} \times (1 + 2)$

17. $(28 + n) \times 4$ when $n = 32$

18. $(9 \times 8) - (n \times 6)$ when $n = 3$

19. $n \times 2 \div 2 + 24$ when $n = 8$

20. $6 + n - 3 \times 6 \div 9$ when $n = 2$

Problem Solving

21. Antonio wants to build a fence around his yard. He will pay $10 for each foot of fence. Simplify $10 \times [(2 \times 8) + (2 \times 12)]$ to find the total cost.

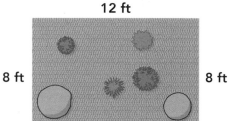

22. Rewrite $9 + 6 \div 3 - 2$ in as many ways as possible by inserting one pair of parentheses around two numbers. Simplify each expression.

23. Explain the difference between $1089 - 50 + 17$ and $1089 - (50 + 17)$. Simplify each expression.

24. A barbell weighs 35 pounds. Beth places a 25-pound weight on each side of the barbell. Write and simplify an expression to represent the total weight.

25. Gwen makes 36 candles. She will keep 4 candles, and then give the same number of candles to each of 8 friends. Which expression shows how many candles each friend will receive?

A. $36 - 4 \div 8$ **B.** $(36 - 4) \div 8$ **C.** $36 - 8 \div 4$ **D.** $36 \div 8 - 4$

Write About It

26. To simplify the expression $100 \div 5 \times 10 \div 2$, Mark first multiplies 5 by 10. Then he divides 100 by 50. Then he divides by 2. Does Mark simplify correctly? Explain.

Expressions

Objective
- Write, evaluate, and compare numerical expressions.

Math Words
expression
grouping symbols

You can write an expression to represent a situation. To show which parts of the expression must be simplified first, use grouping symbols, like parentheses or brackets.

The amount of money Coleman and Javion each have is shown. How much more money does Coleman have than Javion?

Coleman:

$(3 \times 5) + (3 \times 10) \longrightarrow [(3 \times 5) + (3 \times 10)]$

Javion:

$(1 \times 5) + (2 \times 10) \longrightarrow [(1 \times 5) + (2 \times 10)]$

Coleman   **Javion**

Subtract to find the difference in money. Follow the order of operations to simplify the expressions.

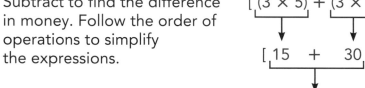

$[(3 \times 5) + (3 \times 10)] - [(1 \times 5) + (2 \times 10)]$

$[15 + 30] \qquad - \qquad [5 + 20]$

$45 \qquad - \qquad 25 \quad = \quad 20$

> Coleman has \$20 more than Javion.

Study these examples.

Write an expression to represent the problem.

Add 3 and 5, and multiply the sum by 2.

$(3 + 5) \times 2$

Compare the two expressions without evaluating.

$4 \times (543 + 2011)$ and $543 + 2011$

The value of the first expression is 4 times the value of the second expression.

PRACTICE

Write an expression to represent each problem.

1. Mila has 3 packs of pens. Each pack has 10 pens. She loses 2 pens.

2. Evelyn has 29 stickers. She gives away 4 and then divides the rest into 5 groups.

Simplify each expression.

3. $[3 \times (4 + 5)] + 9$

4. $7 + [(18 - 3) \div 5]$

5. $[20 - (3 + 4)] \div 13$

6. $[20 \times (5 - 3)] \times (8 \div 4)$

Simplify each expression.

7. $18 + 2 \times 12 + 8$

8. $2 + \left(\dfrac{60 - 5}{5}\right)$

9. $[(3 \times 4) \div (1 + 5)] + 2 \times 8$

10. $8 - 2 \times 2 + 10 \div 5 \times 3$

11. $\dfrac{73 - 58}{3} \times 10$

12. $30 - \dfrac{13 + 27}{8}$

13. $(7 - 24 \div 4) + 9 \times (18 \div 6)$

14. $[56 \div (2 \times 2)] \div [32 - (6 \times 5)]$

Problem Solving

15. Compare $10{,}789 - 487$ and $5 \times (10{,}789 - 487)$ without evaluating.

16. Compare "the sum of 15 and 9" and "the sum of 15 and 9, divided by 3" without evaluating.

17. Lauren says that in the expression $20 \div 10 \div 2$, since the operations are the same, they can be done in any order. Explain her error.

18. Daisy seed packs have 10 seeds each, and bags of lilies have 4 bulbs each. Lyla buys 2 packs of daisy seeds and 4 bags of lily bulbs. She plants 9 plants. How many does she have left to plant?

19. Small building kits have 3 red and 4 blue pieces and the large building kits have 6 red and 8 blue pieces. If Mekhi buys 3 small and 2 large building kits, how many pieces does he have?

Write an expression to represent each problem.

20. Add 3 and 12, and divide the sum by 5.

21. Subtract 8 from 39 divided by 3.

22. In January, Holly sold 16 bracelets and 8 necklaces at a craft fair. In February, she sold three times as many pieces of jewelry, and in March she sold half as many as in January. Write an expression for the number of pieces sold each month. Compare her sales from February and March.

Write About It

23. Consider the expression 6 plus 6 divided by 3. Explain why two students might get answers of 4 and 8. How could you write the expression to avoid any confusion?

Find the quotients.

1. $63 \div 9$
    $630 \div 9$
    $6300 \div 9$

2. $54 \div 6$
    $540 \div 60$
    $5400 \div 600$

3. $35 \div 7$
    $350 \div 7$
    $3500 \div 70$

4. $1600 \div 4$
    $16,000 \div 40$
    $160,000 \div 40$

5. $280 \div 7$
    $2800 \div 70$
    $28,000 \div 700$

6. $90 \div 9$
    $9000 \div 90$
    $90,000 \div 900$

7. $48 \div 8$
    $480 \div 80$
    $4800 \div 80$

8. $65 \div 5$
    $650 \div 5$
    $6500 \div 50$

Divide.

9. $9\overline{)3027}$

10. $479 \div 5$

11. $8\overline{)5866}$

12. $8024 \div 3$

13. $4036 \div 4$

14. $6\overline{)1806}$

15. $841 \div 2$

16. $24\overline{)49}$

17. $41\overline{)984}$

18. $31\overline{)1836}$

19. $8916 \div 9$

20. $15\overline{)945}$

21. $28\overline{)5656}$

22. $7552 \div 2$

23. $4086 \div 7$

24. $17\overline{)3502}$

Determine whether each number is divisible by 2, 3, 4, 5, 6, and/or 9.

25. 90

26. 795

27. 4152

28. 6252

29. 66

30. 184

31. 8436

32. 13,805

Estimate the quotient. Use compatible numbers.

33. $845 \div 9$

34. $1015 \div 29$

35. $1836 \div 15$

36. $1095 \div 11$

37. $651 \div 8$

38. $794 \div 38$

39. $8289 \div 42$

40. $23,805 \div 55$

Use the order of operations to simplify.

41. $(36 - 3) \times 7 + 10 \div 5$

42. $35 \div 7 + 2 \times 3 - 4$

43. $2 \times \dfrac{16 - 7}{3} + 12$

44. $\dfrac{2 \times (6 - 2) + 6}{7}$

Use the order of operations to simplify.

45. $[(3 + 1 \times 5) \div 4] - 2$

46. $(16 + 33) - [24 \div (3 + 1)] - 3$

Write a division sentence for the area model.

47.

	10	+	4
18	252		72
	− 180		−72
	72		0

48.

	20	+	10	+	2
43	1376		516		86
	− 860		−430		−86
	516		86		0

Create an area model to find each quotient.

49. $345 \div 15$

50. $492 \div 12$

Problem Solving

51. A robot can complete a certain task 507 times in 42 minutes. How many times can the robot complete the task each minute? Solve using partial quotients.

In Exercises 52–53, write an expression to represent each problem. Then solve.

52. Luis has a $20 gift card for an online music and video store. He downloads two videos that each cost $3. He downloads 4 songs that each cost $2. How much money is left on Luis' gift card?

53. The table shows the marker sets an art teacher purchases. What is the total number of markers that she purchased?

Set	Number Purchased
16-pack	10
32-pack	5
64-pack	1

54. Audrey creates an array to find the quotient of $182 \div 14$. Identify the error Audrey made. Then find the correct quotient.

A farmer is installing a new irrigation system on his farm. The farm is the shape of a rectangle and has an area of 405 square hectometers (sq hm). A hectometer is 100 meters, or about the length of one soccer field. The farmer will place sprinklers in the centers of square sections of land. Each sprinkler can irrigate 9 square hectometers.

1. The length of the farm is 27 hectometers. What is the width of the farm?

2. How many sprinklers does the farmer need to purchase?

3. What are the dimensions for each square section of land?

4. Draw and label a map of the farm that shows the land sections and placement of each sprinkler.

   - Indicate the length and width of the farm.

   - Indicate the length and width of each parcel.

   - Indicate the placement of each sprinkler with the letter S.

Based on the climate where the farm is located, the farmer estimates that every month he will use 450 gallons of water per sprinkler. To reduce the amount of water needed, the farmer wants to upgrade the sprinklers with one of the following:

   - Soil moisture sensors: Reduce water by $\frac{1}{5}$

   - Rain sensors: Reduce water by $\frac{1}{10}$

   - Advanced technology: Reduces water by $\frac{1}{3}$

5. For each feature listed above, explain how the farmer can use division to determine the amount of water that would be saved per sprinkler each month. (To find $\frac{1}{n}$ of an amount, divide by n.)

6. How could you use mental math to determine which feature would save the most water each month?

7. Make a table that compares the total amount of water that would be saved per sprinkler each month using each of these features.

8. What feature should the farmer purchase in order to save the most water? Determine the total amount of water he will save if he uses this feature on every sprinkler on his farm for 1 year.

9. Suppose the feature that will save the most water is also the most expensive. To help make his decision, the farmer wants to compare how much water would be saved in 1 year using the other two less expensive options. Determine this value for the other two features.

Using the irrigation system, the farmer is able to produce better crops using less water. So, he decides to expand his farm. He wants to add 1152 square hectometers of land to his farm. The new area is roughly the shape of a rectangle.

The farmer will divide the new land into square sections and place sprinklers in the center of each section. For the new land, he will buy larger sprinklers that can each irrigate 16 square hectometers.

10. How many sprinklers does the farmer need to purchase?

11. What are the dimensions for each section of land?

12. Draw a map of the new farmland that shows the land sections and placement of each sprinkler.

- Indicate the overall dimensions of the farm and the dimensions of each parcel.

- Indicate the placement of each sprinkler with the letter S.

13. Compare your map with a map made by a classmate. Is his or her map the same as yours? Do both maps correctly represent the new area of farmland? Explain.

14. The farmer estimates that each 16-square-hectometer section of land will generate $13,920 in revenue every month. What is the expected monthly revenue for each square hectometer?

15. The farmer estimates that the cost to maintain each 16-square-hectometer section of land is $9728 every month. What is the expected monthly maintenance cost for each square hectometer?

Determine the best answer for each problem.

1. What is the value of *n*?

   $65 \times n = 2015$

   A. 25 B. 27
   C. 29 D. 31

2. There are 7200 minutes in 5 days. How many minutes are in 1 day?

   A. 1400
   B. 1440
   C. 1450
   D. 1500

3. What is the height of the rectangle?

   29 units

   464 square units

4. Order the products from least to greatest.

   12×25, 18×16, 32×8

   A. 12×25, 18×16, 32×8
   B. 32×8, 12×25, 18×16
   C. 32×8, 18×16, 12×25
   D. 18×16, 32×8, 12×25

5. Complete the number sentence.

   $2 \times 2 \times \underline{?} \times 5 \times 5 = 300$

   A. 2 B. 3
   C. 4 D. 5

6. Which numbers evenly divide into 2025? Select all that apply.

   A. 2 B. 3
   C. 4 D. 5
   E. 6 F. 9
   G. 10

7. Order the numbers 3081, 2972, and 30,153 from least to greatest.

   A. 30,153; 3081; 2972
   B. 3081; 30,153; 2972
   C. 2972; 30,153; 3081
   D. 2972; 3081; 30,153

8. Which number(s) are a possible remainder for a divisor of 5? Select all that apply.

   A. 1 B. 2
   C. 3 D. 4
   E. 5 F. 6

9. Which two numbers evenly divide into 60?

   A. 15
   B. 20
   C. 25
   D. 35
   E. 40

10. Other than 1 and itself, how many numbers divide evenly into 13?

    A. 0 B. 1
    C. 2 D. 3

Number Theory and Fractions

The Fibonacci sequence is a special list of numbers. The first two numbers are 0 and 1. The third number is $0 + 1 = 1$, the fourth number is $1 + 1 = 2$, the fifth number is $1 + 2 = 3$, the sixth number is $2 + 3 = 5$, and so on. The list continues on forever: 0, 1, 1, 2, 3, 5, 8, 13, 21, 34, …

The Fibonacci Sequence

Fibonacci numbers are sometimes called nature's numbering system because they commonly appear in nature, such as:

♦ in arrangements of plant leaves
♦ in arrangements of seeds on a sunflower
♦ the number of petals on flowers
♦ in spirals on a pinecone or pineapple
♦ in sections inside a piece of fruit
♦ the branching structure of plants and trees

Factors, Primes and Composite Numbers

Objective
- Find the prime factorization of a number.

Math Words
prime number
composite number
prime factor
prime factorization
factor tree
exponent
base

A prime number is a whole number whose only factors are 1 and itself. Composite numbers are whole numbers that have more than two factors. 1 is neither prime nor composite.

You can write a number as a product of all its prime factors. This is called the prime factorization of the number.

You can use a factor tree to find the prime factorizaton of a number. To use a factor tree, write the number as the product of two factors. Repeat the process until the factors are all prime.

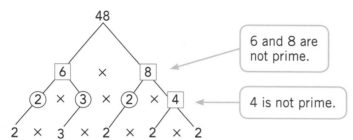

6 and 8 are not prime.

4 is not prime.

Notice that the prime factorization is the same in each factor tree. By the Commutative Property of Multiplication, the order of the factors does not matter.

You can write repeating factors in a prime factorization using an exponent. As with powers of 10, the exponent tells you how many times the base is used as a factor. So, $2 \times 2 \times 2 \times 2 = 2^4$.

The prime factorization of 48 is:

$$2 \times 2 \times 2 \times 2 \times 3 = 2^4 \times 3$$

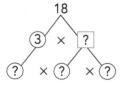

PRACTICE

Complete the factor tree to show the prime factorization.

1.
18
(3) × [?]
(?) × (?) × (?)

2.
90
[?] × [?]
(2) × (3) × (?) × (?)

3.
72
[?] × [9]
(2) × [?] × (?) × (?)
(?) × (?) × (?) × (?) × (?)

Determine whether the number is prime or composite.

4. 49   **5.** 15   **6.** 53   **7.** 111   **8.** 17

Complete the factor tree to find the prime factorization.

9.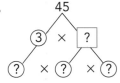

10.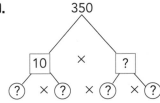

11.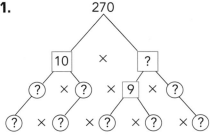

Create a factor tree for each number.

12. 42   **13.** 105   **14.** 24   **15.** 140   **16.** 84

17. 147   **18.** 198   **19.** 100   **20.** 180   **21.** 280

22. 120   **23.** 135   **24.** 195   **25.** 210   **26.** 243

Write the prime factorization of each number. Write repeated factors using an exponent.

27. 78   **28.** 90   **29.** 28   **30.** 75   **31.** 50   **32.** 96

33. 88   **34.** 128   **35.** 108   **36.** 132   **37.** 138   **38.** 144

39. 81   **40.** 93   **41.** 168   **42.** 200   **43.** 1500   **44.** 89

Problem Solving

45. The paper shows Macy's work finding the prime factorization of 360. What is her error?

46. The number 1728 is equal to 12 × 12 × 12. Use this fact to help you write the prime factorization of 1728. Use exponents.

47. What is the least number that has 4 different prime number factors in its prime factorization?

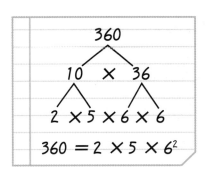

Write About It

48. The number one billion can be written as a power of 10 as 10^9. Use this form to help you write the prime factorization of one billion. Explain your reasoning.

Common Factors

Objective

▪ List the common factors and find the greatest common factor (GCF) of two or more numbers.

Math Words

common factor

greatest common factor (GCF)

Piper is organizing musical instruments in a closet. She wants each shelf to have the same set of instruments. There are 15 recorders and 27 harmonicas. What is the greatest number of shelves Piper can use to store the instruments?

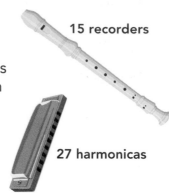

15 recorders

27 harmonicas

The greatest common factor (GCF) of two or more numbers is the greatest number that is a factor of all the numbers.

To find the GCF:

• List the factors of each number.

• Select the greatest factor that the lists have in common.

Find the greatest common factor (GCF) of 15 and 27. The GCF is greatest number of shelves Piper can use.

Factors of 15: 1, 3, 5, 15

Factors of 27: 1, 3, 9, 27

> The common factors of 15 and 27 are 1 and 3.

The GCF of 15 and 27 is 3.

> Piper can use at most 3 shelves. If she uses 3 shelves, each will have 5 recorders and 9 harmonicas.

PRACTICE

Copy and complete the table to find the GCF of each set of numbers. '

	Number	Factors	Common Factors	GCF
1.	10	1, 2, 5, ?	1, ?	?
	12	1, 2, 3, ?, ?, ?		
2.	18	1, 2, 3, ?, ?, ?	?	?
	30	1, 2, 3, ?, ?, ?, ?, ?		
3.	54	?	?	?
	90	?		

List the common factors of each number. Then find the GCF.

4. 6 and 9   **5.** 3 and 15   **6.** 4 and 11   **7.** 18 and 24

8. 16 and 20   **9.** 11 and 26   **10.** 8 and 12   **11.** 10 and 30

12. 15 and 21   **13.** 24 and 32   **14.** 12 and 72   **15.** 27 and 36

16. 24 and 36   **17.** 14 and 20   **18.** 14 and 56   **19.** 18 and 36

Find the GCF of each set of numbers.

20. 45 and 60   **21.** 24 and 40   **22.** 18 and 21   **23.** 16 and 48

24. 30 and 45   **25.** 48 and 56   **26.** 36 and 63   **27.** 36 and 42

28. 3, 9 and 15   **29.** 4, 8 and 12   **30.** 20, 24 and 36   **31.** 6, 9, and 18

32. 12, 15 and 18   **33.** 7, 35 and 49   **34.** 16, 20 and 24   **35.** 10, 14, and 18

Problem Solving

36. Abigail says, "Any two prime numbers always have a GCF of 1." However, her statement is not accurate. How can she adjust her statement so it is true? Explain.

37. Square tiles will be used to fill the rectangular area shown. Only whole tiles will be used. What is the greatest possible whole-number side length of the square tiles? Explain your answer.

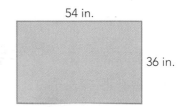

54 in.

36 in.

Leeann has 24 daisies, 32 carnations, and 40 tulips. She wants to make identical arrangements in more than one vase, with no flowers left over. Use this information for Exercises 38–39.

38. Determine the least and greatest number of vases Leeann can use.

39. Describe the flowers in each of the greatest number of vases.

Write About It

40. Describe how divisibility rules can help determine whether a number is prime or composite. Is 112,101 a prime number?

Estimation and Equivalent Fractions

Objectives
- Determine if a fraction is closer to 0, $\frac{1}{2}$, or 1.
- Find equivalent fractions.

Math Words
compatible numbers
equivalent fractions

You can use a number line to help determine if a fraction is closer to 0, closer to $\frac{1}{2}$, or closer to 1.

If the numerator is much less than the denominator, then the fraction is closer to 0.	If the numerator is about half of the denominator, then the fraction is closer to $\frac{1}{2}$.	If the numerator is about equal to the denominator, then the fraction is closer to 1.
$\frac{2}{12}$ is closer to 0.	$\frac{7}{12}$ is closer to $\frac{1}{2}$.	$\frac{11}{12}$ is closer to 1.

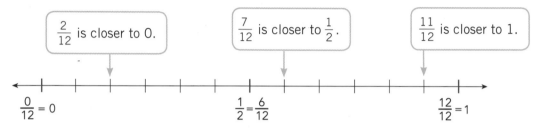

$\frac{0}{12} = 0$ $\frac{1}{2} = \frac{6}{12}$ $\frac{12}{12} = 1$

You can also use compatible numbers to estimate fractions.

$\frac{19}{41}$ is about $\frac{20}{40}$ or $\frac{1}{2}$. $\frac{197}{203}$ is about $\frac{200}{200}$ or 1.

Equivalent fractions are equal and name the same point on the number line.

Study these examples.

Multiply to find equivalent fractions.

$$\frac{2}{6} = \frac{2 \times 2}{6 \times 2} = \frac{4}{12}$$

Divide to find equivalent fractions.

$$\frac{2}{6} = \frac{2 \div 2}{6 \div 2} = \frac{1}{3}$$

PRACTICE

Determine whether the fraction is closer to 0, $\frac{1}{2}$, or 1.

1. $\frac{5}{8}$ **2.** $\frac{1}{9}$ **3.** $\frac{6}{7}$ **4.** $\frac{8}{11}$ **5.** $\frac{7}{15}$ **6.** $\frac{19}{20}$

7. $\frac{21}{43}$ **8.** $\frac{5}{38}$ **9.** $\frac{16}{29}$ **10.** $\frac{45}{47}$ **11.** $\frac{3}{100}$ **12.** $\frac{119}{121}$

Estimate each fraction using compatible numbers.

13. $\frac{6}{13}$ **14.** $\frac{21}{19}$ **15.** $\frac{16}{31}$ **16.** $\frac{23}{24}$ **17.** $\frac{25}{52}$ **18.** $\frac{2}{43}$

19. $\frac{31}{59}$ **20.** $\frac{16}{25}$ **21.** $\frac{87}{91}$ **22.** $\frac{201}{400}$ **23.** $\frac{105}{100}$ **24.** $\frac{498}{500}$

For each fraction, write two equivalent fractions using multiplication.

25. $\frac{1}{4}$ **26.** $\frac{6}{7}$ **27.** $\frac{2}{9}$ **28.** $\frac{5}{8}$ **29.** $\frac{2}{5}$ **30.** $\frac{10}{11}$

For each fraction, write two equivalent fractions using division.

31. $\frac{10}{20}$ **32.** $\frac{16}{24}$ **33.** $\frac{12}{30}$ **34.** $\frac{22}{44}$ **35.** $\frac{15}{75}$ **36.** $\frac{45}{120}$

For each fraction, write three equivalent fractions.

37. $\frac{1}{4}$ **38.** $\frac{2}{5}$ **39.** $\frac{3}{7}$ **40.** $\frac{7}{9}$ **41.** $\frac{10}{12}$ **42.** $\frac{20}{36}$

43. $\frac{2}{3}$ **44.** $\frac{5}{6}$ **45.** $\frac{8}{24}$ **46.** $\frac{15}{30}$ **47.** $\frac{11}{18}$ **48.** $\frac{140}{220}$

Write the missing number or numbers for the equivalent fractions.

49. $\frac{4}{5} = \frac{n}{25}$ **50.** $\frac{7}{8} = \frac{21}{n}$ **51.** $\frac{21}{49} = \frac{n}{7}$ **52.** $\frac{32}{40} = \frac{4}{n}$

53. $\frac{2}{3} = \frac{4}{a} = \frac{8}{b}$ **54.** $\frac{5}{a} = \frac{10}{16} = \frac{20}{b}$ **55.** $\frac{a}{7} = \frac{12}{14} = \frac{b}{28}$ **56.** $\frac{4}{16} = \frac{2}{a} = \frac{1}{b}$

Problem Solving

57. Hannah and her friends eat $\frac{2}{3}$ of the pizza shown. What equivalent fraction best shows how many slices they eat?

58. Chloe has 37 math problems for homework. If she has already completed 17 of them, is she just beginning, about halfway through, or almost done with her homework? Explain.

59. A painter buys one canvas that is $\frac{3}{4}$ of a meter long and one that is $\frac{6}{8}$ of a meter long. Which canvas is longer? Explain.

60. Sandra says a fraction equivalent to $\frac{13}{39}$ cannot be found by dividing since 13 is a prime number. Is her reasoning correct? Explain.

Write About It

61. Madison says that $\frac{6}{14}$ and $\frac{9}{21}$ are not equivalent fractions, since she can't multiply 14 by a number to get 21. Explain to Madison why these fractions are equivalent. (Hint: Use division.)

Determine if each number is prime or composite.

1. 46   **2.** 37   **3.** 131   **4.** 231

5. 53   **6.** 89   **7.** 177   **8.** 711

Identify the factors of each number. Select all that apply.

9. 25

    A. 1   **B.** 2   **C.** 3   **D.** 5   **E.** 25

10. 15

    A. 1   **B.** 2   **C.** 3   **D.** 5   **E.** 15

11. 140

    A. 1   **B.** 2   **C.** 4   **D.** 5   **E.** 7

12. 225

    A. 1   **B.** 2   **C.** 3   **D.** 5   **E.** 225

Match each number with its prime factorization.

13. 28   **A.** $2^4 \times 3$ **17.** 45   **A.** $2^3 \times 5$
    B. $2^2 \times 3^2$ **B.** $3^2 \times 5$
14. 48   **C.** $2^2 \times 7$ **18.** 35   **C.** 5×7
    D. 2^5 **D.** 2×5^2

15. 36   **19.** 50

16. 32   **20.** 40

Match each set of numbers with their greatest common factor.

21. 12 and 18   **A.** 2   **25.** 15, 24, and 75   **A.** 3
    B. 6   **B.** 4
22. 22 and 56   **C.** 7   **26.** 8, 12, and 16   **C.** 7
    D. 12   **D.** 10
23. 14 and 49   **27.** 30, 40, and 80

24. 48 and 60   **28.** 14, 28, and 35

Determine if the fraction is closer to 0, $\frac{1}{2}$, or 1.

29. $\frac{3}{5}$

    A. 0   **B.** $\frac{1}{2}$ **C.** 1

30. $\frac{1}{10}$

    A. 0   **B.** $\frac{1}{2}$ **C.** 1

31. $\frac{7}{9}$

    A. 0   **B.** $\frac{1}{2}$ **C.** 1

Identify any equivalent fractions. Select all that apply.

32. $\frac{18}{34}$

    A. $\frac{8}{14}$ **B.** $\frac{9}{17}$ **C.** $\frac{20}{36}$ **D.** $\frac{27}{51}$

33. $\frac{3}{8}$

    A. $\frac{15}{40}$ **B.** $\frac{1}{3}$ **C.** $\frac{6}{15}$ **D.** $\frac{9}{32}$

34. $\frac{8}{10}$

    A. $\frac{3}{5}$ **B.** $\frac{4}{5}$ **C.** $\frac{24}{40}$ **D.** $\frac{16}{20}$

Problem Solving

35. Stella is making individual servings of trail mix. She has 54 cashews, 63 dried cranberries, and 90 chunks of granola. She wants to split each ingredient equally among the servings. What is the greatest number of servings she can make without having any ingredients left over? How many pieces of each ingredient should go in a serving?

36. Patrick is running a 26.2-mile marathon. The number line shows his progress so far. Is he just beginning, about halfway through, or has he almost completed the marathon? Explain.

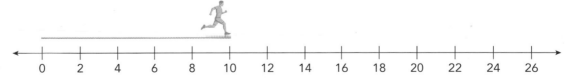

37. Emily says the prime factorization of 108 is $3^2 \times 4$. What is Emily's error? Explain. Then find the correct prime factorization.

Common Multiples and Common Denominators

The multiples of a whole number are the products of that number and 1, 2, 3, 4, ...

$$\begin{array}{cccc} 4 & 4 & 4 & 4 \\ \times 1 & \times 2 & \times 3 & \times 4 \\ \hline 4 & 8 & 12 & 16 \end{array}$$

Multiples of 4 are 4, 8, 12, ...

Multiples that are the same for two or more numbers are called common multiples. What are the common multiples of 2 and 3?

Multiples of 2: 2, 4, 6, 8, 10, 12, 14, 16, 18, ...

Multiples of 3: 3, 6, 9, 12, 15, 18, ...

Common multiples of 2 and 3 are 6, 12, 18, ...

You can find the least common multiple (LCM) of 2, 3, and 4:

Multiples of 2: 2, 4, 6, 8, 10, 12, 14, 16, 18, ...

Multiples of 3: 3, 6, 9, 12, 15, 18, 21, ...

Multiples of 4: 4, 8, 12, 16, 20, 24, ...

The LCM of 2, 3, and 4 is 12.

The least common denominator (LCD) of two or more fractions is the least common multiple of the denominators. What is the LCD of $\frac{3}{4}, \frac{2}{5},$ and $\frac{9}{10}$?

Multiples of 4 for $\frac{3}{4}$: 4, 8, 12, 16, 20, 24...

Multiples of 5 for $\frac{2}{5}$: 5, 10, 15, 20, 25...

Multiples of 10 for $\frac{9}{10}$: 10, 20, 30, 40...

The least common denominator of the fractions $\frac{3}{4}, \frac{2}{5},$ and $\frac{9}{10}$ is 20.

PRACTICE

Find the first eight multiples of each number.

1. 5
2. 7
3. 8
4. 1
5. 9
6. 10
7. 4
8. 13
9. 11
10. 16
11. 14
12. 20

Find the first four common multiples of each set of numbers.

13. 3, 5
14. 6, 9
15. 4, 8
16. 3, 9
17. 5, 6
18. 2, 3
19. 4, 6
20. 3, 8
21. 4, 10
22. 8, 12
23. 3, 4, 9
24. 2, 4, 6
25. 2, 5, 10
26. 3, 5, 9
27. 4, 7, 8

Find the least common multiple of each set of numbers.

28. 2, 4   **29.** 6, 8   **30.** 9, 12   **31.** 3, 10   **32.** 10, 15

33. 5, 11   **34.** 4, 10   **35.** 8, 10   **36.** 7, 15   **37.** 14, 24

38. 3, 4, 9   **39.** 5, 6, 10   **40.** 2, 7, 8   **41.** 4, 5, 12

42. 2, 5, 8   **43.** 3, 8, 12   **44.** 12, 16, 20   **45.** 7, 8, 14

Find the least common denominator of each set of fractions.

46. $\frac{1}{2}, \frac{3}{4}$ **47.** $\frac{2}{3}, \frac{1}{9}$ **48.** $\frac{1}{3}, \frac{3}{5}$ **49.** $\frac{3}{4}, \frac{1}{6}$ **50.** $\frac{5}{6}, \frac{5}{8}$

51. $\frac{1}{3}, \frac{7}{10}$ **52.** $\frac{5}{8}, \frac{7}{12}$ **53.** $\frac{3}{10}, \frac{2}{15}$ **54.** $\frac{2}{3}, \frac{3}{11}$ **55.** $\frac{2}{9}, \frac{4}{15}$

56. $\frac{3}{4}, \frac{2}{5}, \frac{9}{20}$ **57.** $\frac{1}{3}, \frac{5}{6}, \frac{7}{12}$ **58.** $\frac{1}{12}, \frac{3}{16}, \frac{5}{18}$

Problem Solving

Peter is placing rows of square tiles as shown. The yellow tiles are 3 inches long, and the patterned tiles are 4 inches long. Use this information for Exercises 59–61.

59. Peter starts by aligning the left edges next to the wall on the left as shown. How many of each tile will he place before the right edges first line up?

60. What is the distance from the wall on the left to the point where they line up?

61. Write 3 other distances from the wall where the tiles line up again.

62. The table shows a workout schedule. How often will all 3 activities occur on the same day?

Ride Bike	Lift Weights	Yoga Class
every other day	every 3ʳᵈ day	every 7ᵗʰ day

63. What is the least common multiple of any two different prime numbers?

Write About It

64. Katie states that the least common denominator of $\frac{1}{6}$ and $\frac{1}{9}$ is 54. Is she correct? Explain.

Problem Solving
Make a Table

A computer retail store is purchasing cases of laptops and laptop sleeves. The store will offer a free sleeve with each laptop purchase. How many cases of each product should be purchased so that there is a sleeve for each laptop with none left over?

Read and Understand

- What is the question you need to answer?

  How many cases of laptops and cases of laptop sleeves should be purchased?

- What is the key information?

  Laptops come in cases of 8, and laptop sleeves come in cases of 10.

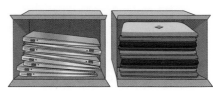

Set of 8   Set of 10

- What math concept can you use to solve the problem?

  Common multiples

Make a Table

Number of cases	1	2	3	4	5	6	7	8	9	10	11	...
Laptops: multiples of 8	8	16	24	32	40	48	56	64	72	80	88	...
Laptop sleeves: multiples of 10	10	20	30	40	50	60	70	80	90	100	110	...

Answer the Question

The numbers of cases corresponding to the common multiples of 8 and 10 can be purchased. For example, 4 cases of laptop sleeves and 5 cases of laptops can be purchased, giving the store 40 sleeves and 40 laptops.

Look Back

Make sure you interpret the table correctly. The common multiples represent the total number of laptops and sleeves, not the number of cases. Also, there is more than one possible answer. For example, the store can also buy 8 cases of sleeves and 10 cases of laptops.

PRACTICE

1. Natalie and Naomi work less than 40 hours per week. Natalie works 4-hour shifts and Naomi works 5-hour shifts. The girls work the same number of hours each week. How many hours do they each work per week? How many shifts do they each work per week? Use a table to find the answer.

2. What are the prime number common factors of 18 and 30? Copy and complete the table to solve the problem.

Prime numbers	2	?	?	?	?	?	?	?
Factors of 18	1	?	?	?	?	?	?	?
Factors of 30	1	?	?	?	?	?	?	?

3. Candles come in packs of 10 and the candle holders come in packs of 15. At least 50 candles are needed to decorate 25 tables. What is the least number of packs of candles and candle holders the party planner can buy if he wants an equal number of candles and candle holders with none left over? Make a table to find your answer.

4. To make a complete revolution around their star, one planet takes 3 years, another takes 4 years, and another takes 8 years. The three planets are now in the same position. Make a table to find how long it will take for the three planets to return to the position they are in now. How many revolutions did each planet make? Explain.

Sebastian collects all the memory cards at the store to organize. He finds different size cards with various numbers of gigabytes (GB) as shown. Fifteen cards are 4 GB, 21 are 8 GB, and 9 are 16 GB. Use this information for Exercises 5–7.

5. Could Sebastian put all the cards in 3 baskets, with the same number of cards in each basket? Explain.

6. Sebastian's boss thought that about half of the memory cards are 8 gigabytes. Is he correct? Explain.

7. Sebastian decides to organize as many of the memory cards as possible into 5 baskets. He wants the same number of each type of card in each basket, and the same total number of cards in each basket. What types of memory cards will be in each basket?

8. Make a table listing all 3-digit numbers that contain each of the digits 1, 3, and 4. Then list each number as prime or composite.

Write About It

9. To find a least common multiple, you make a table of multiples of different numbers. How do you know how long the rows have to be?

Fractions Greater Than or Equal to One

Objectives
- Identify improper fractions.
- Rename improper fractions as a whole or mixed number.

Math Words
improper fraction
proper fraction
mixed number
simplest form

If the numerator of a fraction is greater than or equal to the denominator, it is called an improper fraction. Otherwise it is a proper fraction.

Look at the number line. Fractions greater than or equal to 1 are improper fractions.

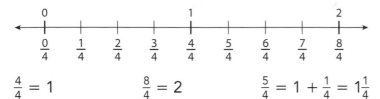

$\frac{4}{4} = 1$ $\frac{8}{4} = 2$ $\frac{5}{4} = 1 + \frac{1}{4} = 1\frac{1}{4}$

You can divide to rename an improper fraction as a whole number or mixed number. The simplest form of a fraction is the equivalent fraction with the least denominator.

- Divide the numerator by the denominator.

- Write the quotient as the whole number part of the mixed number.

- Write the remainder as the numerator and the divisor as the denominator of the fraction part.

- Write the fraction part in simplest form.

$\frac{30}{8} = ?$

$30 \div 8 = 3 \text{ R}6$

$\frac{30}{8} = 3\frac{6}{8}$

$3\frac{6}{8} = 3\frac{3}{4}$

A mixed number is made up of a whole number part and a fraction part.

PRACTICE

Determine whether the fraction is a proper or improper fraction.

1. $\frac{11}{10}$ **2.** $\frac{3}{7}$ **3.** $\frac{9}{9}$ **4.** $\frac{3}{1}$ **5.** $\frac{9}{10}$

Determine if the fraction is greater than or equal to 1.

6. $\frac{9}{8}$ **7.** $\frac{5}{5}$ **8.** $\frac{10}{3}$ **9.** $\frac{6}{4}$ **10.** $\frac{15}{15}$

Write each fraction as a whole number or mixed number in simplest form.

11. $\frac{12}{4}$ **12.** $\frac{7}{5}$ **13.** $\frac{21}{3}$ **14.** $\frac{16}{7}$ **15.** $\frac{16}{12}$ **16.** $\frac{24}{10}$

17. $\frac{26}{8}$ **18.** $\frac{13}{2}$ **19.** $\frac{33}{22}$ **20.** $\frac{14}{5}$ **21.** $\frac{45}{9}$ **22.** $\frac{26}{6}$

Find three values for *n* that make the fraction less than 1, equal to 1, and greater than 1.

23. $\frac{n}{8}$ 24. $\frac{11}{n}$ 25. $\frac{4}{n}$ 26. $\frac{n}{9}$ 27. $\frac{10}{n}$ 28. $\frac{n}{13}$

29. $\frac{6}{n}$ 30. $\frac{16}{n}$ 31. $\frac{n}{14}$ 32. $\frac{18}{n}$ 33. $\frac{n}{21}$ 34. $\frac{n}{17}$

Write each fraction as a whole number or mixed number in simplest form.

35. $\frac{6}{5}$ 36. $\frac{5}{3}$ 37. $\frac{7}{2}$ 38. $\frac{11}{4}$ 39. $\frac{15}{5}$ 40. $\frac{20}{7}$

41. $\frac{53}{6}$ 42. $\frac{42}{10}$ 43. $\frac{81}{40}$ 44. $\frac{36}{6}$ 45. $\frac{15}{2}$ 46. $\frac{30}{8}$

47. $\frac{21}{15}$ 48. $\frac{110}{5}$ 49. $\frac{192}{9}$ 50. $\frac{325}{75}$ 51. $\frac{300}{10}$ 52. $\frac{46}{6}$

Problem Solving

Lobsters captured in Maine must be a certain size, or they need to be released back into the water. The carapace (or body shell) must have a length between $3\frac{1}{4}$ and $\frac{20}{4}$ inches. Use this information for Exercises 53–54.

53. Derek catches a lobster with a carapace that is $\frac{17}{4}$ inches long. Write the length as a mixed number and determine if he is allowed to keep the lobster.

54. Which of the lengths is given as an improper fraction? How do you know? Write the improper fraction as a whole number or mixed number.

Write About It

55. To write the improper fraction $\frac{25}{8}$ as a mixed number, Mariana decides to subtract. Explain why her method works.

$$25 - 8 = 17$$
$$17 - 8 = 9$$
$$9 - 8 = 1$$
3 subtractions, 1 remainder;
$$\frac{25}{8} = 3\frac{1}{8}$$

Compare and Order Fractions and Mixed Numbers

Objective
- Compare and order fractions and mixed numbers.

Math Word
Least common denominator (LCD)

Three friends have the same size hard drive. Jade's hard drive is $\frac{3}{4}$ full. Julia's is $\frac{4}{7}$ full and Amari's is $\frac{5}{8}$ full. Whose hard drive is the fullest?

Compare $\frac{3}{4}, \frac{4}{7}$, and $\frac{5}{8}$.

◆ Compare fractions with unlike denominators.

- Find the least common denominator of the fractions.

- Rename the fractions with the same common denominator.

- Compare the numerators.

- Order the fractions.

The LCM of 4, 7, and 8 is 56. This is the LCD of the fractions.

$\frac{3}{4} = \frac{42}{56}$ $\frac{4}{7} = \frac{28}{56}$ $\frac{5}{8} = \frac{35}{56}$

$28 < 35 < 42$

$\frac{28}{56} < \frac{35}{56} < \frac{42}{56}$ so $\frac{4}{7} < \frac{5}{8} < \frac{3}{4}$

➤ Jade's hard drive is the fullest.

Compare: $1\frac{1}{4}$ _?_ $1\frac{7}{8}$

◆ Compare mixed numbers.

- Compare the whole number parts. $1 = 1$

- If the whole number parts are equal, compare the fraction parts.

$\frac{1}{4} = \frac{2}{8}$ and $\frac{2}{8} < \frac{7}{8}$, so $\frac{1}{4} < \frac{7}{8}$.

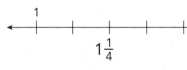 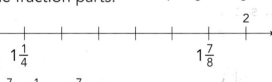

➤ Since $1 = 1$ and $\frac{1}{4} < \frac{7}{8}$, $1\frac{1}{4} < 1\frac{7}{8}$.

PRACTICE

Compare. Write <, =, or >.

1. $\frac{3}{7}$ _?_ $\frac{6}{7}$

2. $\frac{3}{8}$ _?_ $\frac{1}{4}$

3. $\frac{4}{5}$ _?_ $\frac{12}{15}$

4. $1\frac{3}{7}$ _?_ $1\frac{6}{7}$

5. $3\frac{5}{6}$ _?_ $2\frac{7}{8}$

6. $4\frac{1}{2}$ _?_ $4\frac{2}{4}$

7. $1\frac{2}{5}$ _?_ $1\frac{3}{8}$

8. $2\frac{4}{10}$ _?_ $2\frac{4}{9}$

Order the fractions from least to greatest.

9. $\frac{1}{2}, \frac{1}{3}, \frac{1}{4}$

10. $\frac{2}{7}, \frac{5}{7}, \frac{3}{7}$

11. $\frac{2}{9}, \frac{2}{5}, \frac{2}{3}$

12. $\frac{8}{9}, \frac{6}{7}, \frac{4}{5}$

Compare. Write $<$, $=$, or $>$.

13. $2\frac{6}{35}$? $2\frac{2}{11}$

14. $7\frac{5}{21}$? $7\frac{12}{49}$

15. $1\frac{11}{18}$? $1\frac{2}{3}$

16. $4\frac{1}{5}$? $4\frac{3}{15}$

17. $\frac{15}{8}$? $\frac{8}{15}$

18. $1\frac{3}{10}$? $\frac{13}{10}$

19. $1\frac{3}{7}$? $\frac{11}{7}$

20. $\frac{17}{3}$? $5\frac{18}{28}$

21. $\frac{12}{5}$? $1\frac{2}{5}$

22. $2\frac{3}{8}$? $2\frac{5}{11}$

23. $\frac{17}{11}$? $\frac{14}{9}$

24. $\frac{20}{12}$? $1\frac{2}{3}$

Order the fractions from least to greatest.

25. $\frac{1}{5}, \frac{1}{6}, \frac{1}{8}$

26. $\frac{5}{13}, \frac{12}{13}, \frac{8}{13}$

27. $\frac{4}{5}, \frac{1}{4}, \frac{7}{8}$

28. $\frac{4}{5}, \frac{7}{10}, \frac{3}{4}$

29. $\frac{23}{12}, \frac{11}{8}, \frac{11}{6}$

30. $1\frac{3}{4}, 1\frac{2}{3}, 1\frac{4}{5}$

31. $5\frac{3}{5}, 5\frac{7}{10}, 5\frac{3}{4}$

32. $2\frac{7}{9}, 2\frac{5}{6}, 2\frac{2}{3}$

33. $3\frac{5}{7}, 3\frac{8}{9}, 3\frac{10}{13}$

34. $\frac{8}{5}, \frac{10}{7}, \frac{12}{11}$

35. $1\frac{3}{8}, 2, \frac{11}{6}$

36. $\frac{13}{4}, 3, \frac{16}{5}$

Problem Solving

37. Jorge's class uses less clay than Caleb's class, but more than Gio's class. Jorge's class uses $10\frac{1}{4}$ pounds of clay. Whose clay is on the right side of the scale and what is a possible weight of that clay?

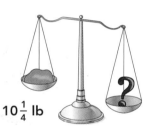

$10\frac{1}{4}$ lb

38. In a long jump competition, Camryn jumped $4\frac{7}{8}$ feet on her first jump and $5\frac{1}{4}$ feet on her second jump. She says that her first jump was longer because $\frac{7}{8} > \frac{1}{4}$. Is she correct? Explain.

39. What is the least fraction with a denominator of 8 that is greater than $\frac{2}{5}$? Explain how you found the fraction.

40. Explain how can you order the four times shown below. Then list the times from shortest to longest. There are 60 seconds in 1 minute. $1\frac{1}{6}$ minutes, 76 seconds, $1\frac{3}{12}$ minutes, 72 seconds

Write About It

41. Jane says that to order fractions that have the same numerator, the denominators can be compared. The greater the denominator, the lesser the fraction. Is she correct? Use an example in your explanation.

Interpret a Remainder

Objective
- Interpret a fraction as a division, and solve word problems involving fractions and mixed numbers.

Math Words
remainder
simplest form

A group of 14 friends are driving to the mall. Each car can hold 4 people. How many cars will they need to take?

When you interpret a remainder in a real-world problem, you have 3 options, depending on what makes sense.

- Keep the fraction.
- Round up.
- Round down.

Divide 14 friends into groups of 4: $14 \div 4 = \frac{14}{4} = 3\frac{2}{4}$.

The friends can split up into 3 groups of 4 people. There will be 2 people left over. Since the 2 leftover people also need to get to the mall, they need to take another car. Round up.

> The friends need 4 cars to get to the mall.

Study these examples.

A teacher purchases 20 cups of gravel to be split among 3 reptile habitats. How much gravel should she place in each habitat?

$$20 \div 3 = \frac{20}{3} = 6\frac{2}{3}$$

> You can measure a fraction of a cup. Keep the fraction. Each habitat gets $6\frac{2}{3}$ cups of gravel.

Tanner has $18 to spend on books. Each book costs $4. How many books can he buy?

$$18 \div 4 = \frac{18}{4} = 4\frac{2}{4}$$

> He cannot buy $\frac{2}{4}$ of a book. Round down. Tanner can buy 4 books.

PRACTICE

Divide. Write each quotient in simplest form.

1. $4 \div 7$ **2.** $1 \div 8$ **3.** $3 \div 9$ **4.** $5 \div 20$

5. $5 \div 3$ **6.** $15 \div 7$ **7.** $12 \div 18$ **8.** $18 \div 12$

9. $6 \overline{)2}$ **10.** $10 \overline{)5}$ **11.** $5 \overline{)1}$ **12.** $9 \overline{)12}$

13. $5 \overline{)12}$ **14.** $6 \overline{)16}$ **15.** $11 \overline{)40}$ **16.** $15 \overline{)18}$

A group of friends go canoeing. The park has 6 canoes available to rent. Each canoe can hold 3 people. Use the information for Exercises 17–19.

17. If there are 10 people on the trip, how many canoes are needed?

18. In this situation, how would you interpret the remainder?

19. A large group rents all 6 of the canoes, and 2 people had to rent kayaks. How many people are in the group?

20. Fourteen friends are in line for a roller coaster. Three people fit in each roller coaster car. How many cars will they need?

21. Antonio divides 15 bags of soil among 4 children to use to plant flowers. How many bags of soil does each child have to use?

Emmanuel wants to cut the piece of canvas as shown to make three equal-sized paintings. Use this information for Exercises 22–23.

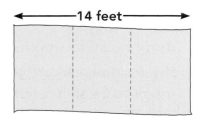

22. How wide will the paintings be?

23. Emmanuel decides that instead of cutting the canvas equally, he wants to cut pieces that are 4 feet wide. How many paintings will there be? How much canvas will be left over?

Problem Solving

24. A ballet company has 15 ballerinas in the corps. Costumes come in packs of 4. How many packs should the producer of the company purchase? How many costumes will be left over?

25. A school buys one snack for each of 94 fifth-graders. Granola bars are sold in boxes of 8. Raisins are sold in packs of 10. Tangerines come with 14 in each box. Which snack can they buy to have the fewest left over? How many of that snack will be left over?

26. Make up two problems that involve the division $100 \div 18$. Each problem must involve interpreting the remainder in a different way.

Write About It

27. Compare rounding a quotient based on the situation with rounding the quotient to the nearest whole number.

Create a factor tree for each number.

1. 38   **2.** 126   **3.** 525   **4.** 110

Write the prime factorization of each number. Write repeated factors using an exponent.

5. 20   **6.** 72   **7.** 70   **8.** 135

9. 200   **10.** 111   **11.** 400   **12.** 360

Identify the greatest common factor and least common multiple of each set of numbers.

13. 12 and 20   **14.** 10 and 15   **15.** 24 and 36   **16.** 18 and 45   **17.** 14 and 21

18. 6, 10, and 12   **19.** 9, 15, and 30   **20.** 4, 12, and 18

Is the fraction closer to 0, $\frac{1}{2}$, or 1? Write two equivalent fractions.

21. $\frac{30}{50}$ **22.** $\frac{2}{9}$ **23.** $\frac{14}{18}$ **24.** $\frac{6}{11}$ **25.** $\frac{2}{13}$ **26.** $\frac{10}{25}$

Identify the least common denominator for each set of fractions.

27. $\frac{2}{3}, \frac{1}{4}$ **28.** $\frac{4}{9}, \frac{5}{6}$ **29.** $\frac{1}{10}, \frac{1}{2}$ **30.** $\frac{3}{5}, \frac{3}{4}$ **31.** $\frac{3}{10}, \frac{1}{6}$

32. $\frac{1}{9}, \frac{2}{4}, \frac{5}{12}$ **33.** $\frac{1}{2}, \frac{1}{3}, \frac{4}{9}$ **34.** $\frac{1}{2}, \frac{2}{5}, \frac{9}{10}$

Determine whether the fraction is a proper or improper fraction.

35. $\frac{6}{8}$ **36.** $\frac{15}{15}$ **37.** $\frac{26}{17}$ **38.** $\frac{35}{36}$ **39.** $\frac{23}{19}$

Find a whole number n that will make each fraction improper.

40. $\frac{4}{n}$ **41.** $\frac{n}{15}$ **42.** $\frac{n}{n}$ **43.** $\frac{28}{n}$ **44.** $\frac{n}{22}$ **45.** $\frac{1}{n}$

Compare. Write <, =, or >.

46. $\frac{1}{8} \, \underline{?} \, \frac{1}{9}$ **47.** $\frac{4}{9} \, \underline{?} \, \frac{1}{3}$ **48.** $\frac{1}{2} \, \underline{?} \, \frac{5}{8}$ **49.** $\frac{2}{7} \, \underline{?} \, \frac{4}{14}$

50. $2\frac{3}{8} \, \underline{?} \, 2\frac{1}{8}$ **51.** $5\frac{5}{10} \, \underline{?} \, 5\frac{6}{12}$ **52.** $10\frac{2}{7} \, \underline{?} \, 10\frac{2}{6}$ **53.** $3\frac{5}{9} \, \underline{?} \, 3\frac{1}{2}$

Write each as a whole number or mixed number in simplest form.

54. $\dfrac{16}{9}$ **55.** $\dfrac{14}{14}$ **56.** $\dfrac{9}{8}$ **57.** $\dfrac{16}{6}$ **58.** $\dfrac{50}{20}$

59. $\dfrac{40}{15}$ **60.** $\dfrac{32}{18}$ **61.** $\dfrac{61}{61}$ **62.** $\dfrac{81}{18}$ **63.** $\dfrac{140}{105}$

Order the numbers from least to greatest.

64. $\dfrac{1}{12}, \dfrac{1}{7}, \dfrac{1}{17}$ **65.** $\dfrac{7}{11}, \dfrac{4}{11}, \dfrac{1}{11}$ **66.** $\dfrac{1}{6}, \dfrac{2}{15}, \dfrac{5}{12}$ **67.** $\dfrac{3}{4}, \dfrac{4}{7}, \dfrac{4}{9}$

68. $\dfrac{12}{7}, \dfrac{13}{7}, \dfrac{13}{8}$ **69.** $2\dfrac{1}{2}, 2\dfrac{3}{4}, 2\dfrac{1}{3}$ **70.** $10\dfrac{3}{7}, 10\dfrac{2}{7}, 10\dfrac{3}{5}$ **71.** $7\dfrac{4}{9}, 7\dfrac{5}{10}, 7\dfrac{7}{11}$

Divide. Write each quotient in simplest form.

72. $4 \div 5$ **73.** $1 \div 7$ **74.** $15 \div 18$ **75.** $4 \div 10$

76. $14 \div 3$ **77.** $20 \div 4$ **78.** $32 \div 10$ **79.** $45 \div 6$

Problem Solving

80. A van can hold 14 students. If 45 students are going on a field trip, how many vans are needed?

81. Preston writes 3 songs in 2 days, working 7 hours each day. He spends the same amount of time on each song. How long does he spend on each song?

The diagram shows the distance a ball travels after launching it at various angles. Use this diagram for Exercises 82–84.

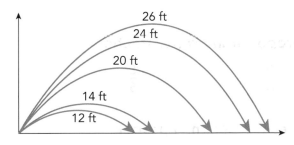

26 ft
24 ft
20 ft
14 ft
12 ft

82. Are the distances prime or composite? Explain.

83. Identify the factors of the greatest distance.

84. Write the LCM of the greatest and least distances.

85. Every 12th person to enter a stadium wins a baseball hat. Every 15th person to enter wins a T-shirt. Describe the first person to enter the stadium and win a baseball hat and a T-shirt.

CHAPTER 5
Performance Assessment

The Fibonacci sequence is defined by the rule "the sum of the previous two numbers." The first two numbers in the sequence are 0 and 1.

1. Complete the list of Fibonacci numbers to the 15th number.

   0, 1, ?, ?, ?, ?, ?, ?, ?, ?, ?, ...

2. Identify each of the first 15 Fibonacci numbers as prime composite, or neither.

3. Identify the factors of each number identified as composite.

4. Determine the prime factorization of each number identified as composite.

5. What is the greatest common factor of these composite numbers? Explain how you know.

Shankar has a part of the Fibonacci sequence shown below. He wants to find the missing numbers.

1597, ?, ?, 6765

His teacher gives him the following property of any 4 consecutive numbers in the sequence: the second greatest number is always equal to half the difference of the greatest and least number.

6. Use the property to find the missing numbers. Explain what you did.

7. One special property of the Fibonacci sequence is tiling. You can use squares with side lengths that are consecutive Fibonacci numbers to tile a plane. Copy the diagram to the bottom middle part of a piece of graph paper. Then continue the pattern using the next three Fibonacci numbers.

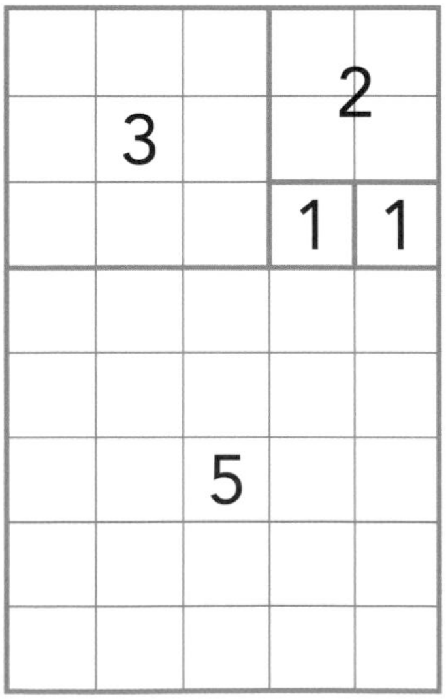

8. Suppose a curve is drawn that passes through opposite diagonal corners of the squares labeled 1, 1, 2, 3, 5, …. Draw this curve on your diagram. How would you describe this shape?

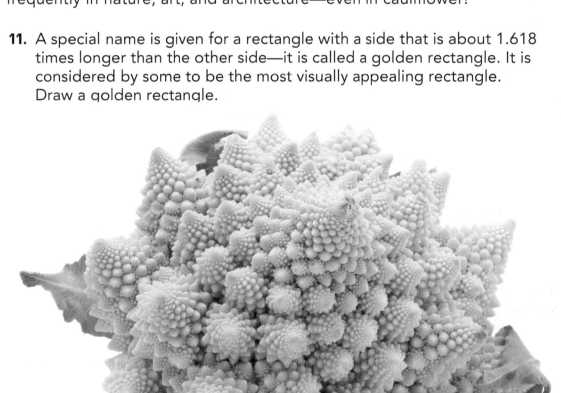

Something special happens when you divide successive numbers in the Fibonacci sequence. For instance, the first 4 quotients are $\frac{1}{1}$, $\frac{2}{1}$, $\frac{3}{2}$, and $\frac{5}{3}$.

9. Use this rule to find the next two fractions in this pattern. Then write each of the 6 fractions as a whole number or mixed number.

10. Plot the fractions on a number line. What do you notice about the values of the fractions?

The fractions created by dividing successive Fibonacci numbers can be approximated by the following decimal values.

1, 2, 1.5, 1.67, 1.6, 1.625, 1.615, 1.619, …

These numbers get closer and closer to a special value called the **golden ratio**. The golden ratio is equal to about 1.618. It appears frequently in nature, art, and architecture—even in cauliflower!

11. A special name is given for a rectangle with a side that is about 1.618 times longer than the other side—it is called a golden rectangle. It is considered by some to be the most visually appealing rectangle. Draw a golden rectangle.

Determine the best answer for each problem.

1. Which fractions are improper? Select all that apply.

   A. $\frac{8}{9}$ B. $\frac{5}{5}$

   C. $\frac{12}{17}$ D. $\frac{9}{1}$

   E. $\frac{3}{4}$ F. $\frac{1}{7}$

2. Identify the prime factorization of 462.

   A. $2 \times 2 \times 7 \times 11$
   B. $2 \times 7 \times 33$
   C. $2 \times 3 \times 7 \times 11$
   D. 2×231

3. What is the greatest common factor of 30 and 42?

4. Fractions can be estimated as 0, $\frac{1}{2}$, or 1. Which fractions are approximately equal to $\frac{1}{2}$? Select all that apply.

   A. $\frac{3}{5}$ B. $\frac{1}{8}$

   C. $\frac{5}{6}$ D. $\frac{67}{100}$

   E. $\frac{23}{25}$ F. $\frac{5}{4}$

5. A group of 5 friends are playing golf. Each golf cart can hold 2 people. What is the least number of golf carts the group needs?

   A. 2   B. 3

   C. 5   D. $\frac{5}{2}$

6. Select the statement that correctly orders the fractions $\frac{5}{6}$, $\frac{1}{3}$, and $\frac{3}{4}$ from least to greatest.

   A. $\frac{5}{6} < \frac{3}{4} < \frac{1}{3}$ B. $\frac{1}{3} < \frac{5}{6} < \frac{3}{4}$

   C. $\frac{3}{4} < \frac{1}{3} < \frac{5}{6}$ D. $\frac{1}{3} < \frac{3}{4} < \frac{5}{6}$

7. What is the least common denominator of the fractions $\frac{3}{8}$ and $\frac{1}{6}$?

   A. 8   B. 16
   C. 24   D. 48

8. Identify the least common multiple of 4, 5, and 6.

9. What fraction is shown by the model?

1 WHOLE			

   A. $\frac{1}{4}$ B. $\frac{2}{4}$

   C. $\frac{3}{4}$ D. $\frac{4}{4}$

10. Identify each fraction that is equivalent to $\frac{2}{3}$. Select all that apply.

   A. $\frac{8}{12}$ B. $\frac{20}{30}$

   C. $\frac{2 \times 3}{3 \times 2}$ D. $\frac{2 \times 2}{3 \times 3}$

   E. $\frac{2 \times 3}{3 \times 3}$ F. $\frac{2 + 2}{3 + 2}$

Fractions: Addition

When little space is available, high-density gardening provides an alternative to a traditional plot. These gardens are planted in a raised bed or containers. This also helps with challenges such as soil quality and weed and pest control.

Top Vegetables for Raised Beds

♦ Root vegetables, such as carrots, beets, radishes, and parsnips, thrive in loose, rock-free soil. In a raised bed, you can customize the soil based on what you plant.

♦ Similarly, tomatoes require nutrient-dense soil, so you can specifically use a soil with the required nutrients.

♦ Leafy greens, such as lettuce, spinach, and kale, prefer soil that drains well. Since the beds are raised, they naturally drain well.

♦ Onions require a longer growing season. High-density gardening allows for soil to warm faster than the ground, so you can plant earlier in a season.

♦ Potatoes benefit from hilling soil around the shoots; hills are easily formed in raised beds.

Model Addition with Unlike Denominators

Objective
- Use models to add fractions with unlike denominators.

Math Words
rename
equivalent fractions
simplest form

A computer programmer is developing new software. He spends $\frac{3}{4}$ of his workday writing code and $\frac{1}{8}$ of his day troubleshooting errors. Altogether, how much of his workday does the computer programmer spend developing software?

Use a model to find $\frac{3}{4} + \frac{1}{8}$.

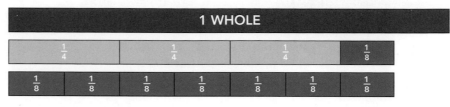

- Model the problem under the strip for 1 whole.

- Use the model to rename the fractions with the same denominator.

The model shows how the parts line up. I can count the parts to see that six $\frac{1}{8}$s are the same as three $\frac{1}{4}$s.

- Write the sum with the equivalent fraction: $\frac{3}{4} + \frac{1}{8} = \frac{6}{8} + \frac{1}{8} = \frac{7}{8}$

The programmer spends $\frac{7}{8}$ of his day developing software.

PRACTICE

Add. Write the answer in simplest form.

1. $\frac{1}{2} + \frac{1}{8}$

1 WHOLE

$\frac{1}{2}$	$\frac{1}{8}$

$\frac{1}{8}$	$\frac{1}{8}$	$\frac{1}{8}$	$\frac{1}{8}$	$\frac{1}{8}$

2. $\frac{2}{3} + \frac{2}{6}$

1 WHOLE

$\frac{1}{3}$	$\frac{1}{3}$	$\frac{1}{6}$	$\frac{1}{6}$

$\frac{1}{6}$	$\frac{1}{6}$	$\frac{1}{6}$	$\frac{1}{6}$	$\frac{1}{6}$	$\frac{1}{6}$

What size fraction strip can you use to find each sum?

3. $\frac{7}{10} + \frac{4}{5}$

4. $\frac{1}{3} + \frac{7}{12}$

5. $\frac{1}{4} + \frac{5}{12}$

6. $\frac{1}{5} + \frac{3}{10}$

7. $\frac{3}{4} + \frac{7}{8}$

8. $\frac{1}{2} + \frac{3}{4}$

Add. Write the answer in simplest form.

9. $\frac{7}{10} + \frac{1}{5}$

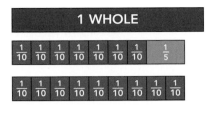

10. $\frac{3}{8} + \frac{1}{4}$

11. $\frac{5}{9} + \frac{1}{3}$

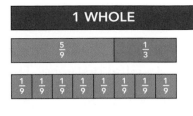

12. $\frac{1}{6} + \frac{2}{3}$

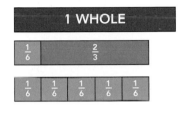

13. $\frac{1}{2} + \frac{3}{10}$

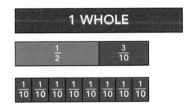

14. $\frac{1}{6} + \frac{1}{2}$

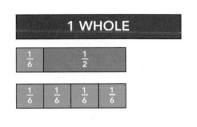

15. $\frac{5}{8} + \frac{1}{2}$

16. $\frac{7}{10} + \frac{1}{2}$

17. $\frac{7}{12} + \frac{2}{3}$

Problem Solving

18. A plumber replaces two sections of pipe. The pipes are $\frac{1}{10}$ yd and $\frac{4}{5}$ yd long. How much pipe will he use?

19. Hector is hanging a 3-panel photo on the wall. He wants to leave $\frac{1}{3}$ meter between each panel. How much wall space will he need from left to right?

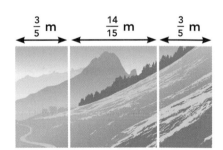

20. Two fractions have a sum of 1. One fraction has a denominator of 4, and the other has a denominator of 12. What could the fractions be?

21. How could you use a model such as fraction strips to find a sum of 3 fractions? Describe using an example.

Write About It

22. Explain how you can use the ruler shown to find $\frac{1}{2} + \frac{5}{8}$.

Add Fractions: Unlike Denominators

Objective
- Add fractions with unlike denominators.

Math Words
equation
unlike denominators
least common denominator (LCD)

The table shows the distances Juan and Tommy run at soccer practice. How far do they run in all?

Distance (miles)	
Juan	$\frac{2}{6}$
Tommy	$\frac{3}{4}$

You can use the letter d to represent the total distance. Then the equation $\frac{2}{6} + \frac{3}{4} = d$ represents this situation.

To add fractions with unlike denominators:

- First, find the least common denominator (LCD) of the fractions.

  Multiples of 6: 6, 12, 18, 24, ...

  Multiples of 4: 4, 8, 12, 16, ...

  LCD of $\frac{2}{6}$ and $\frac{3}{4}$: 12

- Next, use the LCD to rewrite the fractions with the same denominator.

  $$\frac{2}{6} = \frac{2 \times 2}{6 \times 2} = \frac{4}{12}$$

  $$\frac{3}{4} = \frac{3 \times 3}{4 \times 3} = \frac{9}{12}$$

- Add the numerators. Keep the denominator. Write the sum as a mixed number that is in simplest form.

  $$\frac{4}{12} + \frac{9}{12} = \frac{13}{12} = 1\frac{1}{12}$$

Juan and Tommy run a total distance of $1\frac{1}{12}$ miles.

PRACTICE

Rewrite each expression using the LCD.

1. $\frac{5}{8} + \frac{1}{4}$

2. $\frac{1}{3} + \frac{4}{9}$

3. $\frac{7}{12} + \frac{1}{4}$

4. $\frac{3}{4} + \frac{1}{3}$

5. $\frac{1}{2} + \frac{2}{7}$

6. $\frac{1}{6} + \frac{3}{8}$

7. $\frac{5}{8} + \frac{5}{12}$

8. $\frac{3}{5} + \frac{2}{15}$

9. $\frac{2}{5} + \frac{1}{6}$

10. $\frac{1}{15} + \frac{7}{10}$

Find the sum.

11. $\frac{1}{3} + \frac{1}{6}$

12. $\frac{1}{3} + \frac{1}{12}$

13. $\frac{1}{2} + \frac{3}{4}$

14. $\frac{5}{6} + \frac{1}{8}$

15. $\frac{2}{5} + \frac{1}{3}$

16. $\frac{1}{5} + \frac{7}{15}$

17. $\frac{1}{2} + \frac{3}{8}$

18. $\frac{2}{3} + \frac{1}{6}$

19. $\frac{2}{5} + \frac{1}{10}$

20. $\frac{3}{4} + \frac{1}{12}$

21. $\frac{3}{5} + \frac{3}{10}$

22. $\frac{5}{6} + \frac{2}{9}$

23. $\frac{3}{4} + \frac{5}{12}$

24. $\frac{2}{3} + \frac{1}{4}$

25. $\frac{3}{6} + \frac{2}{5}$

Add. Write answers in simplest form.

26. $\dfrac{3}{10} + \dfrac{1}{2}$ **27.** $\dfrac{3}{5} + \dfrac{2}{25}$ **28.** $\dfrac{2}{9} + \dfrac{11}{12}$ **29.** $\dfrac{2}{5} + \dfrac{5}{8}$ **30.** $\dfrac{6}{7} + \dfrac{1}{9}$

31. $\dfrac{2}{5} + \dfrac{1}{10}$ **32.** $\dfrac{3}{8} + \dfrac{1}{2}$ **33.** $\dfrac{2}{3} + \dfrac{4}{15}$ **34.** $\dfrac{3}{4} + \dfrac{5}{6}$ **35.** $\dfrac{2}{3} + \dfrac{3}{5}$

36. $\dfrac{1}{3} + \dfrac{2}{3} + \dfrac{5}{9}$ **37.** $\dfrac{1}{5} + \dfrac{1}{10} + \dfrac{3}{5}$ **38.** $\dfrac{3}{4} + \dfrac{3}{8} + \dfrac{1}{8}$ **39.** $\dfrac{1}{4} + \dfrac{1}{12} + \dfrac{1}{3}$ **40.** $\dfrac{1}{6} + \dfrac{2}{9} + \dfrac{1}{18}$

Find the value of *n*.

41. $\dfrac{4}{7} + \dfrac{3}{14} = n$ **42.** $\dfrac{4}{5} + \dfrac{2}{15} = n$ **43.** $\dfrac{2}{9} + \dfrac{1}{2} = n$

44. $\dfrac{1}{4} + \dfrac{n}{6} - 1\dfrac{1}{12}$ **45.** $\dfrac{n}{2} + \dfrac{5}{7} = 1\dfrac{3}{14}$ **46.** $\dfrac{n}{8} + \dfrac{3}{10} = \dfrac{27}{40}$

Problem Solving

47. Marissa walks from her home to the store, then to the park, then back home. How far does she walk in all?

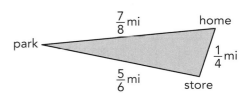

48. An electrical engineer needs $\dfrac{3}{8}$ spool of wire for the first project, $\dfrac{1}{4}$ spool for the second project, and $\dfrac{2}{5}$ spool for the third project. How many spools of wire should he buy from the store? Explain.

49. Write 3 fractions with 3 different denominators that have a sum of 1.

Ashton, Blake, and Manny are working at an ice creamery. The owner wants them to each keep track of how many customers buy sundaes. Use this information for Exercises 50–51.

50. In Blake's line, 3 of 6 customers order a sundae. In Ashton's line, 4 of 10 customers order a sundae. What fraction represents the customers in both lines who order a sundae?

51. Half of all of the customers in the three lines order a sundae. How many customers were in Manny's line and how many bought sundaes?

Write About It

52. Mason adds $\dfrac{1}{6}$ and $\dfrac{4}{9}$. He finds the LCD and writes the equation $\dfrac{1}{18} + \dfrac{4}{18} = \dfrac{5}{18}$. Does Mason get the correct answer? Explain.

Fraction Addition: Estimation and Reasonableness

Objective
- Use benchmarks and number sense to estimate and check answers involving fractions.

Math Words
benchmark
estimate

Victor is making punch for a party. He says the punch will fit in a 2-gallon container. Is he correct?

You can use benchmarks to estimate the sum $\frac{7}{8} + \frac{1}{12} + \frac{3}{5}$.

Think of each fraction on a number line.

Party Punch Recipe
★ ★ ★ ★ ★
- $\frac{7}{8}$ gallon seltzer water
- $\frac{1}{12}$ gallon lemon juice
- $\frac{3}{5}$ gallon grape juice

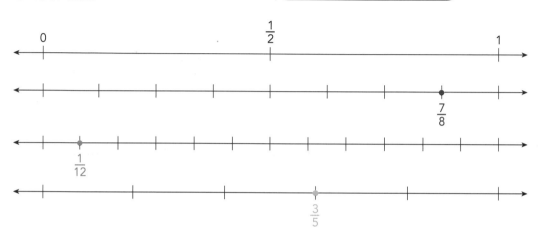

Estimate: $\frac{7}{8} + \frac{1}{12} + \frac{3}{5} \longrightarrow 1 + 0 + \frac{1}{2} = 1\frac{1}{2}$

▷ Victor will make about $1\frac{1}{2}$ gallons of punch. Since $1\frac{1}{2} < 2$, the punch will fit into the 2-gallon container.

PRACTICE

Use benchmark fractions to estimate the sum.

1. $\frac{5}{6} + \frac{7}{10}$

2. $\frac{9}{10} + \frac{11}{12}$

3. $\frac{1}{6} + \frac{8}{9} + \frac{2}{10}$

4. $\frac{7}{12} + \frac{5}{9} + \frac{3}{8}$

5. $\frac{3}{5} + \frac{4}{7}$

6. $\frac{1}{8} + \frac{6}{11}$

7. $\frac{5}{12} + \frac{6}{7} + \frac{2}{5}$

8. $\frac{1}{10} + \frac{8}{15} + \frac{4}{5}$

Determine whether the sum is greater than 1 or less than 1.

9. $\frac{1}{6} + \frac{5}{12}$

10. $\frac{7}{10} + \frac{5}{8}$

11. $\frac{3}{4} + \frac{1}{8} + \frac{7}{16}$

12. $\frac{1}{5} + \frac{2}{7} + \frac{3}{10}$

13. $\frac{6}{11} + \frac{5}{9}$

14. $\frac{3}{8} + \frac{1}{5}$

15. $\frac{2}{3} + \frac{5}{8} + \frac{1}{5}$

16. $\frac{1}{8} + \frac{2}{15} + \frac{1}{5}$

Estimate the sum.

17. $\frac{4}{7} + \frac{6}{10}$

18. $\frac{11}{12} + \frac{8}{9}$

19. $\frac{4}{5} + 3\frac{7}{15}$

20. $\frac{2}{5} + \frac{8}{10} + \frac{1}{6}$

21. $\frac{1}{10} + \frac{3}{8}$

22. $1\frac{2}{9} + \frac{5}{12}$

23. $\frac{5}{8} + \frac{1}{3} + \frac{6}{7}$

24. $\frac{4}{9} + \frac{2}{12} + \frac{9}{10}$

25. $\frac{5}{12} + \frac{4}{7} + \frac{3}{8}$

26. $\frac{9}{10} + \frac{5}{6} + \frac{3}{4}$

27. $\frac{17}{16} + \frac{7}{15} + \frac{13}{14}$

28. $\frac{1}{8} + \frac{5}{6} + \frac{3}{20} + \frac{11}{12}$

29. $\frac{4}{7} + \frac{1}{6} + \frac{15}{16} + \frac{3}{5}$

30. $\frac{1}{2} + \frac{7}{8} + \frac{9}{10} + \frac{3}{5}$

Tell if you agree or disagree with each statement. Explain.

31. The sum of $\frac{6}{7}$ and $\frac{4}{9}$ is about $1\frac{1}{2}$.

32. The sum of $\frac{3}{4}$ and $\frac{11}{12}$ is about 2.

33. The sum of $\frac{5}{6}$, $\frac{7}{8}$ and $\frac{2}{5}$ is about 3.

34. The sum of $1\frac{4}{10}$ and $2\frac{1}{8}$ is about $4\frac{1}{2}$.

Find a value for *n* that would make a proper fraction and the sum greater than 1.

35. $\frac{3}{5} + \frac{n}{7}$

36. $\frac{5}{6} + \frac{n}{9}$

37. $\frac{n}{10} + \frac{2}{3}$

38. $\frac{n}{8} + \frac{3}{4}$

Find a value for *n* that would make the sum less than 1.

39. $\frac{1}{4} + \frac{n}{5}$

40. $\frac{n}{4} + \frac{5}{9}$

41. $\frac{1}{3} + \frac{n}{5}$

42. $\frac{n}{6} + \frac{3}{8}$

Problem Solving

Use the table of ingredients for Exercises 43–45.

43. Kylie adds the sunflower seeds and the granola to a bag. Do the combined ingredients weigh more than or less than 1 pound?

44. Kylie adds the remaining ingredients to her bag. She says her bag now weighs about 3 pounds. Is her estimate reasonable? Explain.

Ingredient	Weight (lb)
Sunflower Seeds	$\frac{3}{8}$
Granola	$\frac{3}{4}$
Dried Fruit	$\frac{13}{16}$
Almonds	$\frac{5}{6}$

45. Confirm your answer to Exercise 43 by finding the exact sum.

Write About It

46. Sarah says $\frac{5}{6} + 5\frac{1}{12}$ is about 6. Is her estimate reasonable? Explain.

Use a fraction model to find the sum.

1. $\frac{1}{4} + \frac{3}{8}$

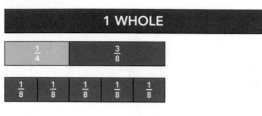

A. $\frac{1}{2}$ **B.** $\frac{5}{8}$

C. $\frac{7}{8}$ **D.** $1\frac{1}{4}$

2. $\frac{2}{9} + \frac{1}{3}$

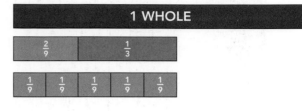

A. $\frac{3}{9}$ **B.** $\frac{4}{9}$

C. $\frac{5}{9}$ **D.** $1\frac{2}{3}$

Find the sum.

3. $\frac{1}{2} + \frac{3}{7}$

A. $\frac{5}{7}$ **B.** $\frac{11}{14}$

C. $\frac{6}{7}$ **D.** $\frac{13}{14}$

4. $\frac{5}{12} + \frac{1}{4}$

A. $\frac{7}{12}$ **B.** $\frac{2}{3}$

C. $\frac{3}{4}$ **D.** $\frac{5}{6}$

5. $\frac{5}{6} + \frac{1}{8}$

A. $2\frac{9}{4}$ **B.** $\frac{21}{24}$

C. $\frac{11}{12}$ **D.** $\frac{23}{24}$

6. $\frac{2}{7} + \frac{2}{5}$

A. 7   **B.** $\frac{22}{35}$

C. $\frac{24}{35}$ **D.** $\frac{5}{7}$

Use benchmark fractions to estimate each sum.

7. $\frac{2}{3} + \frac{4}{5}$

8. $\frac{5}{7} + \frac{5}{12}$

9. $\frac{1}{8} + \frac{2}{5} + \frac{6}{7}$

10. $\frac{7}{12} + \frac{4}{5} + \frac{4}{9}$

11. $\frac{1}{12} + \frac{3}{7}$

12. $\frac{3}{5} + \frac{9}{10}$

13. $\frac{8}{9} + \frac{11}{12} + \frac{9}{10}$

14. $\frac{1}{2} + \frac{9}{20} + \frac{1}{15}$

Determine whether the sum is greater than 1 or less than 1.

15. $\frac{5}{6} + \frac{8}{10}$

16. $\frac{1}{5} + \frac{4}{9}$

17. $\frac{3}{7} + \frac{1}{12}$

18. $\frac{7}{15} + \frac{5}{6}$

19. $\frac{1}{3} + \frac{1}{8}$

20. $\frac{3}{10} + \frac{3}{7}$

21. $\frac{8}{9} + \frac{2}{3}$

22. $\frac{4}{5} + \frac{1}{2}$

Find the sum.

23. $\frac{1}{2} + \frac{1}{6}$

    A. $\frac{1}{3}$ **B.** $\frac{2}{3}$

    C. $\frac{5}{6}$ **D.** $\frac{11}{12}$

24. $\frac{3}{10} + \frac{1}{5}$

    A. $\frac{1}{2}$ **B.** $\frac{3}{5}$

    C. $\frac{7}{10}$ **D.** $\frac{4}{5}$

25. $\frac{5}{12} + \frac{3}{8}$

    A. $\frac{2}{3}$ **B.** $\frac{3}{4}$

    C. $\frac{19}{24}$ **D.** $\frac{11}{12}$

26. $\frac{1}{3} + \frac{5}{9} + \frac{2}{9}$

    A. 1 **B.** $1\frac{1}{9}$

    C. $1\frac{2}{9}$ **D.** $1\frac{1}{3}$

27. $\frac{2}{3} + \frac{2}{9}$

    A. $\frac{5}{9}$ **B.** $\frac{7}{9}$

    C. $\frac{5}{6}$ **D.** $\frac{8}{9}$

28. $\frac{1}{8} + \frac{3}{4}$

    A. $\frac{7}{32}$ **B.** $\frac{3}{4}$

    C. $\frac{13}{16}$ **D.** $\frac{7}{8}$

29. $\frac{1}{5} + \frac{1}{2} + \frac{7}{10}$

    A. $1\frac{1}{10}$ **B.** $1\frac{1}{5}$

    C. $1\frac{2}{5}$ **D.** $1\frac{1}{2}$

30. $\frac{3}{4} + \frac{1}{7}$

    A. $\frac{6}{7}$ **B.** $\frac{9}{14}$

    C. $\frac{6}{7}$ **D.** $\frac{25}{28}$

31. $\frac{4}{9} + \frac{1}{6} + \frac{3}{18}$

    A. $\frac{11}{18}$ **B.** $\frac{2}{3}$

    C. $\frac{13}{18}$ **D.** $\frac{7}{9}$

32. $\frac{5}{7} + \frac{1}{2}$

    A. $1\frac{1}{7}$ **B.** $1\frac{3}{14}$

    C. $1\frac{2}{7}$ **D.** $1\frac{5}{14}$

33. $\frac{3}{5} + \frac{1}{6}$

    A. $\frac{23}{30}$ **B.** $\frac{4}{5}$

    C. $\frac{5}{6}$ **D.** $\frac{13}{15}$

34. $\frac{1}{12} + \frac{3}{5}$

    A. $\frac{2}{15}$ **B.** $\frac{19}{60}$

    C. $\frac{41}{60}$ **D.** $\frac{3}{4}$

Problem Solving

Olivia builds the model. Use the diagram for Exercises 35–37.

35. Estimate the weight of the body tube, payload section, launch lug, and recovery padding.

36. What is the total weight of the fins and engine mount? Show your work.

37. Olivia says the total weight of the nose and payload section is $\frac{2}{7}$ pound. Explain her error. Then find the correct sum.

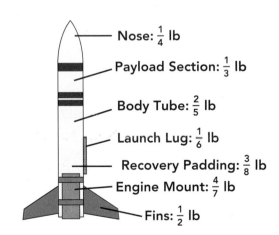

Nose: $\frac{1}{4}$ lb

Payload Section: $\frac{1}{3}$ lb

Body Tube: $\frac{2}{5}$ lb

Launch Lug: $\frac{1}{6}$ lb

Recovery Padding: $\frac{3}{8}$ lb

Engine Mount: $\frac{4}{7}$ lb

Fins: $\frac{1}{2}$ lb

38. Lindsey spends $\frac{1}{2}$ hour cleaning the pool and $\frac{1}{3}$ hour picking up leaves. How long does she spend doing both chores?

39. To sew a pillow, Alex needs $\frac{5}{12}$ yard of one fabric and $\frac{7}{8}$ yard of another fabric. Does he need more than 1 yard of fabric? Explain.

Add Mixed Numbers

Objective
- Add mixed numbers with unlike denominators.

Math Words

mixed number
least common
  denominator (LCD)

An architect makes the scale drawing shown. What is the total height of the house in the drawing?

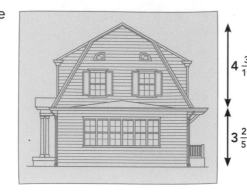

$4\frac{3}{10}$ in.

$3\frac{2}{5}$ in.

The equation $3\frac{2}{5} + 4\frac{3}{10} = h$ represents this sitution.

To add mixed numbers with fractions with unlike denominators:

- Find the LCD of the fractions.

- Rename the fractions as equivalent fractions with the same denominator.

- Add the fraction parts. Then add the whole-number parts.

- Write the sum in simplest form.

LCD of $\frac{2}{5}$ and $\frac{3}{10}$: 10

$$3\frac{2}{5} = 3\frac{2 \times 2}{5 \times 2} = 3\frac{4}{10}$$
$$+\ 4\frac{3}{10} \qquad\qquad = 4\frac{3}{10}$$
$$\rule{4cm}{0.4pt}$$
$$= 7\frac{7}{10}$$

▷ The drawing of the house is $7\frac{7}{10}$ inches tall. The sum is already in simplest form.

Study these examples.

$$5\frac{5}{12} \qquad\qquad = 5\frac{5}{12}$$
$$+\ 2\frac{1}{4} = 2\frac{1 \times 3}{4 \times 3} = 2\frac{3}{12}$$
$$\rule{5cm}{0.4pt}$$
$$= 7\frac{8}{12} = 7\frac{2}{3}$$

Write in simplest form.

$$6\frac{1}{4} + 2\frac{1}{6} + 8\frac{1}{3} = 6\frac{1 \times 3}{4 \times 3} + 2\frac{1 \times 2}{6 \times 2} + 8\frac{1 \times 4}{3 \times 4}$$
$$= 6\frac{3}{12} + 2\frac{2}{12} + 8\frac{4}{12}$$
$$= 16\frac{9}{12} = 16\frac{3}{4}$$

Write in simplest form.

PRACTICE

Complete. Write the sum in simplest form.

1.
$$9\frac{1}{6} = 9\frac{2}{12}$$
$$+ 2\frac{3}{4} = 2\frac{?}{?}$$

2.
$$4\frac{1}{3} = 4\frac{?}{?}$$
$$+ 7\frac{1}{6} = 7\frac{1}{6}$$

3.
$$\frac{4}{5} = \frac{?}{30}$$
$$+ 8\frac{1}{6} = 8\frac{?}{30}$$

4.
$$3\frac{5}{12} = 3\frac{5}{12}$$
$$+ \quad \frac{1}{3} = \frac{?}{?}$$

Add. Write the sum in simplest form.

5. $2\frac{1}{4}$
$+\ 3\frac{2}{5}$

6. 2
$+\ 1\frac{1}{6}$

7. $5\frac{1}{3}$
$+\ 2\frac{1}{6}$

8. $4\frac{1}{10}$
$+\ 4\frac{3}{4}$

9. $1\frac{3}{5}$
$+\ 2\frac{1}{3}$

10. $3\frac{3}{10}$
$+\ \frac{8}{15}$

11. $9\frac{1}{3}$
$2\frac{1}{4}$
$+\ 3\frac{1}{12}$

12. $2\frac{2}{5}$
$6\frac{1}{3}$
$+\ 4\frac{1}{5}$

13. $8\frac{1}{4}$
$2\frac{2}{5}$
$+\ 5\frac{3}{20}$

14. $2\frac{1}{3}$
$5\frac{3}{8}$
$+\ \ \frac{1}{4}$

15. $8\frac{2}{5}$
$7\frac{1}{4}$
$+\ \ \frac{1}{10}$

16. 9
$8\frac{1}{3}$
$+\ 3\frac{1}{12}$

17. $2\frac{2}{5} + 3\frac{1}{15} + 6\frac{1}{5}$

18. $1\frac{3}{8} + 12\frac{1}{4} + 5\frac{1}{16}$

19. $\frac{1}{3} + 5\frac{5}{9} + 5\frac{1}{18}$

Estimate the sum. Then find the value of n.

20. $7\frac{3}{8} + 7\frac{5}{12} = n$

21. $\frac{1}{4} + 20\frac{1}{3} = n$

22. $15\frac{1}{6} + 2\frac{1}{8} + 2\frac{1}{4} = n$

23. $1\frac{1}{6} + 4\frac{2}{3} + 5\frac{1}{12} = n$

24. $5\frac{2}{7} + 6\frac{3}{14} + 2\frac{3}{7} = n$

25. $4\frac{1}{8} + \frac{1}{10} + 3\frac{1}{4} = n$

Problem Solving

26. Meg flies $2\frac{5}{12}$ hours and $2\frac{1}{3}$ hours on Saturday. She flies $2\frac{3}{4}$ hours and $2\frac{1}{6}$ hours on Sunday. On which day does she fly longer?

27. The table shows how much time an audio engineer spends recording. Her plan was to spend an average of 9 hours each day. Did her total hours exceed her plan? Explain.

Day	Time (h)
Monday	$8\frac{1}{4}$
Tuesday	$10\frac{1}{3}$
Friday	$9\frac{1}{4}$

28. Explain how you could use the Associative Property to help you find $\left(2\frac{1}{4} + 1\frac{2}{7}\right) + 4\frac{1}{7}$.

29. Three mixed numbers have a sum of $8\frac{11}{12}$. The first two numbers are $3\frac{1}{2}$ and $2\frac{1}{4}$. What is the third number?

Write About It

30. Miguel finds $2\frac{2}{5} + 1\frac{4}{15}$ and gets a sum of $2\frac{2}{3}$. What is Miguel's error? What is the correct sum?

Problem Solving
Use a Model

Objective
- Focus on using a model to solve problems.

Math Words
reasonable
model
estimate

Harper spends $\frac{1}{3}$ of her allowance on a new shirt. She spends $\frac{1}{5}$ of her allowance going to see a movie. What fraction of her allowance does Harper spend?

- Rewrite the fractions using the LCD. Then add.

$$\frac{1}{3} = \frac{1 \times 5}{3 \times 5} = \frac{5}{15}$$

$$\frac{1}{5} = \frac{1 \times 3}{5 \times 3} = \frac{3}{15}$$

$$\frac{5}{15} + \frac{3}{15} = \frac{8}{15}$$

- Is the answer reasonable? Use a model to estimate.

Use a double number line. Draw to scale and align any equivalent values.

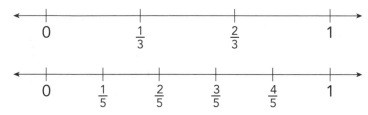

- Show $\frac{1}{3}$ on the top number line. Show $\frac{1}{5}$ on the bottom.

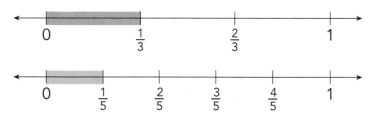

Use the number line models to estimate the sum.

- Imagine the segments representing $\frac{1}{3}$ and $\frac{1}{5}$ are connected.
- Compare the length of the new segment to 0, $\frac{1}{2}$, or 1.

The new segment is close to $\frac{1}{2}$. This is a good estimate for the sum.

Harper spends $\frac{8}{15}$ of her allowance. This is close to $\frac{1}{2}$, so the answer is reasonable.

1. Simon plants cucumbers in $\frac{3}{8}$ of his garden and tomatoes in $\frac{1}{4}$ of his garden. He plants lettuce in the rest of his garden. How much of the garden is used to grow cucumbers and tomatoes? Does the model show that your answer is reasonable? Explain.

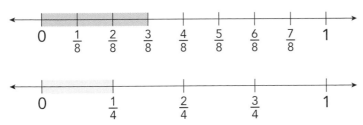

The table shows how long a student studies different subjects. Use the table for Exercises 2–3.

Subject	Study Time (h)
Math	$\frac{5}{6}$
Science	$1\frac{1}{4}$
Social Studies	$\frac{1}{2}$
Reading	$\frac{1}{3}$

2. Estimate the number of hours the student spends studying math and reading. Use a model.

3. How many hours does the student spend studying math, social studies, and reading? Use number line models to check the reasonableness of your answer.

Use the inch ruler shown for Exercises 4–5.

4. Describe a strategy to estimate the sum $1\frac{1}{2} + 2\frac{3}{4} + \frac{5}{8}$. Then write the estimate.

5. Add to find the exact sum. Could you use the model to find the exact sum? If so, explain how.

6. Shayna buys 2 microphone stands, some cables, and some speakers. She spends $989 in all. How many cables and speakers does Shayna buy? Explain any strategies you use to solve the problem.

Item	Price ($)
Microphone stand	182
Cable	5
Speaker	300

7. Would you rather use a number line model or guess and test to divide 1,394 by 34? Explain.

Write About It

8. Explain the importance of aligning the 0 and 1 markers when using number line models to estimate the sum of two fractions.

Rename Mixed Number Sums

Objective
- Add mixed numbers and simplify the sum.

Math Words
rename
mixed number
simplest form

A plane uses $5\frac{3}{4}$ gallons of fuel to travel one mile after reaching its cruising altitude. It then uses $4\frac{5}{6}$ gallons to travel the next mile. How many gallons of fuel does the plane use to travel two miles after reaching its cruising altitude?

Add to find the total fuel used.

$$5\frac{3}{4} + 4\frac{5}{6} = \underline{\;?\;}$$

- Rename the mixed numbers so the fractions have a common denominator.

$$5\frac{3}{4} = 5\frac{3\times3}{4\times3} = 5\frac{9}{12} \qquad 4\frac{5}{6} = 4\frac{5\times2}{6\times2} = 4\frac{10}{12}$$

- Add the whole-number parts. Add the fraction parts.

$$5\frac{9}{12} + 4\frac{10}{12} = (5+4) + \left(\frac{9}{12} + \frac{10}{12}\right) = 9\frac{19}{12}$$

- If the fraction parts have a sum greater than or equal to 1, rename the mixed number in simplest form.

$$9\frac{19}{12} = 9 + 1\frac{7}{12} = 10\frac{7}{12}$$

Add the whole numbers.

Rename: $\frac{19}{12} = \frac{12}{12} + \frac{7}{12} = 1\frac{7}{12}$

The plane uses $10\frac{7}{12}$ gallons of fuel to travel two miles.

PRACTICE

Rename each as a mixed number in simplest form.

1. $6\frac{11}{9}$ **2.** $10\frac{5}{5}$ **3.** $9\frac{10}{8}$ **4.** $8\frac{6}{4}$ **5.** $11\frac{9}{6}$ **6.** $14\frac{7}{7}$

7. $3\frac{20}{15}$ **8.** $21\frac{14}{12}$ **9.** $17\frac{28}{25}$ **10.** $36\frac{9}{9}$ **11.** $42\frac{16}{15}$ **12.** $83\frac{12}{8}$

Add. Write each sum as a mixed number in simplest form.

13. $\quad 4\frac{5}{7}$ **14.** $\quad 4\frac{1}{3}$ **15.** $\quad 6\frac{5}{6}$ **16.** $\quad \frac{3}{8}$ **17.** $\quad 3\frac{8}{9}$ **18.** $\quad 5\frac{2}{4}$

$\underline{+\; 2\frac{3}{7}}$ $\underline{+\; 5\frac{2}{3}}$ $\underline{+\quad \frac{4}{6}}$ $\underline{+\; 3\frac{7}{8}}$ $1\frac{3}{9}$ $4\frac{1}{4}$

                                                          $\underline{+\; 6\frac{2}{9}}$ $\underline{+\; 3\frac{4}{4}}$

19. $1\frac{3}{4} + 6\frac{1}{4}$ **20.** $\frac{6}{8} + 14\frac{5}{8}$ **21.** $2\frac{4}{5} + \frac{3}{5} + \frac{2}{5}$ **22.** $5\frac{5}{7} + 4\frac{5}{7} + 3\frac{1}{7}$

Add. Write each sum as a mixed number in simplest form.

23. $4\frac{3}{4}$ **24.** $8\frac{5}{6}$ **25.** $7\frac{5}{9}$ **26.** $\frac{3}{5}$ **27.** $6\frac{2}{5}$ **28.** $3\frac{5}{12}$

$+2\frac{7}{20}$ $+2\frac{5}{12}$ $+4\frac{8}{18}$ $+9\frac{8}{20}$ $+\frac{2}{3}$ $+9\frac{7}{8}$

29. $4\frac{1}{5} + 6\frac{9}{10} + 2\frac{2}{5}$ **30.** $3\frac{4}{9} + 6\frac{2}{3} + 4\frac{2}{9}$ **31.** $3\frac{3}{4} + 5\frac{3}{8} + 7\frac{5}{8}$

32. $5\frac{1}{8} + \frac{3}{4} + 6\frac{1}{2}$ **33.** $6\frac{1}{2} + 9\frac{1}{4} + 3\frac{2}{3}$ **34.** $2\frac{5}{6} + 9\frac{1}{3} + \frac{1}{12}$

35. $6\frac{5}{9} + 4\frac{2}{3}$ **36.** $\frac{3}{4} + 2\frac{4}{5}$ **37.** $3\frac{5}{8} + 7\frac{2}{3}$ **38.** $6\frac{4}{7} + 8\frac{1}{2}$

39. $\frac{17}{2} + 5\frac{1}{2} + 3\frac{2}{3}$ **40.** $3\frac{3}{10} + 2\frac{3}{4} + 6\frac{1}{5}$ **41.** $4\frac{1}{3} + \frac{5}{8} + \frac{5}{4}$ **42.** $12\frac{1}{2} + \frac{13}{4} + 2\frac{5}{6}$

Problem Solving

43. Lydia's new water filter can filter $2\frac{1}{3}$ gallons of water in 1 minute. Her old filter can filter $1\frac{7}{8}$ gallons in 1 minute. Lydia says that if she uses both filters at the same time, she can filter $3\frac{5}{24}$ gallons in a minute. What is her error?

44. A company has a pizza party for its employees. The table shows the leftover pizza. If a box can hold an 8-slice pizza, how many boxes are needed to save the leftovers? Justify your answer.

Types of Pizza	Leftover Amount
Pepperoni	$3\frac{5}{8}$
Cheese	$1\frac{3}{4}$
Veggie	$2\frac{1}{2}$

45. Corey says that $1\frac{2}{3} + 3\frac{5}{8} = 1 + 3 + \frac{2}{3} + \frac{5}{8}$. Explain the reason why Corey is correct. Include any properties that Corey may have used.

46. Aria renamed $4\frac{13}{6}$ as $5\frac{1}{6}$. Describe her error, and provide the correct answer.

Write About It

47. Samuel uses a different method to add mixed numbers. He changes both mixed numbers to improper fractions with a common denominator. Explain his method using the example $1\frac{3}{8} + 1\frac{7}{10}$.

Use fraction models to add. Write each sum in simplest form.

1. $\dfrac{1}{8} + \dfrac{3}{4}$

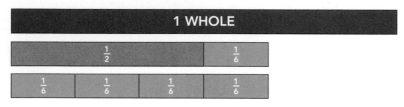

2. $\dfrac{1}{2} + \dfrac{1}{6}$

3. $\dfrac{3}{10} + \dfrac{3}{5}$

4. $\dfrac{1}{2} + \dfrac{3}{8}$

5. $\dfrac{3}{8} + \dfrac{5}{6}$

6. $\dfrac{2}{5} + \dfrac{1}{2}$

Add. Write each sum in simplest form.

7. $\begin{array}{r} \dfrac{3}{8} \\[4pt] +\dfrac{1}{4} \\ \hline \end{array}$

8. $\begin{array}{r} \dfrac{3}{7} \\[4pt] +\dfrac{1}{2} \\ \hline \end{array}$

9. $\begin{array}{r} \dfrac{2}{9} \\[4pt] +\dfrac{5}{6} \\ \hline \end{array}$

10. $\begin{array}{r} \dfrac{2}{15} \\[4pt] +\dfrac{7}{10} \\ \hline \end{array}$

11. $\begin{array}{r} \dfrac{17}{20} \\[4pt] +\dfrac{3}{8} \\ \hline \end{array}$

12. $\dfrac{2}{3} + \dfrac{1}{6}$

13. $\dfrac{1}{4} + \dfrac{5}{8}$

14. $\dfrac{3}{4} + \dfrac{1}{5}$

15. $\dfrac{5}{12} + \dfrac{3}{8}$

16. $\dfrac{1}{10} + \dfrac{3}{4}$

17. $\dfrac{5}{12} + \dfrac{3}{4} + \dfrac{1}{12}$

18. $\dfrac{1}{8} + \dfrac{1}{2} + \dfrac{3}{4}$

19. $\dfrac{1}{6} + \dfrac{1}{2} + \dfrac{1}{3}$

20. $\dfrac{3}{5} + \dfrac{3}{10} + \dfrac{1}{8}$

Estimate each sum.

21. $\dfrac{1}{5} + \dfrac{8}{9}$

22. $\dfrac{2}{3} + \dfrac{11}{12}$

23. $\dfrac{7}{8} + \dfrac{13}{16}$

24. $\dfrac{1}{7} + \dfrac{2}{3}$

25. $\dfrac{1}{2} + \dfrac{7}{10} + \dfrac{9}{11}$

26. $\dfrac{3}{5} + \dfrac{1}{9} + \dfrac{3}{7}$

27. $\dfrac{1}{8} + \dfrac{2}{9} + \dfrac{2}{5}$

28. $\dfrac{4}{15} + \dfrac{3}{10} + \dfrac{3}{5}$

Add. Write each sum as a mixed number in simplest form.

29. $2\frac{1}{5}$
  $+1\frac{3}{5}$
  _____

30. $6\frac{5}{7}$
  $+3\frac{3}{4}$
  _____

31. $4\frac{2}{3}$
  $+1\frac{1}{15}$
  _____

32. $2\frac{1}{2}$
  $+\ \ \frac{2}{3}$
  _____

33. $\frac{7}{10}$
  $+\frac{6}{15}$
  _____

34. $5\frac{5}{7}$
  $1\frac{2}{7}$
  $+2\frac{1}{2}$
  _____

35. $2\frac{1}{2}$
  $\frac{1}{4}$
  $+1\frac{3}{8}$
  _____

36. $2\frac{1}{2}$
  $4\frac{3}{8}$
  $+6\frac{1}{8}$
  _____

37. $2\frac{2}{3}$
  $3\frac{1}{5}$
  $+2\frac{5}{6}$
  _____

38. $3\frac{2}{5}$
  $4\frac{1}{10}$
  $+6\frac{3}{8}$
  _____

39. $6\frac{3}{8} + 2\frac{1}{8}$

40. $12\frac{3}{10} + 5\frac{7}{10}$

41. $1\frac{1}{2} + 4\frac{1}{6}$

42. $2\frac{3}{4} + 5\frac{1}{6}$

43. $6\frac{5}{8} + 2\frac{3}{4}$

44. $6\frac{2}{5} + 4\frac{2}{5} + 1\frac{2}{5}$

45. $7\frac{1}{4} + 10\frac{1}{2} + 3\frac{3}{8}$

46. $2\frac{1}{6} + 3\frac{1}{2} + \frac{1}{3}$

47. $4\frac{2}{9} + 5\frac{2}{3} + 6\frac{5}{6}$

Problem Solving

Use the map for Exercises 48–50.

48. A school bus is traveling from the school to the park. The driver wants to take the shortest route possible. Which route should she take? Explain.

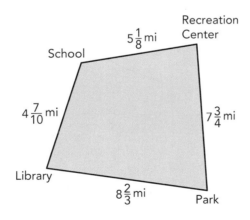

School

$5\frac{1}{8}$ mi

Recreation Center

$4\frac{7}{10}$ mi

$7\frac{3}{4}$ mi

Library

$8\frac{2}{3}$ mi

Park

49. To train for a bicycle race, Justin wants to ride from school to the recreation center to the park, to the library, then back to school. Will his training ride be more than 26 miles? Explain.

50. If Justin started at the park and rode to the recreation center, to the school, to the library, then back to the park, would his distance be farther than the route he took in Exercise 49? Explain.

Lucy wants to plant a vegetable garden but doesn't have a very big yard. To make the most of her space, she decides to use high-density gardening and build a raised garden bed. The bed will be rectangular with the dimensions shown below. She wants to plant carrots, kale, tomatoes, and lettuce.

1. Lucy calculates how much wood she needs to build the garden bed. What is the perimeter of the garden bed?

2. The home improvement store only sells wood in whole-number amounts of feet. What is the fewest number of feet Lucy can buy and still have enough? Explain.

Lucy creates a design to model how she wants to plant the vegetables. First, she splits the garden bed into four sections.

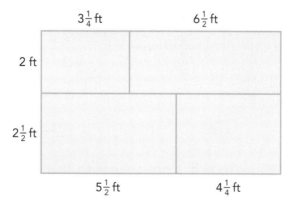

3. Verify that Lucy correctly split the length and width of the bed. Use the overall dimensions of the garden bed and fraction addition. Show your work.

Next, Lucy calculates the area of each section of the garden. She wants to use twice as much area to plant lettuce as to plant kale, and wants to use the largest section for tomatoes.

$6\frac{1}{2}$ sq ft	13 sq ft
$13\frac{3}{4}$ sq ft	$10\frac{5}{8}$ sq ft

4. Explain where each vegetable should be planted.

5. Kale and lettuce are both leafy greens. How many square feet of the garden will be used to grow leafy greens?

6. How many square feet will be used to grow carrots and tomatoes?

7. What is the total area of the garden?

Determine the best answer for each problem.

1. What is the value of n?

$$\frac{5}{10} - \frac{3}{10} = n$$

A. $\frac{1}{10}$ B. $\frac{1}{5}$

C. 1 D. $\frac{4}{5}$

2. What is the least common denominator of $\frac{3}{8}$ and $\frac{1}{6}$?

A. 8 B. 12
C. 24 D. 48

3. What fraction is shown by the model?

A. $\frac{4}{9}$ B. $\frac{5}{9}$

C. $\frac{2}{3}$ D. $\frac{5}{45}$

4. Rename the mixed number $12\frac{22}{18}$ in simplest form.

A. $12\frac{2}{9}$ B. $12\frac{4}{18}$

C. $13\frac{2}{9}$ D. $13\frac{4}{18}$

5. What is the perimeter of the triangle?

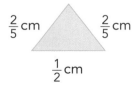

$\frac{2}{5}$ cm $\frac{2}{5}$ cm

$\frac{1}{2}$ cm

6. Which fractions are equivalent to $\frac{1}{3}$? Select all that apply.

A. $\frac{10}{30}$ B. $\frac{3}{10}$

C. $\frac{2}{6}$ D. $\frac{5}{150}$

E. $\frac{4}{12}$ F. $\frac{3}{12}$

7. If $a = \frac{7}{12}$, what is $a + a$?

A. $\frac{1}{6}$ B. $\frac{14}{24}$

C. $1\frac{1}{12}$ D. $1\frac{1}{6}$

8. $1\frac{1}{3}$ plus how much equals $5\frac{2}{3}$?

9. Using the benchmarks 0, $\frac{1}{2}$, and 1, which numbers are closest to $\frac{1}{2}$? Select all that apply.

A. $\frac{2}{3}$ B. $\frac{5}{9}$

C. $\frac{1}{5}$ D. $\frac{1}{3}$

E. $\frac{6}{7}$ F. $\frac{11}{10}$

10. Select the fraction that completes the number sentence.

$$\frac{1}{6} + \underline{\ ?\ } = \frac{17}{30}$$

A. $\frac{2}{5}$ B. $\frac{16}{24}$

C. $\frac{1}{3}$ D. $\frac{5}{30}$

Fractions: Subtraction

A common wood-working tool is a wood planer. It is used to shave thin strips from boards to create a flat surface. At first, wood planers were handheld, but now there are electric planers with large platforms. To use an electric planer, set the cut depth and then feed a piece of wood into the planer, where it will be rolled under fast-spinning blades that trim the board.

Operations with Fractions

Woodworkers must operate with fractions every day to ensure their measurements are accurate, even when working with a sophisticated tool like a wood planer.

♦ The desired thickness is typically displayed on a wood planer and not the depth of a cut. Therefore, to plane a $1\frac{1}{2}$ inch thick piece of wood by $\frac{1}{8}$ inch, the woodworker must subtract to find the desired thickness before operating the machine.

♦ Wood should not planed by more than $\frac{1}{16}$ or $\frac{1}{8}$ inch at a time. This means that a piece of wood may need to be planed multiple times in order to achieve the desired thickness.

Model Subtraction of Fractions with Unlike Denominators

Objective
- Use models to subtract fractions with unlike denominators.

Math Word
equivalent fractions

A nutritionist analyzes the diet of one of her clients who is an athlete. She finds that $\frac{5}{8}$ of the athlete's diet is fruits and vegetables. If $\frac{1}{4}$ of the athlete's diet is fruits, what part of the athlete's diet is vegetables?

Use a model to subtract $\frac{5}{8} - \frac{1}{4}$.

- Model the problem under a strip for 1 whole.

- The model shows how the parts line up. Two $\frac{1}{8}$ strips are the same size as one $\frac{1}{4}$ strip. To subtract $\frac{1}{4}$, remove two $\frac{1}{8}$ strips.

- The three $\frac{1}{8}$ strips remaining represent a difference of $\frac{3}{8}$.

1 WHOLE

| $\frac{1}{8}$ | $\frac{1}{8}$ | $\frac{1}{8}$ | $\frac{1}{8}$ | $\frac{1}{8}$ | | | |

| $\frac{1}{4}$ | | | |

$$\frac{5}{8} - \frac{1}{4} = \frac{3}{8}$$ ← Write the answer in simplest form.

$\frac{3}{8}$ of the athlete's diet is vegetables.

PRACTICE

Subtract. Express the difference in simplest form.

1. $\frac{9}{10} - \frac{3}{5} = \underline{\ ?\ }$

1 WHOLE

| $\frac{1}{10}$ | $\frac{1}{10}$ | $\frac{1}{10}$ | $\frac{1}{10}$ | $\frac{1}{10}$ | $\frac{1}{10}$ | $\frac{1}{10}$ | $\frac{1}{10}$ | $\frac{1}{10}$ | |

| $\frac{1}{5}$ | $\frac{1}{5}$ | $\frac{1}{5}$ | | |

2. $\frac{5}{6} - \frac{1}{3} = \underline{\ ?\ }$

1 WHOLE

| $\frac{1}{6}$ | $\frac{1}{6}$ | $\frac{1}{6}$ | $\frac{1}{6}$ | $\frac{1}{6}$ | |

| $\frac{1}{3}$ | | |

3. $\frac{1}{2} - \frac{5}{12} = \underline{\ ?\ }$

1 WHOLE

| $\frac{1}{2}$ | |

| $\frac{1}{12}$ | $\frac{1}{12}$ | $\frac{1}{12}$ | $\frac{1}{12}$ | $\frac{1}{12}$ | | | | | | | |

Use fraction strips or a model to subtract.

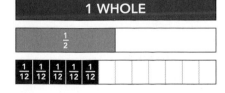

4. $\frac{5}{8} - \frac{1}{2}$

5. $\frac{7}{10} - \frac{2}{5}$

6. $\frac{3}{4} - \frac{5}{12}$

7. $\frac{5}{9} - \frac{1}{3}$

Subtract. Express the difference in simplest form.

8. $\frac{3}{4} - \frac{1}{2}$

1 WHOLE

| $\frac{1}{4}$ | $\frac{1}{4}$ | $\frac{1}{4}$ | |

| $\frac{1}{2}$ | |

9. $\frac{7}{10} - \frac{1}{5}$

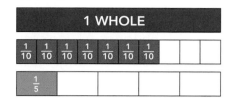

10. $\frac{7}{9} - \frac{1}{3}$

1 WHOLE

| $\frac{1}{9}$ | $\frac{1}{9}$ | $\frac{1}{9}$ | $\frac{1}{9}$ | $\frac{1}{9}$ | $\frac{1}{9}$ | $\frac{1}{9}$ | | |

| $\frac{1}{3}$ | | |

11. $\frac{11}{12} - \frac{1}{4}$

12. $\frac{2}{3} - \frac{7}{12}$

13. $\frac{5}{6} - \frac{1}{2}$

14. $\frac{3}{4} - \frac{1}{8}$

15. $\frac{5}{6} - \frac{2}{3}$

Problem Solving

16. Gabriel designs a robot that can walk $\frac{7}{10}$ meter in a minute. Ian designs a robot that can walk $\frac{3}{5}$ meter in a minute. How much farther does Gabriel's robot walk in one minute? Draw a fraction model to find the difference.

17. A scientist is studying spiders in the rainforest. She measures the fangs of one Goliath birdeater spider as $\frac{13}{16}$ inch. Another has fangs that are $\frac{3}{4}$ inch. How can you use a ruler to find the difference in the lengths? What is the difference?

Write About It

18. Eva and Genesis use different fraction models to show $\frac{1}{2} - \frac{1}{4}$. Whose model is correct? Explain.

Eva

1 WHOLE

| $\frac{1}{8}$ | $\frac{1}{8}$ | $\frac{1}{8}$ | $\frac{1}{8}$ | | |

| $\frac{1}{8}$ | $\frac{1}{8}$ | | |

Genesis

1 WHOLE

| $\frac{1}{4}$ | $\frac{1}{4}$ | | |

| $\frac{1}{4}$ | | |

Subtract Fractions: Unlike Denominators

Objective
- Subtract fractions with unlike denominators.

Math Words

least common denominator (LCD)
difference

A science class observes the growth of a caterpillar over a week. On Monday, Felix's caterpillar was $\frac{1}{2}$ inch long. A week later, Felix's caterpillar was $\frac{3}{5}$ inch long. How much did the caterpillar grow in a week?

To determine the change in length, Felix needs to find $\frac{3}{5} - \frac{1}{2}$.

To subtract fractions with unlike denominators:

- Find the least common denominator (LCD) of the fractions.

- Rename the fractions as equivalent fractions with the LCD as the denominator.

- Subtract the fractions.

- Write the difference in simplest form.

LCD of $\frac{3}{5}$ and $\frac{1}{2}$: 10

$$\frac{3}{5} = \frac{3 \times 2}{5 \times 2} = \frac{6}{10}$$

$$-\frac{1}{2} = \frac{1 \times 5}{2 \times 5} = \frac{5}{10}$$
$$\frac{1}{10}$$

The caterpillar grew $\frac{1}{10}$ inch.

PRACTICE

Complete each subtraction.

1. $\frac{3}{5} = \frac{3 \times ?}{5 \times ?} = \frac{?}{15}$

   $-\frac{1}{3} = \frac{1 \times ?}{3 \times ?} = \frac{?}{15}$
   $\frac{?}{15}$

2. $\frac{5}{6} = \frac{5 \times ?}{6 \times ?} = \frac{?}{24}$

   $-\frac{3}{8} = \frac{3 \times ?}{8 \times ?} = \frac{?}{24}$
   $\frac{?}{24}$

3. $\frac{1}{2} = \frac{1 \times ?}{2 \times ?} = \frac{?}{18}$

   $-\frac{2}{9} = \frac{2 \times ?}{9 \times ?} = \frac{?}{18}$
   $\frac{?}{18}$

Find each difference.

4. $\frac{1}{3}$
   $-\frac{1}{4}$

5. $\frac{4}{5}$
   $-\frac{3}{4}$

6. $\frac{7}{9}$
   $-\frac{1}{2}$

7. $\frac{2}{5}$
   $-\frac{1}{3}$

8. $\frac{4}{5}$
   $-\frac{1}{2}$

9. $\frac{3}{4}$
   $-\frac{1}{6}$

10. $\frac{6}{7} - \frac{2}{3}$

11. $\frac{3}{5} - \frac{1}{8}$

12. $\frac{7}{10} - \frac{2}{3}$

13. $\frac{5}{6} - \frac{1}{3}$

14. $\frac{3}{7} - \frac{1}{3}$

15. $\frac{9}{10} - \frac{1}{4}$

Find each difference.

16. $\dfrac{5}{6}$
    $-\dfrac{2}{9}$

17. $\dfrac{4}{5}$
    $-\dfrac{1}{3}$

18. $\dfrac{8}{9}$
    $-\dfrac{5}{12}$

19. $\dfrac{13}{15}$
    $-\dfrac{4}{9}$

20. $\dfrac{6}{7}$
    $-\dfrac{3}{4}$

21. $\dfrac{9}{10}$
    $-\dfrac{2}{3}$

22. $\dfrac{5}{7} - \dfrac{3}{5}$

23. $\dfrac{7}{9} - \dfrac{2}{3}$

24. $\dfrac{5}{6} - \dfrac{4}{5}$

25. $\dfrac{7}{8} - \dfrac{2}{3}$

26. $\dfrac{4}{5} - \dfrac{3}{7}$

27. $\dfrac{1}{2} - \dfrac{2}{11}$

28. $\dfrac{1}{2} - \dfrac{1}{3} + \dfrac{1}{4}$

29. $\dfrac{3}{4} - \dfrac{2}{5} + \dfrac{1}{3}$

30. $\dfrac{4}{5} - \dfrac{1}{6} - \dfrac{1}{3}$

31. $\dfrac{5}{6} + \dfrac{1}{12} - \dfrac{4}{9}$

Add or subtract. Then, compare using <, =, or >.

32. $\dfrac{1}{4} + \dfrac{2}{8}$ __?__ $\dfrac{9}{10} - \dfrac{1}{6}$

33. $\dfrac{4}{5} - \dfrac{1}{10}$ __?__ $\dfrac{1}{5} + \dfrac{1}{2}$

34. $\dfrac{1}{3} + \dfrac{1}{5}$ __?__ $\dfrac{2}{3} - \dfrac{1}{4}$

Problem Solving

35. Ava is cutting cables. She has a cable that is $\dfrac{11}{12}$ meter long. She cuts two $\dfrac{1}{4}$-meter pieces from the cable. How long is the cable now?

36. A rain gauge can measure up to 6 inches of rain. The picture shows how full the gauge was last month and this month. Assume the gauge was empty before last month. How much rain fell this month? Explain how you know.

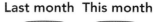
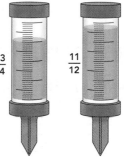

Last month   This month

$\dfrac{3}{4}$ $\dfrac{11}{12}$

37. Write a subtraction problem that has fractions with denominators of 10 and 3. The difference should be $\dfrac{1}{6}$.

Write About It

38. Wendy simplifies the expression $\dfrac{11}{12} - \dfrac{1}{3} + \dfrac{1}{4}$. Her work is shown. She finds a value of $\dfrac{1}{3}$, but her teacher says the correct answer is $\dfrac{5}{6}$. Explain what she did wrong.

$$\dfrac{11}{12} - \dfrac{1}{3} + \dfrac{1}{4}$$
$$= \dfrac{11}{12} - \dfrac{4}{12} + \dfrac{3}{12}$$
$$= \dfrac{11}{12} - \dfrac{7}{12}$$
$$= \dfrac{4}{12} = \dfrac{1}{3}$$

Subtract Fractions: Estimation and Reasonableness

Objective
- Use benchmark fractions to assess the reasonableness of answers.

Math Words

benchmark

estimate

Jorge notices $\frac{4}{5}$ of his tablet's power remains. He can finish his book with about $\frac{1}{4}$ of the power of a fully-charged tablet. After he finishes the book, he says that at least $\frac{1}{2}$ of the power will remain. Is his answer reasonable?

Use the benchmarks 0, $\frac{1}{2}$, and 1.

Compare: $\frac{4}{5}$ is greater than $\frac{3}{4}$.
So $\frac{4}{5} - \frac{1}{4} > \frac{3}{4} - \frac{1}{4} = \frac{1}{2}$. This is supported by the model.

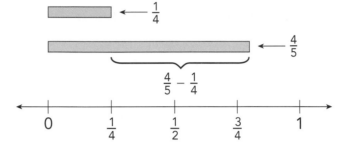

> Jorge's answer is reasonable.

Study these examples.

Is $\frac{8}{9} - \frac{1}{12} = \frac{15}{36}$ reasonable?

$\frac{8}{9}$ is close to 1; $\frac{1}{12}$ is close to 0.

Estimate: $1 - 0 = 1$

> The answer is not reasonable.

Is $\frac{5}{8} - \frac{1}{6} = \frac{11}{24}$ reasonable?

$\frac{5}{8}$ is close to $\frac{1}{2}$; $\frac{1}{6}$ is close to 0.

Estimate: $\frac{1}{2} - 0 = \frac{1}{2}$

> The answer is reasonable.

PRACTICE

Complete the statements to determine if the answer is reasonable.

1. $\frac{7}{8} - \frac{2}{5} = \frac{19}{40}$

Compare: $\frac{7}{8}$ is close to ___?___ .

Compare: $\frac{2}{5}$ is close to ___?___ .

Compare: $\frac{19}{40}$ is close to ___?___ .

2. $\frac{3}{7} - \frac{2}{5} = \frac{5}{12}$

Compare: $\frac{3}{7}$ is close to ___?___ .

Compare: $\frac{2}{5}$ is close to ___?___ .

Compare: $\frac{5}{12}$ is close to ___?___ .

Compare each fraction to 0, $\frac{1}{2}$, or 1 to decide whether the answer is reasonable. Write Yes or No.

3. $\frac{3}{4} - \frac{1}{3} = \frac{5}{12}$

4. $\frac{9}{10} - \frac{2}{3} = \frac{29}{30}$

5. $\frac{7}{10} - \frac{1}{4} = \frac{9}{20}$

6. $\frac{11}{12} - \frac{1}{8} = \frac{5}{24}$

7. $\frac{7}{12} - \frac{1}{3} = \frac{1}{4}$

8. $\frac{4}{6} - \frac{4}{9} = \frac{17}{18}$

Is the answer reasonable? Write Yes or No. If not, explain.

9. $\frac{2}{3} - \frac{1}{5} = \frac{13}{15}$

10. $\frac{7}{12} - \frac{1}{15} = \frac{31}{60}$

11. $\frac{4}{6} - \frac{4}{9} = \frac{11}{18}$

12. $\frac{5}{12} + \frac{1}{2} = \frac{1}{4}$

13. $\frac{3}{10} + \frac{2}{15} = \frac{13}{30}$

14. $\frac{7}{12} + \frac{8}{9} = \frac{19}{36}$

Determine if the answer is about 0, $\frac{1}{2}$, or 1.

15. $\frac{9}{10} - \frac{1}{9}$

16. $\frac{10}{12} - \frac{3}{8}$

17. $\frac{6}{11} - \frac{3}{5}$

18. $\frac{3}{4} - \frac{4}{10}$

19. $\frac{14}{15} - \frac{6}{7}$

20. $\frac{11}{20} - \frac{2}{25}$

21. $\frac{2}{15} - \frac{1}{12}$

22. $\frac{17}{18} - \frac{2}{35}$

Problem Solving

23. The picture shows the fraction of paint remaining in a bottle. An artist thinks he needs $\frac{3}{4}$ of the bottle to finish his painting. Should he buy more paint? Explain.

 ← $\frac{5}{6}$

24. A youth group is picking up recyclables from a local park that is $\frac{9}{10}$ of an acre. They finish $\frac{5}{8}$ of an acre before lunch. A student says that more than half of the work still remains. Is this reasonable? Explain.

25. Marvin says that $\frac{9}{10} - \frac{1}{2} = \frac{1}{2}$ because he can round and use $1 - \frac{1}{2} = \frac{1}{2}$. Do you agree with Marvin's reasoning? Explain.

26. The weight of pure gold needed to create some jewelry is shown in the table. About how much more gold is needed for a necklace than a ring? Use benchmark fractions to justify your answer.

Jewelry	Amount of gold
Necklace	$\frac{5}{6}$ ounce
Ring	$\frac{4}{9}$ ounce
Bracelet	$\frac{1}{4}$ ounce

27. A number is subtracted from $\frac{19}{20}$. The difference is about $\frac{1}{2}$. What could the number be?

Write About It

28. Jordan thinks about a proper fraction greater than $\frac{1}{2}$ minus a proper fraction less than $\frac{1}{2}$. "The difference will always be greater than $\frac{1}{2}$," he says. Is he correct? Explain using examples.

Use the model to find the difference.

1. $\dfrac{5}{9} - \dfrac{1}{3}$

1 WHOLE

| $\frac{1}{9}$ | $\frac{1}{9}$ | $\frac{1}{9}$ | $\frac{1}{9}$ | $\frac{1}{9}$ | | | |

| $\frac{1}{3}$ | | |

2. $\dfrac{7}{8} - \dfrac{1}{4}$

1 WHOLE

| $\frac{1}{8}$ | $\frac{1}{8}$ | $\frac{1}{8}$ | $\frac{1}{8}$ | $\frac{1}{8}$ | $\frac{1}{8}$ | $\frac{1}{8}$ | |

| $\frac{1}{4}$ | | | |

3. $\dfrac{2}{3} - \dfrac{2}{9}$

1 WHOLE

| $\frac{1}{3}$ | $\frac{1}{3}$ | |

| $\frac{1}{9}$ | $\frac{1}{9}$ | | | | | | |

4. $\dfrac{7}{8} - \dfrac{1}{4}$

1 WHOLE

| $\frac{1}{8}$ | $\frac{1}{8}$ | $\frac{1}{8}$ | $\frac{1}{8}$ | $\frac{1}{8}$ | $\frac{1}{8}$ | $\frac{1}{8}$ | |

| $\frac{1}{4}$ | | | |

5. $\dfrac{11}{12} - \dfrac{3}{6}$

1 WHOLE

| $\frac{1}{12}$ | $\frac{1}{12}$ | $\frac{1}{12}$ | $\frac{1}{12}$ | $\frac{1}{12}$ | $\frac{1}{12}$ | $\frac{1}{12}$ | $\frac{1}{12}$ | $\frac{1}{12}$ | $\frac{1}{12}$ | $\frac{1}{12}$ | |

| $\frac{1}{6}$ | $\frac{1}{6}$ | $\frac{1}{6}$ | | | |

6. $\dfrac{8}{10} - \dfrac{2}{5}$

1 WHOLE

| $\frac{1}{10}$ | $\frac{1}{10}$ | $\frac{1}{10}$ | $\frac{1}{10}$ | $\frac{1}{10}$ | $\frac{1}{10}$ | $\frac{1}{10}$ | $\frac{1}{10}$ | | |

| $\frac{1}{5}$ | $\frac{1}{5}$ | | | |

Find the difference.

7. $\dfrac{2}{3} - \dfrac{1}{6}$

  A. $\dfrac{1}{2}$ **B.** $\dfrac{1}{3}$

  C. $\dfrac{1}{6}$ **D.** $\dfrac{1}{9}$

8. $\dfrac{4}{5} - \dfrac{3}{4}$

  A. $\dfrac{1}{5}$ **B.** $\dfrac{1}{9}$

  C. $\dfrac{1}{10}$ **D.** $\dfrac{1}{20}$

9. $\dfrac{3}{8} - \dfrac{1}{10}$

  A. $\dfrac{1}{4}$ **B.** $\dfrac{1}{20}$

  C. $\dfrac{7}{20}$ **D.** $\dfrac{11}{40}$

10. $\dfrac{8}{15} - \dfrac{2}{10}$

  A. $\dfrac{2}{15}$ **B.** $\dfrac{1}{3}$

  C. $\dfrac{6}{15}$ **D.** $\dfrac{3}{5}$

11. $\dfrac{1}{3} - \dfrac{1}{8}$

  A. $\dfrac{5}{24}$ **B.** $\dfrac{1}{4}$

  C. $\dfrac{1}{6}$ **D.** $\dfrac{7}{24}$

12. $\dfrac{11}{12} - \dfrac{3}{4}$

  A. $\dfrac{3}{12}$ **B.** $\dfrac{1}{6}$

  C. $\dfrac{1}{2}$ **D.** $\dfrac{1}{20}$

13. $\dfrac{1}{2} - \dfrac{3}{8}$

  A. $\dfrac{1}{4}$ **B.** $\dfrac{1}{12}$

  C. $\dfrac{3}{16}$ **D.** $\dfrac{1}{8}$

14. $\dfrac{11}{12} - \dfrac{1}{3}$

  A. $\dfrac{5}{12}$ **B.** $\dfrac{7}{12}$

  C. $\dfrac{2}{3}$ **D.** $\dfrac{4}{9}$

Match each subtraction problem with its difference.

A. $\frac{7}{15}$ **B.** $\frac{1}{6}$ **C.** $\frac{1}{2}$ **D.** $\frac{1}{15}$ **E.** $\frac{3}{8}$ **F.** $\frac{5}{24}$ **G.** $\frac{1}{4}$ **H.** $\frac{1}{3}$

15. $\frac{4}{15} - \frac{1}{10}$

16. $\frac{3}{4} - \frac{5}{12}$

17. $\frac{7}{10} - \frac{1}{5}$

18. $\frac{7}{8} - \frac{2}{3}$

19. $\frac{13}{15} - \frac{2}{5}$

20. $\frac{1}{3} - \frac{1}{12}$

21. $\frac{11}{30} - \frac{3}{10}$

22. $\frac{5}{8} - \frac{1}{4}$

Compare each fraction to 0, $\frac{1}{2}$, or 1. Is the difference reasonable? Write Yes or No.

23. $\frac{7}{10} - \frac{1}{5} = \frac{1}{2}$

24. $\frac{8}{9} - \frac{2}{15} = \frac{14}{45}$

25. $\frac{7}{12} - \frac{1}{3} = \frac{3}{4}$

26. $\frac{1}{6} - \frac{1}{8} = \frac{1}{24}$

27. $\frac{5}{7} - \frac{1}{3} = \frac{8}{21}$

28. $\frac{1}{2} - \frac{1}{8} = \frac{3}{8}$

29. $\frac{7}{12} - \frac{3}{7} = \frac{4}{5}$

30. $\frac{11}{18} - \frac{5}{12} = \frac{23}{36}$

Give a reasonable estimate.

31. $\frac{4}{5} - \frac{4}{11}$

32. $\frac{5}{6} - \frac{3}{4}$

33. $\frac{2}{9} - \frac{1}{6}$

34. $\frac{14}{15} - \frac{1}{12}$

35. $\frac{7}{8} - \frac{1}{9}$

36. $\frac{2}{3} - \frac{1}{2}$

37. $\frac{7}{15} - \frac{1}{10}$

38. $\frac{7}{20} - \frac{5}{18}$

39. Which expressions are equal to $\frac{6}{10}$? Choose all that apply.

A. $\frac{1}{2} + \frac{1}{10}$ **B.** $\frac{9}{12} - \frac{1}{12}$ **C.** $\frac{14}{15} - \frac{1}{3}$ **D.** $\frac{9}{10} - \frac{1}{5}$ **E.** $\frac{4}{7} + \frac{2}{3}$

Problem Solving

40. Of incoming freshman at a college, $\frac{5}{14}$ of the class are science majors and $\frac{1}{7}$ of the class are engineering majors. How much more of the class is majoring in science than engineering? Draw a fraction model to find the difference.

41. Reagan and Max go on a road trip together. The table shows the fraction of power on their identical tablets at the start and end of the trip. Write an inequality to show who used more power during the trip.

	Start	End
Reagan	$\frac{9}{10}$	$\frac{2}{5}$
Max	$\frac{4}{5}$	$\frac{1}{3}$

42. Francesca subtracts $\frac{3}{4} - \frac{3}{5}$ to find the difference $\frac{3}{20}$. She uses benchmark fractions to check if her answer is reasonable. She concludes her answer is not reasonable because $1 - \frac{1}{2} = \frac{1}{2}$ and her answer is close to 0. Do you agree?

Model Subtraction with Mixed Numbers

Objective
- Use models to subtract with mixed numbers.

Math Word
mixed number

A science teacher heats $4\frac{3}{4}$ grams of a mineral. The water in the sample evaporates, and $2\frac{1}{2}$ grams of the sample remain. How many grams of water were in the sample?

To solve the problem, subtract.

- Model the mixed numbers using the least common denominator of the fractions.

- Find the difference in the models.

- Express the difference as a mixed number or fraction in simplest form.

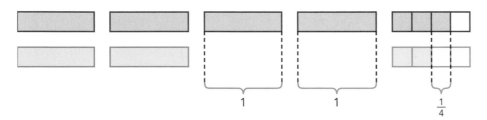

The top model has 2 more wholes and 1 more fourth.
This represents a difference of $2\frac{1}{4}$.

➤ There were $2\frac{1}{4}$ grams of water in the sample.

Study these examples.

$$4\frac{3}{4} - 3 = 1\frac{3}{4}$$

$$3\frac{5}{6} - \frac{1}{3} = 3\frac{3}{6} = 3\frac{1}{2}$$

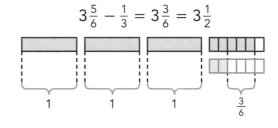

PRACTICE

Subtract. Use the models to help.

1. $3\frac{1}{3} - 1\frac{1}{6}$

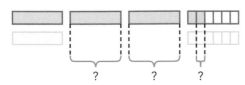

2. $4\frac{1}{4} - 3$

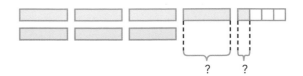

Subtract. Use a model.

3. $2\frac{1}{4} - 1\frac{1}{4}$

4. $3\frac{1}{2} - 3$

5. $2\frac{7}{8} - \frac{1}{2}$

6. $6\frac{3}{5} - 2\frac{3}{10}$

7. $3\frac{7}{10} - \frac{1}{5}$

8. $4\frac{5}{8} - 2$

9. $5\frac{1}{2} - 2\frac{1}{4}$

10. $3\frac{2}{5} - 3\frac{1}{3}$

11. $1\frac{9}{10} - \frac{2}{3}$

12. $6\frac{3}{8} - 4\frac{1}{4}$

13. $4\frac{3}{4} - \frac{3}{5}$

14. $3\frac{5}{6} - 2\frac{1}{4}$

Problem Solving

15. What problem does the model show? Write a subtraction equation. Then rewrite the equation using mixed numbers in simplest form.

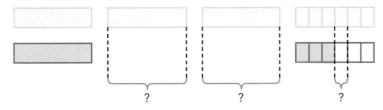

16. Kaylee has $3\frac{9}{10}$ gallons of paint. She uses $1\frac{1}{5}$ gallons to paint a bathroom and $2\frac{1}{2}$ gallons to paint a bedroom. How much paint does she have left over? Use a model to solve.

17. Jasper delivers organic lettuce to different restaurants around the city. He starts with $15\frac{3}{4}$ pounds of lettuce. On the first delivery, he delivers $4\frac{1}{2}$ pounds of lettuce. On the second delivery, he delivers $6\frac{1}{8}$ pounds. How much lettuce does he have now? Describe two different ways to solve the problem.

Write About It

18. Cooper solved the subtraction problem using the following model. Identify any errors and find the correct difference.

$$3\frac{4}{5} - 1\frac{1}{2} = 1\frac{7}{10}$$

Estimate Sums and Differences of Mixed Numbers

Objective
- Use rounding and front-end estimation to estimate sums and differences of mixed numbers.

Math Words
mixed number
rounding
front-end estimation

Hannah and her friend each pick $2\frac{5}{8}$ pints of blueberries. They give $1\frac{1}{5}$ pints to a neighbor. About how many pints of blueberries do they have now?

Estimate $2\frac{5}{8} + 2\frac{5}{8} - 1\frac{1}{5}$.

◆ Use rounding.

Round each mixed number to the nearest whole number.

$2\frac{5}{8} \longrightarrow \frac{5}{8} > \frac{1}{2}$, so $2\frac{5}{8}$ rounds to 3. $1\frac{1}{5} \longrightarrow \frac{1}{5} < \frac{1}{2}$, so $1\frac{1}{5}$ rounds to 1.

$3 + 3 - 1 = 5$, so the estimate is 5 pints.

◆ Use front-end estimation.

Add or subtract the whole-number parts.

$2\frac{5}{8} + 2\frac{5}{8} - 1\frac{1}{5} \longrightarrow 2 + 2 - 1 = 3$

Adjust the estimate with the fraction parts.

$3 + 1 = 4$

The estimate is 4 pints.

Use benchmark fractions:
$\frac{5}{8} + \frac{5}{8} - \frac{1}{5}$ is about
$\frac{1}{2} + \frac{1}{2} - 0$, or about 1.

▷ Hannah and her friend have about 5 pints (using rounding) or about 4 pints (using front-end estimation) of blueberries now.

PRACTICE

Estimate each sum or difference. Use rounding.

1. $10\frac{7}{8} \longrightarrow$?
$+ \ 3\frac{5}{7} \longrightarrow$?
_____

2. $17\frac{2}{5} \longrightarrow$?
$- \ 9\frac{4}{10} \longrightarrow$?
_____

3. $15\frac{7}{8} \longrightarrow$?
$- \ 9\frac{4}{5} \longrightarrow$?
_____

Estimate each sum or difference. Use front-end estimation.

4. $18\frac{5}{6}$
$-13\frac{5}{8}$
_____

5. $14\frac{2}{9}$
$+ \ 8\frac{2}{3}$
_____

6. $7\frac{6}{7}$
$+5\frac{1}{5}$
_____

Estimate by rounding. Then estimate using front-end estimation.

7. $7\frac{1}{2}$
    $-2\frac{2}{3}$

8. $9\frac{3}{4}$
    $+6\frac{1}{3}$

9. $8\frac{5}{10}$
    $-5\frac{3}{8}$

10. $6\frac{5}{6}$
    $-4\frac{1}{5}$

11. $7\frac{1}{4}$
    $+3\frac{4}{5}$

12. $5\frac{1}{12}$
    $+3\frac{9}{10}$

13. $4\frac{5}{12}$
    $+2\frac{7}{12}$

14. $3\frac{1}{8}$
    $-1\frac{2}{5}$

15. $11\frac{5}{8}$
    $-3\frac{3}{5}$

16. $14\frac{9}{11}$
    $-8\frac{4}{7}$

17. $15\frac{1}{2} - 7\frac{1}{12} - 3\frac{6}{11}$

18. $27\frac{5}{6} + 12\frac{2}{3} + 7\frac{2}{15}$

19. $36\frac{1}{2} - 9\frac{5}{9} + 5\frac{4}{7}$

20. $4\frac{7}{8} + 2\frac{1}{5} - 1\frac{3}{7}$

21. $11\frac{4}{5} + 2\frac{1}{8} + \frac{9}{10}$

22. $10\frac{5}{9} - 5\frac{3}{7} - 2\frac{4}{5}$

Problem Solving

23. Austin is fishing and catches three brook trout. Estimate the difference between the longest trout and the shortest trout.

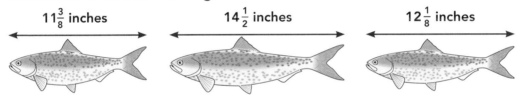

$11\frac{3}{8}$ inches $14\frac{1}{2}$ inches $12\frac{1}{8}$ inches

24. Ariana asks for about 5 pounds of assorted cheeses. The deli worker gives her $1\frac{3}{4}$ pounds of American cheese, $1\frac{5}{8}$ pounds of Swiss cheese, and $1\frac{7}{8}$ pounds of cheddar cheese. She thinks since each cheese weighs more than 1 pound, she has between 3 and 4 pounds of cheese. Should she ask for more? Explain. Then find the exact amount of cheese.

25. Eric wants to estimate $11\frac{5}{8} - 5\frac{15}{16}$ using front-end estimation. However, the fraction parts have estimates of $\frac{1}{2}$ and 1, and he can't subtract them. He decides to write $10\frac{13}{8} - 5\frac{15}{16}$ instead. Estimate the difference using front-end estimation. Explain what you did.

Write About It

26. Give an argument as to whether rounding or front-end estimation gives a better estimate. Do you think this is always true? Include examples to support your answer.

Subtract Fractions and Whole Numbers from Mixed Numbers

Objective
- Subtract whole numbers and proper fractions from mixed numbers.

Math Word

least common denominator (LCD)

Payton and Natalia both play the guitar. The table shows how many hours each practices every week. How much longer does Payton practice than Natalia?

Hours of Practice	
Payton	$2\frac{3}{4}$
Natalia	$\frac{2}{3}$

To find out how much longer Payton practices, find $2\frac{3}{4} - \frac{2}{3}$.

- Write the difference of the fraction parts.

$$\frac{3}{4} - \frac{2}{3}$$

- Find the LCD of the fractions and write equivalent fractions. The LCD of 4 and 3 is 12.

$$\frac{9}{12} - \frac{8}{12}$$

- Subtract.

$$\frac{9}{12} - \frac{8}{12} = \frac{1}{12}$$

- Add the whole-number part to the difference.

$$\frac{1}{12} + 2 = 2\frac{1}{12}$$

▶ Payton practices for $2\frac{1}{12}$ hours longer than Natalia.

Study these examples.

To subtract a whole number from a mixed number, just subtract the whole numbers.

$$7\frac{3}{8} - 4 = 7\frac{3}{8} - 4 = 3\frac{3}{8}$$

$$10\frac{2}{5} - 6 = 10\frac{2}{5} - 6 = 4\frac{2}{5}$$

PRACTICE

Find each missing number.

1. $4\frac{8}{9} - \frac{1}{3}$

$$\frac{8}{9} - \frac{?}{9} = \frac{?}{9}$$

$$4 + \frac{?}{9} = 4\frac{?}{9}$$

2. $7\frac{3}{5} - \frac{3}{8}$

$$\frac{?}{40} - \frac{?}{40} = \frac{?}{?}$$

$$7 + \frac{?}{?} = 7\frac{?}{?}$$

3. $2\frac{1}{4} - \frac{1}{10}$

$$\frac{?}{?} - \frac{?}{?} = \frac{?}{?}$$

$$2 + \frac{?}{?} = 2\frac{?}{?}$$

Find each difference. Write answers in simplest form.

4. $8\frac{1}{4} - 2$

5. $5\frac{2}{3} - 3$

6. $9\frac{5}{6} - 4$

7. $15\frac{7}{10} - 5$

8. $24\frac{15}{16} - 11$

9. $7\frac{5}{6} - \frac{1}{6}$

10. $5\frac{5}{8} - \frac{3}{8}$

11. $4\frac{7}{10} - \frac{3}{10}$

12. $9\frac{3}{4} - \frac{1}{8}$

13. $12\frac{7}{12} - \frac{1}{4}$

14. $4\frac{7}{12} - 4$

15. $6\frac{7}{18} - \frac{1}{6}$

Subtract. Write answers in simplest form.

16. $7\frac{1}{5}$
    -1

17. $6\frac{5}{8}$
    -3

18. $4\frac{4}{9}$
    -2

19. $10\frac{2}{7}$
    $-\,4$

20. $18\frac{5}{16}$
    $-\,9$

21. $6\frac{3}{4}$
    $-\frac{1}{8}$

22. $1\frac{1}{2}$
    $-\frac{3}{8}$

23. $2\frac{3}{4}$
    $-\frac{5}{8}$

24. $11\frac{3}{5}$
    $-\frac{1}{3}$

25. $5\frac{3}{4}$
    $-\frac{2}{3}$

26. $10\frac{1}{3}$
    -10

27. $3\frac{5}{8}$
    $-\frac{1}{4}$

28. $2\frac{5}{6}$
    $-\frac{5}{12}$

29. $5\frac{9}{10}$
    $-\frac{3}{5}$

30. $8\frac{6}{7}$
    $-\frac{1}{5}$

31. $12\frac{11}{15}$
    $-\frac{1}{6}$

Simplify each expression.

32. $2\frac{1}{2} + 3 - \frac{2}{5}$

33. $3\frac{2}{3} + \frac{1}{4} - \frac{5}{12}$

34. $9\frac{3}{4} - \frac{1}{5} - \frac{4}{10}$

35. $5\frac{7}{10} - \frac{2}{5} + 2$

36. $9\frac{11}{12} - \frac{1}{6} - \frac{1}{4}$

37. $8\frac{1}{3} - \frac{2}{7} + \frac{4}{21}$

38. $10\frac{8}{9} + \frac{4}{9} - \frac{3}{10}$

39. $5\frac{3}{10} + \frac{2}{5} - \frac{6}{15}$

Problem Solving

40. Jordan is building this picture frame. The length of the frame is 1 foot longer than the width. How many feet of wood does she need to build the frame?

41. Landon has $4\frac{1}{6}$ gallons of paint now. He used $\frac{2}{3}$ of a gallon for a recent job. How can he use an equation to find the amount of paint he had before the job? Explain.

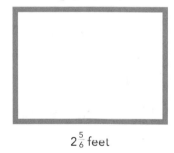

$2\frac{5}{6}$ feet

42. Two trees are $2\frac{7}{8}$ m and $\frac{3}{4}$ m tall. How much taller is the taller tree?

43. Joe has $4\frac{1}{2}$ gallons of water. He uses 1 gallon to make iced tea and $\frac{1}{3}$ gallon to make lemonade. How much water is left?

Write About It

44. How could you use two subtractions to find $5\frac{3}{4} - 3\frac{1}{6}$? Explain, and find the difference. Hint: $3\frac{1}{6}$ is equal to $3 + \frac{1}{6}$.

Subtract Mixed Numbers: Rename Fractions

Objective
- Subtract mixed numbers with like or unlike denominators.

Math Words
mixed number
least common
denominator (LCD)

Faith has $7\frac{3}{4}$ square yards of leftover fabric from last year's play. If she uses $3\frac{1}{8}$ square yards to make a tablecloth, how much fabric will she have left to use to make chair covers?

To solve, find $7\frac{3}{4} - 3\frac{1}{8}$.

To subtract mixed numbers:

- Find the least common denominator (LCD) of the fractions. Rename the fractions.
- Subtract the fractions.
- Subtract the whole numbers.
- Write the difference in simplest form.

LCD of $\frac{3}{4}$ and $\frac{1}{8}$: 8

$$7\frac{3}{4} = 7\frac{3 \times 2}{4 \times 2} = 7\frac{6}{8}$$
$$-3\frac{1}{8} \qquad\qquad = 3\frac{1}{8}$$
$$\overline{\qquad\qquad\qquad 4\frac{5}{8}}$$

▶ Faith has $4\frac{5}{8}$ square yards of fabric left.

Study these examples.

$$9\frac{3}{10}$$
$$-7\frac{3}{10}$$
$$\overline{2\frac{0}{10} = 2}$$

$$5\frac{2}{3} = 5\frac{2 \times 2}{3 \times 2} = 5\frac{4}{6}$$
$$-5\frac{1}{6} \qquad\qquad = 5\frac{1}{6}$$
$$\overline{\qquad\qquad\qquad 0\frac{3}{6} = \frac{1}{2}}$$

$$3\frac{2}{5} = 3\frac{2 \times 2}{5 \times 2} = 3\frac{4}{10}$$
$$-3\frac{4}{10} \qquad\qquad = 3\frac{4}{10}$$
$$\overline{\qquad\qquad\qquad 0\frac{0}{10} = 0}$$

PRACTICE

Subtract. If necessary, rename the fractions first.

1. $3\frac{2}{5}$
$-2\frac{1}{5}$

2. $2\frac{4}{7}$
$-1\frac{3}{7}$

3. $4\frac{7}{8}$
$-2\frac{3}{8}$

4. $5\frac{5}{6}$
$-3\frac{2}{4}$

5. $5\frac{11}{16}$
$-5\frac{2}{4}$

6. $6\frac{8}{9}$
$-3\frac{16}{18}$

7. $6\frac{5}{9}$
$-3\frac{3}{9}$

8. $2\frac{7}{10}$
$-2\frac{4}{10}$

9. $8\frac{5}{8}$
$-2\frac{4}{10}$

10. $7\frac{5}{6}$
$-2\frac{2}{3}$

11. $4\frac{8}{10}$
$-2\frac{5}{10}$

12. $7\frac{4}{6}$
$-3\frac{2}{6}$

PRACTICE

Subtract.

13. $10\frac{9}{14}$
$-\ 4\frac{2}{7}$

14. $6\frac{7}{10}$
$-\ 5\frac{2}{15}$

15. $11\frac{7}{24}$
$-\ 3\frac{1}{6}$

16. $21\frac{11}{16}$
$-\ 5\frac{5}{12}$

17. $5\frac{4}{12} - 5\frac{1}{3}$

18. $6\frac{5}{9} - 4\frac{1}{2}$

19. $6\frac{4}{5} - 2\frac{1}{3}$

20. $8\frac{5}{6} - 8\frac{4}{9}$

21. $9\frac{3}{8} - 4\frac{5}{16}$

22. $6\frac{3}{7} - 2\frac{5}{21}$

23. $2\frac{1}{5} - 1\frac{1}{20}$

24. $8\frac{5}{6} - 5\frac{1}{3}$

25. $5\frac{2}{3} - 5\frac{2}{9}$

26. $3\frac{12}{18} - 3\frac{2}{3}$

27. $7\frac{15}{20} - 4\frac{3}{5}$

28. $2\frac{4}{7} - 1\frac{1}{2}$

Subtract. Then compare using <, =, or >.

29. $9\frac{5}{10} - 6\frac{3}{10} \ \underline{\ ?\ } \ 5\frac{2}{5} - 2\frac{1}{5}$

30. $6\frac{3}{4} - 2\frac{1}{4} \ \underline{\ ?\ } \ 10\frac{2}{3} - 6\frac{1}{3}$

Problem Solving

Molly is shipping several packages. The weights and destinations are shown in the table. Use the information in the table to answer Exercises 31–32.

31. How much heavier is the package going to New York City than Richmond?

32. How much greater is the weight of the package going to Portland than the combined weight of the packages going to Rochester and Richmond?

Destination	Weight (pounds)
New York City	$12\frac{3}{5}$
Richmond	$7\frac{1}{4}$
Rochester	$2\frac{1}{3}$
Portland	$9\frac{2}{3}$

33. On Friday, Petra drives from home to the college, then back home. On Saturday, she drives from home to the park, then back home. Petra says she drives $7\frac{1}{12}$ more miles on Friday than on Saturday. Do you agree? If not, explain her error and find the correct difference.

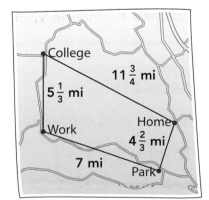

Write About It

34. Describe the steps to find the difference $\frac{29}{3} - 2\frac{1}{2}$. Write your answer as both a mixed number and an improper fraction.

Subtract Mixed Numbers: Rename Whole Numbers and Fractions

Objective
- Subtract mixed numbers by renaming whole numbers and fractions.

Math Words
mixed number
minuend
subtrahend

Sometimes you need to rename fractions before you can subtract. Find $4\frac{1}{2} - 2\frac{5}{6}$.

To subtract mixed numbers:

- If denominators are unlike, rename fractions using a common denominator.

$$4\frac{1}{2} = 4\frac{1 \times 3}{2 \times 3} = 4\frac{3}{6}$$
$$-2\frac{5}{6} \qquad\qquad = 2\frac{5}{6}$$

- $\frac{3}{6} < \frac{5}{6}$, so rename the minuend.

$$4\frac{3}{6} = 3 + 1 + \frac{3}{6}$$
$$= 3 + \frac{6}{6} + \frac{3}{6}$$
$$= 3 + \frac{9}{6}$$
$$= 3\frac{9}{6}$$

Remember to write your answer in simplest form!

- Subtract the fractions. Subtract the whole numbers.

$$4\frac{1}{2} = 4\frac{3}{6} = 3\frac{9}{6}$$
$$-2\frac{5}{6} \qquad\quad = 2\frac{5}{6}$$
$$\overline{\qquad\qquad\qquad 1\frac{4}{6} = 1\frac{2}{3}}$$

Study this example.

$$18 \qquad 17\frac{4}{4}$$
$$-2\frac{1}{4} \qquad -2\frac{1}{4}$$
$$\overline{\qquad\quad 15\frac{3}{4}}$$

$$18 = 17 + 1$$
$$= 17 + \frac{4}{4}$$
$$= 17\frac{4}{4}$$

You cannot subtract a mixed number from 18. So, rename 18 as a mixed number.

PRACTICE

Rename each mixed number.

1. $4\frac{1}{6} = 3 + 1 + \frac{1}{6}$
$$= 3 + \frac{6}{6} + \frac{1}{6}$$
$$= 3\frac{?}{6}$$

2. $4\frac{2}{3} = 3 + 1 + \frac{2}{3}$
$$= 3 + \frac{?}{3} + \frac{2}{3}$$
$$= 3\frac{?}{3}$$

3. $6\frac{4}{9} = 5 + 1 + \frac{4}{9}$
$$= 5 + \frac{?}{9} + \frac{?}{9}$$
$$= 5\frac{?}{9}$$

Subtract. Rewrite the minuend if needed.

4. 4
$-1\dfrac{3}{8}$

5. $8\dfrac{1}{3}$
$-4\dfrac{5}{12}$

6. $7\dfrac{3}{4}$
$-2\dfrac{7}{8}$

7. $6\dfrac{1}{3}$
$-4\dfrac{4}{9}$

8. 9
$-2\dfrac{1}{6}$

9. $12\dfrac{1}{6}$
$-7\dfrac{7}{12}$

10. $5\dfrac{2}{9}$
$-2\dfrac{1}{3}$

11. $10\dfrac{1}{6}$
$-6\dfrac{1}{4}$

12. $2\dfrac{3}{10}$
$-1\dfrac{2}{3}$

13. $8\dfrac{1}{4}$
$-2\dfrac{3}{5}$

14. $12\dfrac{1}{12}$
$-7\dfrac{1}{2}$

15. $13\dfrac{1}{10}$
$-10\dfrac{7}{15}$

16. $4 - 1\dfrac{1}{2}$

17. $6 - 2\dfrac{2}{3}$

18. $10\dfrac{3}{10} - 4\dfrac{3}{5}$

19. $8\dfrac{1}{3} - 3\dfrac{7}{15}$

20. $9\dfrac{1}{4} - 2\dfrac{3}{7}$

21. $12\dfrac{1}{4} - 8\dfrac{2}{3}$

22. $5\dfrac{1}{4} - 2\dfrac{5}{6}$

23. $6\dfrac{1}{9} - 4\dfrac{1}{2}$

24. I am a number. I am $1\dfrac{5}{7}$ less than $3\dfrac{1}{2}$. What number am I?

25. The number $7\dfrac{3}{8}$ is how much greater than $5\dfrac{2}{3}$?

Problem Solving

26. Ashlyn places a rock into a cylinder of water. How can she use the measurements to find the volume of the rock? What is the volume of the rock?

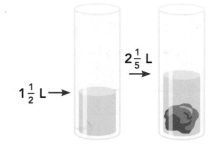

27. Jeffrey buys an 8-foot piece of wood. He cuts off $1\dfrac{2}{3}$-foot pieces to make shelves. How many shelves can he cut? How long is the left over piece of wood?

28. Write a problem that requires renaming the minuend. Explain how you found your numbers.

29. Describe one way to check your answer to a subtraction problem.

Write About It

30. Conrad states that $8 - 3\dfrac{7}{12} = 5\dfrac{5}{12}$. What mistake does he make when subtracting? Determine the correct difference and explain your reasoning.

Problem Solving
Write and Solve An Equation

Objective
- Focus on writing and solving equations to solve problems.

Math Word
equation

On Tuesday, Sadie runs $4\frac{3}{8}$ miles and Violet runs $3\frac{7}{8}$ miles. The next day Sadie runs $3\frac{3}{4}$ miles and Violet runs $4\frac{1}{2}$ miles. Who runs farther on those two days? How much farther?

Read the problem again to organize the information.

- Sadie runs a total of $4\frac{3}{8} + 3\frac{3}{4}$ miles.
- Violet runs a total of $3\frac{7}{8} + 4\frac{1}{2}$ miles.

Make and use a plan.

- First find the total distance that each girl runs.

$$\text{Sadie:} \quad 4\frac{3}{8} \qquad 4\frac{3}{8}$$
$$+3\frac{3}{4} \rightarrow +3\frac{6}{8}$$
$$\overline{\qquad\qquad 7\frac{9}{8} = 8\frac{1}{8}}$$

$$\text{Violet:} \quad 3\frac{7}{8} \qquad 3\frac{7}{8}$$
$$+4\frac{1}{2} \rightarrow +4\frac{4}{8}$$
$$\overline{\qquad\qquad 7\frac{11}{8} = 8\frac{3}{8}}$$

- Then write an equation. Let d represent the difference.

$$d = 8\frac{3}{8} - 8\frac{1}{8}$$
$$d = \frac{2}{8} = \frac{1}{4}$$

- Answer the question.

  Violet runs $\frac{1}{4}$ mile farther than Sadie.

Look back. Check by using addition.

$$\frac{1}{4} \qquad \frac{2}{8}$$
$$+8\frac{1}{8} \rightarrow +8\frac{1}{8}$$
$$\overline{\qquad\qquad = 8\frac{3}{8}} \checkmark \leftarrow \boxed{\text{The subtraction is correct.}}$$

PRACTICE

1. Ms. Ramirez is baking bread, a pie, and muffins today. She uses $4\frac{3}{4}$ cups flour for the bread, $2\frac{1}{2}$ cups flour for the pie, and $1\frac{2}{3}$ cups flour for the muffins. How much more flour does she use for the bread than for the pie and muffins together? Use an equation to help you.

2. Ivy times her practice runs for the 100-meter dash. Her last 3 times are $14\frac{1}{2}$, $13\frac{3}{4}$, and $12\frac{1}{4}$ seconds. Which of these times is the fastest? How much faster is the fastest time than the slowest time? Write an equation.

3. Hector and Jesse both are at the gym today. Hector goes to the gym every fifth day and Jesse goes every third day. In how many days are they both at the gym again on the same day? What strategy helps you to solve this problem?

4. Lucy and Ruby each evaluate the expression shown.

$$(12 + 1) \times 2 - 12 \div 2$$

Lucy gets 7 and Ruby gets 20. Which girl evaluates the expression correctly? Explain the error in the other girl's calculation.

Adam and Jorge hike in a wilderness area. The table shows information for some trails they use. Some trails are flat and easier to hike, while others are steep or have obstacles that require more time. Use the table for Exercises 5–8.

Hiking Trail	Distance (mi)	Usual Time (h)
Spruce	$10\frac{5}{8}$	$4\frac{3}{4}$
Meadow	$18\frac{3}{8}$	$6\frac{1}{4}$
Lake	$16\frac{1}{2}$	$5\frac{1}{2}$
Hilltop	$9\frac{3}{4}$	$3\frac{1}{4}$
Canyon	$6\frac{7}{8}$	$10\frac{3}{4}$

5. On Monday they hike the Meadow Trail. On Wednesday they hike the Hilltop and Canyon trails. On which day do they cover more distance? How much more? Write an equation.

6. What is the total distance of the Hilltop, Spruce, and Lake trails? What is the usual time it takes to hike those trails?

7. Adam and Jorge will have about $14\frac{1}{2}$ hours of daylight. They do not have headlamps to hike in the dark. Why should they not consider hiking the Spruce and Canyon trails on the same day?

8. Write your own question that uses the data in the table. Then write an equation to show the solution.

Write About It

9. How does writing and solving an equation help you to solve problems involving addition or subtraction?

Use the model to subtract. Express the answer in simplest form.

1. $\frac{3}{4} - \frac{7}{12}$

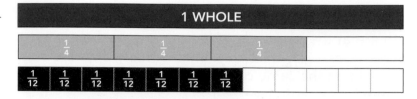

2. $\frac{4}{5} - \frac{3}{10}$

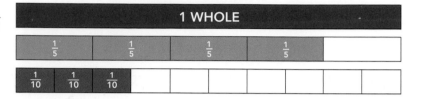

3. $3\frac{1}{2} - 2$

4. $1\frac{7}{8} - 1\frac{1}{4}$

Find the difference. Use benchmark fractions to check whether your answer is reasonable.

5. $\frac{5}{8} - \frac{1}{2}$

6. $\frac{11}{12} - \frac{3}{4}$

7. $\frac{7}{9} - \frac{1}{3}$

8. $\frac{4}{5} - \frac{4}{15}$

9. $\frac{1}{4} - \frac{1}{5}$

10. $\frac{11}{16}$
$-\frac{1}{2}$

11. $\frac{9}{14}$
$-\frac{3}{7}$

12. $\frac{3}{4}$
$-\frac{3}{8}$

13. $\frac{4}{9}$
$-\frac{1}{15}$

14. $\frac{6}{7}$
$-\frac{1}{3}$

Estimate the difference. Use rounding or front-end estimation.

15. $4\frac{2}{5}$
$-3\frac{1}{10}$

16. $6\frac{5}{7}$
$-2\frac{1}{3}$

17. $12\frac{8}{13}$
$-5\frac{6}{11}$

18. $4\frac{3}{5}$
$-1\frac{2}{9}$

19. $7\frac{1}{8}$
$-6\frac{9}{11}$

20. $21\frac{1}{2}$
$-8\frac{4}{7}$

Use estimation to determine if the answer is reasonable. Write Yes or No.

21. $\frac{9}{10}$
$-\frac{2}{5}$
$\frac{1}{2}$

22. $\frac{7}{10}$
$-\frac{7}{12}$
$\frac{37}{60}$

23. $4\frac{3}{4}$
$-\frac{7}{8}$
$2\frac{7}{8}$

24. $9\frac{3}{8}$
$-2\frac{5}{16}$
$7\frac{1}{16}$

25. $6\frac{2}{5}$
$-1\frac{8}{15}$
$4\frac{13}{15}$

26. $5\frac{6}{7}$
$-3\frac{2}{3}$
$2\frac{17}{21}$

Find each difference.

27. $7\frac{2}{3} - \frac{1}{3}$ **28.** $9\frac{4}{5} - 7\frac{1}{2}$ **29.** $4\frac{1}{3} - 2\frac{3}{4}$ **30.** $5\frac{7}{8} - 5\frac{1}{4}$ **31.** $12\frac{3}{8} - 9$

32. $\quad 7\frac{6}{7}$ **33.** $\quad 8\frac{3}{4}$ **34.** $\quad 6\frac{3}{8}$ **35.** $\quad 11\frac{2}{5}$ **36.** $\quad 11\frac{5}{6}$
$\quad \underline{-\ 6\quad}$ $\quad \underline{-\ \ \frac{1}{8}}$ $\quad \underline{-\ 5\frac{1}{4}}$ $\quad \underline{-\ 9\frac{9}{10}}$ $\quad \underline{-\ \ \frac{5}{8}}$

37. $\quad 20\frac{9}{10}$ **38.** $\quad 8$ **39.** $\quad 14\frac{2}{9}$ **40.** $\quad 10\frac{1}{5}$ **41.** $\quad 13\frac{3}{10}$
$\quad \underline{-\ 15\frac{1}{2}}$ $\quad \underline{-\ 5\frac{6}{7}}$ $\quad \underline{-\ 8\quad}$ $\quad \underline{-\ 4\frac{3}{4}}$ $\quad \underline{-\ 10\frac{5}{6}}$

Problem Solving

Use the table for Exercises 42–44.

42. On average, how much more does a hippopotamus weigh than a giraffe?

43. On average, how much more does an African elephant weigh than a walrus?

44. The average weight of a baby giraffe is $\frac{1}{10}$ ton. About how much more does an adult giraffe weigh than a baby giraffe?

Animal	Average Adult Weight (tons)
Hippopotamus	$2\frac{3}{10}$
Giraffe	$1\frac{1}{4}$
African Elephant	$5\frac{2}{5}$
Walrus	$1\frac{11}{20}$

45. Sebastian draws a model to find the difference $3\frac{3}{8} - 1\frac{1}{4}$. He says the difference is $1\frac{1}{4}$. Identify Sebastian's error and correct the model. Then find the correct difference.

A bulletin board has a length of $5\frac{1}{2}$ feet and a width of $3\frac{1}{4}$ feet. Use this information to answer Exercises 46–47.

46. How much greater is the length of the board than its width?

47. Three sheets of the paper are used to cover the bulletin board. Each sheet of paper measures $2\frac{1}{5}$ feet by $3\frac{1}{4}$ feet. By how much does the last piece of paper exceed the length of the board?

A woodworker is building a sandbox according to the specifications in this drawing. The sandbox will be created from three different sized boards: A, B, and C. He will need two pieces of each board to build the sandbox. Each board is 2 inches thick.

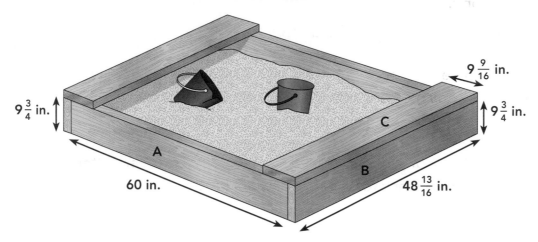

1. Copy and complete the table with the required dimensions of each board.

Board	Length (in.)	Width (in.)	Thickness (in.)
A	?	?	2
B	?	?	2
C	?	?	2

Compare the length, width, and depth of each board. Copy and complete the following statements.

2. Boards __?__ and __?__ have the same __?__ . They are about 1 foot shorter than Board __?__ . The exact difference is __?__ inches.

3. Boards __?__ and __?__ have the same width. They are slightly wider than Board __?__ . The exact difference is __?__ .

4. All three boards have the same __?__ .

The woodworker has some leftover 2 by 10 boards that he wants to use to build the sandbox. These boards have a thickness of 2 inches, a width of 10 inches, and varying lengths. He will use a wood planer to trim the boards to the exact dimensions needed.

BOARD A

The length of the 2 by 10 board that the woodworker will use for board A is 60 inches long.

5. How does this board need to be trimmed?

6. The woodworker's planer can be set to cut $\frac{1}{8}$ inch or $\frac{1}{16}$ inch deep, so he will need to plane the wood more than once. Which depth setting requires fewer passes?

7. Using a cut depth of $\frac{1}{8}$ inch, determine the width of the board after the first pass. How many total passes are needed?

BOARD B

The length of the 2 by 10 board that the woodworker will use for board B is 49 inches long.

8. How does this board need to be trimmed?

9. The woodworker's planer can be set to cut $\frac{1}{8}$ inch or $\frac{1}{16}$ inch deep. Explain how he can use these cut depths to plane the wood to the correct length in two passes.

10. Explain how he can use the available cut depths to plane the wood to the correct length and width in three passes for each dimension.

BOARD C

The length of the 2 by 10 board that the woodworker will use for board C is 49 inches long. The woodworker wants to trim this board to the required dimensions with the wood planer.

11. Draw a diagram of board C that shows the passes required. Indicate the following for each side:
    - existing and desired dimensions
    - number of passes needed
    - cut depth of each pass
    - dimension after each pass

Determine the best answer for each problem.

1. What fraction is shown by the model?

| $\frac{1}{8}$ | $\frac{1}{8}$ | $\frac{1}{8}$ | $\frac{1}{8}$ | $\frac{1}{8}$ | $\frac{1}{8}$ | $\frac{1}{8}$ | $\frac{1}{8}$ |

A. $\frac{1}{8}$ B. $\frac{3}{4}$

C. $\frac{1}{2}$ D. $\frac{5}{8}$

2. Simplify the expression.

$$\frac{1}{4} - \frac{1}{12} - \frac{1}{12}$$

A. $\frac{1}{6}$ B. $\frac{1}{8}$

C. $\frac{1}{12}$ D. $\frac{1}{24}$

3. Identify the greatest common factor of 144 and 148.

A. 2   B. 3
C. 4   D. 8

4. How much longer is the rectangle than it is wide?

$1\frac{5}{6}$ in.

$2\frac{7}{10}$ in.

A. $\frac{2}{15}$ in.   B. $\frac{13}{15}$ in.

C. $1\frac{2}{15}$ in.   D. $1\frac{13}{15}$ in.

5. Select the fractions that are closer to $\frac{1}{2}$ than 0 or 1. Select all that apply.

A. $\frac{2}{3}$ B. $\frac{4}{9}$

C. $\frac{9}{11}$ D. $\frac{1}{8}$

E. $\frac{12}{11}$

6. Simplify. Select all equivalent fractions.

$$\frac{2 \times 8}{4 \times 5}$$

A. $\frac{10}{9}$ B. $\frac{8}{10}$

C. $\frac{4}{5}$ D. $\frac{16}{20}$

E. $\frac{1}{2}$

7. The width of a rectangle is $\frac{1}{2}$ foot shorter than its length. If the length of the rectangle is $\frac{4}{7}$ foot, what expression represents the area of the rectangle?

A. $\frac{4}{7} \times \frac{1}{2}$ B. $\frac{4}{7} \times 1\frac{1}{14}$

C. $\frac{1}{2} \times \frac{1}{14}$ D. $\frac{4}{7} \times \frac{1}{14}$

8. Which best describes the model?

A. 3 groups of $\frac{2}{3}$ B. 4 groups of $\frac{1}{3}$

C. 4 groups of $\frac{2}{3}$ D. 3 groups of $\frac{1}{3}$

Fractions: Multiplication

Car manufacturers commonly use clay models to design cars. These models show how light will interact with a car's surface. The clay model is created at a fraction of the size of the car once it is manufactured. For instance, the clay model may be $\frac{1}{4}$ or $\frac{1}{10}$ the size of the actual car.

How Does the Design Process Work?

◆ Designers sketch illustrations of the car. The top illustrations are turned into clay models.

◆ The base of a clay model is foam and steel. Clay is poured on top of the base.

◆ A milling machine molds the clay into a form that is similar to the model being created.

◆ Sculptors create detailed models of the cars using steel and wooden tools.

◆ A stretchy metallic film is applied to mimic how the car will appear in daylight.

◆ 3D models of mirrors, handles, etc. are applied.

◆ The design of the car is continually refined using the clay model. The design process can take up to 2 years!

Model Multiplying Fractions

Objective
- Use models to multiply a whole number or fraction by a fraction.

Math Words

equal parts

product

Dehlia has 4 bird feeders in her yard. She fills each of them with $\frac{2}{3}$ pound of birdseed. Some birds eat $\frac{1}{4}$ of the birdseed from one of the feeders. How many pounds of birdseed does Dehlia use to fill all the feeders? How many pounds of birdseed do the birds eat?

To write $\frac{8}{3}$ as a mixed number, divide 8 by 3. The remainder 2 is the numerator of the fraction part of the mixed number.

◆ To find the total pounds of birdseed, find $4 \times \frac{2}{3}$.

You can think of $4 \times \frac{2}{3}$ as 4 groups of $\frac{2}{3}$.

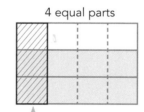

There are $4 \times 2 = 8$ thirds shaded.

▷ Dehlia uses $\frac{8}{3}$, or $2\frac{2}{3}$, pounds of birdseed.

◆ To find the amount of birdseed the birds eat, find $\frac{1}{4} \times \frac{2}{3}$.

Model $\frac{2}{3}$.	Separate $\frac{2}{3}$ into 4 equal parts.	Find 1 of the 4 equal parts.
3 equal parts	4 equal parts	4 equal parts

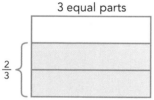

2 out of 12 are double-shaded.

▷ The birds eat $\frac{2}{12}$, or $\frac{1}{6}$, pound of birdseed.

PRACTICE

Use the models to find the value of n.

1. $\frac{2}{4} \times \frac{1}{2} = n$

2. $\frac{1}{3} \times \frac{3}{4} = n$

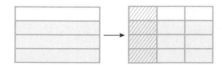

Write a multiplication sentence for the model.

3.  4. 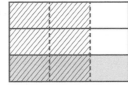 5.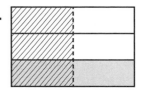

6.

Use a model to multiply.

7. $\dfrac{4}{5} \times \dfrac{1}{3}$ 8. $4 \times \dfrac{3}{8}$ 9. $\dfrac{1}{5} \times \dfrac{2}{3}$

10. $6 \times \dfrac{1}{4}$ 11. $\dfrac{2}{3} \times \dfrac{4}{5}$ 12. $\dfrac{3}{4} \times \dfrac{1}{2}$

Find the model that matches the problem. Then find the product.

A. 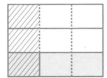 B.  C. 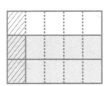 D.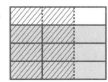

13. $\dfrac{2}{3} \times \dfrac{1}{5}$ 14. $3 \times \dfrac{1}{3}$ 15. $\dfrac{1}{3} \times \dfrac{1}{3}$ 16. $\dfrac{2}{3} \times \dfrac{3}{4}$

Problem Solving

17. Can the product of a nonzero whole number and a fraction less than 1 be greater than or less than 1? Explain using models.

18. A bucket holds $\dfrac{3}{4}$ gallon of water. The bucket is $\dfrac{2}{3}$ full. Explain in words how a student could draw a model to help determine the amount of water in the bucket.

Write About It

19. Write a real-world problem that you could solve using the model shown. Then solve your problem.

Multiply Fractions by Fractions

Objective
- Multiply fractions by fractions.

Math Words
multiply
numerator
denominator

One third of the avocados at the grocery store are not yet ripe. One half of these will be ripe by the end of the week. What fraction of the avocados will be ripe by the end of the week?

Solve the equation $\frac{1}{2} \times \frac{1}{3} = b$.

To multiply a fraction by a fraction:

- Multiply the numerators.
- Multiply the denominators.
- Write the product in simplest form.

$$\frac{1}{2} \times \frac{1}{3} = \frac{1 \times 1}{2 \times 3}$$

$$= \frac{1}{6}$$

▷ One sixth of the avocados will be ripe by the end of the week.

Study these examples.

$$\frac{2}{5} \text{ of } \frac{5}{6} = \frac{2}{5} \times \frac{5}{6}$$

$$= \frac{2 \times 5}{5 \times 6}$$

$$= \frac{10}{30} = \frac{1}{3}$$

Compare:

$$\frac{1}{3} \times \frac{1}{5} \; ? \; \frac{1}{3} \times \frac{1}{6}$$

$$\frac{1 \times 1}{3 \times 5} \; ? \; \frac{1 \times 1}{3 \times 6}$$

$$\frac{1}{15} > \frac{1}{18}$$

PRACTICE

Complete the multiplication.

1. $\frac{2}{3} \times \frac{4}{5} = \frac{2 \times ?}{3 \times ?}$

$= \frac{8}{?}$

2. $\frac{3}{5} \times \frac{1}{2} = \frac{? \times 1}{? \times 2}$

$= \frac{?}{10}$

3. $\frac{5}{7} \times \frac{1}{4} = \frac{? \times ?}{? \times ?}$

$= \frac{?}{?}$

4. $\frac{1}{4} \times \frac{2}{7} = \frac{1 \times ?}{4 \times ?}$

$= \frac{?}{?} = \frac{?}{?}$

5. $\frac{2}{10} \times \frac{7}{10} = \frac{? \times 7}{? \times 10}$

$= \frac{?}{?} = \frac{?}{?}$

6. $\frac{1}{8} \times \frac{4}{9} = \frac{? \times ?}{? \times ?}$

$= \frac{?}{?} = \frac{?}{?}$

Multiply.

7. $\frac{1}{3} \times \frac{1}{8}$

8. $\frac{1}{4} \times \frac{3}{5}$

9. $\frac{4}{5} \times \frac{1}{7}$

10. $\frac{1}{3} \times \frac{2}{9}$

11. $\frac{2}{7} \times \frac{1}{5}$

Find the product. Write in simplest form.

12. $\frac{7}{10} \times \frac{1}{3}$ **13.** $\frac{3}{4} \times \frac{3}{5}$ **14.** $\frac{3}{8} \times \frac{5}{7}$ **15.** $\frac{5}{6} \times \frac{2}{9}$ **16.** $\frac{3}{4} \times \frac{1}{10}$

17. $\frac{8}{9} \times \frac{1}{2}$ **18.** $\frac{4}{5} \times \frac{4}{5}$ **19.** $\frac{10}{11} \times \frac{2}{3}$ **20.** $\frac{6}{7} \times \frac{1}{4}$ **21.** $\frac{4}{9} \times \frac{3}{8}$

22. $\frac{3}{4}$ of $\frac{2}{9}$ **23.** $\frac{4}{5}$ of $\frac{4}{7}$ **24.** $\frac{3}{10}$ of $\frac{2}{5}$ **25.** $\frac{5}{8}$ of $\frac{4}{9}$ **26.** $\frac{3}{5}$ of $\frac{5}{7}$

Find the missing fraction. Check your work by multiplying.

27. $\frac{3}{4} \times n = \frac{5}{6} \times \frac{3}{4}$ **28.** $\frac{6}{7} \times \frac{1}{4} = p \times \frac{6}{7}$ **29.** $q \times \frac{2}{9} = \frac{2}{9} \times \frac{4}{5}$

30. $\frac{5}{7} \times n = \frac{5}{14}$ **31.** $k \times \frac{3}{5} = \frac{21}{40}$ **32.** $\frac{2}{5} \times q = \frac{1}{3}$

Problem Solving

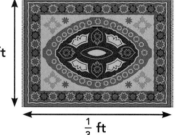

$\frac{1}{4}$ ft

$\frac{1}{3}$ ft

33. Robert makes two of the miniature rugs shown. What is the total area of the two rugs?

34. Danielle is sorting nails. She finds that $\frac{2}{3}$ of the nails are 2 inches long and $\frac{3}{4}$ of the 2-inch nails are made of steel. What fraction of the nails are 2 inches long and made of steel?

35. West Park is $\frac{3}{5}$ of an acre and $\frac{2}{3}$ of the park is covered in trees. East Park is $\frac{7}{8}$ of an acre and $\frac{1}{4}$ of the park is covered in trees. Which park has more land covered in trees?

For Exercises 36–38, use each of the digits 2, 3, 4, and 5 once. Find two fractions that will have a product *p* such that:

$$\frac{?}{?} \times \frac{?}{?} = P$$

36. *p* is as close to 1 as possible.

37. *p* is the greatest product possible.

38. *p* is the least product possible.

Write About It

39. Write a story that relates to the expression $\frac{1}{2} \times \frac{1}{4}$. Explain how the product is related to the story context.

Multiply Fractions and Whole Numbers

One day each week, Sierra's class runs $\frac{1}{4}$ mile in gym class. At the end of nine weeks, how many miles will Sierra's class have run?

I	2		5	6		9	
3	4		7	8			

To solve, find $9 \times \frac{1}{4}$.

To multiply a fraction and a whole number:

- Rename the whole number as a fraction with a denominator of 1.

- Multiply the numerators. Then, multiply the denominators.

- Write the product in simplest form.

$$9 \times \frac{1}{4} = \frac{9}{1} \times \frac{1}{4}$$

$$= \frac{9 \times 1}{1 \times 4}$$

$$= \frac{9}{4} = 2\frac{1}{4}$$

▷ Sierra's class runs $2\frac{1}{4}$ miles by the end of the nine weeks.

Study these examples.

$$5 \times \frac{4}{5} = \frac{5}{1} \times \frac{4}{5}$$

$$= \frac{5 \times 4}{1 \times 5}$$

$$= \frac{20}{5} = 4$$

$$7 \times \frac{5}{21} = \frac{7}{1} \times \frac{5}{21}$$

$$= \frac{7 \times 5}{1 \times 21}$$

$$= \frac{35}{21} = 1\frac{14}{21} = 1\frac{2}{3}$$

PRACTICE

Complete the multiplication.

1. $5 \times \frac{3}{16} = \frac{5}{?} \times \frac{3}{16}$

$\phantom{5 \times \frac{3}{16}} = \frac{15}{?}$

2. $2 \times \frac{2}{9} = \frac{?}{?} \times \frac{2}{9}$

$\phantom{2 \times \frac{2}{9}} = \frac{?}{?}$

3. $8 \times \frac{1}{6} = \frac{?}{?} \times \frac{1}{6}$

$\phantom{8 \times \frac{1}{6}} = \frac{?}{?} = \frac{?}{?} = ?\frac{?}{?}$

4. $6 \times \frac{3}{5} = \frac{?}{?} \times \frac{3}{5}$

$\phantom{6 \times \frac{3}{5}} = \frac{?}{?} = ?\frac{?}{?}$

5. $12 \times \frac{3}{4} = \frac{?}{?} \times \frac{3}{4}$

$\phantom{12 \times \frac{3}{4}} = \frac{?}{?} = ?$

6. $18 \times \frac{3}{10} = \frac{?}{?} \times \frac{3}{10}$

$\phantom{18 \times \frac{3}{10}} = \frac{?}{?} = ?\frac{?}{?} = ?\frac{?}{?}$

Find the product. Write your answer in simplest form.

7. $6 \times \frac{1}{8}$

8. $20 \times \frac{1}{4}$

9. $18 \times \frac{1}{6}$

10. $24 \times \frac{1}{3}$

Find the product. Write your answer in simplest form.

11. $22 \times \frac{1}{2}$

12. $30 \times \frac{1}{10}$

13. $0 \times \frac{1}{5}$

14. $15 \times \frac{2}{3}$

15. $2 \times \frac{3}{8}$

16. $10 \times \frac{3}{50}$

17. $2 \times \frac{3}{7}$

18. $2 \times \frac{4}{12}$

19. $40 \times \frac{7}{16}$

20. $15 \times \frac{4}{25}$

21. $\frac{2}{7}$ of $14

22. $\frac{3}{8}$ of $24

23. $\frac{4}{5}$ of $35

24. $\frac{5}{6}$ of $18

25. $\frac{3}{10}$ of 15

26. $\frac{2}{3}$ of 20

27. $\frac{5}{9}$ of 25

28. $\frac{4}{11}$ of 12

Find the missing fraction. Check your work by multiplying.

29. $4 \times n = \frac{8}{15}$

30. $7 \times n = \frac{7}{12}$

31. $9 \times n = 15$

32. $10 \times n = 6$

33. $4 \times n = 1\frac{5}{7}$

34. $6 \times n = 2\frac{1}{4}$

Compare. Write <, =, or >.

35. $8 \times \frac{3}{4}$? $9 \times \frac{2}{3}$

36. $4 \times \frac{1}{5}$? $5 \times \frac{3}{20}$

37. $12 \times \frac{5}{6}$? $15 \times \frac{1}{2}$

38. $3 \times \frac{7}{9}$? $4 \times \frac{2}{3}$

39. $10 \times \frac{2}{5}$? $20 \times \frac{1}{5}$

40. $6 \times \frac{2}{7}$? $4 \times \frac{2}{5}$

Problem Solving

41. Gabriel is in charge of watering the plants in the school garden. There are 12 tomato seedlings, and each tomato seedling needs $\frac{1}{4}$ cup of water. How many cups of water will Gabriel use if he waters all the seedlings 3 times? Write an equation and solve.

42. A piece of music has 7 quarter notes and 18 eighth notes. What is the equivalent number of whole notes in the piece of music? Explain.

♩ 1 whole note

♩♩♩♩ 4 quarter notes

♪♫♪ 8 eighth notes

43. Write a story that relates to the expression $24 \times \frac{1}{8}$. Explain how the product is related to the story context.

Write About It

44. The product of a nonzero whole number and a proper fraction is a whole number. How do the two whole numbers compare? What can you say about the factors of the original whole number?

Scaling Fractions

Objective
- Understand how the value of one factor affects the size of the product.

Math Words
factor
product

When you multiply two fractions, the product will be less than, equal to, or greater than the first factor.

What happens when $\frac{3}{4}$ is multiplied by another fraction?

Multiply $\frac{3}{4} \times \frac{1}{2}$.

When **one factor is less than 1**, the product is less than the other factor.

$$\frac{1}{2} < 1$$

So, the product is **less than** the first factor.

$$\frac{3}{4} \times \frac{1}{2} < \frac{3}{4}$$

Multiply $\frac{3}{4} \times \frac{2}{2}$.

When **one factor is equal to 1**, use the Identity Property of Multiplication.

$$\frac{2}{2} = 1 \text{ and } \frac{3}{4} \times 1 = \frac{3}{4}$$

So, the product is **equal to** the first factor.

$$\frac{3}{4} \times \frac{2}{2} = \frac{3}{4}$$

Multiply $\frac{3}{4} \times \frac{3}{2}$.

When **one factor is greater than 1**, the product is greater than the other factor.

$$\frac{3}{2} > 1$$

So, the product is **greater than** the first factor, $\frac{3}{4}$.

$$\frac{3}{4} \times \frac{3}{2} > \frac{3}{4}$$

You can also use a model to compare a product to a factor. Think of $\frac{3}{2}$ as $1 + \frac{1}{2}$.

 $\frac{1}{2}$ of $\frac{3}{4}$ is less than $\frac{3}{4}$.

 $\frac{2}{2}$, or 1, of $\frac{3}{4}$ is the same as $\frac{3}{4}$.

The models show that $\frac{3}{2}$ of $\frac{3}{4}$ is greater than $\frac{3}{4}$.

PRACTICE

Complete the comparison or sentence.

1. $\frac{1}{8} \times \frac{4}{4}$

$\frac{4}{4} \underline{\quad?\quad} 1$

The product is $\underline{\quad?\quad} \frac{1}{8}$.

2. $\frac{5}{6} \times \frac{1}{3}$

$\frac{1}{3} \underline{\quad?\quad} 1$

The product is $\underline{\quad?\quad} \frac{5}{6}$.

3. $\frac{2}{3} \times \frac{4}{3}$

$\frac{4}{3} \underline{\quad?\quad} 1$

The product is $\underline{\quad?\quad} \frac{2}{3}$.

4. $\frac{5}{9} \times \frac{5}{4}$

The product is $\underline{\quad?\quad} \frac{5}{9}$.

5. $\frac{7}{9} \times \frac{6}{6}$

The product is $\underline{\quad?\quad} \frac{7}{9}$.

6. $\frac{3}{4} \times \frac{7}{10}$

The product is $\underline{\quad?\quad} \frac{3}{4}$.

Determine if the product is less than, equal to, or greater than the first factor.

7. $\dfrac{1}{10} \times \dfrac{1}{2}$ **8.** $\dfrac{4}{7} \times \dfrac{3}{7}$ **9.** $\dfrac{6}{5} \times \dfrac{3}{3}$ **10.** $\dfrac{12}{15} \times \dfrac{8}{5}$ **11.** $\dfrac{4}{9} \times \dfrac{10}{10}$

12. $\dfrac{4}{3} \times \dfrac{1}{4}$ **13.** $\dfrac{1}{8} \times \dfrac{12}{7}$ **14.** $\dfrac{2}{9} \times \dfrac{5}{5}$ **15.** $\dfrac{10}{3} \times \dfrac{5}{2}$ **16.** $\dfrac{2}{5} \times \dfrac{7}{2}$

17. $\dfrac{3}{1}$ of $\dfrac{3}{2}$ **18.** $\dfrac{4}{9}$ of $\dfrac{5}{9}$ **19.** $\dfrac{7}{4}$ of $\dfrac{1}{8}$ **20.** $\dfrac{6}{1}$ of $\dfrac{4}{4}$ **21.** $\dfrac{7}{2}$ of $\dfrac{7}{2}$

22. $\dfrac{6}{11}$ of $\dfrac{5}{5}$ **23.** $\dfrac{2}{3}$ of $\dfrac{3}{5}$ **24.** $\dfrac{10}{7}$ of $\dfrac{9}{10}$ **25.** $\dfrac{3}{4}$ of $\dfrac{9}{5}$ **26.** $\dfrac{14}{25}$ of $\dfrac{12}{12}$

Write a fraction that makes a true statement.

27. $\dfrac{1}{2} \times \underline{\ ?\ } > \dfrac{1}{2}$ **28.** $\dfrac{1}{7} \times \underline{\ ?\ } = \dfrac{1}{7}$ **29.** $\dfrac{3}{3} \times \underline{\ ?\ } < \dfrac{3}{3}$ **30.** $\dfrac{5}{3} \times \underline{\ ?\ } = \dfrac{5}{3}$

31. $\dfrac{2}{11} \times \underline{\ ?\ } < \dfrac{2}{11}$ **32.** $\dfrac{8}{1} \times \underline{\ ?\ } > \dfrac{8}{1}$ **33.** $\dfrac{1}{4} \times \underline{\ ?\ } < \dfrac{1}{4}$ **34.** $\dfrac{9}{2} \times \underline{\ ?\ } < \dfrac{9}{2}$

Problem Solving

35. The product of $\dfrac{7}{5}$ and a number is less than 1. Which of the following could describe the number?

    A. proper fraction   **B.** whole number
    C. nonzero whole number   **D.** improper fraction

36. A recipe makes enough salad for 6 people. Suppose the amount of each ingredient is multiplied by $\dfrac{5}{4}$. Will there be less than 6 servings of salad, exactly 6 servings, or more than 6 servings? Explain.

37. How does the product of two proper fractions compare to either of the factors? Explain.

38. Janet multiplies a fraction by the same fraction, and then multiplies by the same fraction again, and continues in this way. If the product keeps getting smaller, how would you describe the fraction? Will the product eventually equal zero? Explain.

Write About It

39. Meghan studies the equation $\dfrac{8}{5} \times \dfrac{3}{4} = n$. She concludes that n is less than $\dfrac{8}{5}$ but greater than $\dfrac{3}{4}$. How does she know this?

Common Factors in Products

Objective
- Divide common factors.
  before multiplying fractions.

Math Words

simplify
greatest common
  factor

Tessa and Alivia are identifying rock samples based on their properties. There are 10 samples to analyze, and the girls will spend $\frac{1}{4}$ hour on each sample. How long will it take them to classify all of the samples?

You can simplify fractions before multiplying:

- Divide any numerator and denominator by their greatest common factor.

- Multiply the numerators. Then, multiply the denominators.

- Write the product in simplest form.

$$t = 10 \times \frac{1}{4}$$

$$= \frac{10}{1} \times \frac{1}{4} = \frac{10 \times 1}{1 \times 4}$$

$$= \frac{\overset{5}{\cancel{10}} \times 1}{1 \times \underset{2}{\cancel{4}}} = \frac{5 \times 1}{1 \times 2}$$

$$= \frac{5}{2} = 2\frac{1}{2}$$

▶ Tessa and Alivia will spend $2\frac{1}{2}$ hours classifying the 10 samples.

Study these examples.

$$49 \times \frac{5}{14} = \frac{49}{1} \times \frac{5}{14}$$

$$= \frac{\overset{7}{\cancel{49}} \times 5}{1 \times \underset{2}{\cancel{14}}} = \frac{35}{2} = 17\frac{1}{2}$$

$$\frac{3}{10} \times 5 \times \frac{2}{3} = \frac{3}{10} \times \frac{5}{1} \times \frac{2}{3}$$

$$= \frac{\overset{1}{\cancel{3}}}{\underset{2}{\cancel{10}}} \times \frac{\overset{1}{\cancel{5}}}{1} \times \frac{2}{\underset{1}{\cancel{3}}} = \frac{2}{2} = 1$$

PRACTICE

Simplify the factors, if possible. Then write the product in simplest form.

1. $\frac{4}{7} \times \frac{35}{36} = \frac{\overset{1}{\cancel{4}}}{\underset{?}{\cancel{7}}} \times \frac{\overset{5}{\cancel{35}}}{\underset{?}{\cancel{36}}} = ?$

2. $\frac{3}{8} \times 16 = \frac{3}{\underset{?}{\cancel{8}}} \times \frac{\overset{?}{\cancel{16}}}{?} = ?$

3. $\frac{4}{7} \times \frac{1}{4}$

4. $\frac{1}{5} \times \frac{10}{13}$

5. $\frac{8}{9} \times \frac{3}{7}$

6. $\frac{2}{5} \times \frac{3}{8}$

7. $12 \times \frac{3}{4}$

8. $\frac{5}{8} \times 24$

9. $\frac{15}{16} \times 8$

10. $33 \times \frac{3}{22}$

11. $\frac{2}{15} \times \frac{5}{8}$

12. $\frac{12}{15} \times \frac{3}{8}$

13. $\frac{10}{21} \times \frac{14}{25}$

14. $\frac{30}{45} \times \frac{15}{20}$

Write the product in simplest form.

15. $\frac{1}{2} \times \frac{2}{3}$

16. $\frac{1}{4} \times \frac{2}{7}$

17. $\frac{2}{9} \times \frac{1}{6}$

18. $\frac{3}{4} \times \frac{1}{9}$

19. $\frac{4}{9} \times \frac{3}{5}$

20. $32 \times \frac{5}{6}$

21. $33 \times \frac{4}{11}$

22. $35 \times \frac{5}{42}$

23. $24 \times \frac{3}{8}$

24. $25 \times \frac{2}{15}$

25. $\frac{3}{10} \times \frac{25}{27}$

26. $\frac{8}{27} \times \frac{9}{20}$

27. $\frac{9}{14} \times \frac{7}{15}$

28. $\frac{7}{8} \times \frac{6}{21}$

29. $\frac{2}{9} \times \frac{21}{26}$

30. $14 \times \frac{3}{7}$

31. $\frac{3}{19} \times 30$

32. $\frac{3}{4} \times 18$

33. $8 \times \frac{5}{12} \times \frac{3}{10}$

34. $\frac{4}{9} \times \frac{5}{36} \times \frac{3}{20}$

35. $\frac{1}{8} \times 4 \times \frac{2}{3}$

36. $\frac{6}{7} \times \frac{1}{2} \times \frac{14}{15}$

37. $3 \times \frac{2}{9} \times \frac{27}{30}$

38. $\frac{9}{14} \times \frac{7}{12} \times 2$

Find the missing numbers to complete the equation.

39. $\frac{2}{9} \times \frac{?}{?} = \frac{1}{6}$

40. $\frac{?}{?} \times \frac{5}{8} = \frac{1}{12}$

41. $\frac{15}{?} \times \frac{?}{10} = \frac{21}{32}$

42. $\frac{5}{?} \times \frac{?}{20} = \frac{1}{8}$

43. $\frac{15}{24} \times \frac{?}{?} = \frac{3}{8}$

44. $\frac{?}{10} \times \frac{15}{?} = \frac{9}{20}$

45. $\frac{?}{4} \times \frac{8}{?} = \frac{2}{11}$

46. $\frac{8}{?} \times \frac{?}{10} = \frac{1}{3}$

Problem Solving

There are 24 people in Nylah's class. The graph shows how they get to school. Use this information and graph for Exercises 47–49.

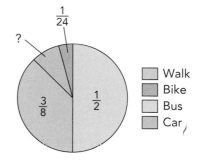

47. What fraction of the students gets to school by car?

48. How many students in Nylah's class walk to school? Explain how to find the answer.

49. Of the students who take the bus, $\frac{2}{3}$ of them live 4 or more miles from school. How many students who take the bus live less than 4 miles from school?

50. Find three fractions that, when multiplied by $\frac{5}{6}$, have a product of $\frac{1}{3}$.

Write About It

51. Jack wants to simplify the expression $\frac{4}{21} \times \left(\frac{7}{8} + \frac{3}{2}\right)$. He uses common factors and writes $\frac{1}{3} \times \left(\frac{1}{2} + \frac{3}{2}\right)$. What error did Jack make?

Use the model to find the product.

1. $\frac{2}{5} \times \frac{2}{3}$

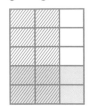

   A. $\frac{2}{15}$ **B.** $\frac{4}{15}$

   C. $\frac{2}{5}$ **D.** $\frac{2}{3}$

2. $\frac{3}{4} \times \frac{1}{6}$

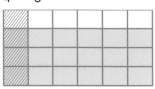

   A. $\frac{1}{8}$ **B.** $\frac{1}{4}$

   C. $\frac{5}{8}$ **D.** $\frac{3}{4}$

3. $\frac{5}{6} \times \frac{1}{2}$

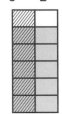

   A. $\frac{1}{6}$ **B.** $\frac{1}{5}$

   C. $\frac{5}{12}$ **D.** $\frac{5}{6}$

Find the product.

4. $\frac{1}{6} \times \frac{4}{5}$ **5.** $8 \times \frac{1}{4}$ **6.** $\frac{2}{7} \times \frac{1}{2}$ **7.** $\frac{5}{8} \times \frac{2}{3}$ **8.** $12 \times \frac{5}{8}$ **9.** $\frac{6}{7} \times \frac{1}{3}$

10. $7 \times \frac{5}{7}$ **11.** $\frac{3}{5} \times \frac{1}{9}$ **12.** $9 \times \frac{1}{10}$ **13.** $\frac{3}{4} \times \frac{4}{7}$ **14.** $15 \times \frac{2}{30}$ **15.** $12 \times \frac{3}{5}$

16. $\frac{6}{11} \times \frac{3}{4}$ **17.** $\frac{3}{10} \times \frac{15}{23}$ **18.** $\frac{4}{7} \times \frac{7}{8}$ **19.** $\frac{4}{5} \times \frac{10}{12}$ **20.** $\frac{7}{9} \times \frac{18}{35}$ **21.** $\frac{2}{5} \times \frac{20}{21}$

22. $16 \times \frac{1}{4}$ **23.** $5 \times \frac{3}{10}$ **24.** $\frac{5}{6} \times 12$

25. $\frac{1}{3} \times 4 \times \frac{3}{8}$ **26.** $\frac{5}{8} \times \frac{3}{10} \times \frac{12}{13}$ **27.** $\frac{1}{2} \times \frac{3}{4} \times \frac{5}{6}$

Identify the expression that simplifies the fractions completely.

28. $\frac{1}{8} \times \frac{4}{9}$ **A.** $\frac{1}{8} \times \frac{1}{9}$ **B.** $\frac{1}{4} \times \frac{2}{9}$ **C.** $\frac{1}{2} \times \frac{4}{9}$ **D.** $\frac{1}{2} \times \frac{1}{9}$

29. $12 \times \frac{5}{6}$ **A.** $2 \times \frac{5}{1}$ **B.** $6 \times \frac{5}{1}$ **C.** $2 \times \frac{5}{6}$ **D.** $12 \times \frac{5}{1}$

30. $\frac{3}{10} \times \frac{1}{3}$ **A.** $\frac{3}{1} \times \frac{1}{3}$ **B.** $\frac{1}{10} \times \frac{1}{3}$ **C.** $\frac{1}{10} \times \frac{1}{1}$ **D.** $\frac{3}{10} \times \frac{1}{1}$

31. $\frac{21}{32} \times \frac{4}{7}$ **A.** $\frac{21}{8} \times \frac{1}{7}$ **B.** $\frac{3}{16} \times \frac{2}{1}$ **C.** $\frac{3}{8} \times \frac{1}{1}$ **D.** $\frac{3}{32} \times \frac{4}{1}$

32. $25 \times \frac{8}{25}$ **A.** $25 \times \frac{8}{1}$ **B.** $5 \times \frac{8}{5}$ **C.** $1 \times \frac{8}{25}$ **D.** $1 \times \frac{8}{1}$

Decide if the product will be less than, equal to, or greater than the first factor.

A. less than   **B.** equal to   **C.** greater than

33. $\frac{2}{3} \times \frac{9}{9}$ **34.** $\frac{1}{5} \times \frac{3}{2}$ **35.** $\frac{3}{3} \times \frac{1}{8}$ **36.** $\frac{5}{9} \times \frac{3}{4}$ **37.** $\frac{4}{1} \times \frac{10}{10}$

38. $\frac{4}{3} \times \frac{5}{4}$ **39.** $\frac{7}{4} \times \frac{1}{7}$ **40.** $\frac{8}{5} \times \frac{3}{3}$ **41.** $\frac{12}{7} \times \frac{12}{7}$ **42.** $\frac{9}{11} \times \frac{9}{11}$

Select all the fractions that make the statement true.

43. $\frac{1}{5} \times \underline{\ ?\ } > \frac{1}{5}$ **A.** $\frac{4}{4}$ **B.** $\frac{2}{3}$ **C.** $\frac{8}{5}$ **D.** $\frac{4}{1}$

44. $\frac{3}{8} \times \underline{\ ?\ } < \frac{3}{8}$ **A.** $\frac{1}{9}$ **B.** $\frac{6}{6}$ **C.** $\frac{8}{3}$ **D.** $\frac{3}{8}$

45. $\frac{4}{7} \times \underline{\ ?\ } = \frac{4}{7}$ **A.** $\frac{4}{7}$ **B.** $\frac{1}{1}$ **C.** $\frac{7}{7}$ **D.** $\frac{7}{4}$

46. $\frac{12}{7} \times \underline{\ ?\ } > \frac{12}{7}$ **A.** $\frac{7}{7}$ **B.** $\frac{1}{7}$ **C.** $\frac{1}{12}$ **D.** $\frac{12}{7}$

47. $\frac{3}{2} \times \underline{\ ?\ } < \frac{3}{2}$ **A.** $\frac{1}{4}$ **B.** $\frac{2}{1}$ **C.** $\frac{3}{3}$ **D.** $\frac{3}{2}$

Problem Solving

The table shows how much college students use each device when completing schoolwork that requires Internet access. Use the table for Exercises 48–49.

Device	Usage
Smartphone	$\frac{2}{5}$
Tablet	$\frac{1}{4}$
Computer	$\frac{7}{20}$

48. Suppose a student typically spends 4 hours per week using a device to complete schoolwork. How many schoolwork hours does a student spend on each device in 1 week?

49. Suppose a student typically spends $\frac{5}{2}$ hours each week doing research on the Internet. How much research time does a student spend on each device in 1 week?

50. Caden practices guitar for $\frac{5}{6}$ hour. Micah practices for $\frac{5}{3}$ hour. Does Micah spend half as much time practicing as Caden? Explain.

51. Two fractions are multiplied, and the product is less than 1. Can one of the fractions be greater than 1? Explain.

Rename Mixed Numbers as Fractions

Objective
- Rename mixed numbers as improper fractions.

Math Words
mixed number
improper fraction

Peyton runs $2\frac{5}{6}$ miles. What is another way to express how many miles Peyton runs?

A mixed number includes a whole number part and a fraction part. Any mixed number can be rewritten as an improper fraction.

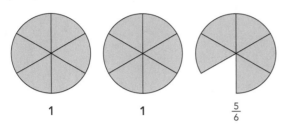

| 1 | 1 | $\frac{5}{6}$ |

There are 6 sixths in 1 whole. You can use the model to count the total number of sixths: $6 + 6 + 5 = 17$ sixths, or $\frac{17}{6}$.

Rename $2\frac{5}{6}$ as an improper fraction.

$2\frac{5}{6}$

$6 \times 2 = 12$ • Multiply the whole number by the denominator.

$12 + 5 = 17$ • Add the product to the numerator.

$\frac{17}{6}$ • Write the sum as the numerator. Keep the denominator.

Peyton runs $\frac{17}{6}$ miles.

PRACTICE

Rename as an improper fraction.

1. $2\frac{1}{4} = \frac{(4 \times ?) + ?}{4}$

$= \frac{?}{4}$

2. $6\frac{3}{7} = \frac{(7 \times ?) + ?}{7}$

$= \frac{?}{7}$

3. $1\frac{2}{3} = \frac{(3 \times ?) + ?}{3}$

$= \frac{?}{3}$

4. $3\frac{3}{5} = \frac{(? \times 3) + ?}{?}$

$= \frac{?}{?}$

5. $9\frac{1}{2} = \frac{(? \times 9) + ?}{?}$

$= \frac{?}{?}$

6. $5\frac{1}{6} = \frac{(? \times 5) + ?}{?}$

$= \frac{?}{?}$

7. $8\frac{1}{5} = \frac{(? \times ?) + ?}{?}$

$= \frac{?}{?}$

8. $4\frac{3}{7} = \frac{(? \times ?) + ?}{?}$

$= \frac{?}{?}$

9. $7\frac{3}{4} = \frac{(? \times ?) + ?}{?}$

$= \frac{?}{?}$

Identify the improper fraction shown by the model.

10.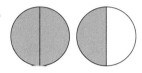

11.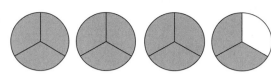

12.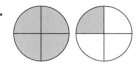

13.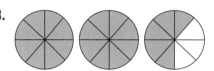

Rename as an improper fraction.

14. $10\frac{2}{5}$

15. $6\frac{7}{10}$

16. $8\frac{2}{3}$

17. $7\frac{4}{11}$

18. $2\frac{4}{7}$

19. $5\frac{2}{9}$

20. $15\frac{1}{4}$

21. $4\frac{2}{17}$

22. $3\frac{7}{25}$

23. $7\frac{5}{21}$

24. $4\frac{5}{12}$

25. $12\frac{1}{6}$

26. $2\frac{7}{10}$

27. $12\frac{4}{7}$

28. $11\frac{9}{14}$

29. $6\frac{3}{11}$

Problem Solving

Use the tablet for Exercises 30–31.

30. Rename the length and width as improper fractions.

31. How many inches longer is the tablet than it is wide? Express your answer as an improper fraction in simplest form.

length = $9\frac{1}{2}$ in.

width = $7\frac{3}{10}$ in.

32. An improper fraction has a denominator of 8 and simplifies to $3\frac{1}{2}$. What is the improper fraction?

Write About It

33. When renaming to subtract fractions, Seamus writes the mixed number $10\frac{8}{5}$. Does the method described in this lesson change this fraction into an equivalent improper fraction? Justify your answer.

Estimate Products with Mixed Numbers

Objective
- Use rounding and compatible numbers to estimate products of mixed numbers.

Math Words
round
mixed number
compatible numbers

Hector uses $16\frac{1}{4}$ pounds of cement to make a batch of mortar. He makes a second batch with $\frac{2}{3}$ as much cement. About how many pounds of cement does Hector use in the second batch of mortar?

You can use strategies to estimate the product $\frac{2}{3} \times 16\frac{1}{4}$.

◆ Use rounding.

- Round each factor to the nearest whole number. Compare the fractions to $\frac{1}{2}$.

    $\frac{2}{3} \longrightarrow \frac{2}{3} > \frac{1}{2}$, so $\frac{2}{3}$ rounds to 1.

    $16\frac{1}{4} \longrightarrow \frac{1}{4} < \frac{1}{2}$, so $16\frac{1}{4}$ rounds to 16.

- Find the product of the rounded numbers.

    $1 \times 16 = 16$

If a fraction is equal to or greater than $\frac{1}{2}$, round up. Otherwise round down!

◆ Use compatible numbers.

- Think of nearby numbers that are compatible.

    $\frac{2}{3}$ is close to $\frac{3}{4}$.

    $16\frac{1}{4}$ is close to 16. ←—— Compatible numbers are easy to compute with mentally.

- Multiply to find the estimate. $\dfrac{3}{\underset{1}{4}} \times \overset{4}{\cancel{16}} = 12$

▷ Hector uses about 16 pounds of cement (using rounding) or about 12 pounds of cement (using compatible numbers) in the second batch.

◆ Use number sense to compare the estimates.

$\frac{2}{3}$ is close to 1, but it is closer to $\frac{1}{2}$. The estimate of 1 for $\frac{2}{3}$ is high. So in this case, compatible numbers gives a better estimate.

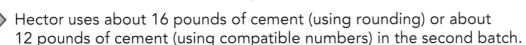

PRACTICE

1. Use rounding to estimate $6\frac{7}{8} \times 2\frac{1}{3}$.

    $6\frac{7}{8}$ rounds to __?__ .

    $2\frac{1}{3}$ rounds to __?__ .

    So $6\frac{7}{8} \times 2\frac{1}{3}$ is about __?__ .

2. Use compatible numbers to estimate $\frac{3}{4} \times 12\frac{1}{6}$.

    $12\frac{1}{6}$ is close to __?__ .

    So $\frac{3}{4} \times 12\frac{1}{6}$ is about __?__ .

Use rounding to estimate the product.

3. $6\frac{1}{3} \times 2\frac{3}{4}$

4. $2\frac{1}{3} \times 6\frac{3}{4}$

5. $8\frac{5}{8} \times 8\frac{5}{8}$

6. $1\frac{2}{3} \times 5\frac{3}{4}$

7. $4\frac{7}{8} \times 10\frac{3}{7}$

8. $2\frac{1}{3} \times 6\frac{3}{4}$

9. $6\frac{1}{3} \times 2\frac{3}{4}$

10. $3\frac{5}{8} \times 7\frac{3}{8}$

11. $9\frac{5}{7} \times 8\frac{1}{8}$

Use compatible numbers to estimate the product. Is the actual product less than or greater than the estimate?

12. $\frac{2}{3} \times 8\frac{1}{5}$

13. $25\frac{3}{5} \times \frac{3}{8}$

14. $\frac{9}{10} \times 28\frac{1}{2}$

15. $82\frac{3}{5} \times \frac{7}{8}$

16. $\frac{1}{3} \times 5\frac{3}{4}$

17. $\frac{2}{3} \times 14\frac{3}{4}$

18. Choose one exercise from Exercises 3–11. Compute the product and compare it with your estimate.

Problem Solving

19. Diane collects $\frac{3}{4}$ dozen eggs from her hens today. Sabrina collects $3\frac{2}{3}$ times as many eggs as Diane. About how many dozen eggs does Sabrina collect?

20. Shelby buys $1\frac{3}{4}$ pounds of cheese. Derek buys $1\frac{5}{8}$ pounds more than Shelby. Erik buys $1\frac{7}{8}$ times as much cheese as Derek. About how much cheese does Erik buy? Explain how you found your estimate.

21. An ecologist estimates the population of prairie dogs. In this area, the animals have a density of about $23\frac{1}{2}$ animals per acre. What is the approximate prairie dog population? Explain.

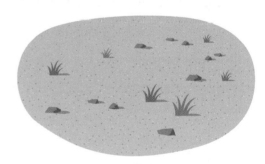

$1242\frac{2}{3}$ acres

Write About It

22. Compare rounding with using compatible numbers to estimate products of mixed numbers and fractions. Which method do you like better? Explain why.

Multiply Fractions and Mixed Numbers

Objective
- Multiply fractions and mixed numbers.

Math Word

mixed number

In a set of gears in a clock, the smaller gear turns $8\frac{1}{2}$ times in one minute. The larger gear turns $\frac{1}{4}$ times as fast as the smaller gear. How many times does the larger gear turn in one minute?

To find out how many times the larger gear turns, calculate $8\frac{1}{2} \times \frac{1}{4}$.

To multiply a fraction and a mixed number:

- Rename the mixed number as a fraction.
- Simplify before multiplying, if possible.
- Multiply the numerators. Then, multiply the denominators.
- Write the answer in simplest form.

$$8\frac{1}{2} \times \frac{1}{4} = \frac{17}{2} \times \frac{1}{4}$$

$$= \frac{17 \times 1}{2 \times 4} = \frac{17}{8}$$

$$= 2\frac{1}{8}$$

The larger gear turns $2\frac{1}{8}$ times in one minute.

Study these examples.

$$\frac{6}{11} \times 2\frac{2}{9} = \frac{6}{11} \times \frac{20}{9}$$

$$= \frac{\overset{2}{\cancel{6}} \times 20}{11 \times \underset{3}{\cancel{9}}}$$

$$= \frac{2 \times 20}{11 \times 3}$$

$$= \frac{40}{33} = 1\frac{7}{33}$$

$$3\frac{3}{5} \times \frac{5}{6} = \frac{18}{5} \times \frac{5}{6}$$

$$= \frac{\overset{3}{\cancel{18}} \times \overset{1}{\cancel{5}}}{\underset{1}{\cancel{5}} \times \underset{1}{\cancel{6}}}$$

$$= \frac{3 \times 1}{1 \times 1}$$

$$= \frac{3}{1} = 3$$

PRACTICE

Find the product. Simplify as necessary.

1. $\frac{4}{7} \times 3\frac{1}{2} = \frac{4}{7} \times \frac{?}{2}$

2. $6\frac{2}{5} \times \frac{3}{8} = \frac{?}{5} \times \frac{?}{8}$

3. $\frac{8}{9} \times 2\frac{3}{4} = \frac{?}{9} \times \frac{?}{?}$

4. $3\frac{1}{3} \times \frac{2}{5}$

5. $\frac{5}{8} \times 1\frac{6}{7}$

6. $2\frac{8}{11} \times \frac{1}{4}$

7. $\frac{1}{8} \times 4\frac{4}{5}$

8. $1\frac{7}{12} \times \frac{4}{5}$

9. $4\frac{2}{3} \times \frac{11}{14}$

10. $\frac{3}{4} \times 6\frac{8}{9}$

11. $\frac{5}{6} \times 9\frac{3}{10}$

Find the product. Simplify before you multiply, if possible.

12. $3\frac{1}{2} \times \frac{1}{3}$

13. $2\frac{1}{2} \times \frac{3}{5}$

14. $\frac{5}{14} \times 2\frac{1}{3}$

15. $\frac{1}{9} \times 5\frac{1}{3}$

16. $\frac{2}{3} \times 4\frac{1}{5}$

17. $\frac{3}{7} \times 5\frac{3}{5}$

18. $2\frac{1}{5} \times \frac{4}{11}$

19. $1\frac{5}{7} \times \frac{5}{12}$

20. $\frac{3}{4} \times 1\frac{2}{6}$

21. $\frac{7}{8} \times 2\frac{2}{7}$

22. $2\frac{1}{2} \times \frac{2}{15}$

23. $2\frac{4}{5} \times \frac{5}{7}$

24. $\frac{1}{8} \times 8\frac{8}{11}$

25. $\frac{1}{6} \times 12\frac{3}{5}$

26. $\frac{1}{5} \times 10\frac{5}{9}$

27. $\frac{1}{3} \times 15\frac{3}{8}$

Problem Solving

28. Natalia's art class is learning about pottery. Each student makes a mug with $\frac{5}{8}$ pound clay. If Natalia's teacher determined that one pack of clay will make $6\frac{2}{5}$ mugs, how much does one pack of clay weigh? Explain how you know.

29. A chemist prepares a compound by reacting the two chemicals shown in these beakers. Once the chemicals are combined, only $\frac{3}{4}$ of the solution will remain. How much of the compound will she get from this reaction?

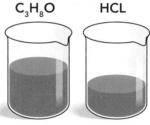

C_3H_8O HCL

$5\frac{3}{5}$ mL $2\frac{3}{8}$ mL

30. Darlene picks $9\frac{1}{2}$ pounds of apples. Anaya picks $\frac{1}{2}$ the amount of apples as Darlene. If the girls donate $\frac{1}{4}$ of all the apples to a local food bank, how many pounds of apples do they donate?

Write About It

31. Erik determined that $2\frac{5}{6} \times \frac{3}{4} = 2$. What mistake did Erik make in his multiplication? Find the correct product.

$$2\frac{5}{6} \times \frac{3}{4}$$
$$= \frac{(2 \times 5) + 6}{6} \times \frac{3}{4}$$
$$= \frac{16}{6} \times \frac{3}{4}$$
$$= \frac{48}{24}$$
$$= 2$$

Multiply Mixed Numbers

Objective
- Multiply mixed numbers by mixed numbers and whole numbers.

Math Words

mixed number

improper fraction

The density of Neptune is $1\frac{3}{5}$ g/cm³. The density of Earth is $3\frac{7}{16}$ times the density of Neptune. What is the density of Earth?

To find out, find the value of $1\frac{3}{5} \times 3\frac{7}{16}$.

To multiply mixed numbers:

- Rename both factors as improper fractions.

- Simplify by dividing any common factors.

- Multiply the numerators. Then, multiply the denominators.

- Write as a mixed number.

$$1\frac{3}{5} \times 3\frac{7}{16} = \frac{8}{5} \times \frac{55}{16}$$

$$= \frac{\overset{1}{\cancel{8}} \times \overset{11}{\cancel{55}}}{\underset{1}{\cancel{5}} \times \underset{2}{\cancel{16}}}$$

$$= \frac{11}{2}$$

$$= 5\frac{1}{2}$$

 Earth

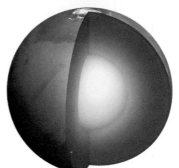

Neptune

▷ The density of Earth is $5\frac{1}{2}$ g/cm³.

Study these examples.

$$8 \times 4\frac{1}{2} = \frac{8}{1} \times \frac{9}{2}$$

$$= \frac{\overset{4}{\cancel{8}} \times 9}{1 \times \underset{1}{\cancel{2}}} = \frac{4 \times 9}{1 \times 1}$$

$$= \frac{36}{1} = 36$$

$$4\frac{4}{6} \times 3\frac{3}{7} = \frac{28}{6} \times \frac{24}{7}$$

$$= \frac{\overset{4}{\cancel{28}} \times \overset{4}{\cancel{24}}}{\underset{1}{\cancel{6}} \times \underset{1}{\cancel{7}}} = \frac{4 \times 4}{1 \times 1}$$

$$= \frac{16}{1} = 16$$

PRACTICE

Find the product. Simplify as necessary.

1. $9 \times 1\frac{1}{6} = \frac{?}{1} \times \frac{?}{6}$

   $= \frac{? \times ?}{1 \times 6}$

   $= ?$

2. $1\frac{5}{10} \times 5\frac{1}{2} = \frac{?}{10} \times \frac{?}{2}$

   $= \frac{? \times ?}{10 \times 2}$

   $= ?$

3. $3\frac{1}{2} \times 3\frac{1}{3} = \frac{?}{?} \times \frac{?}{?}$

   $= \frac{? \times ?}{? \times ?}$

   $= ?$

Find the product. Simplify before you multiply, if possible.

4. $2\frac{5}{8} \times 2\frac{1}{7}$

5. $4\frac{1}{3} \times 3\frac{3}{7}$

6. $1\frac{7}{10} \times 5\frac{1}{3}$

7. $6\frac{2}{11} \times 4\frac{1}{8}$

Find the product. Simplify before you multiply.

8. $9 \times 1\frac{2}{3}$

9. $4 \times 1\frac{1}{4}$

10. $4 \times 2\frac{2}{5}$

11. $7\frac{1}{2} \times 2\frac{2}{5}$

12. $4\frac{1}{6} \times \frac{1}{5}$

13. $5\frac{1}{2} \times 5$

14. $4\frac{2}{5} \times 25$

15. $3\frac{3}{8} \times 4\frac{2}{4}$

16. $8\frac{2}{3} \times \frac{5}{2}$

17. $3\frac{3}{5} \times 1\frac{2}{3}$

18. $4\frac{2}{7} \times 3$

19. $6\frac{1}{8} \times \frac{16}{7}$

20. $2\frac{1}{8} \times 6 \times \frac{1}{2}$

21. $1\frac{3}{5} \times 1\frac{1}{2} \times \frac{3}{4}$

22. $6\frac{1}{3} \times 1\frac{1}{5} \times 2$

23. $3 \times 2\frac{1}{5} \times 5\frac{5}{6}$

24. $1\frac{1}{4} \times 5\frac{2}{5} \times 1\frac{3}{5}$

25. $5\frac{3}{5} \times \frac{5}{7} \times 3\frac{1}{2}$

Problem Solving

26. A technology company has two and a half million dollars in revenue this year. The company plans to have three and half times this amount next year. By how much will the revenue increase?

27. Maggie builds websites. She works $5\frac{1}{2}$ hours each day from Monday through Friday, and works $8\frac{3}{4}$ hours on Saturday. How many hours does she work in all? Explain how you know.

28. Yemi can read about $1\frac{1}{5}$ pages per minute. Study period is from 1:00 to 2:15. If he takes a break for 10 minutes, how much can he read during study period?

29. A fashion designer is creating 4 skirts and 3 shirts. The amount of fabric needed for each item is shown in the table. How much fabric is needed to make all 7 garments?

Garment	Amount of fabric
Skirt	$2\frac{1}{5}$ yd
Shirt	$1\frac{2}{3}$ yd

30. You can use mental math to find $12\frac{1}{2} \times 4\frac{1}{2}$. Find 12×4 and $12 \times \frac{1}{2}$. Then find $4 \times \frac{1}{2}$ and $\frac{1}{2} \times \frac{1}{2}$. Show the final answer as a sum of these products.

Write About It

31. Audrey determined that $5 \times 1\frac{2}{3}$ is the same as $5 \times 1 + 5 \times \frac{2}{3}$, which equals $5 + 3\frac{1}{3} = 8\frac{1}{3}$. Do you agree with Audrey's reasoning? Explain.

Find the Area of a Rectangle

Objective
- Use tiling or a formula to find the area of a rectangle with fractional side lengths.

Math Words
tile
formula
unit square

Vanessa makes a map of her neighborhood. The map is a rectangle $1\frac{1}{2}$ feet long and $1\frac{1}{4}$ feet wide. What is the area of Vanessa's map?

You can tile a rectangle or use a formula to find the area.

◆ Tile a rectangle.

- Draw a rectangle to represent the map.

- You can use a $\frac{1}{4}$-ft square to tile the rectangle. The area of each square tile is $\frac{1}{16}$ square foot, or $\frac{1}{16}$ ft². 30 square tiles of area $\frac{1}{16}$ ft² are needed to tile the rectangle. So the area is $\frac{30}{16} = \frac{15}{8}$ or $1\frac{7}{8}$ ft².

$1\frac{1}{2}$ ft $= \frac{3}{2}$ ft $= \frac{6}{4}$ ft

$\frac{1}{4}$ ft {

$1\frac{1}{4}$ ft $= \frac{5}{4}$ ft

◆ Use the area formula.

$A = \ell \times w$
$\quad = 1\frac{1}{2} \times 1\frac{1}{4}$
$\quad = \frac{3}{2} \times \frac{5}{4}$
$\quad = \frac{15}{8}$, or $1\frac{7}{8}$

A unit square has a side length of 1 unit. Its area is 1 square unit.

▷ The tiling method and the area formula give the same area. The area of Vanessa's map is $1\frac{7}{8}$ ft².

PRACTICE

1. In the rectangle, find the area of the each square, the number of squares, and the area of the rectangle.

2. Use the formula to find the area. Do you get the same area with both methods?

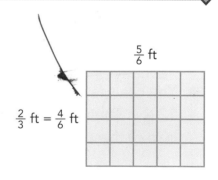

$\frac{5}{6}$ ft

$\frac{2}{3}$ ft $= \frac{4}{6}$ ft

Find the area of the rectangle by tiling.

3.
$2\frac{2}{3}$ in.

$3\frac{1}{3}$ in.

4.
$1\frac{1}{4}$ in.

$4\frac{1}{2}$ in.

Find the area of the rectangle by tiling.

5.

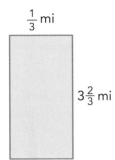

$\frac{1}{3}$ mi

$3\frac{2}{3}$ mi

6.

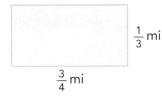

$\frac{1}{3}$ mi

$\frac{3}{4}$ mi

7.

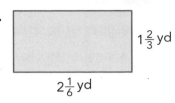

$1\frac{2}{3}$ yd

$2\frac{1}{6}$ yd

8. $2\frac{1}{3}$ mi by $1\frac{2}{3}$ mi

9. $3\frac{1}{4}$ cm by $2\frac{1}{2}$ cm

10. $1\frac{1}{2}$ ft by $\frac{3}{4}$ ft

11. $1\frac{2}{5}$ in. by 5 in.

Find the area of the rectangle by using the formula.

12. $5\frac{1}{3}$ ft by $3\frac{3}{4}$ ft

13. $3\frac{5}{6}$ ft by $4\frac{4}{5}$ ft

14. $\frac{5}{6}$ yd by $\frac{7}{12}$ yd

15. $2\frac{1}{2}$ ft by $4\frac{3}{4}$ ft

16. $4\frac{3}{8}$ ft by $4\frac{4}{5}$ ft

17. $\frac{5}{8}$ yd by $\frac{4}{15}$ yd

Problem Solving

18. The figure represents the plans for a new patio. Find its area.

19. A postcard that is $5\frac{5}{8}$ inches long and $3\frac{3}{5}$ inches wide is cut in half. What is the area of a piece of the postcard?

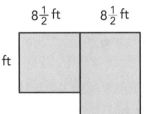

$8\frac{1}{2}$ ft $8\frac{1}{2}$ ft

$8\frac{1}{2}$ ft

$12\frac{1}{2}$ ft

20. Yoshi tiles a rectangle with 48 squares that each have a side length of $\frac{1}{2}$ inch. Give two sets of possible dimensions for the rectangle.

Write About It

21. A rectangle is cut diagonally to form the triangle shown. Find the area of the triangle. Explain what you did.

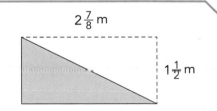

$2\frac{7}{8}$ m

$1\frac{1}{2}$ m

Problem Solving
Use Logical Reasoning

The heights of four herb plants are described as follows:

- Parsley is shorter than oregano.
- Basil is a quarter inch shorter than coriander, which is 6 inches tall.
- Either parsley or oregano is half the height of basil. The other is two thirds the height of basil.

Find the height of each herb.

Read and Understand

What is the question you need to answer?

How tall is each herb plant?

What is the key information?

Coriander is 6 inches tall.

The relationships between the heights of the herb plants are given.

Make and Use a Plan

How can I use logical reasoning?

Analyze and organize the facts to devise a plan.

The height of the coriander plant is given.

The height of the basil plant can be determined since the height of coriander is given.

The heights of oregano and parsley can be determined once the height of basil is known.

Determine the height of each plant.

The height of coriander is given: 6 inches.

Basil is one quarter inch shorter than coriander:
$6 - \frac{1}{4} = 5\frac{3}{4}$ *or* $5\frac{3}{4}$ *inches.*

Parsley is half the height of basil: $\frac{1}{2} \times 5\frac{3}{4} = 2\frac{7}{8}$, *or* $2\frac{7}{8}$ *inches.*

Oregano is two-thirds the height of basil:
$\frac{2}{3} \times 5\frac{3}{4} = 3\frac{5}{6}$, *or* $3\frac{5}{6}$ *inches.*

Look back.

Check each given statement with your final answers to see if each statement is true. For example: Parsley is $2\frac{7}{8}$ inches and oregano is $3\frac{5}{6}$ inches. Yes, parsley is shorter than oregano.

1. Ivan is making curtain panels for 4 different windows. He bought the fabric for the windows that are $1\frac{5}{8}$ meters, $\frac{4}{5}$ meter, $\frac{5}{4}$ meters, and $2\frac{1}{6}$ meters in length.

   - The living room window is the longest window.
   - The kitchen window is less than a meter long.
   - The bedroom window is $\frac{3}{4}$ the length of the living room window.
   - The playroom window's length is between the length of the kitchen and the length of the bedroom.

   Which fabric size goes with which room? Use logical reasoning and a table to organize your answer.

2. Micah is finding the masses of different mineral samples. The anthracite sample has $1\frac{1}{2}$ times the mass of the shale sample. The basalt has $\frac{4}{5}$ times the mass of the shale. The three masses are 5 grams, $6\frac{1}{4}$ grams, and $9\frac{3}{8}$ grams. Find the mass of each sample. Explain your reasoning.

3. A class is playing a numbers game. The teacher writes the six numbers shown on the board and hands out the index cards.

$$\frac{2}{3} \qquad \frac{7}{4} \qquad 2\frac{1}{5} \qquad 1\frac{5}{8} \qquad \frac{1}{4} \qquad \frac{7}{7}$$

The product of two numbers is less than 1.	The product of two numbers is between 1 and 2.	The product of two numbers is greater than 2.

   What are the three pairs of different numbers?

4. Wyatt walks twice as far as Cooper. Cooper walks $1\frac{1}{3}$ miles more than Victor. Victor walks three quarters the distance of Cristian. Cristian walks $3\frac{1}{3}$ miles. Explain why work backward is an effective strategy to solve this problem. Then solve.

Write About It

5. Explain how logical reasoning can be used to solve Exercise 3 without completing each multiplication.

Write a multiplication sentence for each model.

1.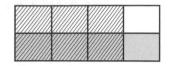

2.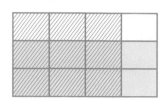

3.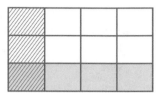

Use rounding to estimate the product.

4. $\frac{2}{3} \times 4\frac{1}{4}$

5. $5\frac{3}{5} \times 2\frac{2}{5}$

6. $7\frac{4}{9} \times 3\frac{1}{3}$

Use compatible numbers to estimate.

7. $4\frac{2}{5} \times 2\frac{7}{8}$

8. $9\frac{8}{9} \times \frac{1}{2}$

9. $3\frac{5}{6} \times 1\frac{5}{7}$

10. $\frac{3}{8} \times 8\frac{7}{9}$

11. $\frac{4}{9} \times 10\frac{1}{4}$

12. $\frac{2}{5} \times 11\frac{4}{5}$

13. $\frac{2}{5} \times 10\frac{1}{4}$

14. $\frac{4}{7} \times 6\frac{8}{9}$

15. $7\frac{1}{3} \times 2\frac{9}{10}$

Find each product.

16. $\frac{2}{3} \times \frac{6}{7}$

17. $2\frac{1}{4} \times 3\frac{1}{3}$

18. $1\frac{1}{3} \times \frac{1}{2}$

19. $\frac{4}{5} \times \frac{10}{11}$

20. $4 \times \frac{2}{7}$

21. $\frac{3}{8} \times 2$

22. $\frac{2}{3} \times 30$

23. $\frac{2}{9} \times \frac{3}{4}$

24. $1\frac{5}{7} \times 4\frac{1}{2}$

25. $12 \times \frac{11}{12}$

26. $1\frac{2}{7} \times 1\frac{2}{5}$

27. $6\frac{1}{4} \times \frac{2}{3}$

28. $\frac{3}{5} \times \frac{7}{8}$

29. $\frac{1}{8} \times 56$

30. $2\frac{4}{5} \times \frac{1}{3}$

31. $5\frac{1}{3} \times 4\frac{2}{3}$

32. $2\frac{2}{5} \times 4\frac{1}{5}$

33. $\frac{3}{8} \times 4\frac{1}{2}$

34. $6\frac{1}{4} \times 8\frac{1}{2}$

35. $\frac{7}{12} \times \frac{1}{6}$

36. $\frac{9}{10} \times 5\frac{1}{5}$

37. $2\frac{2}{3} \times \frac{5}{6}$

38. $\frac{3}{4} \times 100$

39. $\frac{3}{8} \times \frac{5}{7}$

Simplify the fractions. Then multiply.

40. $\frac{9}{10} \times \frac{2}{7}$

41. $8 \times \frac{5}{22}$

42. $\frac{5}{8} \times \frac{16}{25}$

43. $\frac{4}{21} \times \frac{9}{20}$

44. $\frac{1}{7} \times 14$

45. $\frac{10}{11} \times \frac{9}{15}$

46. $\frac{14}{25} \times \frac{5}{21}$

47. $\frac{6}{15} \times \frac{5}{8}$

Write a fraction that makes a true statement.

48. $\frac{2}{5} \times$ ___ $> \frac{2}{5}$

49. $\frac{4}{9} \times$ ___ $= \frac{4}{9}$

50. $\frac{3}{2} \times$ ___ $< \frac{3}{2}$

51. $\frac{7}{6} \times$ ___ $> \frac{7}{6}$

52. $\frac{3}{1} \times$ ___ $= \frac{3}{1}$

53. $\frac{15}{18} \times$ ___ $< \frac{15}{18}$

54. $\frac{2}{2} \times$ ___ $> \frac{2}{2}$

55. $\frac{10}{10} \times$ ___ $= \frac{10}{10}$

Rename the mixed number as an improper fraction.

56. $2\frac{3}{8}$

57. $7\frac{1}{4}$

58. $10\frac{1}{3}$

59. $5\frac{7}{9}$

60. $6\frac{5}{6}$

61. $11\frac{2}{5}$

Use the formula $A = \ell \times w$ or tiling to find the area of the rectangle.

62.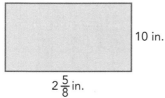
10 in.
$2\frac{5}{8}$ in.

63.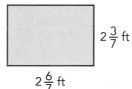
$2\frac{3}{7}$ ft
$2\frac{6}{7}$ ft

64.
$5\frac{2}{3}$ mi
$3\frac{3}{4}$ mi

65.
$\frac{15}{18}$ m
$8\frac{1}{10}$ m

66. $2\frac{1}{6}$ in. by $4\frac{1}{2}$ in.

67. $3\frac{3}{4}$ ft by $5\frac{2}{3}$ ft

68. $6\frac{1}{5}$ in. by $3\frac{2}{5}$ in.

Find each product.

69. $4\frac{2}{9} \times 27$

70. $3\frac{3}{5} \times \frac{4}{9}$

71. $1\frac{11}{12} \times 1\frac{1}{2}$

72. $2\frac{2}{3} \times 3\frac{1}{8}$

73. $4\frac{9}{10} \times 1\frac{5}{7}$

74. $2\frac{11}{12} \times \frac{18}{35}$

75. $5\frac{1}{10} \times 4\frac{3}{8}$

76. $3\frac{8}{9} \times 2\frac{2}{5}$

Problem Solving

77. Zoey describes how to begin to draw a model to find $\frac{7}{8}$ of $\frac{3}{5}$. Identify the missing numbers from each blank.

> *Split a rectangle into _____ equal rows and shade 7 rows. Then split the rectangle into 5 equal columns and shade _____ columns.*

78. Natalie estimates the product $\frac{5}{8} \times 12\frac{1}{9}$ using compatible numbers: $\frac{1}{2} \times 12 = 6$. Benjamin estimates the same product using rounding: $1 \times 12 = 12$. The estimates are not close. Did one or both students make an error? Which method gives a more reasonable estimate? Explain.

A car manufacturer is designing a new model of car. As part of the design process they will create clay models of the car. Once the car is manufactured, it will have the dimensions shown in the diagram below.

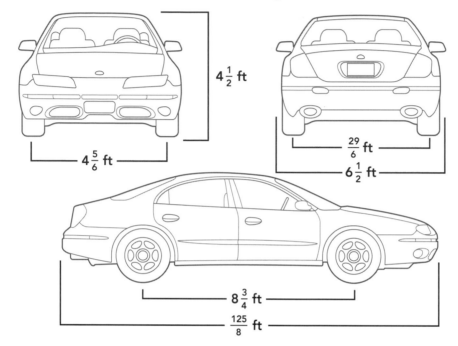

There will be a few different design teams creating models of the car.

- Team A will design a model that is $\frac{1}{4}$ the size of the actual car.

- Team B will design a model that is $\frac{1}{10}$ the size of the actual car.

1. Which team will create a larger model? Explain.

2. Which two dimensions given in the diagram are equal? Why does this make sense?

3. Team A and B each need to determine the dimensions of their model. Copy and complete the front/rear table shown. Then make a similar table for the side view.

Front/Rear View		
Actual	Team A Model	Team B Model
$4\frac{5}{6}$ ft	?	?
$4\frac{1}{2}$ ft	?	?
$6\frac{1}{2}$ ft	?	?

4. The teams also need to create a cover for each model using the dimensions below. Use rounding to estimate the volume of the cover needed for each model. Hint: multiply length, width, and height to find volume.

- Height from bottom of tire to roof

- Width from outside of left tire to outside of right tire

- Length from bumper to bumper

Models are also used when designing buildings, landmarks, and parks.

5. A model of the Statue of Liberty with approximately $\frac{1}{10}$ the actual size of the landmark has the following dimensions:

- Foundation of the pedestal to the torch: $30\frac{1}{2}$ ft

- Base to the torch: $15\frac{1}{6}$ ft

- Heel to top of head: $11\frac{3}{20}$ ft

Use the information to determine the actual dimensions of the statue of liberty.

6. Research two famous buildings, landmarks, or parks. Identify some key dimensions of each. Then calculate the dimensions of a model that is $\frac{1}{4}, \frac{1}{8}$, or $\frac{1}{10}$ the actual size.

7. The Empire State Building is 1454 feet tall. A company wants to create toy replicas of the iconic building. Does it make sense to create the replicas at $\frac{1}{10}$ the actual size of the building? Explain why or why not.

Determine the best answer for each problem.

1. What multiplication sentence is shown by the model?

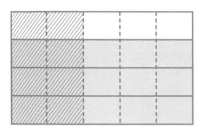

A. $\dfrac{1}{4} \times \dfrac{3}{5} = \dfrac{3}{20}$ **B.** $\dfrac{3}{4} \times \dfrac{2}{5} = \dfrac{3}{10}$

C. $\dfrac{1}{4} \times \dfrac{2}{5} = \dfrac{1}{10}$ **D.** $\dfrac{3}{4} \times \dfrac{3}{5} = \dfrac{9}{20}$

2. What is the area of the rectangle?

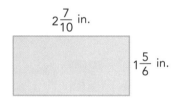

$2\dfrac{7}{10}$ in.

$1\dfrac{5}{6}$ in.

A. $2\dfrac{7}{12}$ in.² **B.** $4\dfrac{8}{15}$ in.²

C. $4\dfrac{19}{20}$ in.² **D.** $5\dfrac{1}{20}$ in.²

3. Find the product.

$$\dfrac{2}{5} \times \dfrac{3}{4} \times \dfrac{1}{7}$$

4. Identify each product that is equivalent to $6\dfrac{3}{4}$. Select all that apply.

A. $2\dfrac{1}{2} \times 2\dfrac{7}{10}$ **B.** $2\dfrac{3}{4} \times 2\dfrac{5}{11}$

C. $4\dfrac{5}{8} \times 1\dfrac{1}{2}$ **D.** $6\dfrac{7}{8} \times \dfrac{3}{4}$

E. $5\dfrac{1}{4} \times 1\dfrac{2}{7}$

5. Which of the following orders these products from least to greatest?

$$1\dfrac{4}{5} \times \dfrac{2}{2},\ 1\dfrac{4}{5} \times \dfrac{6}{5},\ 1\dfrac{4}{5} \times \dfrac{4}{5}$$

A. $1\dfrac{4}{5} \times \dfrac{2}{2} < 1\dfrac{4}{5} \times \dfrac{4}{5} < 1\dfrac{4}{5} \times \dfrac{6}{5}$

B. $1\dfrac{4}{5} \times \dfrac{4}{5} > 1\dfrac{4}{5} \times \dfrac{2}{2} > 1\dfrac{4}{5} \times \dfrac{6}{5}$

C. $1\dfrac{4}{5} \times \dfrac{2}{2} > 1\dfrac{4}{5} \times \dfrac{6}{5} > 1\dfrac{4}{5} \times \dfrac{4}{5}$

D. $1\dfrac{4}{5} \times \dfrac{4}{5} < 1\dfrac{4}{5} \times \dfrac{2}{2} < 1\dfrac{4}{5} \times \dfrac{6}{5}$

6. How can you simplify before multiplying? Select all that apply.

$$\dfrac{4}{15} \times \dfrac{9}{14}$$

A. Divide 4 and 14 by 2.
B. Divide 9 and 15 by 5.
C. Divide 4 and 14 by 4.
D. Divide 9 and 15 by 3.
E. Nothing can be simplified.

7. Find the product.

$$2\dfrac{1}{4} \times \dfrac{5}{2} \times 3\dfrac{2}{3}$$

8. Which statement is true?

A. Multiplication is commutative.
B. Division is commutative.
C. Both multiplication and division are commutative.
D. Neither multiplication nor division is commutative.

Fractions: Division

City planners work with others to build successful communities. They make sure there are enough places for people to live and work, while also ensuring a city has enough space for roads, parks, trees, wildlife, and stores. City planners make decisions based on how the community will be affected currently as well as 5 or 20 years in the future.

Other Types of Planners

◆ A *community planner* makes sure there is a plan for growth and development that the people in the community support.

◆ An *environmental planner* ensures natural features, such as lakes, rivers, and wetlands, are protected during development.

◆ A *transportation planner* plans the transportation system of a city, including its roads, highways, bike paths, and sidewalks.

Divide Whole Numbers by Unit Fractions

Objective
- Divide whole numbers by unit fractions.

Math Words
unit fraction
dividend
divisor

An art teacher has 5 pints of red paint. Each student needs $\frac{1}{4}$ pint of red paint for an art project. How many students can complete the art project?

Use fraction models to divide 5 by the unit fraction $\frac{1}{4}$. A unit fraction has a numerator of 1.

$$5 \div \frac{1}{4} = \underline{\ ?\ }$$

- Model the dividend using 5 wholes.
- Model the divisor $\frac{1}{4}$ by dividing each whole into fourths.
- Count the fourths in 5 wholes.

$$5 \div \frac{1}{4} = 20$$

There are 4 fourths in each whole. There are 20 fourths in 5 wholes.

▷ There is enough paint for 20 students to complete the project.

PRACTICE

Divide. Use the model to find the quotient.

1. $2 \div \frac{1}{8}$

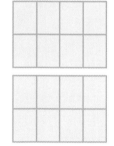

2. $4 \div \frac{1}{3}$

3. $6 \div \frac{1}{8}$

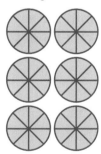

4. $3 \div \frac{1}{4}$

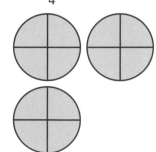

5. $4 \div \frac{1}{2}$

6. $5 \div \frac{1}{6}$

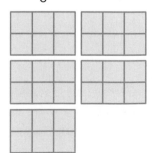

Use fraction circles or strips to model the quotient. Then write a division sentence.

7. $3 \div \dfrac{1}{5}$

8. $2 \div \dfrac{1}{9}$

Draw a model to answer the question.

9. How many fourths are in 2?

10. How many halves are in 5?

Find the quotient.

11. $10 \div \dfrac{1}{3}$

12. $7 \div \dfrac{1}{2}$

13. $8 \div \dfrac{1}{5}$

14. $12 \div \dfrac{1}{4}$

15. $8 \div \dfrac{1}{8}$

16. $15 \div \dfrac{1}{5}$

17. $12 \div \dfrac{1}{10}$

18. $10 \div \dfrac{1}{15}$

Problem Solving

Use the information for Exercises 19–20. A plot of 24 acres of land will be used for wind turbines. A wind energy engineer recommends placing a wind turbine on each quarter acre.

19. How many wind turbines can be placed on this plot of land? Write a division problem. Then find the quotient.

20. Explain how you would draw a model to represent this problem.

21. Frank makes 12 quiches. He cuts half of them into fourths, and half of them into sixths. He sells the large pieces for $5 each and the small pieces for $3 each. If he sells all the pieces, how much money does he make?

Marcia used this model to divide 14 by $\dfrac{1}{4}$. Use the model for Exercises 22–23.

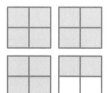

22. Explain why Marcia's model is incorrect.

23. What is the correct quotient?

Write About It

24. Gerald says that a whole number divided by a proper fraction always results in a whole number. How could you revise Gerald's statement so that it is true?

Reciprocals

Objective
- Determine the reciprocal of a fraction or whole number.

Math Words
reciprocal
product

The force of gravity on Jupiter is $2\frac{1}{2}$ times the force of gravity on Earth. What is the reciprocal of $2\frac{1}{2}$?

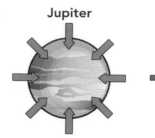

Jupiter   Earth

Two numbers with a product of 1 are called reciprocals of each other.

$$\frac{\cancel{2}^{1}}{\cancel{7}_{1}} \times \frac{\cancel{7}^{1}}{\cancel{2}_{1}} = \frac{1}{1} = 1$$

$\frac{2}{7}$ and $\frac{7}{2}$ are reciprocals.

$$1\frac{1}{4} \times \frac{4}{5} = \frac{\cancel{5}^{1}}{\cancel{4}_{1}} \times \frac{\cancel{4}^{1}}{\cancel{5}_{1}} = \frac{1}{1} = 1$$

$1\frac{1}{4}$ and $\frac{4}{5}$ are reciprocals.

What is the reciprocal of $2\frac{1}{2}$?

To determine the reciprocal of a number:

- Write the number as a fraction.

$$2\frac{1}{2} = \frac{5}{2}$$

- Switch the numerator and the denominator of the fraction.

$$\frac{5}{2} \diagup \diagdown \frac{2}{5}$$

- Check that the product of the numbers is 1.

$$\frac{\cancel{5}^{1}}{\cancel{2}_{1}} \times \frac{\cancel{2}^{1}}{\cancel{5}_{1}} = \frac{1}{1} = 1 \longrightarrow 2\frac{1}{2} \times \frac{2}{5} = 1$$

▷ The reciprocal of $2\frac{1}{2}$ is $\frac{2}{5}$.

Study these examples.

$$\frac{5}{9} \diagup \diagdown \frac{9}{5} \qquad \frac{\cancel{5}^{1}}{\cancel{9}_{1}} \times \frac{\cancel{9}^{1}}{\cancel{5}_{1}} = \frac{1}{1} = 1$$

$$2\frac{1}{3} = \frac{7}{3} \qquad \frac{7}{3} \diagup \diagdown \frac{3}{7} \qquad \frac{\cancel{7}^{1}}{\cancel{3}_{1}} \times \frac{\cancel{3}^{1}}{\cancel{7}_{1}} = \frac{1}{1} = 1$$

$\frac{9}{5}$ or $1\frac{4}{5}$ is the reciprocal of $\frac{5}{9}$. | $\frac{3}{7}$ is the reciprocal of $2\frac{1}{3}$.

PRACTICE

Find the value of the missing reciprocal in the multiplication sentence.

1. $7 \times n = 1$

2. $z \times 3 = 1$

3. $\frac{1}{6} \times p = 1$

4. $s \times \frac{1}{8} = 1$

5. $\frac{7}{11} \times m = 1$

6. $\frac{8}{9} \times k = 1$

7. $a \times \frac{3}{2} = 1$

8. $t \times \frac{7}{3} = 1$

Write the reciprocal of the number.

9. 11

10. 8

11. 2

12. 23

13. 60

14. 100

15. $\frac{1}{5}$

16. $\frac{5}{8}$

17. $\frac{15}{7}$

18. $\frac{9}{2}$

19. $6\frac{3}{5}$

20. $2\frac{8}{9}$

Write *always*, *sometimes*, or *never* to make the statement true.

21. The reciprocal of a nonzero whole number __?__ can be written with a numerator of 1.

22. The reciprocal of a mixed number is __?__ a fraction greater than one.

23. The reciprocal of a fraction is __?__ a whole number.

Use the fractions below for Exercises 24–26.

$$\frac{1}{4} \qquad \frac{9}{8} \qquad \frac{3}{10} \qquad \frac{6}{5} \qquad \frac{2}{7}$$

24. Write the fractions that are less than 1. Then write the reciprocal of each of these fractions.

25. Do the same for the fractions that are greater than 1.

26. Did you notice any patterns in your answer? If so, write a rule to describe the pattern.

Problem Solving

27. Only one whole number is its own reciprocal. What number is that? Why?

28. Is there any whole number that does *not* have a reciprocal? Explain your answer.

Write About It

29. A number plus its reciprocal is equal to $3\frac{1}{3}$. Use a guess and check strategy to find the number and its reciprocal. Does it matter which one is which? Explain.

Divide Whole Numbers by Fractions

A 6-foot length of elastic is to be cut into $\frac{3}{4}$-foot pieces for a jewelry designer to make bracelets. How many pieces of elastic will be made?

To determine the number of $\frac{3}{4}$-foot pieces, find $6 \div \frac{3}{4}$.

◆ You can use a diagram to find how many $\frac{3}{4}$s are in 6:

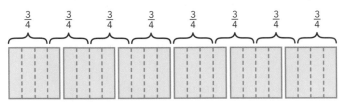

The diagram shows that there are eight $\frac{3}{4}$s in 6. So $6 \div \frac{3}{4} = 8$.

◆ You can also multiply by the reciprocal of the divisor.

- Rename the whole number as a fraction with a denominator of 1.

- Multiply by the reciprocal of the divisor.

- Simplify where possible.

- Multiply the numerators and multiply the denominators.

- Rename the product as a whole or mixed number, if necessary.

$$6 \div \frac{3}{4} = \frac{6}{1} \div \frac{3}{4}$$

$$= \frac{6}{1} \times \frac{4}{3}$$

$$= \frac{6 \times 4}{1 \times 3}$$

$$= \frac{2 \times 4}{1 \times 1}$$

$$= \frac{8}{1} = 8$$

> Dividing by a number is the same as multiplying by the reciprocal of the number.

➤ The jewelry designer will have 8 pieces of elastic that are $\frac{3}{4}$-foot long.

PRACTICE

Find the reciprocal of the divisor.

1. $8 \div \frac{3}{10}$ **2.** $5 \div \frac{8}{9}$ **3.** $3 \div \frac{2}{5}$ **4.** $6 \div \frac{3}{2}$ **5.** $1 \div \frac{4}{7}$

Rewrite the division problem as multiplication by the reciprocal.

6. $5 \div \frac{4}{9}$ **7.** $2 \div \frac{3}{5}$ **8.** $4 \div \frac{6}{7}$ **9.** $11 \div \frac{1}{3}$ **10.** $3 \div \frac{8}{5}$

Divide.

11. $3 \div \frac{2}{3}$ **12.** $5 \div \frac{6}{7}$ **13.** $8 \div \frac{5}{6}$ **14.** $10 \div \frac{4}{5}$

15. $2 \div \frac{4}{7}$ **16.** $6 \div \frac{8}{3}$ **17.** $3 \div \frac{3}{5}$ **18.** $9 \div \frac{2}{9}$

19. $1 \div \frac{5}{8}$ **20.** $4 \div \frac{8}{9}$ **21.** $8 \div \frac{1}{10}$ **22.** $5 \div \frac{2}{5}$

23. $4 \div \frac{2}{7}$ **24.** $9 \div \frac{4}{3}$ **25.** $6 \div \frac{8}{7}$ **26.** $12 \div \frac{8}{9}$

27. $20 \div \frac{4}{9}$ **28.** $5 \div \frac{4}{9}$ **29.** $20 \div \frac{8}{9}$ **30.** $13 \div \frac{3}{10}$

Problem Solving

31. How many $\frac{3}{4}$-cup servings of milk can be poured from the jug? Will there be any milk left over? There are 16 cups in a gallon.

MILK

$\frac{1}{2}$ gal

32. A chef mixes $4\frac{1}{2}$ cups oil, $3\frac{1}{2}$ cups balsamic vinegar, and 1 cup orange juice to make a marinade. She divides the marinade into $\frac{2}{3}$-cup servings. How many full servings can she make?

33. The model represents division of a whole number by a fraction. What division sentence does it show?

34. The model represents the division of a whole number by a fraction. Does this problem have a whole-number quotient? Explain how you know. Then find the quotient.

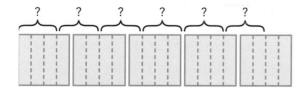

Write About It

35. The division problems shown all have whole-number quotients. Analyze each problem and look for a pattern. When will dividing a whole number by a proper fraction result in a whole number?

$$12 \div \frac{6}{7} = 14 \qquad 5 \div \frac{5}{6} = 6 \qquad 29 \div \frac{1}{3} = 87$$

Use the model to find the quotient.

1. $4 \div \frac{1}{3}$

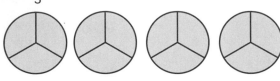

A. 5   **B.** 12
C. 15   **D.** 20

2. $2 \div \frac{1}{6}$

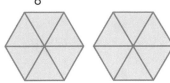

A. 2   **B.** 6
C. 12   **D.** 16

3. $3 \div \frac{1}{3}$

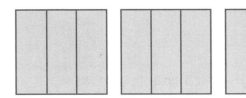

A. 1   **B.** 9   **C.** 12   **D.** 15

4. $4 \div \frac{2}{3}$

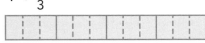

A. 2   **B.** 3
C. 6   **D.** 12

5. $3 \div \frac{3}{5}$

A. 3   **B.** 5
C. 9   **D.** 15

6. $2 \div \frac{10}{15}$

Match the reciprocals.

7. $\frac{1}{4}$ **A.** 9

8. $\frac{9}{4}$ **B.** $\frac{4}{9}$

       C. 1

9. $\frac{1}{9}$ **D.** 4

10. 1

11. $2\frac{2}{3}$ **A.** $\frac{8}{3}$

       B. $\frac{5}{3}$

12. $1\frac{2}{3}$ **C.** $\frac{3}{8}$

13. $\frac{3}{8}$ **D.** $\frac{3}{5}$

14. $\frac{3}{5}$

15. $\frac{1}{10}$ **A.** $\frac{2}{11}$

       B. $\frac{3}{10}$

16. $5\frac{1}{2}$ **C.** 10

17. $1\frac{3}{10}$ **D.** $\frac{10}{13}$

18. $\frac{10}{3}$

Find the value of n.

19. $14 \times n = 1$ **20.** $\frac{1}{2} \times n = 1$ **21.** $n \times 8 = 1$ **22.** $n \times \frac{4}{3} = 1$ **23.** $1 \times n = 1$

24. $n \times \frac{7}{10} = 1$ **25.** $\frac{4}{5} \times n = 1$ **26.** $n \times 3\frac{1}{2} = 1$ **27.** $\frac{3}{8} \times n = 1$ **28.** $n \times 2\frac{1}{5} = 1$

Find the quotient.

29. $7 \div \frac{1}{3}$ **30.** $8 \div \frac{1}{2}$ **31.** $12 \div \frac{1}{4}$

32. $9 \div \frac{1}{7}$ **33.** $10 \div \frac{1}{8}$ **34.** $6 : \frac{1}{5}$

35. $9 \div \frac{3}{4}$ **36.** $5 \div \frac{4}{7}$ **37.** $10 \div \frac{2}{5}$

38. $7 \div \frac{3}{4}$ **39.** $10 \div \frac{3}{5}$ **40.** $8 \div \frac{3}{10}$

41. $3 \div \frac{6}{11}$ **42.** $4 \div \frac{2}{5}$ **43.** $6 \div \frac{2}{3}$

44. $9 \div \frac{3}{7}$ **45.** $6 \div \frac{8}{9}$ **46.** $11 \div \frac{3}{4}$

Problem Solving

47. A 16-c bag of pretzel twists has a serving size of $\frac{2}{3}$ c. A 14-c bag of pretzel rods has a serving size of $\frac{1}{2}$ c. Which snack has more servings? How many more?

48. Emily runs laps around a building. Each lap is $\frac{2}{5}$ mile. How many laps must Emily run in order to run 1 mile?

49. Explain two different ways you could find the quotient $8 \div \frac{2}{3}$.

50. A jump rope competition has a checkpoint every $\frac{3}{4}$ of a minute, where the number of remaining participants are counted. Sarah lasts in the competition for 15 minutes. How many checkpoints include Sarah? Write a division problem to solve.

51. Jordan says the model below shows $5 \div \frac{1}{8} = 40$. Is Jordan correct? Explain.

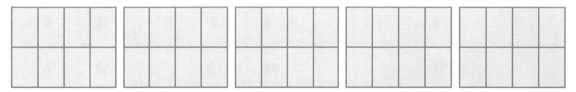

Divide Unit Fractions by Whole Numbers

Objective
- Divide a fraction by a whole number.

Math Words
algorithm
reciprocal

A hair stylist equally separates half a bottle of styling product into three separate containers. How much product does he put in each container?

Use division. Find $\frac{1}{2} \div 3$.

◆ Use a model.

- Shade $\frac{1}{2}$ of the diagram.

- Divide each half into 3 equal parts.

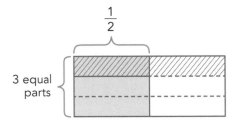

$\frac{1}{2}$

3 equal parts

1 out of 6 parts is double-shaded.

◆ Use the algorithm.
Multiply by the reciprocal of the divisor.

$$\frac{1}{2} \div 3 = \frac{1}{2} \times \frac{1}{3}$$
$$= \frac{1}{2} \times \frac{1}{3}$$
$$= \frac{1 \times 1}{2 \times 3}$$
$$= \frac{1}{6}$$

The stylist puts $\frac{1}{6}$ bottle of hair product in each container.

PRACTICE

Draw a model to find the quotient.

1. $\frac{1}{2} \div 5$

2. $\frac{1}{4} \div 2$

3. $\frac{1}{5} \div 3$

Write the division problem shown by the model. Find the quotient.

4.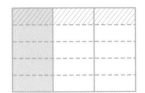

5.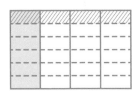

6.

Use the algorithm to divide.

7. $\frac{1}{9} \div 2$

8. $\frac{1}{4} \div 3$

9. $\frac{1}{3} \div 4$

10. $\frac{1}{2} \div 8$

11. $\frac{1}{6} \div 5$

12. $\frac{1}{2} \div 4$

13. $\frac{1}{10} \div 2$

14. $\frac{1}{3} \div 6$

PRACTICE

Divide.

15. $\frac{1}{4} \div 5$

16. $\frac{1}{6} \div 2$

17. $\frac{1}{2} \div 9$

18. $\frac{1}{5} \div 1$

19. $\frac{1}{5} \div 5$

20. $\frac{1}{2} \div 2$

21. $\frac{1}{11} \div 2$

22. $\frac{1}{6} \div 9$

23. $\frac{1}{9} \div 3$

24. $\frac{1}{8} \div 5$

25. $\frac{1}{12} \div 5$

26. $\frac{1}{10} \div 1$

27. $\frac{1}{15} \div 3$

28. $\frac{1}{15} \div 5$

29. $\frac{1}{10} \div 10$

Compare. Use <, >, or =.

30. $\frac{1}{6} \div 4 \;\underline{\;?\;}\; \frac{1}{4} \div 6$

31. $\frac{1}{3} \div 5 \;\underline{\;?\;}\; \frac{1}{4} \div 5$

32. $\frac{1}{3} \div 7 \;\underline{\;?\;}\; \frac{1}{3} \div 8$

33. $\frac{1}{3} \div 3 \;\underline{\;?\;}\; \frac{1}{2} \div 3$

34. $\frac{1}{2} \div 8 \;\underline{\;?\;}\; \frac{1}{4} \div 4$

35. $\frac{1}{10} \div 4 \;\underline{\;?\;}\; \frac{1}{10} \div 3$

Problem Solving

36. Kaitlyn has half of a bottle of liquid soap. She hopes that the soap will last for 4 more weeks. Can she use $\frac{1}{6}$ of the bottle each week? Explain your reasoning.

37. Ariana has a $\frac{1}{3}$-acre farm. She uses half of the land to grow vegetables and the other half to grow grains. She plants equal areas of 4 different vegetables and equal areas of 2 different grains. How much land is used to grow each vegetable and each grain?

38. The model represents division of a fraction by a whole number. What is the division sentence?

Write About It

39. Hector says $\frac{1}{8} \div 1$ is equal to 8, which is the reciprocal of $\frac{1}{8}$. Describe Hector's mistake. What is the quotient?

Divide Fractions by Whole Numbers

Objective
- Divide a fraction by a whole number.

Math Words
reciprocal
whole number
divisor

A recycling plant recycles $\frac{2}{3}$ ton of plastic each year. The plant recycles about the same amount each month of the year. How much plastic does the plant recycle each month?

To find out how much plastic is recycled each month, find $\frac{2}{3} \div 12$.

◆ Use a diagram.

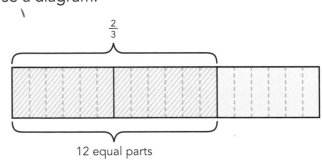

12 equal parts

There are 18 total parts, so $\frac{2}{3} \div 12 = \frac{1}{18}$.

◆ Divide.

- Rename the whole number as a fraction with a denominator of 1.

$$\frac{2}{3} \div 12 = \frac{2}{3} \div \frac{12}{1}$$

- Rewrite as multiplication by the reciprocal.

$$= \frac{2}{3} \times \frac{1}{12}$$

- Simplify where possible. Then multiply the numerators and multiply the denominators.

$$= \frac{\overset{1}{2} \times 1}{3 \times \underset{6}{12}} = \frac{1}{18}$$

- Write the answer in simplest form.

The plant recycles about $\frac{1}{18}$ ton of plastic each month.

PRACTICE

Complete the division.

1. $\frac{5}{8} \div 2 = \frac{5}{8} \div \frac{2}{?}$

$= \frac{5}{8} \times \frac{?}{?}$

$= ?$

2. $\frac{3}{4} \div 5 = \frac{3}{4} \div \frac{5}{?}$

$= \frac{3}{4} \times \frac{?}{?}$

$= ?$

3. $\frac{8}{9} \div 4 = \frac{8}{9} \div \frac{4}{?}$

$= \frac{8}{9} \times \frac{?}{?}$

$= ?$

Rewrite the division problem as multiplication by the reciprocal.

4. $\frac{5}{8} \div 2$

5. $\frac{3}{4} \div 5$

6. $\frac{8}{9} \div 4$

7. $\frac{1}{8} \div 3$

8. $\frac{2}{5} \div 7$

Divide.

9. $\frac{4}{5} \div 3$ 10. $\frac{5}{8} \div 2$ 11. $\frac{2}{7} \div 5$ 12. $\frac{3}{10} \div 4$

13. $\frac{9}{10} \div 3$ 14. $\frac{12}{33} \div 4$ 15. $\frac{12}{25} \div 6$ 16. $\frac{6}{7} \div 15$

17. $\frac{15}{19} \div 6$ 18. $\frac{9}{10} \div 81$ 19. $\frac{4}{9} \div 36$ 20. $\frac{10}{11} \div 15$

21. $\frac{5}{8} \div 5$ 22. $\frac{12}{25} \div 4$ 23. $\frac{2}{3} \div 50$ 24. $\frac{2}{9} \div 6$

25. $\frac{10}{11} \div 5$ 26. $\frac{12}{7} \div 6$ 27. $\frac{8}{5} \div 12$ 28. $\frac{6}{2} \div 5$

Draw a model to find the quotient. Then divide to confirm that your model is correct.

29. $\frac{3}{4} \div 6$ 30. $\frac{4}{5} \div 4$ 31. $\frac{5}{8} \div 3$

Problem Solving

32. Find the missing whole number in the equation. $\frac{7}{10} \div n = \frac{1}{20}$. Explain how you found the number.

33. Peter says that $\frac{1}{2} \div 1 \div 2 = \frac{1}{2} \div \frac{1}{2} = 1$. Do you agree? Explain.

Use the diagram for Exercise 34. About $\frac{1}{3}$ of the beach shown is suitable for swimming. The rest is too rocky and is not suitable for swimming.

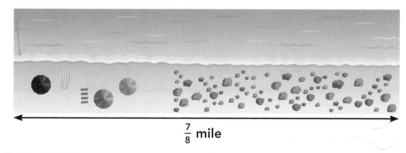

$\frac{7}{8}$ mile

34. What is the length of the beach that is not suitable for swimming?

Write About It

35. Is $\frac{3}{5} \div 2$ the same as $\frac{3}{5} \div 1 + 1$? Explain.

Word Problems Involving Fraction Division

To solve division word problems, read carefully to decide which number to divide.

Seth cuts 6 yards of wrapping paper into pieces that are $\frac{1}{3}$ yard long for wrapping small packages in his store. How many pieces does he cut?

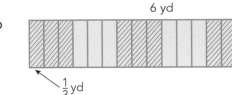
6 yd

- Seth is cutting a whole-number length into fractional lengths, so for this problem you divide the whole number by the fraction.

- Let p be the number of pieces.

$\frac{1}{3}$ yd

$$p = 6 \div \frac{1}{3}$$ Write an equation.

$$p = \frac{6}{1} \div \frac{1}{3}$$ Write 6 as a fraction.

$$p = \frac{6}{1} \times \frac{3}{1} = 18$$ Multiply by the reciprocal of $\frac{1}{3}$.

▷ Seth cuts 18 pieces of wrapping paper.

Tristan cuts $\frac{1}{3}$ yard of poster board into 6 equal pieces to make note cards. How long is each smaller piece of poster board?

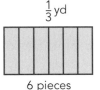
$\frac{1}{3}$ yd

6 pieces

- Tristan is cutting a fractional length into a whole number of pieces, so for this problem you divide the fraction by the whole number.

- Let b be the length of a smaller piece of poster board.

$$b = \frac{1}{3} \div 6$$ Write an equation.

$$b = \frac{1}{3} \div \frac{6}{1}$$ Write 6 as a fraction.

$$b = \frac{1}{3} \times \frac{1}{6} = \frac{1}{18}$$ Multiply by the reciprocal of $\frac{6}{1}$.

▷ Each smaller piece of poster board is $\frac{1}{18}$ yard long.

PRACTICE

Use the problem for Exercises 1–2. Signs are placed every $\frac{3}{4}$ mile along a 6-mile bicycle path. There is no sign at the start but there is one at the end. How many signs are placed along the path?

1. Should you divide $\frac{3}{4}$ by 6 or 6 by $\frac{3}{4}$? How do you know?

2. What is the answer?

3. Breanna makes salad dressing by mixing $\frac{1}{2}$ cup oil and $\frac{1}{4}$ cup vinegar. She uses all the salad dressing as she puts equal amounts on 6 salads. How much salad dressing does Breanna put on each salad?

4. A group of 6 scouts works in pairs to pick up trash along $\frac{7}{8}$ mile of a trail. Each pair of scouts cleans up an equal distance along the trail. How long is the part of the trail that one pair of scouts cleans?

   Miguel and Riley both write equations to solve this problem:

   Miguel's Equation: $t = \frac{7}{8} \div 3$ Riley's Equation: $p = \frac{7}{8} \div 6$

   Whose equation represents the problem situation? Why?

5. During one week, a jewelry maker spent 18 hours making necklaces and 12 hours making bracelets. It takes her $\frac{1}{2}$ hour to make each necklace and $\frac{1}{3}$ hour to make each bracelet. How many necklaces and bracelets did she make?

Problem Solving

6. Summer uses the formula shown to make some natural insect repellent. Then she uses it to put the same amount of repellent into 3 small spray bottles. How much insect repellent is in each spray bottle? Hint: Write the mixed number as an improper fraction.

Formula for Natural Insect Repellent

Mix together:

4 fl oz distilled water,

$3\frac{1}{2}$ fl oz witch hazel,

$\frac{1}{6}$ fl oz or 1 teaspoon glycerin,

$\frac{1}{10}$ fl oz or 60 drops peppermint oil,

$\frac{1}{15}$ fl oz or 45 drops eucalyptus oil

7. A trail is $\frac{1}{2}$ mile long. A fence with 17 equally-spaced fence posts runs along the trail. There are fence posts at both ends of the trail. How far apart are the fence posts?

8. Ms. Greene mixes $\frac{3}{4}$ cup of borax, $\frac{3}{4}$ cup of washing soda, $\frac{3}{8}$ cup citric acid, and $\frac{1}{8}$ cup salt to make a batch of dishwasher detergent. She uses $\frac{1}{16}$ cup for each dishwasher load. How many loads of dishes can she wash with 1 batch?

Write About It

9. A problem involves division of a fraction and a whole number. Explain how to decide whether to divide the fraction by the whole number or the whole number by the fraction.

Problem Solving
More Than One Way

Objective
- Use more than one strategy to solve.

Math Words

strategy
model
diagram

Nathan has $\frac{1}{2}$ pound of wildflower seeds. He plans to divide the seeds equally to make 12 packets of seeds for members of the local conservation club. How much wildflower seed goes in each packet?

You can choose from different strategies to solve this problem.

Use a Model

Draw a diagram to model the problem situation.

12 packets

$\frac{1}{2}$ lb {

The diagram shows 24 parts. So, each shaded part represents $\frac{1}{24}$ lb of seeds in each packet.

Guess and Test

Make a table to record the guesses and the results.

Guess	Amount in 1 Packet	Amount in 12 Packets	Result
1	$\frac{1}{12}$ lb	1 lb	Too much
2	$\frac{1}{48}$ lb	$\frac{1}{4}$ lb	Too little
3	$\frac{1}{24}$ lb	$\frac{1}{2}$ lb	Correct

Guess $\frac{1}{12}$ lb because it is easy to multiply.

Guess a number less than $\frac{1}{12}$ lb.

Write and Solve an Equation

Let w be the weight of the seeds in 1 packet.

$$w = \frac{1}{2} \div 12$$
$$= \frac{1}{2} \div \frac{12}{1}$$
$$= \frac{1}{2} \times \frac{1}{12} = \frac{1}{24}$$

The answer is the same with the three different strategies.

Gage has $\frac{1}{2}$ yard of maple framing material. He wants to cut it into 6 equal pieces to finish his shop project. Gage needs to know how long each piece will be. Use this information for Exercises 1–2.

1. What strategy would you choose to solve this problem?

2. How long will each piece be?

Julia and Anna use different strategies to solve this problem: Mary writes $\frac{1}{2}$ page of an essay in $\frac{1}{3}$ hour. At that rate, how long will it take Mary to write a 3-page essay? Use this information for Exercises 3–4.

Julia makes a table.

Session	Total Pages	Total Hours
1	$\frac{1}{2}$	$\frac{1}{3}$
2	1	$\frac{2}{3}$
3	$1\frac{1}{2}$	1
4	2	$1\frac{1}{3}$
5	$2\frac{1}{2}$	$1\frac{2}{3}$
6	3	2

Anna writes and solves two equations.

First find the number of sessions, s.

$$3 \div \frac{1}{2} = s$$
$$3 \times 2 = s$$
$$6 = s$$

Then find the number of hours, h, in s sessions.

$$6 \times \frac{1}{3} = h$$
$$2 = h$$

3. Which strategy is more efficient? Why?

4. With which strategy is it easier to visualize the problem? Why?

5. A waiter has 36 fl oz of orange juice. He pours $4\frac{1}{2}$ fl oz of juice in each glass. The table he is serving has 10 guests. Will he have enough juice? Explain how you know.

Write About It

6. Katherine's math teacher tells the class that a guess and test strategy works better for missing-factor problems with whole numbers than problems with fractions. Why do you think this is the case?

Use the model to find the quotients.

1.

$1 \div \dfrac{1}{3}$

$2 \div \dfrac{1}{3}$

$3 \div \dfrac{1}{3}$

$4 \div \dfrac{1}{3}$

2.

$1 \div \dfrac{1}{5}$

$2 \div \dfrac{1}{5}$

$3 \div \dfrac{1}{5}$

$4 \div \dfrac{1}{5}$

3.

$1 \div \dfrac{1}{6}$

$2 \div \dfrac{1}{6}$

$3 \div \dfrac{1}{6}$

$4 \div \dfrac{1}{6}$

Write the division sentence shown by the model.

4.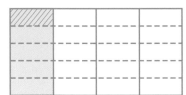

5.

6.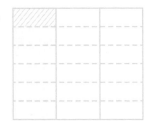

Determine the reciprocal of the number.

7. 12

8. 3

9. $\dfrac{1}{10}$

10. $\dfrac{7}{4}$

11. $3\dfrac{1}{5}$

12. $\dfrac{5}{21}$

13. $\dfrac{1}{8}$

14. $\dfrac{6}{5}$

15. $2\dfrac{1}{9}$

16. $\dfrac{4}{11}$

17. $\dfrac{8}{13}$

18. $1\dfrac{6}{7}$

Rewrite each division problem as multiplication by the reciprocal.

19. $7 \div \dfrac{1}{3}$

20. $\dfrac{5}{6} \div 4$

21. $5 \div \dfrac{2}{9}$

22. $\dfrac{1}{3} \div 9$

23. $12 \div \dfrac{3}{4}$

24. $6 \div \dfrac{1}{7}$

25. $\dfrac{1}{2} \div 11$

26. $\dfrac{3}{8} \div 5$

Find each quotient.

27. $14 \div \dfrac{1}{2}$

28. $20 \div \dfrac{1}{3}$

29. $8 \div \dfrac{1}{9}$

30. $100 \div \dfrac{1}{4}$

31. $10 \div \dfrac{5}{9}$

32. $4 \div \dfrac{2}{7}$

33. $15 \div \dfrac{2}{3}$

34. $9 \div \dfrac{3}{7}$

35. $8 \div \dfrac{5}{6}$

36. $2 \div \dfrac{3}{5}$

37. $4 \div \dfrac{3}{8}$

38. $6 \div \dfrac{4}{5}$

39. $\dfrac{1}{5} \div 4$

40. $\dfrac{1}{8} \div 7$

41. $\dfrac{1}{6} \div 10$

42. $\dfrac{1}{3} \div 8$

43. $\dfrac{2}{3} \div 7$

44. $\dfrac{7}{8} \div 3$

45. $\dfrac{3}{5} \div 8$

46. $\dfrac{2}{7} \div 5$

47. $\dfrac{4}{9} \div 2$

48. $\dfrac{3}{10} \div 6$

49. $\dfrac{10}{11} \div 5$

50. $\dfrac{3}{4} \div 11$

Problem Solving

In Exercises 51–54, use the notes to complete the statement.

whole	half	quarter	eighth	sixteenth
1	$\dfrac{1}{2}$	$\dfrac{1}{4}$	$\dfrac{1}{8}$	$\dfrac{1}{16}$

51. 2 half notes = __?__ eighth notes

52. 5 whole notes = __?__ quarter notes

53. 16 eighth notes = __?__ half notes

54. 10 half notes = __?__ sixteenth notes

55. Spencer lives $\dfrac{4}{5}$ mile from his office. In one week, Spencer commutes a total of 16 miles to and from work. How many round trips does Spencer make between his home and office?

56. Predict a division rule for the pattern below. Then determine the next number in the pattern. Explain how you found the pattern.

4, 6, 9, __?__

A city planner is leading the development of a new suburban community. A billboard sign advertises the features of the community to potential residents.

The city planner must submit initial plans for the new community to the board for approval. The plans must include the following information.

Lots

- $\frac{2}{3}$ of the community's land will be used for lots.

- 10 acres will be dedicated to 1-acre lots; the remaining lot acreage will be split equally into $\frac{1}{2}$-acre lots and $\frac{1}{4}$-acre lots.

Amenities

- $\frac{1}{6}$ of the community's land will be used for amenities.
- The athletic complex will occupy 7 acres of land.
- The rest will be used for playgrounds that are each $\frac{3}{4}$ acre.

Retail Shops

- $\frac{1}{18}$ of the community's land will be used for retail.
- $\frac{1}{3}$ acre be used for a community gift shop.
- The rest of the space will be available for lease; each space will be $\frac{1}{4}$ acre.

Green Space

- $\frac{1}{9}$ of the community's land will be green space.
- $\frac{2}{3}$ acre will be used to develop a man-made lake.
- The rest of the green space will be used to plant trees; 10 trees will be planted on every $\frac{1}{5}$ of an acre.

The table organizes the acreage breakout for the new community.
Some information is missing.

Falls Landing

Falls Landing: Initial Plans for Development
Drafted August 29

		Total Acreage:	?	
LOTS		Lot Size	Acreage Breakout	Total Count
		$\frac{1}{4}$-acre lots	?	?
		$\frac{1}{2}$-acre lots	?	?
		1-acre lots	?	?
AMENITIES		Total Acreage:	?	
		Features	Acreage Breakout	Total Count
		Athletic Complex	?	N/A
		Playgrounds	?	?
RETAIL SHOPS		Total Acreage:	?	
		Features	Acreage Breakout	Total Count
		Gift Shop	?	N/A
		Spaces for Lease	?	?
GREEN SPACE		Total Acreage:	?	
		Features	Acreage Breakout	Total Count
		Lake	?	N/A
		Trees	?	?

1. Copy the table and complete the plans using the given information.

Determine the best answer for each problem.

1. Find the missing number.

$$\frac{4}{5} \times n = 1$$

A. $\frac{1}{5}$ **B.** $\frac{1}{4}$

C. 5   **D.** $\frac{5}{4}$

2. To divide a whole number by a fraction, _____.

A. multiply by the reciprocal of the fraction

B. divide by the reciprocal of the fraction

C. multiply by the reciprocal of the whole number

D. divide by the reciprocal of the whole number

3. Which of the following orders these quotients from least to greatest?

$$\frac{6}{7} \div 3,\ 3 \div \frac{6}{7},\ \frac{1}{7} \div 3,\ 3 \div \frac{1}{6}$$

A. $\frac{1}{7} \div 3,\ \frac{6}{7} \div 3,\ 3 \div \frac{6}{7},\ 3 \div \frac{1}{6}$

B. $\frac{1}{7} \div 3,\ \frac{6}{7} \div 3,\ 3 \div \frac{1}{6},\ 3 \div \frac{6}{7}$

C. $3 \div \frac{1}{6},\ 3 \div \frac{6}{7},\ \frac{6}{7} \div 3,\ \frac{1}{7} \div 3$

D. $3 \div \frac{6}{7},\ 3 \div \frac{1}{6},\ \frac{1}{7} \div 3,\ \frac{6}{7} \div 3$

4. Simplify.

$$6 \div \frac{1}{2} \div \frac{4}{5}$$

A. $3\frac{3}{4}$ **B.** $9\frac{3}{5}$

C. 12   **D.** 15

5. A track is $\frac{1}{4}$ mile long. How many laps around the track equal 7 miles?

A. $\frac{4}{7}$ lap   **B.** $1\frac{3}{4}$ laps

C. 11 laps   **D.** 28 laps

6. Identify each expression that is equivalent to 12. Select all that apply.

A. $3 \div \frac{1}{4}$

B. $8 \div \frac{3}{2}$

C. $2 \div \frac{1}{6}$

D. $9 \div \frac{3}{4}$

E. $8 \div \frac{2}{3}$

7. Find the quotient.

$$\frac{1}{5} \div 9$$

A. $\frac{1}{45}$ **B.** $\frac{5}{9}$

C. $\frac{9}{5}$ **D.** 45

8. Identify the expression that is equivalent to $\frac{6}{7} \div 4$.

A. $\frac{7}{6} \times 4$ **B.** $\frac{6}{7} \times 4$

C. $\frac{6}{7} \times \frac{1}{4}$ **D.** $\frac{7}{6} \times \frac{1}{4}$

Decimals: Addition

A budget can show how money is being spent and can also help to reduce spending. Budgets can help you reach a financial goal, such as saving for a vacation or a college education.

Every budget is unique based on the needs of an individual, family, or business.

Personal Expenses to Consider

- Home: mortgage, rent
- Utilities: electric, gas, water, cell phone, Internet, cable
- Food: groceries, dining out
- Transportation: car payment, gas

- Debt: credit card payments, college tuition payments
- Travel and Entertainment
- Insurance and Taxes
- Miscellaneous: personal care, household items, gifts

Business Expenses to Consider

- Wages
- Employee benefits
- Insurance and taxes

- Office supplies
- Maintenance and repairs
- Advertising

Use Models to Add Decimals

Objective
■ Use base-ten models to add decimals.

Math Words
decimal
hundredth
tenth

You can use models to help you calculate a decimal sum.
Find 1.26 + 0.95.

 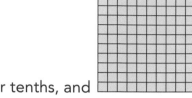

Use ☐ for hundredths, ▯ for tenths, and ▦ for ones (wholes).

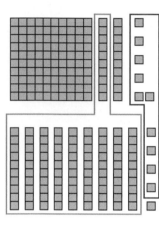 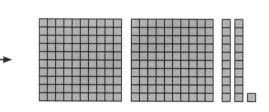

11 hundredths = 1 tenth and 1 hundredth

12 tenths = 1 whole and 2 tenths

So, 1.26 + 0.95 = 2.21.

PRACTICE

Use the model to find the sum.

1. 1.2 + 0.88

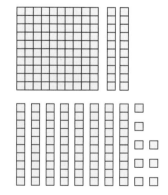

2. 1.68 + 1.77

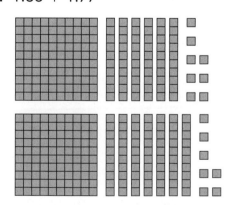

Draw a model to find the sum.

3. 0.5 + 0.14

4. 1.7 + 0.5

5. 0.7 + 1.02

6. 0.37 + 0.08

Write the addition sentence shown by the model.

7. $\underline{\ ?\ } + \underline{\ ?\ } + \underline{\ ?\ } = \underline{\ ?\ }$

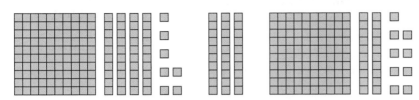

Use a model to find each sum.

8. 0.43 + 0.1

9. 0.38 + 0.2 + 0.35

10. 0.8 + 1.6 + 0.66

11. 1.48 + 0.77

12. 2.4 + 0.77 + 0.09

13. 0.19 + 0.83 + 2

14.
$$\begin{array}{r} 0.53 \\ 0.8 \\ +\,0.62 \\ \hline \end{array}$$

15.
$$\begin{array}{r} 5.3 \\ 0.09 \\ +\,4.61 \\ \hline \end{array}$$

16.
$$\begin{array}{r} 0.88 \\ 4.9 \\ +\,0.02 \\ \hline \end{array}$$

17.
$$\begin{array}{r} 0.81 \\ 0.16 \\ +\,1.1 \\ \hline \end{array}$$

18.
$$\begin{array}{r} 2.2 \\ 1.07 \\ +\,0.37 \\ \hline \end{array}$$

19.
$$\begin{array}{r} 2.08 \\ 1.7 \\ +\,1.5 \\ \hline \end{array}$$

20. 2.08 + 1.3 + 4.43 + 3.8

21. 5.5 + 1.65 + 0.25 + 3.2

Problem Solving

22. It rains 1.05 inches on Monday, 0.85 inch on Tuesday, and 1.44 inches on Wednesday. How much does it rain in all?

23. How can you use base-ten blocks to find the sum 1.53 + 1.78?

24. Destiny models the sum 0.72 + 0.040 as shown. Will her model help her find the answer? Explain.

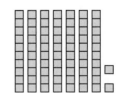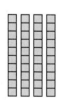

Write About It

25. Describe how you can use models to find 43.05 + 36.41. Assume that you do not want to draw more than 10 of any particular picture.

Use Properties to Add Decimals

Objective
- Use properties and strategies to add decimals.

Math Words
place value
Commutative Property
Associative Property

The Sun is Earth's closest star. The next closest star, Alpha Centauri, is 4.24 light-years away from the Sun. If Sirius is 4.34 more light-years away from the Sun than Alpha Centauri is, how far away is Sirius from the Sun?

To find the total distance from the Sun to Sirius, find 4.24 + 4.34.

◆ Use properties of addition.   4.24 + 4.34

- Use place value to write the addends in expanded form.   4 + 0.2 + 0.04 + 4 + 0.3 + 0.04

- Use the Commutative Property.   4 + 4 + 0.2 + 0.3 + 0.04 + 0.04

- Use the Associative Property.   (4 + 4) + (0.2 + 0.3) + (0.04 + 0.04)

- Simplify inside the parentheses.   8 + 0.5 + 0.08

- Add to simplify.   8.58

◆ Use place value to find partial sums.

- Add the ones.   8 ones

- Add the tenths.   4.2 4   5 tenths

- Add the hundredths.   + 4.3 4   + 8 hundredths
                                           ———————   ————————
- Add the three partial sums.   8.58

▷ Sirius is 8.58 light-years away from the Sun.

PRACTICE

Find the sum using the given method.

1. Use properties of addition.

0.4 + 0.9 + 0.6

_?_ + _?_ + 0.9

_?_ + 0.9 = 1.9

2. Use place value and properties of addition.

0.54 + 0.52

_?_ + 0.04 + _?_ + 0.02

_?_ + 0.06 = _?_

3. Add by place value.

  0.8 4
+ 0.6 7
————————

4. What property did you use in Exercise 1?

Find the sum using any method.

5. 2.92 + 1.16

6. 8.03 + 0.86

7. 3.04 + 4.6

8. 7.35 + 4.7 + 5.25

9. 3.30 + 3.03 + 3.33

10. 1.4 + 2.04 + 1.60

11.
```
  2.5 4
  1.5
+4.2 9
```

12.
```
 1 3.7 9
    4.2
+   4.0 1
```

13.
```
  6.2
  9.0 9
+1.8 0
```

14.
```
  5.0 5
  8.9
  1.0 5
+2.0 0
```

15.
```
 6 0.3 8
 1 0.2 3
 2 0.3 7
+  5.0 2
```

16.
```
  3.8
  0.0 2
  1.4
+6.0 6
```

17. 2.85 + 0.43 + 1.15

18. 3.9 + 1.02 + 0.08

19. 13.3 + 21.90 + 3.1 + 12.08

20. 13.49 + 9.8 + 10.51 + 1.10

Problem Solving

21. Samir adds several decimals. The decimals are all written to the nearest hundredth. Is it possible that he will need to write the sum to the thousandths place? Explain.

22. What is the perimeter of the basketball court?

23. A tennis court is 23.77 meters by 8.23 meters. Jenna walks around the perimeter of the court two times. How far does she walk?

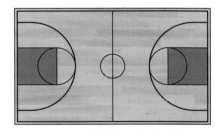

28.65 m

15.24 m

24. Create an addition problem with 3 addends where using properties would be an appropriate strategy.

25. Barry hikes three trails. The trails are 0.44 mile long, 0.9 mile long, and 2 miles long. How many total miles does he hike?

Write About It

26. When using place value to add decimals, can you add the digits in each place in any order? Explain.

Estimate Decimal Sums

Objective
- Use front-end estimation and rounding to estimate decimal sums.

Math Words
nonzero place
front-end estimation
rounding

John is competing in a duathlon. He needs to run 1.35 miles, bike 3.1 miles, and run 0.75 mile. What is the approximate length of the duathlon?

To solve, estimate the value of 1.35 + 3.1 + 0.75.

◆ Use front-end estimation.

- Identify the front digits in the greatest nonzero place of each number.   1.35 + 3.1 + 0.75

- Add the values of those front digits.   1.00 + 3.0 + 0.70 = 4.7

◆ Use rounding.

- Round the decimals to the greatest nonzero place of the least number. The least number is 0.75 and its greatest nonzero place is tenths. So, round each decimal to the nearest tenth.

$$
\begin{array}{rcl}
1.35 & \rightarrow & 1.4 \\
3.1 & \rightarrow & 3.1 \\
+0.75 & \rightarrow & +0.8 \\
\hline
& & 5.3
\end{array}
$$

- Add the rounded numbers.

▷ The duathlon is approximately 5 miles long.

Study these examples.

Front-End Estimation	Rounding
$324.54 → $300	$324.54 → $300
$276.37 → $200	$276.37 → $300
+$436.93 → +$400	+$436.93 → +$400
about $900	about $1000

PRACTICE

Estimate the sum by front-end estimation.

1.
$$
\begin{array}{rcl}
2.1 & \rightarrow & ? \\
4.2 & \rightarrow & ? \\
+1.9 & \rightarrow & +? \\
\end{array}
$$

2.
$$
\begin{array}{rcl}
13.2 & \rightarrow & ? \\
1.7 & \rightarrow & ? \\
+\ 8.9 & \rightarrow & +? \\
\end{array}
$$

3.
$$
\begin{array}{rcl}
\$12.75 & \rightarrow & ? \\
\$26.23 & \rightarrow & ? \\
+\$35.43 & \rightarrow & +? \\
\end{array}
$$

Estimate the sum by rounding.

4. 2.1 + 4.2 + 1.9

5. 13.2 + 1.7 + 8.9

6. 12.75 + 26.23 + 35.43

Estimate the sum by front-end estimation.

7. $\begin{array}{r} 1.19 \\ +1.8 \\ \hline \end{array}$
8. $\begin{array}{r} 7.8 \\ +4.4 \\ \hline \end{array}$
9. $\begin{array}{r} 2.65 \\ +5.93 \\ \hline \end{array}$
10. $\begin{array}{r} 0.23 \\ 0.38 \\ +0.59 \\ \hline \end{array}$
11. $\begin{array}{r} 3.79 \\ 4.38 \\ +7.33 \\ \hline \end{array}$

12. 3.2 + 6.43

13. 0.26 + 0.65

14. 1.71 + 6.39 + 3.94

Estimate the sum by rounding.

15. $\begin{array}{r} 0.57 \\ +1.3 \\ \hline \end{array}$
16. $\begin{array}{r} 6.6 \\ +4.2 \\ \hline \end{array}$
17. $\begin{array}{r} 8.57 \\ +0.59 \\ \hline \end{array}$
18. $\begin{array}{r} 0.77 \\ 0.57 \\ +0.48 \\ \hline \end{array}$
19. $\begin{array}{r} 5.41 \\ 2.80 \\ +0.14 \\ \hline \end{array}$

20. 7.39 + 5.3

21. 0.55 + 0.94

22. 3.07 + 7.5 + 4.27

Estimate using front-end estimation and by rounding.

23. 17.08 + 25.9

24. 30.07 + 2.54

25. 374.91 + 592.6

26. $\begin{array}{r} 12.35 \\ +52.67 \\ \hline \end{array}$
27. $\begin{array}{r} 27.35 \\ +41.19 \\ \hline \end{array}$
28. $\begin{array}{r} 73.62 \\ +\ 2.81 \\ \hline \end{array}$
29. $\begin{array}{r} 128.55 \\ +\ 57.34 \\ \hline \end{array}$
30. $\begin{array}{r} 698.22 \\ +346.46 \\ \hline \end{array}$

31. Is it possible that an estimate for a decimal sum is equal to the exact answer? Use an example to justify your answer.

Problem Solving

32. Use front-end estimation and rounding to estimate 9.86 + 21.409. Which estimate do you think is more accurate? Explain how you know.

33. Which estimation technique would be best for estimating the sum of 3.85 + 6.95 + 5.98? Justify your choice.

34. Create an addition problem with two addends that will lead to different estimates using front-end estimation and rounding.

Write About It

35. Seamus wants to estimate the sum 235.243 + 89.4 + 1342.68. He writes 200 + 100 + 1300 and gets an estimate of 1600. Did Seamus use the rounding rules described in this lesson? Explain.

Use the model to find the sum.

1. 2.3 + 1.8

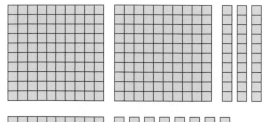

A. 3.1   **B.** 3.3
C. 4.1   **D.** 4.3

2. 1.55 + 0.7

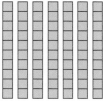
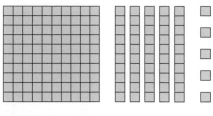

A. 1.75   **B.** 2.25
C. 3.25   **D.** 3.75

3. 0.64 + 0.38

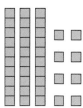
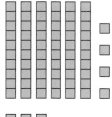

A. 0.2   **B.** 0.92
C. 0.98   **D.** 1.02

4. 2.14 + 1.62

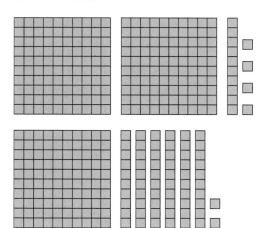

A. 3.62   **B.** 3.74
C. 3.76   **D.** 3.86

Write the addition sentence shown by the model.

5. _?_ + _?_ + _?_ = _?_

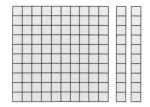
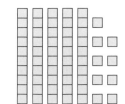
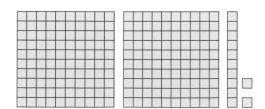

Match. Add using place value or properties of addition.

6. 2.24 + 1.83

7. 1.35 + 1.01 + 1.91

8. 3.22 + 0.68 + 0.8

9. 1.37 + 3.4

A. 4.27
B. 4.7
C. 4.07
D. 4.77

10. 0.33 + 2.17

11. 0.69 + 0.83 + 0.78

12. 2.27 + 0.43

13. 1.07 + 0.64 + 0.39

A. 2.7
B. 2.5
C. 2.1
D. 2.3

Estimate the sum by front-end estimation.

14.
$$\begin{array}{r} 3.42 \\ +5.05 \\ \hline \end{array}$$

15.
$$\begin{array}{r} 10.6 \\ +7.9 \\ \hline \end{array}$$

16.
$$\begin{array}{r} 7.24 \\ +7.9 \\ \hline \end{array}$$

17.
$$\begin{array}{r} 0.32 \\ 0.46 \\ +0.37 \\ \hline \end{array}$$

18.
$$\begin{array}{r} 5.2 \\ 1.66 \\ +9.45 \\ \hline \end{array}$$

Estimate the sum by rounding.

19.
$$\begin{array}{r} 0.56 \\ +3.17 \\ \hline \end{array}$$

20.
$$\begin{array}{r} 2.83 \\ +7.67 \\ \hline \end{array}$$

21.
$$\begin{array}{r} 2.25 \\ +0.14 \\ \hline \end{array}$$

22.
$$\begin{array}{r} 0.32 \\ 0.91 \\ +0.55 \\ \hline \end{array}$$

23.
$$\begin{array}{r} 1.74 \\ 0.26 \\ +5.95 \\ \hline \end{array}$$

Problem Solving

A technology company offers three different smartphones. Use the information for Exercises 24–26.

- The diagonal for the display of phone B is 0.7 inch longer than phone A.
- The diagonal for the display of phone C is 0.82 inch longer than phone B.
- Phone C is 0.24 mm thicker than phone B.
- Phone A is 1.13 mm thicker than phone C.

Phone A — 4.2 in. — 6.8 mm

Phone B

Phone C

24. How much longer is the display of phone C than phone A?

25. What is the length of the display of phone B? of phone C?

26. What is the thickness of phone C? of phone A?

27. Write two different ways to estimate the sum 6.4 + 1.85 + 3.44. Do the estimates differ? If so, explain why.

Problem Solving
Draw a Picture

Objective
- Solve problems by drawing pictures.

Math Words
tenth
hundredth

Zoey is buying some items at the market. The items are shown in the table. What is the total weight of the items?

Read and Understand

What is the question you need to answer?

What is the total weight of the items?

What is the key information?

The weight of each item: 2.65 lb, 2 lb, 3.8 lb

Item	Weight (lb)
Cantaloupe	2.65
Grapes	2
Swiss Cheese	3.8

Make a Plan

How can I draw a picture to solve the problem?

Sketch base-ten blocks. Draw circles to regroup.

I can use ☐ *for each one.*

I can use | *for each tenth.*

I can use ■ *for each hundredth.*

Be careful counting the blocks when you regroup!

Draw a Picture to Solve

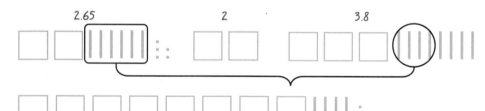

$2.65 + 2 + 3.8 = 8.45$

Answer the Question

The total weight of the items is 8.45 pounds.

PRACTICE

1. Suppose Toni buys two of the same item from the table. Which item would require regrouping hundredths as a tenth? Explain.

2. Suppose Zoey buys 2 pineapples that each weigh 3.17 lb. What is their total weight? Draw a picture.

A quarter, a penny, and a dime are lined up in a row. Use the diagram for Exercises 3–5.

← 0.96 in. →   ← 0.75 in. →   ← 0.71 in. →

3. Draw a picture to find the total length of the coins.

4. If the coins were lined up in a different order, would the total length change? Explain.

5. Suppose one more penny is added to the end of the coins. What is the total length of the coins now?

6. Jorge wants to go to the beach this week. He is waiting for the temperature to climb above 80°F. On Monday, it was 77.3°F. It was 0.5°F hotter on Tuesday. On Wednesday, the temperature climbed by another 1.9°F. Should Jorge go to the beach on Wednesday? Use the number line to help you.

7. Particle A and Particle B start in the same location. Particle A moves 3.2 cm north while Particle B moves 1.9 cm south. Then Particle A moves another 1.4 cm north. What is the distance between the particles now?

8. For a medical test, a patient must drink a glucose solution within 5 minutes. After an hour, the patient's blood will be tested. One patient drinks the solution in 3 sips. The table shows how many grams she drinks in each sip. What is the amount of glucose solution used for the test?

Sip	Amount of Solution Drank
Sip #1	12.8 grams
Sip #2	15.5 grams
Sip #3	21.7 grams

9. There are 2.54 centimeters in one inch. How many centimeters are there in 3 inches?

Write About It

10. To add 3.54 and 1.8, Rebecca wants to use base ten blocks, and Lindsey wants to draw a picture. Describe a reason why each method may be preferable.

Add Decimals: Hundredths

Objective
- Use an algorithm to add decimals to hundredths.

Math Words
hundredth
sum

Brian went grocery shopping with his dad. The receipt shows part of the produce they purchased. How many pounds of onions did they purchase altogether?

To find the total number of pounds Brian and his dad purchased, determine the sum of 0.37 and 1.26.

RECEIPT
....
YELLOW ONIONS
0.37 lb @ 1.49/lb 0.55

WHITE ONIONS
1.26 lb @ 1.49/lb 1.88

◆ Use place value. Add the same way you add whole numbers.

Line up the decimal points.	Add the hundredths. Regroup.	Add the tenths.	Add the ones.	Write the decimal point in the sum.
0.37 +1.26	1 0.37 +1.26 3	1 0.37 +1.26 63	1 0.37 +1.26 1 63	0.37 +1.26 1.63

◆ Use a model to check. Regroup as needed.

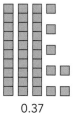 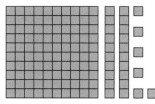 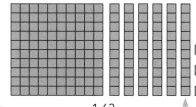

0.37   +   1.26   =   1.63

Regroup 10 hundredths as 1 tenth.

▷ Brian and his dad bought 1.63 pounds of onions.

PRACTICE

Add. Use base-ten blocks to check.

1. 2.2
   +5.5

2. 0.63
   +0.03

3. 4.42
   +5.54

4. 1.24
   +2.69

5. 1.63
   +2.73

6. 1.24
   0.9
   +3.39

7. 1.05
   3.82
   +2.12

8. 1.3
   0.4
   +2.2

9. 0.28
   1.6
   +0.09

10. 1.53
    0.4
    +3

Add.

11.
$$\begin{array}{r} 1.39 \\ +\ 3.05 \end{array}$$

12.
$$\begin{array}{r} 4.49 \\ +10.38 \end{array}$$

13.
$$\begin{array}{r} 3.8 \\ +1.39 \end{array}$$

14.
$$\begin{array}{r} 1.98 \\ +9.32 \end{array}$$

15.
$$\begin{array}{r} 10.87 \\ +20.48 \end{array}$$

16.
$$\begin{array}{r} 3.6 \\ 1.5 \\ +\ 6.8 \end{array}$$

17.
$$\begin{array}{r} 1.09 \\ 0.75 \\ +1.24 \end{array}$$

18.
$$\begin{array}{r} 3.7 \\ 1.29 \\ +0.43 \end{array}$$

19.
$$\begin{array}{r} 3.4 \\ 1.75 \\ +4.6 \end{array}$$

20.
$$\begin{array}{r} 1.07 \\ 4.3 \\ +5.9 \end{array}$$

Align the addends and determine the sum.

21. $10.2 + 15.79$

22. $2.03 + 9.9$

23. $1.54 + 3.05$

24. $12.38 + 8.06$

25. $1.72 + 0.3$

26. $5.7 + 3.97$

27. $3.6 + 6.54 + 3.05$

28. $2.82 + 3.6 + 4.05$

29. $8.2 + 10.08 + 1.32$

30. $2.9 + 0.01 + 1.65$

31. $0.41 + a$ when $a = 1.09$

32. $2.98 + p$ when $p = 1.2$

33. $1.51 + 3.3 + w$ when $w = 2.08$

34. $5.73 + k + 5.2$ when $k = 1.13$

Problem Solving

35. The highest active volcano on Earth is Ojos del Salado. If Mount Everest is 1.96 kilometer taller than Ojos del Salado, how tall is Mount Everest?

36. Manaus, Brazil is a city on the edge of the Amazon rainforest. On average, the city of Manaus receives 6.3 cm of rain in September. In October, the rainfall average increases by 4.81 cm. What is the total average rainfall for both months in Manaus?

Write About It

37. Margo is adding 7.88 and 5.24. She says that she can switch the tenths digits in the two numbers, and the sum would not change. Will this be true for any two numbers? Explain, using properties.

LESSON 10-6 Add Decimals: Thousandths

Objective
- Use an algorithm to add decimals to thousandths.

Math Words

estimate
thousandth

The table shows where most of Earth's water is located. What total percent of Earth's water is found in ice caps, glaciers, permanent snow, groundwater, and lakes?

Water Source	Percent of Total Water
Oceans, Seas, and Bays	96.5
Ice Caps, Glaciers, and Permanent Snow	1.74
Groundwater	1.7
Ground Ice and Permafrost	0.022
Lakes	0.013
Atmosphere, Swamp Water, Rivers, and Biological Water	0.024

Find the sum 1.74 + 1.7 + 0.013.

Line up the decimal points. Insert zeros as needed.	Add the thousandths, hundredths, and tenths. Regroup as needed.	Add the whole numbers. Write the decimal point in the sum.

```
                                                    1              1
  1.740      1.740      1.740      1.740        1.740
  1.700      1.700      1.700      1.700        1.700
+ 0.013    + 0.013    + 0.013    + 0.013      + 0.013
                3          53         453        3.453
```

Ice caps, glaciers, permanent snow, groundwater, and lakes make up 3.453 percent of Earth's total water.

Study these examples.

```
                        1 1          2 1            1
  5.173      0.365      18.41      213.000
+ 3.215    + 0.680    + 37.05      451.400
  8.388      1.045    + 24.90    + 381.071
                        80.36      1045.471
```

PRACTICE

Use rounding to estimate. Then determine the sum.

1.   3.6
      + 2.8

2.   3.02
      + 4.06

3.   4.12
      + 5.63

4.   0.597
      + 0.802

5.   3.125
      + 7.431

Use rounding to estimate. Then determine the sum.

6.	5.4	7.	7.36	8.	0.825	9.	16.3	10.	911.435
	3.02		9.43		0.914		25.07		79.362
	+7.601		+5.721		+0.203		+32.044		+812.417

11.	3.45	12.	0.458	13.	4.4	14.	179.65	15.	919.435
	4.2		0.42		8.056		67.142		2.812
	+7.034		+0.31		+9.14		+571.23		+ 73.764

Align addends and determine the sum.

16. 7.05 + 9.505

17. 17 + 4.5 + 1.153

18. 2.114 + 4 + 1.07

19. 97.602 + 5.98 + 6.8

20. 635 + 27.314 + 9.5

21. 902.4 + 0.391 + 12.003

22. w + 7.825 when w = 5.6

23. y + 24.08 when y = 35.195

24. 32.571 + k when k = 5.429

25. g + 4.23 when g = 53.291

Problem Solving

A batting average is written as a decimal from 0 to 1, rounded to the nearest thousandth. Use this information for Exercises 26–27.

26. A team's batting average is 0.273. If the team improves this by 0.014 each of the next two years, what will be the average in two years?

27. A softball player has a batting average of 0.319. She wants to improve it to an average of 0.375. If she increases her average by 0.066, will she reach her goal? Write an equation to explain.

28. A mortgage is a type of loan. The 30-year fixed rate is 0.696 percentage points higher than the Veterans Affairs' rate. The 5-year adjustable rate is 0.09 points higher than the 30-year rate. Find the missing numbers.

Mortgage Rate Type	Annual Percentage Points
5-Year Adjustable	?
30-Year Fixed	?
Veterans Affairs' Adjustable	2.933

Write About It

29. Why is it especially important to align decimal points when adding decimals to thousandths?

Addition with Money

Objective
- Use estimation, models, and addition strategies to add amounts of money.

Math Words
dollar
cent

A class is building model roller coasters to learn more about forces. The teacher purchases the materials shown in the table.

Item	Cost
Foam Insulation	$19.20
Masking Tape	$6.69
Marbles	$6.13

How much does the teacher spend on materials?

Add money amounts with dollars and cents the same way you add all decimal numbers.

A good estimate can help to ensure you have enough money before making a purchase.

- Use rounding to estimate the sum. $19 + $7 + $6 = $32
- Determine the exact sum.

Line up the decimal points.	Add the hundredths. Regroup.	Add the tenths. Regroup.	Add the whole numbers. Write the decimal point in the sum.
$19.20 6.69 + 6.13	¹ $19.20 6.69 + 6.13 $ 2	¹ ¹ $19.20 6.69 + 6.13 $ 02	² ¹ ¹ $19.20 6.69 + 6.13 $32.02

▷ The teacher spends $32.02. This is close to the estimate.

Study these examples.

$7.00
+   5.21
$12.21

¹ ¹ ¹
$26.34
14.72
+ 37.18
$78.24

¹ ¹
$247.00
+ 166.72
$413.72

PRACTICE

Use rounding to estimate. Then, determine the sum.

1. $6.00
   + 3.92

2. $8.38
   + 2.97

3. $5.09
   + 1.35

4. $4.83
   + 5.43

5. $9.02
   + 1.24

Add.

6. $19.57
          70.46
       + 13.12

7. $52.09
          43.17
       + 17.45

8. $23.21
           1.92
       + 17.64

9. $56.25
           9.18
       + 13.46

10. $23.86
          13.96
       + 21.76

11. $621.21
       + 354.25

12. $516.83
       + 378.35

13. $357.97
       + 689.80

14. $721.63
       + 494.09

15. $270.05
       + 179.71

16. $235.52
       +   25.97

17. $979.75
       +   34.55

18. $274.89
       + 274.89

19. $246.24
          28.72
       +   69.47

20. $174.73
          424.25
       + 284.54

Simplify for $n = \$4.09$.

21. $\$1.80 + n$

22. $n + n + \$2$

23. $(\$5.08 + n) + \$0.55$

24. double the sum of $n + \$12.87$

Problem Solving

Kennedy makes and sells jewelry at the school carnival. Use the table for Exercises 25–27.

Jewelry	Cost
Necklace	$7.25
Earrings	$3.75
Bracelet	$4.50
Ring	$3.50

25. Sofia buys a necklace and Alana buys a pair of earrings. How much money does Kennedy earn?

26. Jasmine buys a bracelet and two rings. How much change will she get from $15?

27. If Sofia, Alana, and Jasmine are the only people who bought jewelry, how much money did Kennedy make altogether?

28. Hailey needs to find $5.55 + $1.51. She uses several steps. Her work is shown. Is Hailey's work correct? Explain.

> $5.55 + $1 = $6.55
> $6.55 + $0.50 = $7.05
> $7.05 + $0.01 = $7.06

Write About It

29. Explain how you could use the Associative or Commutative Property to simplify $4.25 + $3.32 + $5 + $0.75.

Use the model to find the sum.

1. 2.14 + 1.67

2. 0.82 + 0.53

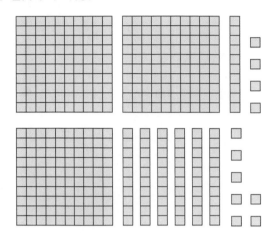

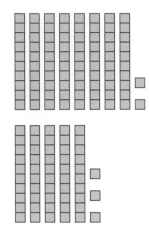

Draw a model to find the sum.

3. 0.71 + 0.25

4. 1.42 + 1.66

5. 2.4 + 0.78

6. 1.09 + 1.9 + 1

7. 1.05 + 1.87 + 3.4

8. 2.45 + 1.8 + 2.2

Estimate the sum by front-end estimation.

9.	**10.**	**11.**	**12.**	**13.**
2.18	12.2	4.7	0.6	3.08
+7.54	+ 8.9	+9.61	3.3	5.2
			+0.4	+6.33

14. 5.1 + 3.29 + 4.17

15. 0.48 + 7.3 + 0.55

16. 4.23 + 8.12 + 2.24

17. 12.45 + 28.17 + 6.94

Estimate the sum by rounding.

18.	**19.**	**20.**	**21.**	**22.**
8.6	10.3	6.38	2.38	0.25
+4.1	+ 5.41	+0.71	0.56	0.22
			+0.11	+0.29

23. 12.35 + 7.88 + 1.44

24. 9.57 + 4.81 + 6.75

25. 5.24 + 4.7 + 12.61

26. 12.68 + 8.3 + 38.63

Find the sum.

27.
```
  6.1
+ 4.9
```

28.
```
  0.48
+ 7.2
```

29.
```
  3.85
+ 1.14
```

30.
```
  6.01
+ 2.74
```

31.
```
  0.45
+ 12.6
```

32.
```
  0.201
+ 1.574
```

33.
```
  6.5
+ 4.291
```

34.
```
  0.472
+ 0.28
```

35.
```
  7.128
+ 0.405
```

36.
```
  12.521
+  3.712
```

37.
```
  7.8
  1.5
+ 4.22
```

38.
```
  0.48
  0.59
+ 0.6
```

39.
```
  7.22
  3.5
+ 6.08
```

40.
```
  10.54
   5.16
+  8.91
```

41.
```
  0.58
  0.76
+ 0.99
```

42.
```
  1.542
  2.6
+ 8.5
```

43.
```
  3.495
  2.17
+ 5.92
```

44.
```
  7.234
  6.77
+ 8.418
```

45.
```
   5.419
  10.276
+  3.621
```

46.
```
   7.254
  11.318
+  9.648
```

Align addends and determine the sum.

47. 5.8 + 4.31 + 4.8

48. 4.56 + 4.1 + 56.71

49. 23.723 + 5.813 + 54.1

50. 4.682 + 54.23 + 251.3

51. 0.345 + 6 + 35.1

52. 3.274 + 4.12 + 81

53. 2.58 + 6.87 + w when w = 0.47

54. 0.21 + 0.9 + t when t = 1.595

55. 12.4 + k + 7.86 when k = 0.622

56. a + 13.647 + 0.84 when a = 9.5

57. s + 2.649 + 5.178 when s = 4.237

58. 0.417 + t + 5.215 when t = 3.667

Problem Solving

Lydia has saved $45 to buy model kits. Use the table for Exercises 59–61.

Model Kit	Cost
Jet	$25.98
Sea Plane	$3.75
Helicopter	$22.50
Rocket	$15.95

59. Can Lydia buy all four kits? Explain why or why not.

60. Can Lydia buy three of the available kits? Explain why or why not.

61. Lydia saves an additional $20.50. Does she have enough for 3 helicopter kits? Explain.

62. Explain how the sum 2.14 + 0.51 + 3.22 can be found using properties of addition.

Maxwell wants to create a budget so he can save $200 each month for a down payment on a house. His budget will categorize spending and assign an amount to each expense on a monthly basis.

Part 1: Determine Maxwell's Monthly Income

1. Maxwell is paid bi-monthly (two times per month). The net amount of each paycheck is $1432.16. What is Maxwell's total monthly income?

2. Should Maxwell's total monthly expenses be less than, equal to, or greater than his total monthly income? Explain.

Part 2: Create Maxwell's Budget

Maxwell reviews his bills and expenses for previous months and enters them into a budget spreadsheet.

Maxwell's Monthly Budget			
Home	Budget	Transportation	Budget
Rent	$750.00	Car Payment	$347.51
Renter's Insurance	$27.42	Auto Insurance	$82.74
Gas & Electric	$156.85	Fuel	$125.00
Water & Trash	$35.67	Subtotal:	?
Phone	$64.92		
Cable TV	$58.24	Food & Entertainment	
Internet	$45.99	Groceries	$315.00
House Supplies	$60.00	Dining Out	$125.00
Subtotal:	?	Clothing	$50.00
		Movies	$30.00
Loans		Subtotal:	?
Credit Card Payment	$241.65		
Student Loan Payment	$184.06	Total Monthly Income:	?
Subtotal:	?	Total Monthly Expenses:	?

3. Find the following totals to complete Maxwell's budget:

- Home
- Food & Entertainment
- Transportation
- Loans

4. Complete the budget by identifying Maxwell's total monthly income and total monthly expenses.

Part 3: Analyze Maxwell's Budget

5. Does Maxwell's budget allow him to reach his goal of saving $200 per month? Explain.

6. Suppose Maxwell stops going to the movies and buying new clothing. He also disconnects his cable TV. Determine the new totals. Will these changes to Maxwell's lifestyle allow him meet his savings goal?

7. Unexpected expenses can occur in any given month. What are some other categories Maxwell should consider adding to his budget?

Part 4: Create Your Own Budget

8. Suppose you receive a set allowance each month. Think about how you would spend your money (school supplies, clothes, presents, snacks, etc.). Create your own budget using a table or spreadsheet. Organize expenses into categories. Make sure your total monthly expenses do not exceed your monthly allowance.

Determine the best answer for each problem.

1. Find the sum when $j = 0.009$.

$$6.47 + 0.21 + j$$

5. Determine the perimeter.

8.25 cm

5.1 cm

A. 13.35 cm   **B.** 18.45 cm

C. 21.6 cm   **D.** 26.7 cm

2. Which property is illustrated?

$$4 + 0.5 + 2 + 0.7 = 4 + 2 + 0.5 + 0.7$$

A. Associative Property
B. Commutative Property
C. Distributive Property
D. Multiplication Property

6. What value of m would make the statement true?

$$7.098 + m = 7.45$$

3. Identify the pattern rule.

$$2.5, 3.51, 4.52, 5.53, \ldots$$

A. Add 1.001
B. Add 1.01
C. Add 1.1
D. Add 1.11

7. Which of the following is equivalent to the given expression?

$$6.329 + 0.307$$

A. $(6.3 + 0.02 + 0.009) + (0.3 + 0.07)$
B. $(6.3 + 0.2 + 0.09) + (0.3 + 0.07)$
C. $(6.3 + 0.02 + 0.009) + (0.3 + 0.007)$
D. $(6.3 + 0.29) + (0.3 + 0.07)$

4. Which week had the most rainfall?

Week	Saturday Rainfall (in.)	Sunday Rainfall (in.)
1	0.67	0.84
2	0	1.49
3	0.97	0.43
4	1.06	0.5

A. Week 1   **B.** Week 2
C. Week 3   **D.** Week 4

8. Hayden buys a 10-pack of pencils for $1.79 and 2 pens for $1.29 each. How much does he spend in all?

Decimals: Subtraction

It is important to track budgeted amounts against actual expenses so that you can determine if any amount needs to be adjusted. This type of analysis is especially helpful at the end of each month.

How to Handle Unexpected Expenses

♦ Not all expenses are controllable or predictable. For instance, home and car repairs may arise unexpectedly. It is important to budget for these each month so that when an issue does arise, you have money set aside to cover any needed replacements or repairs.

Use Models to Subtract Decimals

Objective
- Use concrete models to subtract decimals.

Math Words
minuend
subtrahend
regroup

◆ Use a model to find 1.57 − 0.34.

Model the minuend. Take away the blocks that represent the subtrahend. Count the blocks that remain.

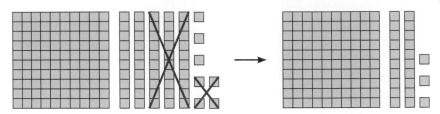

▷ 1.57 − 0.34 = 1.23

◆ Use a model to find 0.72 − 0.56.

Regroup the minuend before you take away the blocks that represent the subtrahend.

1 tenth = 10 hundredths

▷ 0.72 − 0.56 = 0.16

◆ Use addition to find 0.93 − 0.64.

To find the difference, you can count from 0.64 to 0.93 by adding.

- Add to count to the next tenth, 0.70.   0.64 + 0.06 = 0.70
- Add to count to the tenth in 0.93.   0.70 + 0.20 = 0.90
- Add to count to 0.93.   0.90 + 0.03 = 0.93
- Find the total that you added to 0.64.   0.29

▷ 0.93 − 0.64 = 0.29

PRACTICE

Use a model or addition to find the difference.

1. 0.58 − 0.35

2. 1.31 − 0.13

3. 3.42 − 1.81

4. Use the model to find 1.26 − 0.89.

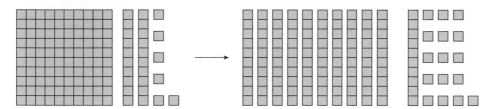

Find the difference. Use a model or addition.

5. 2.85 − 0.61

6. 1.38 − 1.19

7. 0.8 − 0.37

Simplify the expression.

8. 3.08 + 1.3 − 3.8

9. 5.5 − 1.65 + 0.25 − 3.2

10. Write the subtraction sentence shown by the model.

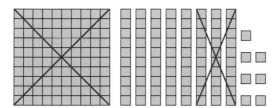

_?_ − _?_ = _?_

Problem Solving

Various space missions have had the goal of collecting dust and studying comets. Use the table for Exercises 11–12.

Comet	Orbit around the Sun	Average radius
Wild 2	6.4 years	2.13 km
Tempel 1	5.52 years	3 km

11. Jen is using a model to find out how much longer the orbit of Wild 2 is. Will she need to regroup when subtracting? Explain.

12. How much greater is Tempel 1's diameter than Wild 2? Hint: The diameter is double the radius.

Write About It

13. Sam uses addition to find 2.28 − 1.34. Is he correct? Justify your answer.

```
1.34 + 0.06 = 1.40
1.40 + 0.60 = 2.00
2.00 + 0.28 = 2.28
        ————
         0.84
2.28 − 1.34 = 0.84
```

Estimate Decimal Differences

Objective
- Estimate decimal differences.

Math Words
front-end estimation
rounding

Blue Morpho butterflies live in the tropical rainforests of Latin America. During one study, the smallest buttefly found had a wingspan of 4.67 inches and the largest had a wingspan of 7.28 inches. What is the approximate difference in wingspans?

To estimate the difference:

◆ Use front-end estimation.

- Identify the nonzero front digits.
- Subtract the values of those digits.

$$\begin{array}{ll} 7.28 \rightarrow & 7 \\ -4.67 \rightarrow & -4 \\ \hline & 3 \end{array}$$

◆ Use rounding.

- Round the decimals to the greatest nonzero place of the lesser number.
- Subtract the rounded numbers.

$$\begin{array}{ll} 7.28 \rightarrow & 7 \\ -4.67 \rightarrow & -5 \\ \hline & 2 \end{array}$$

The difference between wingspans is about 2 to 3 inches.

Study this example.

$$\begin{array}{llll} \$3.46 & \rightarrow \$3 & \rightarrow & \$3.50 \\ -\$3.20 & \rightarrow \$3 & \rightarrow & \$3.20 \\ \hline & \text{about } \$0 & \text{about} & \$0.30 \end{array}$$

If rounding gives a difference of 0, try rounding to the next place.

PRACTICE

Use rounding to estimate the difference.

1. $\begin{array}{l} 0.93 \rightarrow \underline{\quad?\quad} \\ -0.52 \rightarrow \underline{\quad?\quad} \\ \hline \quad\quad\quad ? \end{array}$

2. $\begin{array}{l} 1.26 \rightarrow \underline{\quad?\quad} \\ -0.64 \rightarrow \underline{\quad?\quad} \\ \hline \quad\quad\quad ? \end{array}$

Use front-end estimation to estimate the difference.

3. $\begin{array}{l} \$0.57 \rightarrow \underline{\quad?\quad} \\ -\$0.41 \rightarrow \underline{\quad?\quad} \\ \hline \quad\quad\quad ? \end{array}$

4. $\begin{array}{l} 0.808 \rightarrow \underline{\quad?\quad} \\ -0.23 \rightarrow \underline{\quad?\quad} \\ \hline \quad\quad\quad ? \end{array}$

Use rounding to estimate the difference.

5.
$$0.464$$
$$-0.24$$

6.
$$0.73$$
$$-0.5$$

7.
$$0.631$$
$$-0.39$$

8.
$$0.9$$
$$-0.36$$

9.
$$4.72$$
$$-2.003$$

Use front-end estimation to estimate the difference.

10.
$$0.576$$
$$-0.42$$

11.
$$0.8$$
$$-0.263$$

12.
$$8.43$$
$$-6.82$$

13.
$$0.392$$
$$-0.04$$

14.
$$1.201$$
$$-0.18$$

Use either method to estimate.

15.
$$0.882$$
$$-0.21$$

16.
$$0.91$$
$$-0.704$$

17.
$$2.17$$
$$-2.03$$

18.
$$62.8$$
$$-29.12$$

19.
$$\$0.93$$
$$-\$0.48$$

20.
$$\$2.85$$
$$-\$2.14$$

21.
$$\$18.43$$
$$-\$13.82$$

22.
$$\$54.80$$
$$-\$54.22$$

23. $0.673 - 0.41$

24. $0.7 - 0.38$

25. $2.47 - 1.31$

26. $35.54 - 21.68$

27. $23.45 - 9.87$

28. $8.89 - 2.33$

29. $46.8 - 22.95$

30. $11.13 - 9.39$

31. $\$65.79 - \$24.20$

32. $\$8.90 - \$3.29$

33. $\$15.50 - \$8.85$

34. $\$10.82 - \$10.29$

Problem Solving

35. Canadian Lynx are common in Canada and Alaska. One female in a zoo had 5 kittens. The table shows the weight of each kitten. What is the estimated difference in weight between the two lightest kittens?

36. Katie receives a paycheck for $63.24. She buys a pair of jeans for $23.89 and puts $30.00 into her savings account. About how much money does she have left?

Kitten	Weight (oz)
Caleb	7.12
Dakota	7.71
Omar	7.45
Preston	7.28
Wesley	7.6

Write About It

37. A student uses front-end estimation as shown. How could the student improve the estimate?

$$1.89 \rightarrow 1$$
$$-1.08 \rightarrow 1$$
$$\text{about} \quad 0$$

Use the model to help find the difference.

1. 0.74 − 0.32

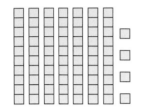

A. 0.24 **B.** 0.32
C. 0.40 **D.** 0.42

2. 0.41 − 0.27

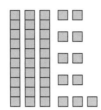

A. 0.13 **B.** 0.14
C. 0.24 **D.** 0.27

3. 1.25 − 0.14

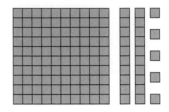

A. 0.11 **B.** 0.91
C. 1.11 **D.** 1.21

4. 1.63 − 0.58

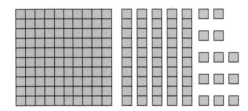

A. 0.05 **B.** 0.95
C. 1.05 **D.** 1.15

5. 1.29 − 0.53

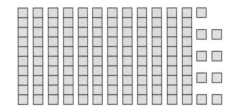

A. 0.76 **B.** 0.86
C. 0.96 **D.** 1.16

Use addition to find the difference.

6. 3.51 − 1.76
 1.76 + _?_ = 1.80
 1.80 + _?_ = 2.00
 2.00 + _?_ = 3.00
 3.00 + _?_ = 3.51
 3.51 − 1.76 = _?_

7. 4.09 − 2.47
 2.47 + _?_ = 2.50
 2.50 + _?_ = 3.00
 3.00 + _?_ = 4.00
 4.00 + _?_ = 4.09
 4.09 − 2.47 = _?_

8. 7.31 − 4.89
 4.89 + _?_ = 4.90
 4.90 + _?_ = 5.00
 5.00 + _?_ = 7.00
 7.00 + _?_ = 7.31
 7.31 − 4.89 = _?_

9. 4.32 − 2.17

10. 1.18 − 0.33

11. 0.82 − 0.79

Find the difference. Use a model or addition.

12. 5.12 − 4.98

13. 3.11 − 1.28

14. 5.5 − 3.65

15. 8.41 − 6.7

16. 12.58 − 9.39

17. 2.7 − 1.81

Choose the subtraction sentence shown by the model.

18.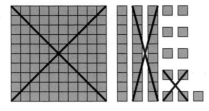

A. 1.31 − 1.24 = 0.07
B. 1.41 − 1.24 = 0.17
C. 1.31 − 1.14 = 0.17
D. 1.41 − 1.14 = 0.27

19.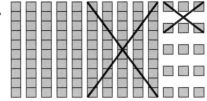

A. 1.05 − 0.59 = 0.46
B. 1.05 − 0.56 = 0.49
C. 1.15 − 0.59 = 0.56
D. 1.15 − 0.56 = 0.59

Use rounding to estimate the difference.

20.   0.5 8 4
     − 0.3 1 2

21.   0.9
     − 0.7 5

22.   0.2 8
     − 0.2 1

23.   1.7 4 1
     − 0.6 4 8

24.   6.3 2
     − 2.6 8

25.   1.3 4 5
     − 0.5 6 1

26.   0.0 6 9
     − 0.0 4 1

27.   0.2 3 1
     − 0.1 4 6

28.   2.3 5 1
     − 2.1 9 1

29.   4.2 4 1
     − 0.0 2 8

Use front-end estimation to estimate the difference.

30.   0.9 8 4
     − 0.4 4 2

31.   0.4 7
     − 0.3

32.   4.9
     − 1.4 4

33.   5.4 9 8
     − 0.5 6

34.   1 0.5 1 4
     −   6.0 0 9

35.   2.3 4 1
     − 1.1 4 2

36.   3.3 4 5
     − 0.6 7 2

37.   8.1 6 3
     − 2.1 5 7

38.   0.0 3 6
     − 0.0 1 4

39.   1.2 5 8
     − 0.9 5 2

Problem Solving

Rings form inside tree trunks as they age. The line graph shows the length of some rings from an oak tree. Use the line graph for Exercises 40–41.

40. About how much greater is the length of the ring formed at 400 years than 300 years? Use front-end estimation and rounding.

41. Write statements that describe how the rings of this tree change from 100 to 200 years of age, and 200 to 300 years of age.

42. Explain how to find 2.52 − 1.84 using addition.

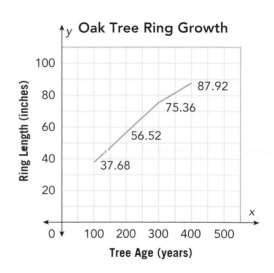

Oak Tree Ring Growth

Subtract Decimals: Hundredths

Objective
- Subtract decimals through hundredths.

Math Word
regroup

Diego heats 0.8 liter of water in a pot until the water boils. After a few minutes, he turns the heat off and measures the remaining water. There is 0.44 liter of water remaining. How much water has evaporated?

To find the amount of water that evaporated, find $0.8 - 0.44$.

◆ Subtract using a model.

 → Regroup a tenth as 10 hundredths.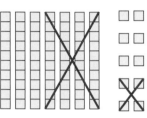

Cross out 4 tenths and 4 hundredths to subtract 0.44.

$$0.8 - 0.44 = 0.36$$

◆ Subtract using place value.

Line up the decimal points. $0.8 = 0.80$	Regroup. Subtract the hundredths.	Subtract the tenths.	Write the decimal point in the difference.
$\begin{array}{r} 0.8\,0 \\ -\,0.4\,4 \\ \hline \end{array}$	$\begin{array}{r} {}^{7\ 10} \\ 0.\cancel{8}\,\cancel{0} \\ -\,0.4\,4 \\ \hline 6 \end{array}$	$\begin{array}{r} {}^{7\ 10} \\ 0.\cancel{8}\,\cancel{0} \\ -\,0.4\,4 \\ \hline 3\,6 \end{array}$	$\begin{array}{r} {}^{7\ 10} \\ 0.\cancel{8}\,\cancel{0} \\ -\,0.4\,4 \\ \hline 0.3\,6 \end{array}$

▷ 0.36 liter of water has evaporated.

PRACTICE

Regroup. Find the difference.

1. $\begin{array}{r} 0.3\,2 \\ -\,0.1\,5 \\ \hline \end{array}$ $\begin{array}{r} ? \\ -\,0.1\,5 \\ \hline \end{array}$

Regroup 32 hundredths as _?_ tenths _?_ hundredths. The difference is _?_ .

2. $\begin{array}{r} 1.8\,4 \\ -\,0.3\,9 \\ \hline \end{array}$ $\begin{array}{r} ? \\ -\,0.3\,9 \\ \hline \end{array}$

Regroup 1 and 84 hundredths as _?_ one _?_ tenths _?_ hundredths. The difference is _?_ .

3. $\begin{array}{r} 2.3\,8 \\ -\,1.8\,4 \\ \hline \end{array}$

4. $\begin{array}{r} 5.1\,1 \\ -\,0.6\,5 \\ \hline \end{array}$

5. $\begin{array}{r} 10.9\,2 \\ -\ \ 7.3\,9 \\ \hline \end{array}$

6. $\begin{array}{r} 0.5\,3 \\ -\,0.2\,8 \\ \hline \end{array}$

Find the difference.

7.   0.08
     − 0.03

8.   12.28
     − 0.16

9.   6.53
     − 6.38

10.   10.87
      − 5.59

11.   9.61
      − 0.35

12.   1.9
      − 0.6

13.   0.63
      − 0.2

14.   0.8
      − 0.09

15.   3.4
      − 2.23

16.   0.78
      − 0.3

17. 5.84 − n when $n = 0.3$

18. 0.7 − n when $n = 0.27$

19. 0.5 − n when $n = 0.12$

20. 11.62 − n when $n = 0.38$

Write a pattern rule. Find the next 2 terms in the set.

21. 0.1, 0.4, 0.7, 1.0, _?_ , _?_

22. 0.7, 0.75, 0.8, 0.85, _?_ , _?_

23. 0.54, 0.46, 0.38, 0.3, _?_ , _?_

24. 0.55, 0.48, 0.41, 0.34, 0.27 _?_ , _?_

Simplify the expression.

25. 0.4 − 0.28 + 3.2

26. 0.3 + (0.28 − 0.19)

27. 0.87 − (0.2 + 0.19)

28. 0.14 + 0.58 − 0.62

Problem Solving

Two common pollutants and their maximum allowable levels are listed in the table. These levels are measured in the same house. Use the table for Exercises 29–30.

Pollutant	Maximum Level
Lead	0.15 micrograms per cubic meter
Ozone	0.07 parts per million

29. A reading for ozone is at 0.11 parts per million. How much does the level need to decrease to be at a safe level?

30. A first measure for lead is 0.11 micrograms per cubic meter. A second measure shows an improvement of 0.04 micrograms. How far below the maximum level is the second reading?

Write About It

31. When is regrouping necessary when subtracting decimals?

Subtract Decimals: Thousandths

Objective
- Subtract decimals through thousandths.

Math Word
regroup

A certain test measures the acidity, or pH level, of blood. The pH of blood is usually between 7.35 and 7.45. The table shows the results of two tests. How much did the pH level decrease?

Lab Results	
Test Time	pH
Morning	7.416
Afternoon	7.358

To find the decrease of the pH level, find 7.416 − 7.358.

- Line up the decimal points.

```
  7.416
− 7.358
```

- Subtract in each place. Regroup as needed.

```
      0 16              3 10 16
  7.4 1 6          7.4 1 6
− 7.3 5 8        − 7.3 5 8
        8            0 5 8
```

- Write the decimal point in the difference.

```
      3 10 16
  7.4 1 6
− 7.3 5 8
  0.0 5 8
```

➤ The pH level decreased by 0.058.

Study these examples.

```
                  2 16  14                                    0  15 9 10
  2 4.9        3 7.4 2          9.2 5 8          1 5 1.8 0 0
− 1 3.7      − 1 9.8 0        − 2.1 3 4        −   1 0.7 1 8
  1 1.2        1 7.6 2          7.1 2 4          1 4 0.8 8 2
```

PRACTICE

Regroup. Find the difference.

1.
```
  0.825      ?
− 0.348    − 0.348
```

Regroup 825 thousandths as ? thousandths ? hundredths ? tenths. The difference is ? .

2.
```
  7.642      ?
− 6.574    − 6.574
```

Regroup 7 and 642 thousandths as ? thousandths ? hundredths ? tenths ? ones. The difference is ? .

Find the difference.

3.
```
  0.388
− 0.23
```

4.
```
  8.51
− 4.32
```

5.
```
  2.285
− 0.196
```

6.
```
  6.123
− 5.765
```

7.
```
  14.682
−  8.395
```

8.
```
  4.809
− 2.315
```

9.
```
  3.102
− 0.416
```

10.
```
  15.051
−  8.199
```

11.
```
  2.523
− 0.46
```

12.
```
  0.45
− 0.293
```

Find the difference.

13. 0.647
− 0.562

14. 6.495
− 2.397

15. 23.915
− 20.508

16. 3.172
− 0.59

17. 41.6
− 10.67

18. 0.431
− 0.381

19. 6.501
− 3.448

20. 9.093
− 8.41

21. 10.003
− 8.692

22. 1.59
− 1.499

23. 1.852 − 0.963

24. 13.4 − 11.812

25. 81.171 − n when $n = 20.83$

26. 51.7 − n when $n = 36.816$

Simplify the expression.

27. 0.729 − 0.483 + 0.72

28. 0.741 + (0.632 − 0.377)

29. 0.93 − (0.526 + 0.32) − 0.02

30. (0.284 + 0.197) − 0.228

Compare. Write <, =, or >.

31. 5.6 ? 9.4 − 4.72

32. 11.24 ? 21.4 − 10.79

33. 12.6 − 4 ? 46.2 − 36.479

34. 9.607 − 3.9 ? 16.547 − 7.8

Problem Solving

35. Use mental math to find 7.506 − 1.003 − 2.403.

36. If there is a zero in the minuend, will regrouping always be necessary? Give an example.

37. The table shows data for two baseball players. Which statistic, batting average or on-base percentage, has the greater difference for the players? By how much?

Player	Batting Average	On-Base Percentage
Caprara	0.338	0.440
Henderson	0.299	0.402

Write About It

38. When using base ten blocks to model a difference, how will a zero in a place in the minuend affect the model? Use an example in your explanation.

Subtraction with Money

Objective
■ Use estimation and addition strategies to subtract with money.

Math Word
difference

Jasmin's family buys a new television. They pay $640.93 incuding tax. How much is the tax for the television?

To find the cost of the tax, find $640.93 − $599. Subtract money amounts the same way you subtract all decimal numbers.

SALE $599

First, use rounding to estimate the difference: $640 − $600 = $40.

Line up the decimal points.	Regroup as needed. Subtract the hundredths.	Regroup as needed. Subtract the tenths.	Regroup as needed. Subtract the whole numbers. Write the decimal point in the difference.
$640.93 − 599.00	$640.93 − 599.00 $ 3	$640.93 − 599.00 $ 93	13 5 3 10 $640.93 − 599.00 $ 41.93

The tax on the television is $41.93. This is close to the estimate.

Study these examples.

```
    9  9
 6 10 10 12
 $70.02
− 32.58
 $37.44
```

```
   9  15
 8 10 5 13
 $90.63
− 43.76
 $46.87
```

```
   9  9  9
 6 10 10 10 11
 $700.01
− 549.34
 $150.67
```

PRACTICE

Estimate. Then determine the difference.

1. $45.16
− 36.14

2. $20.40
− 10.69

3. $97.73
− 32.84

4. $98.53
− 23.85

5. $77.17
− 38.74

6. $6.00
− 3.92

7. $5.09
− 1.35

8. $87.00
− 64.27

9. $48.00
− 7.03

10. $30.20
− 4.53

Use rounding to estimate. Then determine the difference.

11.	12.	13.	14.	15.
$57.43 − 28.15	$54.10 − 37.84	$23.85 − 10.69	$94.31 − 9.83	$270.05 − 179.71

16.	17.	18.	19.	20.
$7.75 − 5.79	$50.00 − 05.47	$19.99 − 14.79	$1.25 − 0.87	$134.92 − 89.59

Align. Then determine the difference.

21. $73.20 − $45.05

22. $370.05 − $151.29

23. $721.63 − $494.09

24. $900 − $357.97

Simplify the expression when $n =$ $13.23.

25. $100 − ($62.16 + n)

26. $32.81 + ($89.28 − n)

27. n − ($5.09 + $2.39)

28. $100 − n − $24.99

Problem Solving

A store sells kits that students can use to learn more about science and engineering. Use the advertisement for Exercises 29–31.

ON SALE NOW!

Egg Drop Kit $38.00

Balloon Rocket Kit $19.95

Roller Coaster Kit $67.00

Crystal Growing Kit $43.75

29. Andres buys a roller coaster kit and a crystal growing kit. He spends $118.50 in all. How much tax does he pay?

30. Malachi buys an egg drop kit and a crystal growing kit. He pays $5.72 tax and pays with a $100 bill. How much change should he get?

31. The store's website has free shipping on orders over $200. Otherwise, shipping is $24.50. Explain why Mr. Cho should add to his order of two crystal kits, an egg drop kit, and a roller coaster kit.

Write About It

32. Explain what ones, tenths, and hundredths represent in the context of money.

Problem Solving
Use a Model

Objective
- Use a diagram to represent the situation when solving a problem.

Math Word

bar diagram

Paige is making 3 batches of soap for her science fair project. How many kilograms of the three oils does Paige use in Batch 1? How much greater is the amount of olive oil in Batch 3 than the amount of olive oil in Batch 2?

You can use bar diagrams to model the situation.

To find the total amount of the three oils in Batch 1, refer to the table. The three parts go in the bottom bar of the bar diagram.

Batch	Olive Oil (kg)	Coconut Oil (kg)	Palm Oil (kg)
1	0.525	0.095	0.095
2	0.565	0.075	0.075
3	0.605	0.055	0.055

total amount = ?		
0.525	0.095	0.095

The diagram shows that the total amount is the sum 0.525 + 0.095 + 0.095. Align the decimal points and add. Regroup as needed.

$$
\begin{array}{r}
{\scriptstyle 2\ 1} \\
0.5\,2\,5 \\
0.0\,9\,5 \\
+\,0.0\,9\,5 \\
\hline
0.7\,1\,5
\end{array}
$$

▷ Paige uses 0.715 kg of the three oils in Batch 1.

To find the difference of the amounts of olive oil in Batches 2 and 3, refer to the table. Place the unknown part in the bottom bar.

0.605	
0.565	?

The diagram shows that the unknown part is the difference 0.605 − 0.565. Align decimal points and subtract. Regroup as needed.

$$
\begin{array}{r}
{\scriptstyle 5\ 10} \\
0.\,\cancel{6}\,\cancel{0}\,5 \\
-\,0.5\,6\,5 \\
\hline
0.0\,4\,0
\end{array}
$$

▷ The amount of olive oil in Batch 3 is 0.040 kg greater than the amount in Batch 2.

PRACTICE

1. As an earthworm crawls, its length is observed and measured. It measures 8.43 cm at its shortest length and 11.19 cm at its longest length. Use a bar diagram to determine how many centimeters it stretches as it crawls.

Henry uses decimals to record the distances he rows on the rowing machine. His brother spilled some paint on Henry's table. Henry decides that he can find find his distance from Thursday by performing some calculations. Use this information for Exercises 2–5.

Day	Distance (mi)
Monday	2.25
Tuesday	3.375
Wednesday	2.875
Thursday	
Total	11.625

2. Copy and complete this bar diagram to represent the data in Henry's table.

?			
?	3.375	?	?

3. How far does Henry row on Thursday?

4. How much farther does Henry row on Tuesday than on Monday?

5. How far must Henry row on Friday to total 15 miles for the 5 days?

The table shows the ingredients for Makayla's favorite salad dressing. She also adds salt and pepper after she mixes the dressing. Use the table for Exercises 6–8. Draw a bar diagram to solve each problem.

Ingredient	Amount (L)
Olive Oil	0.625
Vinegar	0.375
Orange Juice	0.125

6. What is the total volume of all the ingredients for the salad dressing?

7. How much greater is the amount of olive oil than the amount of vinegar and orange juice combined?

8. Makayla makes the dressing in a large bowl. She pours some out and fills a 0.5-liter bottle. Is there more dressing in the bowl or in the bottle? Explain.

9. Becky wants to find the values missing from the bar diagram. Does she have enough information to solve the problem? Explain.

?		
1.05	0.367	?

Write About It

10. How can a bar diagram help in solving a problem? What operations do you plan to use when solving a problem using bar diagrams? Explain.

Use the model to help find the difference.

1. $0.55 - 0.24$

2. $0.64 - 0.49$

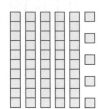 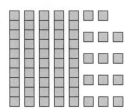

3. What subtraction sentence does the model show?

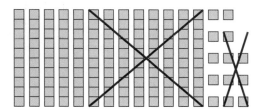

Use rounding to estimate the difference.

4. $\begin{array}{r} 0.728 \\ -0.55 \\ \hline \end{array}$
5. $\begin{array}{r} 0.89 \\ -0.67 \\ \hline \end{array}$
6. $\begin{array}{r} 0.433 \\ -0.109 \\ \hline \end{array}$
7. $\begin{array}{r} 6.48 \\ -2.71 \\ \hline \end{array}$
8. $\begin{array}{r} 10.576 \\ -\;\;5.442 \\ \hline \end{array}$

Use front-end estimation to estimate the difference.

9. $\begin{array}{r} 0.72 \\ -0.38 \\ \hline \end{array}$
10. $\begin{array}{r} 0.842 \\ -0.199 \\ \hline \end{array}$
11. $\begin{array}{r} 6.21 \\ -5.84 \\ \hline \end{array}$
12. $\begin{array}{r} 7.295 \\ -2.483 \\ \hline \end{array}$
13. $\begin{array}{r} 2.628 \\ -1.335 \\ \hline \end{array}$

Regroup. Find the difference.

14. $\begin{array}{r} 0.93 \\ -0.47 \\ \hline \end{array}$

Regroup 93 hundredths as ?
hundredths and ? tenths.
The difference is ? .

15. $\begin{array}{r} 6.81 \\ -2.73 \\ \hline \end{array}$

Regroup 6 and 81 hundredths as ?
hundredths ? tenths and ? ones.
The difference is ? .

16. $\begin{array}{r} 0.714 \\ -0.426 \\ \hline \end{array}$

17. $\begin{array}{r} 8.529 \\ -5.685 \\ \hline \end{array}$

Find the difference.

18. 0.05 −0.01	**19.** 6.782 −4.351	**20.** $5.42 − 2.31	**21.** 7.409 −1.202	**22.** 4.83 −0.67
23. $2.15 − 1.48	**24.** 10.548 − 6.285	**25.** 1.9 −1.048	**26.** 12.684 − 9.59	**27.** $15.28 − 8.79
28. 22.007 −13.842	**29.** 14.574 −13.894	**30.** 74.2 −39.05	**31.** 84.219 −16.506	**32.** 17.111 − 8.444

33. $26.91 − $19.87

34. $5.22 − $0.89

Simplify.

35. $15.79 + $2.75 − $11.99

36. $5.50 − $4.21 − $1.09

37. 45.792 + (11.61 − 4.451)

38. 21.49 − (2.269 + 3.26)

39. 17.09 − n when $n = 1.88$

40. 5.638 − n when $n = 0.759$

41. n − 0.775 when $n = 0.823$

42. $14.07 − n when $n = 11.46

Problem Solving

The table shows rainfall totals from some of the wettest U.S. hurricanes. Use the table for Exercises 43–46.

Hurricane	Rainfall (inches)
Danny	36.71
Paul	38.76
Allison	40.68

43. The recorded rainfall for Paul is __?__ inches more than the recorded rainfall for Danny.

44. The recorded rainfall for Allison is __?__ inches more than the recorded rainfall for Paul.

45. The rainfall for Allison is __?__ inches more than the rainfall for Danny.

46. What method other than subtraction could be used to complete Exercise 45? Explain.

47. Julia orders a pizza. Her total comes to $14.57. She pays the delivery person using a $20 bill. How much change should she get back? Explain how to regroup the $20 bill using $1 bills, dimes, and pennies.

Recall that Maxwell created a budget so he can save $200 each month for a down payment on a house. He made some final adjustments to his budget, and will begin using the budget in September.

Maxwell wants to monitor his spending each month to ensure he stays on budget. He downloads an app on his smartphone that automatically links purchases and payments from his bank account to different categories of his budget. On September 15th, the app displays the data shown.

	Budget	Actual
Category		
🏠 **Home** $1,140.85		$754.23
💲 **Loans and Savings** $625.71		$376.95
🚗 **Transportation** $555.25		$597.36
🍴 **Food and Entertainment** $440.00		$387.64
Total Expenses $2,761.81		$2,116.18

1. How much money does Maxwell have left to spend this month?

2. How much money does Maxwell have left to spend in each category?

- Home ?
- Loans and Savings ?
- Transportation ?
- Food and Entertainment ?

3. In what category has Maxwell overspent? By how much has he exceeded his budget?

Maxwell is also concerned that he has already spent most of the money he budgeted for Food and Entertainment. He uses his smartphone to look at the spending for this category in detail.

4. What does a blue bar in the smartphone app tell Maxwell? What does a red bar tell him?

5. In which category does Maxwell have money left to spend? How much is left?

	Budget	Actual
Food and Entertainment		
🛍️ **Groceries** $315.00		$176.48
🍴 **Dining Out** $125.00		$149.71
👕 **Clothing** $0.00		$61.45
🎬 **Movies** $0.00		$0.00
Total Expenses $440.00		$387.64

6. Will Maxwell meet his grocery budget this month? Explain.

7. In what categories has Maxwell overspent? By how much?

8. When Maxwell created his budget, he decided to remove all spending on clothing. Based on his September expenses so far, was this a reasonable decision? Explain.

When September ends, Maxwell analyzes and adjusts his budget based on his spending habits. He cuts back in other areas so he can allocate more money to Food and Entertainment. He also tries to dine out less. On October 15th, Maxwell's smartphone displays the details shown for this category.

	Budget	Actual
Food and Entertainment		
Groceries $315.00		$169.12
Dining Out $150.00		$72.83
Clothing $50.00		$31.09
Movies $0.00		$0.00
Total Expenses $515.00		$273.04

9. Use the given data to analyze Maxwell's current budget for October. Determine how much money he has left to spend in each category.

10. Overall, how much money does Maxwell have left to spend on Food and Entertainment in the month of October? Should he be concerned about meeting his Food & Entertainment budget this month? Explain.

11. The table shows Maxwell's spending as of the 15th of the month. Copy the table. Then complete the table by first estimating expenses as of the 15th. Then calculate the remaining budget. Identify areas where Maxwell should be concerned about meeting his budget.

	Total Budget	Expenses as of 15th	Remaining Budget
Rent	$750.00	?	?
Renter's Insurance	$27.42	?	?
Gas & Electric	$156.85	?	?
Water & Trash	$35.67	?	?
Phone	$64.92	?	?
Cable TV	$0.00	?	?
Internet	$45.99	?	?
House Supplies	$60.00	?	?
Total	$1140.85	?	?

Determine the best answer for each problem.

1. Identify the pattern rule.

   6.25, 5.77, 5.29, 4.81

   A. Subtract 0.42.
   B. Subtract 0.48.
   C. Subtract 0.52.
   D. Subtract 0.58.

2. Which is equal to 0.829? Select all that apply.

   A. 5.355 − 4.526
   B. 7.87 − 7.041
   C. 5.135 − 4.206
   D. 0.928 − 0.199
   E. 12.476 − 11.647

3. Hannah buys a glue stick that costs $0.92 and a paintbrush that costs $2.87. How much more expensive is the paintbrush?

4. Find the difference.

   12.076 − 4.638

   A. 6.642
   B. 7.438
   C. 8.438
   D. 8.642

5. The length of the rectangle is how much longer than the width?

   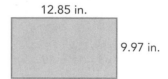

   12.85 in.

   9.97 in.

6. Find the missing value.

   41.08 − _?_ = 3.927

   A. 37.153
   B. 37.873
   C. 38.153
   D. 38.873

7. On Sunday, a family's bank account balance is $482.41. The next day, the account balance is $527.10. Describe how the account balance changed.

   A. The balance increased by $165.31.
   B. The balance decreased by $165.31.
   C. The balance increased by $44.69.
   D. The balance decreased by $44.69.

8. Subtract.

   41.24 − 6.739 − 12.085

   A. 21.651
   B. 22.416
   C. 29.155
   D. 34.501

Decimals: Multiplication

A budget can help you save money and better understand your spending. Over time, you can see how your spending habits change. When you see how much money has been spent on certain expenses over an extended period of time, you may choose to cut back in some areas.

Budget Analysis

After using a budget for 6 to 12 months, ask yourself these questions and then update your budget accordingly.

♦ How difficult has it been to meet my budget each month? Have I saved any money?

♦ Is it possible to decrease my expenses in order to save more money each month?

♦ In what categories did my spending exceed what I expected? Are there categories that need spending limits increased?

Multiply by Powers of 10

Objective
- Observe and use patterns of zeros when multiplying by a power of 10.

Math Word
power of 10

A cotton fiber is a single cell. It can be 1000 times as long as its diameter. If the diameter of a cotton fiber is 0.0165 mm, how long could the cotton fiber be?

To find the length of the cotton fiber in millimeters, find 0.0165×1000.

To multiply 0.0165 by 1000, move the decimal point to the right 3 places because there are 3 zeros in 1000.

$$0.0165 \times 1000 = 0.016.5 = 16.5$$

The cotton fiber could be about 16.5 mm long.

To multiply by a power of 10 written in standard form, move the decimal point to the right as many places as there are zeros in the power of 10.

$$0.125 \times 10 = 0.1.25 = 1.25$$
$$0.125 \times 100 = 0.12.5 = 12.5$$
$$0.125 \times 1000 = 0.125. = 125$$

To multiply by a power of 10 written with an exponent, move the decimal point to the right as many places as the exponent.

$$0.47 \times 10^1 = 0.4.7 = 4.7$$
$$0.47 \times 10^2 = 0.47. = 47$$
$$0.47 \times 10^3 = 0.470. = 470$$

Write one or more zeros to the right of the last digit if there are not enough places in the number.

Study these examples.

$$0.2 \times 50 = 0.2 \times 10 \times 5 = 0.2. \times 5 = 10$$
$$0.2 \times 500 = 0.2 \times 100 \times 5 = 0.20. \times 5 = 100$$
$$0.2 \times 5000 = 0.2 \times 1000 \times 5 = 0.200. \times 5 = 1000$$

PRACTICE

1. 3.68×1000

How many 0s are there?

What is the product?

2. 0.395×10^2

What is the exponent?

What is the product?

3. 5.7×20

How do you factor 20?

What is the product?

Find the product.

4. 0.752×10

5. 2.29×10^2

6. 3.14×800

7. 0.627×100

8. 0.037×10^3

9. 5.06×400

10. 3.747×10^2

11. 0.831×10^4

12. 90.17×300

13. 0.598×10^5

14. 0.578×10^1

15. 0.081×9000

16. 99.34×10^3

17. 0.725×10^7

18. 586.1×200

Find the value of n.

19. $0.032 \times n = 3.2$

$n = \underline{\ ?\ }$

20. $12.345 \times n = 12,345$

$n = \underline{\ ?\ }$

21. $n \times 0.013 = 13,000$

$n = \underline{\ ?\ }$

Problem Solving

22. When a certain number is multiplied by 10^5, the product is 340,900. What is the number?

23. Ms. Victor buys 1000 shares of Stock A and 500 shares of Stock B. How much does she pay for all the shares?

Stock	Cost per Share ($)
A	5.72
B	10.50

24. The weight of a carriage bolt is 0.175 pound. These bolts are packaged in boxes of 50. What is the weight of the bolts in 200 boxes?

25. A marble company makes 10^6 marbles a day. If each marble weighs 4.5 grams, how many kilograms of marbles does the company make in a day? Hint: There are 1000 grams in one kilogram.

26. Sergio says that 0.082×10^9 is greater than 100 million. Is Sergio's statement correct? Explain how you know.

Write About It

27. Do 1.05×10^7 and $10,000,000 \times 1.05$ have the same value? Justify your reasoning.

12-2 Use Properties to Multiply a Decimal by a Whole Number

Objective
• Use properties of multiplication to multiply a decimal by a whole number.

Math Words
repeated addition
Distributive Property

Manuel buys 2 packages that each contain 0.45 kilogram of rice. How much rice does Manuel have in all?

• Model 2 × 0.45 as repeated addition.

0.45 + 0.45

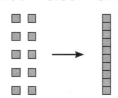

• Model 2 × 0.45 with the Distributive Property.

Break apart 0.45.
2 × (0.40 + 0.05)

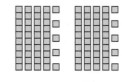

• Add the tenths.
0.4 + 0.4 = 0.8

• Use the Distributive Property.
(2 × 0.40) + (2 × 0.05)

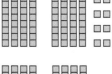

• Add the hundredths. Regroup.
0.05 + 0.05 = 0.10

• Find how many tenths.
8 tenths ⟶ 2 × 0.4 = 0.8

• Add the two sums.
0.8 + 0.10 = 0.90

• Find how many hundredths.
10 hundredths ⟶ 2 × 0.05 = 0.10

• Add the tenths and hundredths.
0.8 + 0.10 = 0.90

Write 0.45 as a fraction to check your work.

$$2 \times 0.45 = 2 \times \frac{45}{100}$$
$$= \frac{90}{100}$$
$$= 0.90 \checkmark$$

Manuel has 0.90 kilogram of rice.

PRACTICE

Complete the statement.

1. 5 × 0.17 = 5 × (0.10 + _?_) = (5 × 0.10) + (5 × _?_)

2. 12 × 0.25 = 12 × (_?_ + 0.05) = (12 × _?_) + (12 × 0.05)

Use repeated addition to find the product for the model.

3.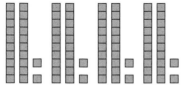

4.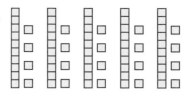

Use the Distributive Property to find the product for the model.

5.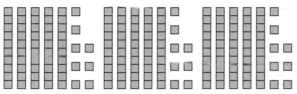

6.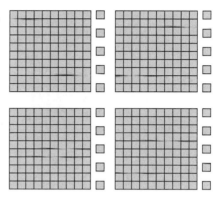

Use base-ten models or diagrams to find the product.

7. 2 × 0.53

8. 3 × 0.82

9. 4 × 1.91

10. 5 × 0.01

11. 2.36 × 6

12. 0.33 × 7

Problem Solving

13. Ruby buys six 1.75-liter bottles of olive oil and three 0.30-liter bottles of walnut oil for her restaurant. How much oil does she buy?

14. Micah uses a mixture of 0.25 cup of detergent and 3 cups of water to wash his bicycle. He makes 4 times as much of the mixture to wash the family car. How much detergent does he need to wash the car? How much mixture does he make to wash the car?

Write About It

15. Compare using repeated addition and using the Distributive Property to find products of decimals and whole numbers.

Estimate Decimal Products

Objective
- Estimate decimal products.

Math Words
front-end estimation
rounding

Fernando's family just got a new car. According to the sticker on the window, the car averages 32.1 miles per gallon. If the car's gas tank can hold 12.4 gallons, about how many miles can Fernando's family drive on one full tank of gas?

◆ Use front-end estimation.

- Determine the nonzero front digits.
- Write zeros for the other digits and multiply.

$$
\begin{array}{r}
32.1 \longrightarrow 30 \\
\times 12.4 \longrightarrow \times 10 \\
\hline
\text{about } 300
\end{array}
$$

◆ Use rounding.

- Round each decimal to its greatest place.
- Multiply the rounded numbers.

$$
\begin{array}{r}
32.1 \longrightarrow 30 \\
\times 12.4 \longrightarrow \times 10 \\
\hline
\text{about } 300
\end{array}
$$

▷ Fernando's family can drive about 300 miles on one full tank of gas.

Study these examples.

Front-end Estimation	Rounding	Clustering
$\begin{array}{r} 1.63 \longrightarrow 1 \\ \times\ 8.6 \longrightarrow 8 \\ \hline \text{about } 8 \end{array}$	$\begin{array}{r} 1.63 \longrightarrow 2 \\ \times\ 8.6 \longrightarrow 9 \\ \hline \text{about } 18 \end{array}$	When addends cluster around a certain value, estimate by multiplying that value by the number of addends.
Both factors are less than the actual factors.	Both factors are greater than the actual factors.	$1.42 + 1.39 + 1.403 + 1.37$
The estimate is *less than* the actual product.	The estimate is *greater than* the actual product.	$1.4 + 1.4 + 1.4 + 1.4$
		$4 \times 1.4 = 5.6$

PRACTICE

Use front-end estimation to estimate the product.

1. $\begin{array}{r} 4.81 \longrightarrow \text{nonzero front digit } \underline{\ ?\ } \\ \times\ \ 2.6 \longrightarrow \text{nonzero front digit } \underline{\ ?\ } \\ \text{Estimate: } \underline{\ ?\ } \end{array}$

2. $\begin{array}{r} 3.45 \longrightarrow \text{nonzero front digit } \underline{\ ?\ } \\ \times\ \ 4.3 \longrightarrow \text{nonzero front digit } \underline{\ ?\ } \\ \text{Estimate: } \underline{\ ?\ } \end{array}$

Use rounding to estimate the product.

3. 0.88×9.8

4. 4.376×8.2

5. 9.135×12.7

Use front-end estimation to estimate the product.

6. 24.891 × 0.68

7. 89.2 × 0.345

8. 72.008 × 4.24

Use rounding to estimate the product.

9. 31.12 × 0.8

10. 27.876 × 19.2

11. 0.099 × 0.16

Use front-end estimation to estimate the product. Determine whether the estimate is *less than* or *greater than* the actual product.

12. 45.186 × 0.35

13. 83.607 × 0.64

14. 92.487 × 0.92

Use rounding to estimate the product. Determine whether the estimate is *less than* or *greater than* the actual product.

15. 17.68 × 0.55

16. 0.096 × 29.34

17. 0.341 × 32.49

Use clustering to estimate the sum.

18. 2.05 + 1.986 + 2.014 + 1.895 + 2.1

19. 0.93 + 1.1 + 1.08 + 0.9

Problem Solving

On average, Mercury is about 0.39 Astronomical Unit (AU) from the sun. Jupiter is about 13.4 times as far away from the sun as Mercury. Use this information for Exercises 20–21.

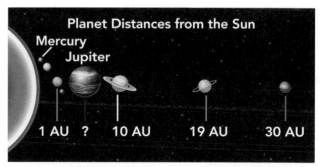

Planet Distances from the Sun

20. Use rounding to show that Jupiter is about 4 AU from the sun.

21. Improve your estimate by rounding one of the factors to the second greatest place.

Write About It

22. Does front-end estimation usually lead to overestimates or underestimates? Justify your answer.

Multiply Decimals by Whole Numbers

Objective
- Multiply decimals to hundredths using models and strategies.

Math Words
multiply
decimal
whole number

A sandwich shop uses 0.25 pound of meat per medium sandwich. How many pounds of meat does the shop need to make 23 sandwiches for a catering order?

♦ First, estimate the product by rounding: $20 \times 0.3 = 6$.

Use the model to help you. It shows 23 groups of 0.25. There are less than 7 whole grids shaded, so the product should be less than 7. To find the exact amount, multiply 23 by 0.25.

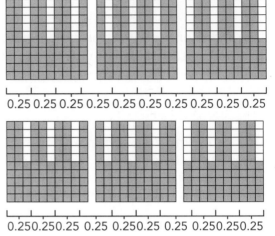

0.25 0.25 0.25 0.25 0.25 0.25 0.25 0.25 0.25 0.25

0.25 0.25 0.25 0.25 0.25 0.25 0.25 0.25 0.25 0.25

♦ To multiply a decimal by a whole number:

- Multiply as you would with whole numbers.

- Count the number of decimal places in the decimal factor.

- Mark off the same number of decimal places in the product.

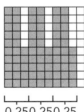

0.25 0.25 0.25

$$
\begin{array}{r}
0.2\,5 \\
\times\quad 2\,3 \\
\hline
7\,5 \\
+\,5\ 0\,0 \\
\hline
5.7\,5
\end{array}
$$

2 decimal places

▷ The sandwich shop needs 5.75 pounds of meat for the catering order.

Study these examples.

$$
\begin{array}{r}
0.1\,2\,1 \\
\times\qquad 4 \\
\hline
0.4\,8\,4
\end{array}
$$
3 decimal places

$$
\begin{array}{r}
9.3 \\
\times\quad 5 \\
\hline
4\,6.5
\end{array}
$$
1 decimal place

$$
\begin{array}{r}
4.5\,5 \\
\times\qquad 9 \\
\hline
4\,0.9\,5
\end{array}
$$
2 decimal places

PRACTICE

Write the decimal point in each product.

1.
$$
\begin{array}{r}
2.8 \\
\times\ \ 3 \\
\hline
8\,4
\end{array}
$$

2.
$$
\begin{array}{r}
6.3\,1 \\
\times\quad 1\,6 \\
\hline
1\,0\,0\ 9\,6
\end{array}
$$

3.
$$
\begin{array}{r}
0.7\,9 \\
\times\quad 3 \\
\hline
2\ 3\,7
\end{array}
$$

4.
$$
\begin{array}{r}
4.1\,7 \\
\times\quad 7\,2 \\
\hline
3\,0\,0\ 2\,4
\end{array}
$$

5.
$$
\begin{array}{r}
0.5\,4 \\
\times\quad 5 \\
\hline
2\ 7\,0
\end{array}
$$

6. How did you know where to place the decimal point in the product of Exercise 5?

Use rounding to estimate. Then, find the product.

7.
```
   0.6
×  1 3
```

8.
```
   0.4 9
×    2 9
```

9.
```
   0.0 8
×    3 5
```

10.
```
   9.2
× 3 9
```

11.
```
   3.0 5
×    2 6
```

12.
```
   5.0 5 2
×      1 9
```

13.
```
   7.8 9 1
×      5 6
```

14.
```
   0.7 4
×    1 2
```

15.
```
   8.3 9
×    6 2
```

16.
```
   1 4.5 5
×        8 9
```

Find the product.

17. 3×0.4

18. 0.49×5

19. 9×0.019

20. 0.153×8

21. 2×0.8519

22. 35×35.02

23. 15×0.67

24. 49×15.19

25. $24,000 \times 4.25$

26. $0.47 \times 360,000$

27. six times nineteen thousandths

28. two times five and two tenths

29. $n \times 3.29$ when $n = 3$

30. $18.29 \times w$ when $w = 27$

31. $p \times 43$ when $p = 26.514$

32. $36 \times r$ when $r = 1.03$

33. $a \times 3.673$ when $a = 21$

34. $3.2 \times m$ when $m = 41$

Problem Solving

The table shows the nutrients in one banana. Use the table to answer Exercises 35–38. (1 g = 1000 mg)

Nutrient	Amount (mg)
Vitamin B6	0.5
Manganese	0.3
Potassium	450
Iron	0.3

35. How much iron will a dozen bananas contain?

36. How many grams of potassium will 4 bananas contain?

37. Brooke wants to get 2 mg of manganese each day. This week she eats 5 bananas. How much more manganese should she get from other foods this week?

38. Sarah says that 8 bananas have about 8 mg of Vitamin B6. Do you agree with Sarah? Explain.

Write About It

39. Where do you place the decimal point in a product of a decimal and whole number? Describe in your own words.

Multiplication with Money

Objective
■ Multiply money amounts using the place-value algorithm.

Math Words
decimal point
dollar sign

A teacher is ordering recorders for her music class. How much does it cost to order 22 of the recorders?

First, round to estimate the product: $7 × 20 = $140.

The estimate $140 will be less than the actual product since both factors were rounded down.

$7.49

To find the total cost of the recorders, multiply 22 by $7.49.

To multiply a whole number by an amount of money:

- Multiply as usual.

- Write a decimal point in the product two places from the right.

- Write the dollar sign in the product.

```
  $ 7 . 4 9
×      2 2
  1 4 9 8
1 4 9 8 0
$ 1 6 4 . 7 8
```

▷ The recorders cost $164.78.

Study these examples.

```
  $ 0 . 8 8
×      4 7
    6 1 6
  3 5 2 0
$ 4 1 . 3 6
```

```
  $ 2 . 1 3
×      8 7
  1 4 9 1
1 7 0 4 0
$ 1 8 5 . 3 1
```

```
  $ 3 . 1 5
×    4 4 1
    3 1 5
  1 2 6 0 0
1 2 6 0 0 0
$ 1 3 8 9 . 1 5
```

PRACTICE

Find the product. Write the dollar sign and the decimal point.

1. $2.80
    ×   3

2. $3.54
    ×   9

3. $0.66
    ×   4

4. $7.38
    ×   6

5. $8.69
    ×   8

6. $0.74
    ×   8

7. $0.39
    ×   7

8. $12.38
    ×   9

9. $10.47
    ×   6

10. $2.63
    ×   9

11. $0.57
    ×   38

12. $2.90
    ×   70

13. $9.80
    ×   55

14. $0.69
    ×   43

15. $0.86
    ×   30

Use rounding to estimate. Then, find the product.

16. $3.73
×   9

17. $5.46
×   7

18. $3.14
×   8

19. $9.03
×   5

20. $7.80
×   6

21. $4.50
×   605

22. $2.19
×   341

23. $9.06
×   214

24. $7.16
×   416

25. $6.18
×   524

Find the product.

26. 43 × $3.04

27. 79 × $8.47

28. 86 × $9.32

29. 51 × $7.46

30. 62 × $5.78

31. 93 × $6.85

Simplify.

32. three times as much as $5.60, increased by $4.30

33. twice the sum of $10.56 and $133.05

34. 6 groups of $5.67 plus 3 groups of $100.89

Problem Solving

Use the weekly advertisement for Exercises 35–37.

35. Isabelle buys 1 bunch of kale and two 6-ounce packs of blueberries. How much does she spend?

36. Shawn buys one container of spring mix, 3 pounds of grapes, and 2 pounds of butternut squash. How much does he spend?

37. Isaac buys one bunch of kale, two 6-ounce packs of blueberries, and two 14-oz containers of baby spinach. If he pays with $40, how much change does he receive?

Local organic green kale **$3.39**/bunch
Grapes **$3.49**/lb
Butternut Squash **$1.29**/lb
Blueberries **$3.99**/6oz
Organic baby spinach or spring mix **$6.99**/14oz
Roma tomatoes **$2.99**/lb

Write About It

38. When you multiply a whole number by an amount of money, the decimal point is two places from the right in the product. Explain why. When might you place the decimal point differently?

Solve.

1. 1.84×100
How many 0s are there?
What is the product?

2. 2.6×40
How do you factor 40?
What is the product?

3. 0.742×10^3
What is the exponent?
What is the product?

4. 0.24×1000

5. 400.209×10^5

6. 3.06×10^4

Use repeated addition to find the product for each model.

7.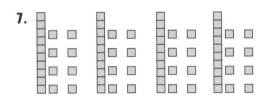

8.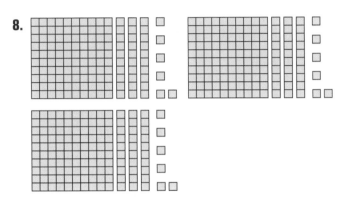

Complete the statement.

9. $7 \times 0.31 = 7 \times (0.30 + \underline{?}) = (7 \times 0.30) + (7 \times \underline{?})$

10. $11 \times 0.67 = 11 \times (\underline{?} + 0.07) = (11 \times \underline{?}) + (11 \times 0.07)$

Use front-end estimation to estimate the product.

11. 5.19×9.872

12. 10.203×6.4

13. 8.724×1.942

Use rounding to estimate the product.

14. 5.19×9.872

15. 10.203×6.4

16. 8.724×1.942

Use clustering to estimate the sum.

17. $7.16 + 6.924 + 7.093 + 6.899 + 6.9$

18. $9.88 + 10.041 + 10.102 + 9.946$

Match the description with its total.

19. 7 groups of $2.54 plus 3 groups of $10.28

20. four times as much as $6.75, plus $12.85

21. five times the sum of $2.39 and $7.62

22. ten times the difference of $7.95 and $3.48

A. $39.85
B. $44.70
C. $48.62
D. $50.05

Use the Distributive Property to find the product for the model.

23.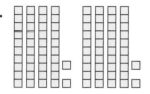

24.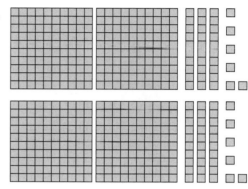

Find the product.

25. 0.87×10

26. 4×0.57

27. 0.2×12

28. 7.42×8

29. 1.429×12

30. 12.50×14

31. 3.5×10^3

32. 8×0.95

33.
$$\begin{array}{r} 5.23 \\ \times\ \ \ 50 \\ \hline \end{array}$$

34.
$$\begin{array}{r} \$0.87 \\ \times\ \ \ \ \ 52 \\ \hline \end{array}$$

35.
$$\begin{array}{r} 16 \\ \times 5.34 \\ \hline \end{array}$$

36.
$$\begin{array}{r} \$10.09 \\ \times\ \ \ \ \ \ \ 25 \\ \hline \end{array}$$

37.
$$\begin{array}{r} 13 \\ \times 0.84 \\ \hline \end{array}$$

38.
$$\begin{array}{r} 4.07 \\ \times 100 \\ \hline \end{array}$$

39.
$$\begin{array}{r} \$6.99 \\ \times\ \ \ 108 \\ \hline \end{array}$$

40.
$$\begin{array}{r} 7.821 \\ \times\ \ \ \ \ 22 \\ \hline \end{array}$$

Problem Solving

The table shows the monthly rainfall in a certain region of a tropical rainforest. Use the table for Exercises 41–43.

Month	Total Rainfall (in.)
January	51.25
February	48.6
March	50.8
April	49

41. Use clustering to estimate the total rainfall January through April.

42. The rainfall in May is a quarter of the rainfall in April. How many inches of rainfall occurs in May?

43. The rainfall in November is three times the rainfall in May. How many inches of rainfall occurs in November?

Model Multiplying Two Decimals

Objective
- Use models to multiply a decimal by a decimal.

Math Words
product
factors

Seth's cat Jasper has a body that is 0.4 meter long. Jasper's tail is 0.6 times as long as his body. How long is Jasper's tail?

You can find the product 0.4 × 0.6 by modeling the multiplication on a grid.

- Use a 10 × 10 grid. The grid represents 1 whole.

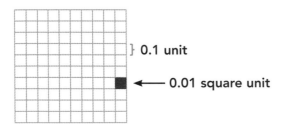

} 0.1 unit

← 0.01 square unit

- Shade to show the factors.

  Shade 4 rows red to show 0.4.

  Shade 6 columns blue to show 0.6.

- Find the product.

  The overlapping area represents the product.

  The 24 overlapping squares show that the product is 0.24.

- Check by multiplying equivalent fractions.

$$\frac{4}{10} \times \frac{6}{10} = \frac{24}{100}$$

$$\frac{24}{100} = 0.24 \checkmark$$

▷ Jasper's tail is 0.24 meter long.

PRACTICE

Write a multiplication sentence for the model.

1.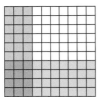

2.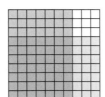

3.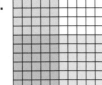

Tell how many rows and columns to shade on a 10 × 10 grid. Then find the product.

4. 0.5 × 0.9   **5.** 0.6 × 0.3   **6.** 0.8 × 0.7   **7.** 0.9 × 0.3

8. 0.7 × 0.5   **9.** 0.5 × 0.7   **10.** 0.2 × 0.4   **11.** 0.1 × 0.9

Multiply. Use a 10 × 10 grid to model the product.

12. 0.3 × 0.7   **13.** 0.7 × 0.2   **14.** 0.5 × 0.5   **15.** 0.7 × 0.4

16. 0.8 × 0.5   **17.** 0.5 × 0.6   **18.** 0.1 × 0.6   **19.** 0.2 × 0.3

20. A grid models the product of two decimals that are tenths. The overlapping area has 30 squares shaded. Write a possible number sentence that the model represents.

Problem Solving

21. A chef uses mustard that comes in jars. A full jar has 0.4 pound of mustard. Two jars of mustard are in the kitchen. One is half full and the other is 0.8 full. How much mustard is in the two jars?

22. Stephen shades 9 rows and 9 columns of a 10 × 10 grid. He states that because there is one unshaded square on the grid, it shows that 0.9 × 0.9 = 0.99. Do you agree with Stephen? Explain.

23. Haley shades all the rows and all the columns of a 10 × 10 grid. What multiplication fact does this represent? Explain.

24. Jenna knits a scarf with the dimensions shown. After she washes it, it shrinks. Each dimension is now 0.8 times its original length. What are the dimensions of the scarf now?

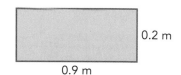

0.2 m

0.9 m

25. Spencer draws a number line from 0 to 1. He places a tick mark at each 0.1. He draws an arrow from 0 that lands halfway between 0 and 0.8. Write a multiplication sentence that Spencer models.

Write About It

26. Choose any two decimal factors that are tenths. Use a grid to find the product. How does the product compare to the two factors? Do you think this will always be true for any two tenths? Why?

Multiply Decimals by Decimals

Objective
- Multiply a decimal number by another decimal number.

Math Words
decimal
multiply

From 2009 to 2011, approximately 0.8 million hybrid vehicles were sold in the United States. From 2012 to 2014, the total number of hybrid vehicles sold was about 1.9 times the total for the previous three years. Approximately how many hybrid vehicles were sold in the U.S. from 2012 to 2014?

To find the answer, multiply 1.9 by 0.8.

To multiply a decimal by another decimal:

- Multiply as you would with whole numbers.

$$19 \times 8 = 152$$

- Count the total number of decimal places in both factors.

- Mark off the same number of decimal places in the product.

$$
\begin{array}{r}
1.9 \\
\times\ 0.8 \\
\hline
1.5\ 2
\end{array}
$$

1.9 ← **1** decimal place
× 0.8 ← **1** decimal place
1.5 2 ← **2** decimal places

▷ Approximately 1.52 million hybrid vehicles were sold from 2012 to 2014.

Study these examples.

$$
\begin{array}{r}
0.3\ 9 \\
\times\ 0.4\ 5 \\
\hline
1\ 9\ 5 \\
1\ 5\ 6\ 0 \\
\hline
0.1\ 7\ 5\ 5
\end{array}
$$

0.3 9 ← **2** decimal places
× 0.4 5 ← **2** decimal places
0.1 7 5 5 ← **4** decimal places

$$
\begin{array}{r}
2.1\ 5 \\
\times\ 4.5 \\
\hline
1\ 0\ 7\ 5 \\
8\ 6\ 0\ 0 \\
\hline
9.6\ 7\ 5
\end{array}
$$

2.1 5 ← **2** decimal places
× 4.5 ← **1** decimal place
9.6 7 5 ← **3** decimal places

PRACTICE

Find the product.

1.
2.8
× 5.1

2.
8.3
× 0.2 4

3.
1 0.2
× 0.7

4.
0.5 7
× 0.4 1

5.
4.2 6
× 0.9 2

6.
4.6
× 9.1

7.
1 7.9
× 2.1

8.
5.8 1
× 3.5

9.
1 1.2
× 6.7

10.
8.2 5
× 0.4 3

11.
6.5
× 0.5 3

12.
5.5 1
× 0.3 4

13.
4.3 9
× 2.3 6

14.
6 3.2
× 2.8 1

15.
2 3.2
× 1 2.3

Find the product.

16.
$$\begin{array}{r} 12.8 \\ \times\,10.3 \\ \hline \end{array}$$

17.
$$\begin{array}{r} 6.24 \\ \times\quad 0.9 \\ \hline \end{array}$$

18.
$$\begin{array}{r} 0.92 \\ \times\,0.81 \\ \hline \end{array}$$

19.
$$\begin{array}{r} 3.55 \\ \times\,7.82 \\ \hline \end{array}$$

20.
$$\begin{array}{r} 4.26 \\ \times\,0.92 \\ \hline \end{array}$$

21. 6.6×2.47 **22.** 0.94×12.7 **23.** 0.87×0.6 **24.** 0.36×0.77 **25.** 1.58×5.61

26. $n \times 8.7$ when $n = 0.4$

27. $n \times 0.56$ when $n = 1.7$

28. $14.3 \times n$ when $n = 0.24$

29. $4.82 \times n$ when $n = 10.74$

30. $n \times 0.66$ when $n = 7.3$

31. $0.92 \times n$ when $n = 0.15$

Simplify using the order of operations.

32. $(3.7 + 2.6) \times 0.34$ **33.** $1.4 \times 6.84 - 5.2$ **34.** $(12.78 - 11.44) \times 9.2$

35. $(3.6 \times 0.7 + 2.4) \times 1.3$ **36.** $0.89 \times 3.42 + 2.5$ **37.** $0.8 \times 0.82 - 0.64 \times 0.9$

Problem Solving

Use the blueprint for Exercises 38–40.

38. What is the area of the garage?

39. How much carpet is needed to cover the family room and den?

40. How much greater is the area of the dining area/kitchen than the den?

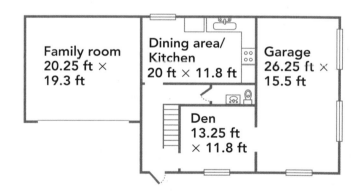

Family room
20.25 ft ×
19.3 ft

Dining area/
Kitchen
20 ft × 11.8 ft

Garage
26.25 ft ×
15.5 ft

Den
13.25 ft
× 11.8 ft

41. Karen runs 3.5 miles. Her running app is calibrated incorrectly. It records every mile run as 1.18 miles. What will be the error in the total number of miles the app shows?

42. The product 2.90×3.4 is 9.86. Explain why the factors have a total of three decimal places, but the product has two decimal places.

Write About It

43. The digits in the product 23.51×8.08 are 1899608, but the decimal point is missing. Use an estimate to decide where to put the decimal point. How can you check your answer without multiplying?

12-8 Zeros in the Product

Objective
- Write zeros as placeholders in decimal products.

Math Words

decimal

multiply

The cost of driving an electric car depends on the cost of electricity and how much electricity is used per mile. Suppose an electric car uses 0.34 kilowatt-hour to travel 1 mile. If electricity costs $0.10 for each kilowatt-hour, what is the cost for each mile?

Find 0.34 × 0.10.

Sometimes you need to write zeros to the left of nonzero digits in the product in order to place the decimal point correctly.

- Multiply as with whole numbers.   34 × 1 = 34

- Write 1 zero to the left of the 3.

- Place the decimal point in the product.

The product is $0.034.

$$
\begin{array}{r}
0.3\ 4 \\
\times\quad\ 0.1 \\
\hline
0.0\ 3\ 4
\end{array}
$$

← 2 decimal places
← 1 decimal place
← 3 decimal places

▷ Rounded to the nearest cent, the cost for each mile is about $0.03.

Study these examples.

$$
\begin{array}{r}
0.0\ 3 \\
\times\quad\ 0.2 \\
\hline
0.0\ 0\ 6
\end{array}
$$

← 2 decimal places
← 1 decimal place
← 3 decimal places

Write 2 zeros to the left of 6.

$$
\begin{array}{r}
0.0\ 0\ 5 \\
\times\qquad 2 \\
\hline
0.0\ 1\ 0
\end{array}
$$

← 3 decimal places

Write 1 zero to the left of 1.

PRACTICE

Write the decimal point in the product. Write zeros in the product where necessary.

1.
$$
\begin{array}{r}
0.2 \\
\times 0.2 \\
\hline
4
\end{array}
$$

2.
$$
\begin{array}{r}
0.0\ 9 \\
\times\quad 0.4 \\
\hline
3\ 6
\end{array}
$$

3.
$$
\begin{array}{r}
0.2\ 5 \\
\times\quad 0.3 \\
\hline
7\ 5
\end{array}
$$

4.
$$
\begin{array}{r}
0.0\ 0\ 3 \\
\times\qquad 3 \\
\hline
9
\end{array}
$$

5.
$$
\begin{array}{r}
0.0\ 2 \\
\times\quad 3\ 8 \\
\hline
7\ 6
\end{array}
$$

Multiply.

6.
$$
\begin{array}{r}
0.2 \\
\times 0.4
\end{array}
$$

7.
$$
\begin{array}{r}
0.0\ 5 \\
\times\quad 0.2
\end{array}
$$

8.
$$
\begin{array}{r}
0.0\ 7 \\
\times\quad 0.5
\end{array}
$$

9.
$$
\begin{array}{r}
0.0\ 4\ 2 \\
\times\qquad 0.4
\end{array}
$$

10.
$$
\begin{array}{r}
0.1\ 3 \\
\times\quad 0.2
\end{array}
$$

11. 0.2 × 0.1   **12.** 0.03 × 0.8   **13.** 0.05 × 0.2   **14.** 0.002 × 0.4   **15.** 0.18 × 0.4

Find the product.

16. 1.1×0.004 **17.** 2.5×0.03 **18.** 3.2×0.02 **19.** 2.3×0.01 **20.** 1.8×0.03

21. 2.7×0.03 **22.** 0.94×0.02 **23.** 0.09×0.04 **24.** 3×0.004 **25.** 0.07×0.06

26. 5.3×0.004 **27.** 0.09×0.18 **28.** 0.4×0.003 **29.** 2.4×0.05 **30.** 0.009×7

31. 0.06×0.41 **32.** 0.2×0.014 **33.** 2.2×0.06 **34.** 0.005×4 **35.** 0.18×0.02

36. $n \times 0.5$ when $n = 0.065$ **37.** $n \times 2$ when $n = 0.009$

38. $0.08 \times n$ when $n = 0.08$ **39.** $3.5 \times n$ when $n = 0.005$

Simplify using the order of operations.

40. $(2 - 0.75) \times 0.04$ **41.** $(0.09 \times 0.8) + (0.3 \times 0.6)$

42. $1.9 - 0.4 \times 0.2 + 0.03$ **43.** $(0.005 + 0.025) \times 0.89$

Problem Solving

44. A small lamp uses 0.009 kilowatt-hour of electricity each day. How much electricity does it use in 1 week?

45. For an art project, a craft punch is used to punch out 4 small squares from a piece of construction paper. What is the total area that is punched out?

0.1 in.
0.1 in.→

46. A decorative plate has a radius of $r = 4.6$ inches. The distance around the plate is approximately equal to $2 \times 3.14 \times r$. A small glass bead is placed at about every inch along the outside of the plate. About how many beads are needed?

47. Anwar wants to find the product $\frac{7}{100} \times 0.5$. Describe two ways that he can do this. Write the product in two ways.

Write About It

48. How can the rules for multiplying two decimals be extended to multiplying three decimals? Use your explanation to help you find the product $0.5 \times 0.03 \times 0.2$.

Problem Solving
More Than One Way

Cassandra weighs four packages before they are shipped. Three weigh 1.5 pounds each and the other one weighs 4.5 pounds. How much do the four packages weigh?

You can use two strategies to solve this problem and then compare the strategies to see which is faster or easier to use.

Strategy: Use a Model

Draw a number line to model the problem situation.

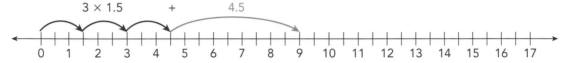

The first three jumps represent the weight of the three packages weighing 1.5 pounds each. The fourth jump represents the weight of the package weighing 4.5 pounds. The total is 9.0 pounds.

Strategy: Write and Solve an Equation

Let w represent the total weight of the four packages. Write and solve an equation.

$$w = (3 \times 1.5) + 4.5$$
$$= 4.5 + 4.5$$
$$= 9.0$$

The order of operations tells you to work inside the parentheses first.

▷ The four packages weigh 9.0 pounds.

Compare the Strategies

The number line does not require any calculations. Drawing and labeling a number line does take time.

Solving an equation does require some calculations. It is faster to write and solve an equation than to draw and label a number line.

The answer is the same using either strategy.

PRACTICE

1. Five blocks are stacked on top of one another. Three of the blocks are each 1.25 inches tall and the other two blocks are 1.5 inches tall. How tall is the stack? Use a number line or an equation to solve the problem.

Paul makes a table of the times that the sun rises and sets. He thinks that there is a pattern he can use to predict the length of time between sunrise and sunset on October 14, which is 20 days away. Use the information for Exercises 2–4.

Date	Sunrise	Sunset
9/19	6:29 A.M.	6:46 P.M.
9/20	6:30 A.M.	6:44 P.M.
9/21	6:31 A.M.	6:42 P.M.
9/22	6:32 A.M.	6:40 P.M.
9/23	6:33 A.M.	6:38 P.M.
9/24	6:34 A.M.	6:36 P.M.

2. What patterns do you observe in the data?

3. Paul decides that he can extend the table or write and solve an equation to predict the length of time between sunrise and sunset on October 14. Which strategy do you think he should use? Why?

4. Use your strategy to predict the length of time between sunrise and sunset on October 14.

Ricardo is making and testing paper airplanes for a science project. The first plane is 25 cm long. The next plane is 0.5 cm shorter. The third plane is 0.5 cm shorter than the second, and so on. How long is the tenth airplane? Naomi and Anna solve the problem as shown. Use the information for Exercises 5–6.

Naomi uses a number line.

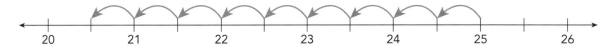

Anna writes and solves an equation.

$L = 25 - (9 \times 0.5)$

$\quad = 25 - 4.5$

$\quad = 20.5$

5. Compare the strategies. Which strategy would you use? Why?

6. Why are there only 9 jumps on the number line?

7. Jessie buys 5 granola bars and 4 water bottles. Each water bottle costs $1.09 and each granola bar costs $0.79. Write an equation that you could use to find the total amount Jessie spends. Let c represent the cost. How much does she spend?

Write About It

8. Why do you have to think about the problem situation before choosing the best strategy to use?

Solve.

1. 0.67 × 1000

How many 0s are there?

What is the product?

2. 10.84 × 30

How do you factor 30?

What is the product?

3. 2.075 × 10²

What is the exponent?

What is the product?

Write a multiplication sentence for the model.

4. 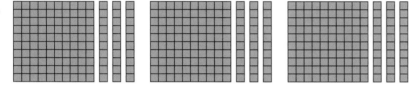   **5.**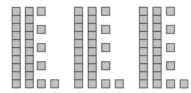

6.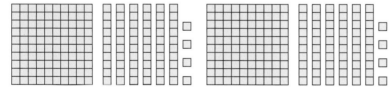

7.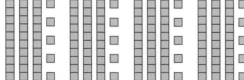

Use front-end estimation and rounding to estimate the product.

8. 6.45 × 11.204

9. 7.509 × 8.67

10. 10.391 × 5.728

11. 2.06 × 8.784

12. 11.006 × 4.82

13. 24.76 × 3.114

Use clustering to estimate the sum.

14. 4.18 + 3.8 + 3.92 + 4.075

15. 24.96 + 25.095 + 24.899

16. 9.08 + 8.9 + 8.91 + 9.085

17. 0.34 + 0.297 + 0.316

Simplify.

18. five times as much as $11.37, decreased by $20.08

Write a multiplication sentence for the model.

19.

20.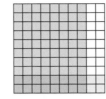

21.

Find the product.

22. 0.27 × 100

23. 8 × 0.91

24. 0.6 × 15

25. $10.50 × 12

26. 3.724 × 15

27. 0.7 × 0.7

28. 6.9 × 10³

29. 2.72 × 1.6

30. 0.4 × 8.26

31. 0.8 × 0.3

32. 0.709 × 10

33. 1.29 × 0.05

34. 1 1.0 4
      ×   6 0

35. $5.99
      ×   7

36. 7.2 1
      ×   5 1

37. 0.0 9
      × 0.8 5

38. 4.8
      × 2.3

39. 2.8 3
      × 6.0 4

40. $1 1.5 8
      ×   0.5 0

41. 4.5 1 9
      ×   1 7

42. 3.1 5
      × 0.0 6

43. 0.0 7
      × 0.0 9

44. 1 1.4 4
      ×   5.8 7

45.   3.1
      × 0.0 4

Problem Solving

Leah is planning to host a graphic design seminar. She will charge an admission fee of $59.50. There are 24 seats available. Use this information for Exercises 46–48.

46. How much will Leah earn if she fills all available seats?

47. One week before the seminar, there are some seats still available. Leah cuts the fee to half price. How much is the fee to attend now?

48. Leah sells 15 seats at the original fee, and 9 seats after the markdown. How much does Leah earn from the seminar?

49. Madison and Brianna both draw a model to show 0.9 × 0.3. They compare their models and notice they are different. Whose model is correct? Explain.

Madison   Brianna

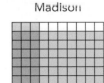

Now that Maxwell has a realistic monthly budget in place, he wants to find how much he will spend in each category every quarter (3 months) and annually (12 months). Maxwell will use a spreadsheet program where he can enter formulas that will automatically calculate these amounts.

1. How can Maxwell determine how much he spends in each category every quarter?

2. Maxwell's rent is $750 per month. What formula should Maxwell enter into the program to calculate how much he spends on rent every quarter? Find the missing values.

$$= \$ \underline{\ ?\ } \times \underline{\ ?\ }$$

3. How can he find how much he spends in each category every year?

4. What formula should Maxwell enter into the program to calculate how much he spends on rent every year?

$$= \$ \underline{\ ?\ } \times \underline{\ ?\ }$$

5. Suppose Maxwell calculates the quarterly amounts first. What is another way he could determine how much he spends in each category every year? Write an equation to show that both ways give the same total for how much Maxwell spends on rent every year.

Copy the table from the next page. Determine the quarterly and annual budget for each category. Be sure to show the formula Maxwell should enter for each calculation. Then answer the following questions.

6. Maxwell's credit card balance is $2398.45. How many more months will it take to pay off the balance if he continues to pay the current amount?

7. His student loan balance is $5,496.22. How many more months will it take to pay off the balance if he continues to pay the current amount?

8. If Maxwell were to increase his credit card payment by $25 per month, how much quicker could he pay off the balance?

9. If Maxwell were to increase his student loan payment by $45 per month, how much quicker could he pay off the balance?

10. After Maxwell pays off his credit card and student loan, his monthly bills will decrease. He plans to put this extra money into his savings account. How much more money will Maxwell be able to save every month? Every quarter? Every year?

11. Complete each statement: Maxwell spends about _?_ times as much on home expenses as on any other category. This is mostly due to his _?_ expense.

12. If he continues to rent the same apartment for 3 more years, how much more money will he spend on rent?

13. Maxwell saves $200 each month for the first year. After 1 year, Maxwell pays off his credit card and can now save about $440 per month. After 2 years, Maxwell pays off his school loan and can now save about $625 per month. How much money does Maxwell save in 3 years?

14. If Maxwell decides to put off buying a house for 5 years so he can save more money, how much more money will Maxwell save?

		Monthly Amount	Quarterly Amount	Annual Amount
1	**Home**			
2	Rent	$750.00	?	?
3	Renter's Insurance	$27.42	?	?
4	Gas & Electric	$156.85	?	?
5	Water & Trash	$35.67	?	?
6	Phone	$64.92	?	?
7	Cable TV	$0.00	?	?
8	Internet	$45.99	?	?
9	House Supplies	$60.00	?	?
10	**TOTAL:**	**$1140.85**	?	?
12	**Loans & Savings**			
13	Credit Card Payment	$241.65	?	?
14	Student Loan Payment	$184.06	?	?
15	Savings Contribution	$200.00	?	?
16	**TOTAL:**	**$625.71**	?	?
18	**Transportation**			
19	Car Payment	$347.51	?	?
20	Auto Insurance	$82.74	?	?
21	Fuel	$125.00	?	?
22	**TOTAL:**	**$555.25**	?	?
24	**Food & Entertainment**			
25	Groceries	$315.00	?	?
26	Dining Out	$150.00	?	?
27	Clothing	$50.00	?	?
28	Movies	$0.00	?	?
29	**TOTAL:**	**$515.00**	?	?
30				
31	**TOTAL INCOME:**	**$2864.32**	?	?
32	**TOTAL EXPENSES:**	**$2836.81**	?	?

Determine the best answer for each problem.

1. Which expressions are equal to 8.125? Select all that apply.

   A. 3.75 × 2.25
   B. 4.25 × 2
   C. 0.5 × 16.25
   D. 0.25 × 32.5
   E. 2.5 × 3.25

2. Identify the pattern rule.
   $$3, 3.3, 3.63, 3.993$$

   A. Add 0.11.
   B. Add 0.31.
   C. Multiply by 0.11.
   D. Multiply by 1.1.

3. Which multiplication sentence is shown by the model?

   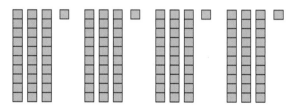

   A. 3.1 × 4 = 12.4
   B. 0.13 × 5 = 0.65
   C. 0.31 × 4 = 1.24
   D. 1.3 × 5 = 6.5

4. Find the product.
   $$2.1 \times 6.7 = \underline{\ ?\ }$$

5. Estimate the product by using front-end estimation.
   $$4.28 \times 7.95$$

6. Estimate the product by using rounding.
   $$12.53 \times 7.76$$

7. Ava is 1.2 times as tall as Grace. Grace is 1.4 times as tall as Kiara. How many times as tall as Kiara is Ava?

8. What is the area of the square?

   0.08 in.

9. Find the product.
   $$0.8 \times 0.4 \times 9.57$$

10. While on vacation, Marco spends $84.29 on Thursday, $85.25 on Friday, $83.97 on Saturday, and $86.09 on Sunday. About how much does Marco spend altogether?

Decimals: Division

Many bills are due once a month, such as car payments or electric bills. However, there are also unexpected expenses that come up such as car and home repairs. It is important to budget for these each month so that when an issue does arise, you have money set aside to cover the expense.

Other Variable Expenses

Bills and repairs are not the only kinds of expenses that will vary month to month. A lot of expenses may vary depending on the time of year and your lifestyle, such as those listed below. Try thinking of some others to add to this list!

♦ **Gifts for friends and family**

♦ Back-to-school supplies

♦ Summer vacations

♦ License plate and driver's license renewal fees

♦ Annual subscription costs

Divide by Powers of 10

Objective
- Divide decimals and whole numbers by powers of 10.

Math Word

power of 10

Hector measures 1350 mL of a baking soda and water mixture. He adds the mixture to an aquarium to regulate the pH level. How many liters of the mixture does he measure?

Since 1 L = 1000 mL, divide 1350 by 1000 to solve.

To divide 1350 by 1000, move the decimal point to the left 3 places because there are 3 zeros in 1000.

$$1350 \div 1000 = 1.350. = 1.35 \longleftarrow$$ Remove the end zero to the right of the decimal point.

▷ Hector measures 1.35 L of the mixture.

To divide a number by 10, 100, or 1000, move the decimal point to the left as many places as there are zeros in the power of 10.

$$35 \div 10 = 3.5. = 3.5$$
$$35 \div 100 = .35. = 0.35 \longleftarrow$$
$$35 \div 1000 = .035. = 0.035 \longleftarrow$$

Include a zero in the ones place when the number is less than 1.

To divide a number by a power of 10 written with an exponent, move the decimal point to the left as many places as the exponent.

$$7 \div 10^1 = .7. = 0.7$$
$$7 \div 10^2 = .07. = 0.07$$
$$7 \div 10^3 = .007. = 0.007$$

Study these examples.

$$1285 \div 1000 = 1.285. = 1.285$$
$$8734 \div 10^4 = .8734. = 0.8734$$
$$490,000,000 \div 10^6 = 490.000000. = 490$$

PRACTICE

1. $52.4 \div 10$

How many 0s are there?

What is the quotient?

2. $8.3 \div 100$

How many 0s are there?

What is the quotient?

3. $6120 \div 10^3$

What is the exponent?

What is the quotient?

4. Describe how to divide a number by a power of 10.

Find the quotient.

5. $341 \div 10$

6. $483 \div 10$

7. $235 \div 10^2$

8. $52 \div 100$

9. $0.1 \div 10^2$

10. $8207 \div 10^3$

11. $3100 \div 1000$

12. $320 \div 100$

13. $0.6 \div 10^1$

14. $2.7 \div 10$

15. $2752.1 \div 10^2$

16. $0.23 \div 10^2$

17. $924 \div 1000$

18. $0.04 \div 10$

19. $150.1 \div 10^3$

20. $12{,}564{,}000 \div 10{,}000$

21. $820{,}100 \div 10^5$

Compare. Write <, =, or >.

22. $18{,}561{,}000 \div 10^5 \ \underline{\ ?\ }\ 18.561 \times 10^2$

23. $0.109 \times 100{,}000 \ \underline{\ ?\ }\ 10{,}900{,}000 \div 10^4$

Problem Solving

24. David purchases seeds to plant in his garden. He buys 100 pepper seeds and 1000 tomato seeds. Which type of seed is more expensive? Explain.

Vegetable Seed	Total Cost ($)
Tomato	21.24
Pepper	3.21

25. Veronica uses $\frac{2}{5}$ of the bag of rice shown. She will use the same portion from the remaining amount each day over 10 days. How much rice can she use each day?

RICE
20 lb

26. The water level of a lake is being analyzed during a drought. Over a 100-day study, the water level decreases 21.7 inches. It decreases the same amount each day. How much does the water level decrease each day?

27. A test has 22 multiple choice questions and 18 fill in the blank questions. Each question is worth the same number of points. The test is worth 100 points. How many points is each question worth?

Write About It

28. A number has nonzero digits in the tens, ones, and tenths places, but not in any other place. If the number is divided by 100, what places will have nonzero digits? Explain.

Model Dividing a Decimal by a Whole Number

Objective
- Model division of a decimal by a whole number.

Math Words
tenth
hundredth
regroup

Lilly separates 1.54 kilograms of pumpkin seeds into 7 plastic bags. How many kilograms of seeds are in each bag?

Use models to divide 1.54 by 7.

- Model 1.54.

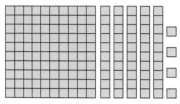

> There are not enough ones to divide into 7 equal groups.

- Regroup the 1 as 10 tenths. Make 7 equal groups of tenths.

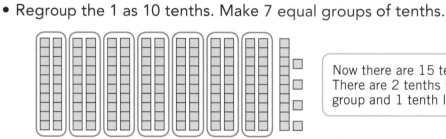

> Now there are 15 tenths. There are 2 tenths in each group and 1 tenth left over.

- Regroup the extra tenth as 10 hundredths. Make 7 equal groups.

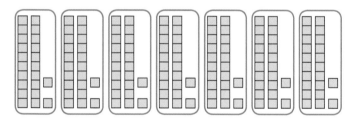

> Using the 14 hundredths put 2 hundredths in each group.

There are 7 equal groups. So 1.54 ÷ 7 = 0.22.

> Each bag contains 0.22 kilogram of pumpkin seeds.

PRACTICE

Use the model to find the quotient.

1. 0.24 ÷ 3

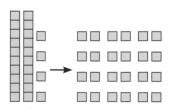

2. 1.24 ÷ 4

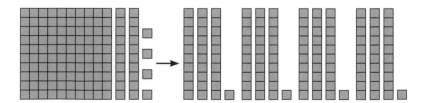

Use the model to find the quotient. Regroup as needed.

3. 2.48 ÷ 4

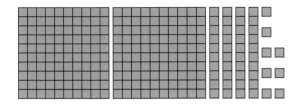

4. 1.35 ÷ 3

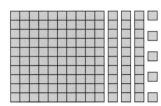

Write the division sentence shown by the model.

5. __?__ ÷ __?__ = __?__

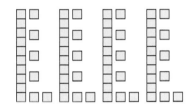

6. __?__ ÷ __?__ = __?__

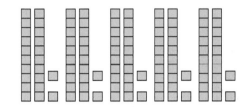

Use models or base-ten blocks to divide.

7. 3.24 ÷ 6

8. 0.87 ÷ 3

9. 1.26 ÷ 7

10. 0.78 ÷ 6

11. 2.56 ÷ 4

12. 3)6.42

13. 5)3.8

14. 3)1.47

15. 8)1.36

16. 6)3.84

Problem Solving

17. Eight students are painting a mural. The area of the mural is 17.28 square feet. Each student paints an equal part of the mural. What is the area that each student paints?

18. Half an acre of land is split in half. How many acres is each part of land?

19. What is the unknown dimension of the rectangle?

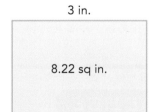

3 in.

8.22 sq in.

Write About It

20. Choose a division problem from this page that divides a decimal by a whole number and requires regrouping. Explain how you know when to regroup when using a model.

LESSON 13-3 Estimate Decimal Quotients

Objective
- Estimate decimal quotients.

Math Words
quotient
compatible numbers

A square plot of land has a perimeter of 23.64 meters. About how long is each side of the plot?

To estimate the length of each side, estimate 23.64 ÷ 4.

◆ Estimate using place value.
- Write the decimal point in the quotient.
- Decide in which place the first nonzero digit of the quotient begins.
- Find the first nonzero digit of the quotient.
- Write zeros for the remaining digits.

$$\frac{5.00}{4)\overline{23.64}}$$

4 > 2 Not enough tens

4 < 23 Enough ones

How many 4s in 23? 5

◆ Estimate using compatible numbers.
- Think of nearby numbers that are compatible.
- Divide the compatible numbers.

$$4)\overline{23.64} \longrightarrow \frac{6.00}{4)\overline{24.00}}$$

The plot of land is between 5 and 6 meters on a side.

Study these examples.

$$8)\overline{3.118} \qquad \frac{0.300}{8)\overline{3.118}}$$

$$6)\overline{0.314} \qquad \frac{0.050}{6)\overline{0.314}}$$

$$39)\overline{158.067} \qquad 39)\overline{158.067} \longrightarrow \frac{4.0}{40)\overline{160.0}}$$

8 > 3 Not enough ones
8 < 31 Enough tenths
How many 8s in 31? 3

6 > 3 Not enough tenths
6 < 31 Enough hundredths
How many 6s in 31? 5

40 and 160 are compatible numbers.
The quotient is about 4.

PRACTICE

Estimate the quotient.

1. $6)\overline{0.234}$ 2. $5)\overline{0.244}$ 3. $7)\overline{0.746}$ 4. $3)\overline{0.917}$

5. $6)\overline{14.287}$ 6. $8)\overline{8.107}$ 7. $9)\overline{46.3}$ 8. $4)\overline{0.051}$

Estimate the quotient.

9. $4\overline{)0.872}$ **10.** $7\overline{)0.566}$ **11.** $6\overline{)2.472}$ **12.** $3\overline{)2.976}$

13. $8\overline{)3.295}$ **14.** $5\overline{)3.315}$ **15.** $3\overline{)29.506}$ **16.** $9\overline{)36.279}$

Estimate the quotient. Use compatible numbers.

17. $4\overline{)2.302}$ **18.** $9\overline{)1.935}$ **19.** $7\overline{)4.351}$ **20.** $8\overline{)4.253}$

21. $62.158 \div 28$ **22.** $36.751 \div 61$ **23.** $461.651 \div 53$

Estimate. Determine if the estimate is less than or greater than the actual quotient.

24. $5\overline{)0.874}$ **25.** $3\overline{)0.855}$ **26.** $4\overline{)5.364}$

27. $9\overline{)47.372}$ **28.** $4\overline{)23.018}$ **29.** $8\overline{)58.761}$

Problem Solving

Use the map for Exercises 30–31.

30. Serenity and her family are driving to their family reunion. They need to arrive by the end of the day on Friday to be on time. If they leave on Tuesday morning and drive 400 miles each day, will they arrive on time? Explain.

31. The family will drive 500 miles each day instead. What day should they leave to make sure they arrive in time? Explain.

32. William has a balance of $128.06 left on his gift card for Photo Frames Plus. He needs to buy one multi-photo frame for $31.49. He wants to spend the rest of the balance on small frames that cost $8.75 each. About how many small frames can he buy?

Write About It

33. When you estimate decimal quotients using compatible numbers, how can you tell whether the estimate is greater or less than the actual quotient?

Estimate with Money

Objective
- Estimate quotients of money amounts.

Math Word
compatible numbers

Four cell phone screen protectors cost $7.45. About how much is one screen protector?

To find the approximate cost of one screen protector, estimate $7.45 ÷ 4.

Use compatible numbers.

$$4 \overline{)\$7.45} \longrightarrow 4 \overline{)\$7.20}^{\$1.80}$$

4 and 72 are compatible numbers.

Think
Since $7.20 < $7.45, the exact quotient must be greater than $1.80.

The price of one screen protector is about $1.80.

72 and 76 are both compatible with 4, since they are multiples of 4. Notice that $7.20 is less than the exact price and $7.60 is greater than the exact price.

$$4 \overline{)\$7.45} \longrightarrow 4 \overline{)\$7.60}^{\$1.90}$$

Sometimes you use different sets of compatible numbers to estimate a quotient involving money.

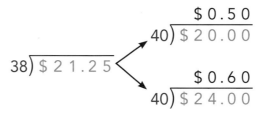

▷ The price of one screen protector is between $1.80 and $1.90.

Study these examples.

Estimate $4.95 ÷ 3.

$$3 \overline{)\$4.95} \begin{cases} 3\overline{)\$4.80}^{\$1.60} \\ 3\overline{)\$5.10}^{\$1.70} \end{cases}$$

Estimate $21.25 ÷ 38.

$$38 \overline{)\$21.25} \begin{cases} 40\overline{)\$20.00}^{\$0.50} \\ 40\overline{)\$24.00}^{\$0.60} \end{cases}$$

▷ The exact quotient is between $1.60 and $1.70.

▷ The exact quotient is about $0.50 or $0.60.

PRACTICE

Write the compatible numbers you would use. Estimate the quotient.

1. $6 \overline{)\$1.32}$

2. $5 \overline{)\$8.29}$

3. $8 \overline{)\$19.99}$

4. $3 \overline{)\$0.88}$

5. $7 \overline{)\$22.19}$

6. $4 \overline{)\$1.59}$

Write the compatible numbers you would use. Estimate the quotient.

7. $12\overline{)\$27.36}$

8. $37\overline{)\$65.81}$

9. $25\overline{)\$134.50}$

10. $\$128.88 \div 9$

11. $\$88.57 \div 17$

12. $\$419.15 \div 83$

Estimate the quotient.

13. $2\overline{)\$7.21}$

14. $4\overline{)\$5.99}$

15. $7\overline{)\$31.92}$

16. $16\overline{)\$37.79}$

17. $32\overline{)\$8.27}$

18. $55\overline{)\$289.89}$

The number of items and their total cost are given. Estimate the cost for each item.

19. 4.5 pounds of apples for $13.25

20. 8 bananas for $3.60

Problem Solving

Six roommates buy the appliances shown in the table and will equally share the cost. Use the table for Exercises 21–23.

Appliance	Cost ($)
Microwave	79.95
Oven	358.50

21. About how much will each roommate pay to purchase the two appliances in the table?

22. If they decide to also buy a juicer for $109.36, about how much does each person owe for all three appliances?

23. Two of the roommates decide to move out before the two appliances are purchased. How much more do each of the 4 remaining roommates owe? Use your estimate from Exercise 21.

24. A sports team is raising money for new equipment that costs $2559. They have already raised $1813.50. For their final fundraiser, they are selling coupon cards. About how much money will each of the 18 teammates need to raise to reach their goal?

Write About It

25. Jada is estimating $\$37.75 \div 58$. Analyze Jada's work. Explain how her estimate can be improved.

$$58\overline{)\$37.75} \longrightarrow 50\overline{)\$40.00} = \$0.80$$

Divide Decimals by Whole Numbers

Marshall divides 8.55 kg of dry soup mix into 5 bags. How much dry soup mix goes into each bag? Find 8.55 ÷ 5.

To divide a decimal by a whole number:

Write the decimal point of the quotient above the decimal point of the dividend.

$$5\overline{)8.55}$$

5 < 8 Enough ones

The quotient begins in the ones place.

Divide as you would with whole numbers.

```
       1.71
   5) 8.55
    - 5
      3 5
    - 3 5
        0 5
      - 0 5
          0
```

Multiply to check.

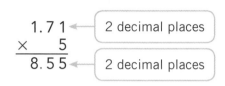

```
     1.71  ←  2 decimal places
   ×    5
     8.55  ←  2 decimal places
```

Use a model to check. Divide 8.55 into 5 equal groups. Regroup.

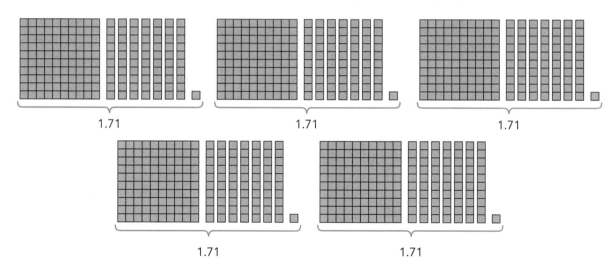

1.71   1.71   1.71

1.71   1.71

Each bag contains 1.71 kg of soup mix.

Study these examples.

```
      1.1              0.555             0.42            1.25
   8) 8.8          5) 2.775         23) 9.66         2) 2.50
    - 8              - 2 5            - 9 2            - 2
      0 8              27               46              0 5
    - 8              - 25             - 46             - 4
      0                25               0               1 0
                     - 25                             - 1 0
                        0                                 0
```

Use the model to complete the statement.

1. $\underline{\ ?\ } \div 2 = \underline{\ ?\ }$

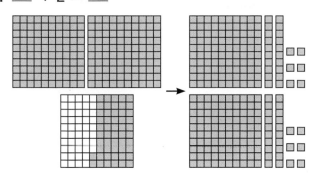

2. $0.93 \div \underline{\ ?\ } = \underline{\ ?\ }$

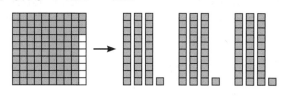

Determine the quotient. Check your answer.

3. $8\overline{)5.6}$ **4.** $9\overline{)5.4}$ **5.** $6\overline{)0.96}$ **6.** $5\overline{)0.75}$ **7.** $12\overline{)8.4}$

8. $0.924 \div 4$ **9.** $2.214 \div 9$ **10.** $28.05 \div 33$ **11.** $14.24 \div 16$

Compare. Write <, =, or >.

12. $1.2 \div 3 \underline{\ ?\ } 0.84 \div 2$

13. $31.92 \div 4 \underline{\ ?\ } 23.55 \div 5$

14. $15.6 \div 2 \underline{\ ?\ } 21.72 \div 3$

15. $9.84 \div 12 \underline{\ ?\ } 18.86 \div 23$

Problem Solving

The barbell without added weights weighs 2.54 lb.
Weights of different sizes and can be added to the
barbell. Use the information for Exercises 16–17.

16. Caitlyn adds two identical circular weights to the barbell
for a total weight of 16.14 lb. What is the weight of each
circular weight?

17. Caitlyn adds four identical circular weights to the barbell for a
total weight of 20.14 lb. What is the weight of each circular weight?

Write About It

18. Find the quotient $3\frac{3}{5} \div 6$ by writing the dividend as a decimal and
then dividing. Use your decimal answer to write the quotient as a
fraction. Compare with dividing the mixed number.

Objective
- Divide decimals using zeros as placeholders.

Math Words

quotient
remainder

Scientists use chips like the one shown to analyze very small samples. A scientist is using a device that draws in 0.368 mL of fluid at a time. The fluid is directed into four different channels to analyze the sample. How much fluid flows through each channel?

To find the volume, find 0.368 ÷ 4.

Sometimes you must write zeros in the quotient to show the correct place value.

To divide:

- Write the decimal point in the quotient. Then divide until you have a remainder of 0.

- Check: 4 × 0.092 = 0.368 ✓

▷ The volume in each channel is 0.092 mL.

$$
\begin{array}{r}
4\overline{)0.368} \\
\end{array}
$$

$$
\begin{array}{r}
0.092 \\
4\overline{)0.368} \\
-36 \\
\hline
08 \\
-8 \\
\hline
0 \\
\end{array}
$$

> 4 > 3 Not enough tenths
>
> Write 0 in the tenths place.

> 4 < 36 Enough hundredths
>
> The quotient begins in the hundredths place.

Sometimes you must write zeros in the dividend.

Find 3.2 ÷ 5.

- Write the decimal point in the quotient. Divide until you have a remainder of 0.

- Check: 5 × 0.64 = 3.2 ✓

$$
\begin{array}{r}
0.64 \\
5\overline{)3.20} \\
-30 \\
\hline
20 \\
-20 \\
\hline
0 \\
\end{array}
$$

> Write a zero in the dividend to complete the division.
>
> 3.2 = 3.20

Study these examples.

$$
\begin{array}{r}
1.08 \\
14\overline{)15.12} \\
-14 \\
\hline
11 \\
-0 \\
\hline
112 \\
-112 \\
\hline
0 \\
\end{array}
$$

> Not enough tenths
>
> Write 0 in the tenths place.

$$
\begin{array}{r}
0.125 \\
8\overline{)1.000} \\
-8 \\
\hline
20 \\
-16 \\
\hline
40 \\
-40 \\
\hline
0 \\
\end{array}
$$

> Write zeros in the dividend to complete the division.

PRACTICE

Divide. Multiply to check.

1. $\overset{?.??}{5\overline{)3.25}}$

2. $\overset{?.??}{28\overline{)1.96}}$

3. $\overset{?.??}{4\overline{)7.40}}$

4. $\overset{?.??}{52\overline{)18.20}}$

Divide and check.

5. $2\overline{)0.16}$ **6.** $6\overline{)3.06}$ **7.** $3\overline{)1.08}$ **8.** $8\overline{)14}$ **9.** $5\overline{)0.06}$

10. $21\overline{)6.72}$ **11.** $68\overline{)4.08}$ **12.** $4\overline{)16.2}$ **13.** $33\overline{)67.32}$ **14.** $25\overline{)16}$

15. $23.17 \div 7$ **16.** $0.164 \div 8$ **17.** $5.1 \div 12$ **18.** $0.112 \div 14$

19. $146.88 \div 36$ **20.** $18.27 \div 6$ **21.** $32.84 \div 8$ **22.** $25.848 \div 6$

Find the quotient.

23. $n \div 4$ when $n = 12.36$

24. $3.84 \div n$ when $n = 5$

25. $n \div 75$ when $n = 111$

26. $6.88 \div n$ when $n = 86$

Problem Solving

27. Kimberly makes gifts for 6 of her teachers. She buys the supplies shown on the receipt. How much does she spend on each gift?

28. Kasey studies birds. She finds a bird's nest with 5 eggs in it. If the nest and eggs weigh 10 ounces and the nest is assumed to be 6.5 ounces, how much does each egg weigh?

```
RECEIPT
.....................
Candy:     $3.20
Candles:   $8.74
Baskets:   $6.54
```

29. What is the first nonzero digit in the quotient of $2.35 \div 5$? Which place is the digit in? Explain how you know.

30. Jennie is having trouble finding the error in her division. She knows her quotient is incorrect because she checked using multiplication. Analyze her work and explain her error.

```
        3.4
   45)15.3
     −135
      180
    − 180
        0
```

Write About It

31. Create a division problem where zeros will need to be written in the dividend and the quotient when solving. Explain how you determined your answer.

Check Your Progress

Solve.

1. 9.57 ÷ 10

How many 0s are there?

What is the quotient?

2. 84.9 ÷ 1000

How many 0s are there?

What is the quotient?

3. 0.65 ÷ 10²

What is the exponent?

What is the quotient?

Find the quotient.

4. 3084 ÷ 100

5. 99.8 ÷ 100

6. 8007 ÷ 10⁴

7. 52.45 ÷ 10

8. 21.3 ÷ 1000

9. 889.2 ÷ 10³

10. Divide these blocks into 5 equal groups. How much is in each group?

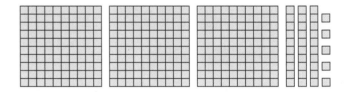

Use the model to find the quotient. Regroup as needed.

11. 1.38 ÷ 3

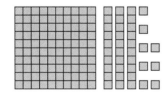

12. 1.4 ÷ 4

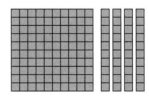

13. 2.35 ÷ 5

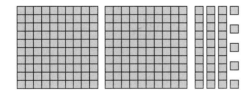

14. 1.7 ÷ 2

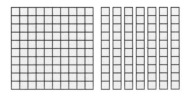

Match the division problem with the best estimate of the quotient.

    A. 0.14   **B.** 0.31   **C.** 0.5   **D.** 5.3

15. $7\overline{)3.482}$

16. $6\overline{)0.814}$

17. 26.48 ÷ 5

18. 2.785 ÷ 9

Write the compatible numbers you would use to divide. Then estimate the quotient.

19. $5\overline{)\$3.81}$

20. $\$29.74 \div 7$

21. $3\overline{)\$4.79}$

22. $\$78.96 \div 41$

23. $16\overline{)\$118.49}$

24. $\$203.18 \div 9$

Find the quotient. Use a model when needed.

25. $25 \div 10$

26. $36.4 \div 1000$

27. $7.5 \div 10^2$

28. $826.3 \div 10^3$

29. $96.5 \div 100$

30. $0.726 \div 10^1$

31. $0.54 \div 10^3$

32. $86.08 \div 1000$

33. $4.68 \div 6$

34. $0.72 \div 3$

35. $4.5 \div 9$

36. $1.48 \div 4$

37. $6.4 \div 8$

38. $2.05 \div 5$

39. $3.1 \div 2$

40. $2.64 \div 6$

Find the quotient.

41. $12\overline{)25.092}$

42. $5\overline{)25.16}$

43. $8\overline{)327.08}$

44. $21\overline{)399.42}$

45. $7\overline{)840.21}$

46. $45\overline{)272.25}$

47. $17\overline{)306.204}$

48. $33\overline{)662.31}$

Problem Solving

49. Three servers work at a café. On Friday night, they earn $176.49 in tips altogether. If they split the tips equally, how much money will each server earn?

50. A community newspaper reports the average monthly snowfall for the months shown. What was the average monthly snowfall this winter? To find an average, find the total and divide the sum by the number of addends.

Month	Snowfall (in.)
December	7
January	9.2
February	8.82

51. The area of a pantry is 10.8 square feet. If the width of the pantry is 3 feet, what is the approximate length of the pantry?

52. How many centimeters are equivalent to 230.5 millimeters? How many meters is this?

53. Explain how to use base-ten blocks to find $1.41 \div 3$. Draw a model to show the division.

Think
10 mm = 1 cm
1000 mm = 1 m

LESSON

13-7 Division with Money

Objective
- Divide money amounts.

Math Word
quotient

A music teacher is buying 24 guitar tuners that cost $173.52 in all. How much is each tuner?

To find the cost of one tuner, find $173.52 ÷ 24.

To divide money:

- Place the dollar sign and the decimal point in the quotient.

- Divide as usual.

- Check:

  24 × $7.23 = $173.52 ✓

```
        $   7.23
   24) $ 1 7 3.5 2
       − 1 6 8 ↓
           5 5
         − 4 8 ↓
             7 2
           − 7 2
               0
```

▷ The price of each guitar tuner is $7.23.

Study these examples.

```
      $ 1.7 0 8
   5) $ 8.5 4 0
     − 5 ↓
       3 5
     − 3 5 ↓
         0 4 ↓
       −   0 ↓
           4 0
         − 4 0
             0
```

Round to the nearest cent.

$1.708 rounds to $1.71 since 8 > 5.

Insert a zero in the dividend and keep dividing.

$8.54 = $8.540

$8.54 ÷ 5 is about $1.71.

```
      $ 0.5 5 5
   9) $ 5.0 0 0
     − 4 5 ↓
         5 0
       − 4 5 ↓
           5 0
         − 4 5
```

The answer is numbers that repeat. Round to the nearest cent.

$5.00 ÷ 9 is about $0.56.

PRACTICE

Complete each division.

```
        $  2.??
1.  5) $ 1 2.8 5
       − 1 0
           2 8
         − ? ?
             ? ?
           − ? ?
               ?
```

```
          $  4.??
2.  18) $ 7 6.8 6
        − ? ?
            ? ?
          − ? ?
              ? ? ?
            − ? ? ?
                  ?
```

```
          $    6.??
3.  33) $ 2 0 0.9 7
        − ? ? ?
              ? ?
            − ? ?
                ? ? ?
              − ? ? ?
                    ?
```

Divide and check.

4. $4\overline{)\$10.28}$ **5.** $3\overline{)\$9.42}$ **6.** $7\overline{)\$58.17}$ **7.** $6\overline{)\$24.54}$

8. $5\overline{)\$34.05}$ **9.** $11\overline{)\$65.34}$ **10.** $28\overline{)\$169.96}$ **11.** $57\overline{)\$527.82}$

12. $84\overline{)\$451.08}$ **13.** $45\overline{)\$641.25}$ **14.** $38\overline{)\$383.04}$ **15.** $4\overline{)\$952.84}$

Divide. Round the quotient to the nearest cent.

16. $4\overline{)\$13.09}$ **17.** $5\overline{)\$59.47}$ **18.** $20\overline{)\$45.20}$ **19.** $25\overline{)\$305.75}$

20. $12\overline{)\$32.73}$ **21.** $72\overline{)\$85.47}$ **22.** $44\overline{)\$205.09}$ **23.** $52\overline{)\$532.87}$

Problem Solving

Julia works part-time. The table shows how many hours she worked last week. She receives a paycheck for $140.30. Use this information for Exercises 24–25.

Julia's Hours	
Monday	5.5
Tuesday	4.25
Wednesday	0
Thursday	5.25

24. How much does Julia earn per hour?

25. Suppose Julia worked 4 hours on Wednesday. How would this change Julia's total earnings?

Use the photo for Joe's Pet Store for Exercises 26–28.

26. Jan buys 1 clownfish and pays with a $20 bill. What is her change?

27. Pet City sells 4 clownfish for $70.48. Which store has the better buy? Explain how you found your answer.

28. Joe's Pet Store has a sale today. The cost for 3 clownfish has decreased to $50.54. Also, if you buy 6 fish, you get 1 free. Jack buys 7 fish today. How much money does he save per fish, compared to the original price?

Joe's Pet Store

3 for $52.92

Write About It

29. To find $12.42 divided by 3, Hank divides $12 by 3 and $0.42 by 3. Explain how Hank can continue his work to find the exact quotient.

Objective
- Use the Work Backward strategy to solve problems.

Math Word

number line

Valeria walks for exercise. She walks the same distance on Monday and Tuesday. On Wednesday, Thursday, and Friday, she walks 3.5 miles each day. After she walks 5.0 miles on Saturday, her total for the 6 days is 18.5 miles. How far does she walk each day on Monday and Tuesday?

You can work backward using a number line to solve this problem.

- Start at 18.5, the number of miles Valeria walks in all. First jump back 5.0, the distance she walks on Saturday. $18.5 - 5.0 = 13.5$

- Then jump back 3.5 three times, the number of miles Valeria walks each day Wednesday through Friday. $13.5 - (3 \times 3.5) = 3.0$

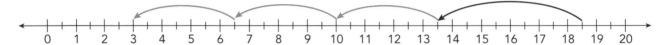

The distance that is left, 3.0 miles, shows how far Valeria walks in all on the two days, Monday and Tuesday.

- Now find how far she walks each day on Monday and Tuesday. Divide 3.0 miles by 2.

$$3.0 \div 2 = 1.5$$

➢ Valeria walks 1.5 miles each day on Monday and Tuesday.

You can find the total distance walked to check your work.

$$\text{total} = (2 \times 1.5) + (3 \times 3.5) + 5.0$$
$$= 3.0 + 10.5 + 5.0$$
$$= 18.5 \checkmark$$

PRACTICE

1. Breana spends 3 hours and 45 minutes reading during one week. On Monday and Tuesday, she reads for 25 minutes each day. On Wednesday and Thursday, she reads for 40 minutes each day. On Friday and Saturday, she reads for a total of 1 hour. How much time does she spend reading on Sunday?

The table shows the cost of beef and turkey at Manny's Market this week. Use the table for Exercises 2–5.

Manny's Market	
Meat	Cost for 1 lb
beef	$6.76
turkey	$4.45

2. Bianca buys 3 pounds of beef and 2 pounds of turkey. When she pays for her purchase, she receives $10.82 in change. How much money does Bianca give the clerk?

3. Oliver buys some beef and 6 pounds of turkey. His change from $100 is $12.46. How many pounds of beef does Oliver buy?

4. Trevor pays $52.82 for 3 pounds of apples, 4 pounds of beef, and 4 pounds of turkey. How much does 1 pound of apples cost?

5. Without calculating an exact answer, explain how to decide whether $55 is enough to buy 5 pounds of beef and 5 pounds of turkey.

6. A softball coach has a $1000 uniform budget. She buys 24 jerseys and has $189.04 left to spend. How much does each jersey cost?

7. After school, Max goes to the library for 45 minutes, to the swimming pool for an hour, and to the bookstore for 25 minutes. He arrives home at 5:15 PM after a 20-minute walk. What time does Max leave school?

8. Jessica buys a container of liquid plant fertilizer. She puts 0.125 liter of fertilizer into each of 4 small bottles. Then she pours half of what is left of the container into another bottle. There is now 0.5 liter of fertilizer left in the container. How much fertilizer was in the container that Jessica bought?

9. The pep club is decorating the 50-foot long bleachers shown. There are 10 rows of seats. The club will put a green streamer and a white streamer along each row of seats. Streamer rolls are 81 feet long. How many streamer rolls does the pep club need?

50 ft

10. Beth combines 16 ounces ground turkey with two 14.5-ounce cans of beans and 1 can tomatoes to make chili. She makes 73 ounces of chili in all. How many ounces of tomatoes does she use?

Write About It

11. How can you recognize a problem situation where using Work Backward would be a good strategy to use?

Model Dividing a Decimal by a Decimal

Objective
- Use a model to divide a decimal by a decimal.

Math Words
quotient
hundredths

Find 0.80 ÷ 0.05. Use a model to divide.

Model 0.80.

Identify 0.05, or 5 hundredths.

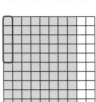

Count the number of groups of 5 hundredths in 80 hundredths.

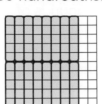

There are 16 groups of 5 hundredths.

So, 0.80 ÷ 0.05 = 16.

Study this example.

Find 3.6 ÷ 1.2.

Model 3 and 6 tenths.

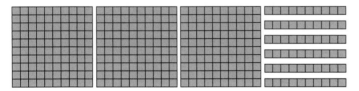

How many groups of 1 and 2 tenths are in 3.6?

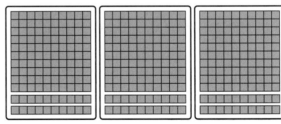

There are 3 groups of 1.2 in 3.6, so 3.6 ÷ 1.2 = 3.

PRACTICE

The model shows a decimal divided by a decimal. Write a division sentence for the model.

1.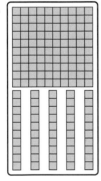

2.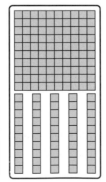

Use the model to find the quotient.

3. 0.64 ÷ 0.08

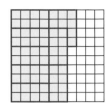

4. 0.36 ÷ 0.04

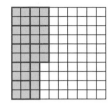

5. 5.1 ÷ 1.7

6. 3.2 ÷ 0.2

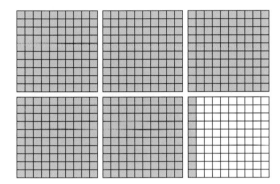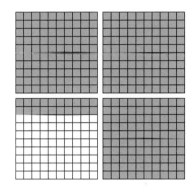

Use base-ten blocks or draw a model to find the quotient.

7. 4.2 ÷ 1.4   **8.** 0.88 ÷ 0.11   **9.** 0.96 ÷ 0.08   **10.** 7.2 ÷ 1.8

Problem Solving

Rebecca's class is on a field trip. One experiment includes collecting stream water. They collected 0.96 liter of stream water to analyze. Use this information for Exercises 11–13.

11. They divide the water into 3 equal samples. How much water is in each sample?

12. The students realize they should have 4 equal samples of water, not 3. How much water should be in each sample?

13. How much water could the students pour from each of the 3 equal samples to create a fourth sample?

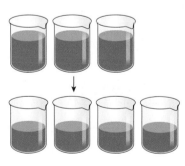

Write About It

14. Ben needs to find 45.5 ÷ 3.5. He knows that in a previous exercise, he found 45.5 ÷ 7 = 6.5. How can he use this to find the quotient?

13-10 Divide a Decimal by a Decimal

Objective
- Divide by a decimal.

Math Words
divisor
quotient

How many times greater is the mass of the half-dollar than the mass of the penny?

To solve the problem, divide 12.5 by 2.5.

Rewrite the division problem so that the divisor is a whole number.

- Move the decimal point of the divisor enough places to form a whole number.

- Move the decimal point in the dividend to the right the same number of places.

$$\begin{array}{r} 5 \\ 2.5\overline{)12.5} \\ -\underline{12\ 5} \\ 0 \end{array}$$

- Place the decimal point in the quotient and divide.

12.5 grams   **2.5 grams**

▷ So, the half-dollar has 5 times the mass of the penny.

Moving decimal points is like multiplying or dividing by a power of 10:
$12.5 \div 2.5 =$
$(12.5 \times 10) \div (2.5 \times 10) =$
$125 \div 25 = 5$

Study these examples.

$$\begin{array}{r} 27.6 \\ 0.3\overline{)8.2.8} \\ -\underline{6} \\ 2\ 2 \\ -\underline{2\ 1} \\ 1\ 8 \\ -\underline{1\ 8} \\ 0 \end{array}$$

$8.28 \div 0.3 = 27.6$

$$\begin{array}{r} 27.1 \\ 0.21\overline{)5.69.1} \\ -\underline{4\ 2} \\ 1\ 49 \\ -\underline{1\ 47} \\ 21 \\ -\underline{21} \\ 0 \end{array}$$

$5.691 \div 0.21 = 27.1$

PRACTICE

Complete each division.

1. $0.4\overline{)9.2.4}$

2. $0.4\overline{)92.4.}$

3. $0.04\overline{)0.92.4}$

4. $441.6 \div 1.2$

5. $44.16 \div 1.2$

6. $4.416 \div 1.2$

7. $0.6\overline{)1.74}$

8. $2.4\overline{)4.32}$

9. $0.3\overline{)92.7}$

10. $4.1\overline{)90.2}$

11. $0.9\overline{)0.432}$

12. $0.02\overline{)17.4}$

Divide and check.

13. $0.7 \overline{)0.28}$ **14.** $0.4 \overline{)0.96}$ **15.** $0.3 \overline{)5.7}$ **16.** $1.6 \overline{)21.6}$

17. $0.9 \overline{)8.73}$ **18.** $0.05 \overline{)3.25}$ **19.** $0.74 \overline{)0.814}$ **20.** $6.2 \overline{)2.604}$

21. $5.75 \div 0.25$ **22.** $32.4 \div 0.2$ **23.** $74.16 \div 1.8$

24. $6.452 \div 0.4$ **25.** $30.78 \div 1.8$ **26.** $64.116 \div 5.2$

27. $3.5 \overline{)22.68}$ **28.** $0.6 \overline{)111.6}$ **29.** $0.7 \overline{)32.809}$

Compare without computing. Write <, >, or =.

30. $55.2 \div 0.3 \underline{} 26.08 \div 0.4$ **31.** $0.96 \div 0.08 \underline{} 6.06 \div 0.06$

32. $1.848 \div 0.22 \underline{} 9.24 \div 0.33$ **33.** $8.08 \div 0.2 \underline{} 80.8 \div 2$

Problem Solving

34. Eliza grows basil and oregano in her herb garden. The heights of the flower pots including the plants are shown. She says the basil plant (without the pot) is more than twice as tall as the oregano plant. Do you agree? Justify your answer.

35. A chef is separating 7.2 pounds of rice into smaller servings. Each serving should contain 1.2 ounces of rice. How many servings will there be in all? There are 16 ounces in 1 pound.

36. When a number is divided by 0.5, the quotient is a whole number. When the same number is multiplied by 0.5, the product is 1.25. What is the quotient when the number is divided by 0.5? Explain.

Write About It

37. Mandy wants to find $12.8 \div 3.2 \div 2$. Her work is shown. Did Mandy make a mistake? If so, explain and correct the error.

> $12.8 \div 3.2 \div 2 =$
> $12.8 \div 1.6 =$
> $128 \div 16 = 8$

Use the model to find the quotient.

1. 3.1 ÷ 5

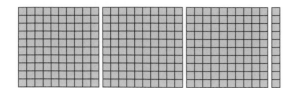

2. 2.96 ÷ 4

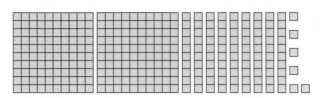

3. 1.26 ÷ 7

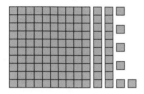

4. 3.12 ÷ 6

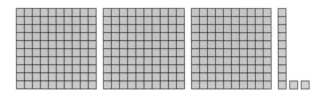

5. 0.92 ÷ 0.23

6. 1.62 ÷ 0.27

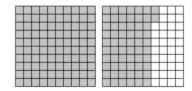

7. 0.84 ÷ 0.12

8. 2.4 ÷ 0.48

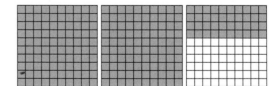

Estimate the quotient.

9. 9$\overline{)5.396}$ **10.** 3$\overline{)1.174}$ **11.** 5$\overline{)6.602}$ **12.** 7$\overline{)0.293}$

13. 4$\overline{)\$3.58}$ **14.** \$151.20 ÷ 14 **15.** 11$\overline{)\$401.25}$ **16.** \$5.56 ÷ 8

17. 11$\overline{)85.441}$ **18.** 21$\overline{)\$123.08}$ **19.** 8$\overline{)\$100.48}$ **20.** 14$\overline{)460.008}$

Divide.

21. $37 \div 100$

22. $0.08 \div 10$

23. $4.82 \div 1000$

24. $364.89 \div 10^2$

25. $109.5 \div 10^1$

26. $117.06 \div 10^3$

27. $6.86 \div 7$

28. $2.64 \div 8$

29. $20.8 \div 16$

30. $8.25 \div 33$

31. $26.51 \div 11$

32. $26.8 \div 20$

33. $6\overline{)0.3\,6}$

34. $3\overline{)0.2\,4}$

35. $22\overline{)0.8\,8}$

36. $5\overline{)5.2}$

37. $0.6\overline{)0.4\,8}$

38. $0.5\overline{)0.3\,5}$

39. $0.2\overline{)3.4}$

40. $2.5\overline{)1.3\,2\,5}$

41. $7.56 \div 2.1$

42. $8.5 \div 3.4$

43. $51.41 \div 5.3$

44. $27.328 \div 3.2$

Find the quotient.

45. $42.5 \div n$ when $n = 10^3$

46. $n \div 100$ when $n = 33.02$

47. $n \div 12$ when $n = 8.76$

48. $7.56 \div n$ when $n = 7$

49. $26.65 \div n$ when $n = 4.1$

50. $n \div 7.8$ when $n = 71.916$

Divide. Round to the nearest cent.

51. $13\overline{)\$6\,5.2\,2}$

52. $6\overline{)\$1\,9.5\,8}$

53. $18\overline{)\$4\,8\,7.0\,9}$

54. $30\overline{)\$8\,6.1\,5}$

55. $5\overline{)\$4\,8\,2.4\,7}$

56. $7\overline{)\$2\,0\,0.6\,4}$

57. $22\overline{)\$5\,8\,0.9\,3}$

58. $52\overline{)\$9\,0\,0.1\,4}$

Problem Solving

A graphic designer specializes in making flyers. She charges different amounts depending on the size of the flyer. Use this information for Exercises 59–61.

Flyer Size	Price ($)
5-inch × 7-inch	101.50
6.5-inch × 9-inch	157.95
8.5-inch × 11-inch	233.75

59. How can you find the price the designer charges per square inch of a flyer?

60. How much more per square inch does the 5-inch × 7-inch flyer cost than the 6.5-inch × 9-inch flyer?

61. How much more per square inch does the 5-inch × 7-inch flyer cost than the 8.5-inch × 11-inch flyer?

62. Julie wants to use a model to divide 154.96 by 5.2. Explain to Julie why a different method would be better. Then find the quotient.

After using his budget for five months, Maxwell notices that other expenses have also come up that he did not consider when creating his budget. He makes a list of these expenses so he can adjust his budget to include them.

- Soccer club membership: $39.99 (every 6 months)
- Gifts: $149.64 (total amount spent over 5 months)
- Car registration: $126.90 (every 24 months)

- Airfare: $264.78 (one trip every 12 months)
- Tuition and books for one class: $726.75 (2 classes each year)
- Car repair: $487.09
- Dental work: $318.52

Maxwell decides to add a **Miscellaneous** category to his monthly budget spreadsheet to account for these types of expenses.

1. In order to budget for each category, Maxwell needs to find the cost of each expense on a monthly basis. How can he find these amounts? Explain using an example from the list above.

2. Some of the expenses Maxwell lists are predictable but others are not, such as car repairs and dental work. How should Maxwell plan for these expenses in his monthly budget?

3. Maxwell takes one class a semester (or two classes each year). He knows how much he must pay for tuition and books for each class. How can he convert this expense into a monthly amount?

4. Copy and complete the table below. Use compatible numbers.

Miscellaneous	Compatible Numbers	Estimate (Monthly)
Soccer club membership	42 ÷ 6	
Gifts	150 ÷ 5	
Car registration	?	
Airfare	?	
Tuition and books	?	
Car repairs	?	
Dental work	?	
	TOTAL:	

5. Copy and complete the table below. Be sure to include the formula that Maxwell will need to enter into the spreadsheet program for each calculation. Round answers to the nearest cent when necessary.

The formulas should look like this: = $ _?_ ÷ _?_ = $ _?_

Miscellaneous	
SOCCER CLUB MEMBERSHIP	= $39.99 ÷ 6 = $6.67
GIFTS	= $149.64 ÷ 5 = ?
CAR REGISTRATION	?
AIRFARE	?
TUITION AND BOOKS	?
CAR REPAIRS	?
DENTAL WORK	?
TOTAL:	?

6. Compare your estimate for each miscellaneous category to the actual amount. Why are some estimates greater than the actual amount and others are less than the actual amount? Explain.

7. Compare your estimated total for Miscellaneous costs with the actual total. How do the values compare? Is your exact total a reasonable answer?

8. Maxwell is surprised to see how many expenses he did not include in his original budget. He wants to determine how much he will spend on miscellaneous expenses each week. Describe how can he calculate this cost. Then calculate how much money Maxwell will spend on miscellaneous expenses each week. Round to the nearest cent. There are 52 weeks in a year.

9. Name three other expenses that may vary from month to month. For each, create an amount and how often it must be paid (similar to the list on the previous page). Then calculate the corresponding monthly cost. Use a table similar to the one below to organize your response.

Expense	Cost	Frequency	Monthly Cost
?	?	?	?
?	?	?	?
?	?	?	?

Determine the best answer for each problem.

1. Find the quotient.

$$8.64 \div 8 \div 0.2$$

A. 0.216
B. 1.08
C. 5.4
D. 40

2. The dimensions of a small bedroom are shown by the diagram. How wide is the bedroom?

8.4 feet

66.36 square feet

3. Divide the money into 3 equal groups. How much money is in each group?

A. $0.51   B. $0.86
C. $0.93   D. $1.29

4. Find the missing value.

$$\underline{\ ?\ } \times 9.4 = 66.74$$

A. 6.3   B. 7.1
C. 57.34   D. 627.356

5. Which statements are correct? Select all that apply.

A. $4.48 \div 1.4 > 6 \div 2.4$
B. $17.52 \div 3 < 30.6 \div 4.5$
C. $2.79 \div 0.9 < 7.5 \div 2.5$
D. $68.08 \div 7.4 = 62.72 \div 6.4$
E. $0.34 \div 0.5 = 1.36 \div 2$

6. Half of the rectangle shown is shaded. What is the area of the shaded part?

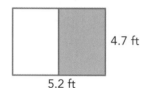

4.7 ft

5.2 ft

7. Determine the best estimate of the quotient. Is the estimate greater than or less than the actual quotient?

$$8\overline{)1.752}$$

A. 0.2; less than
B. 0.2; greater than
C. 0.3; less than
D. 0.3; greater than

8. Identify the pattern rule.

$$3.25, 6.5, 13, 26$$

A. Multiply by 0.5.
B. Divide by 0.5.
C. Multiply by 2.5.
D. Divide by 2.5.

Measurement

Early humans developed systems of measurement, some of which still exist today. Measurement systems were developed even before people knew how to write or count.

To measure distance or length, early humans used their hands and feet.

♦ inch: the width of the thumb

♦ foot: the length of the foot

♦ yard: the distance from the center of the body to the fingertips of the outstretched arm

♦ mile: one thousand paces (pace = two steps)

These lengths are part of the customary system of measurement, and are still used in the United States today.

Determining early standards for capacity, weight, and temperature were more complicated. Early humans often used elements of nature to standardize measures.

Relate Customary Units of Length

Objective
- Convert customary units of length.

Math Words
convert
inch
foot
yard
mile

The length of a pickleball court is 44 feet. How long is the court in yards? How long is the court in inches?

Non-Volley Zone
↓

44 ft

Different units can be used to measure length. Sometimes one unit makes more sense than another unit.

♦ To convert a smaller unit to a larger unit, *divide*.

44 ft = ? yd

44 ft = (44 ÷ 3) yd   3 feet = 1 yard

$= 14\frac{2}{3}$ yd

Units of Length

12 inches (in.) = 1 foot (ft)

3 feet = 1 yard (yd)

5280 ft = 1760 yd = 1 mile (mi)

♦ To convert a larger unit to a smaller unit, *multiply*.

44 ft = ? in.

44 ft = (44 × 12) in.   12 inches = 1 foot

= 528 in.

▷ The length of a pickleball court is $14\frac{2}{3}$ yards, or 528 inches.

It is difficult to visualize 528 inches, so feet or yards may be better units to use for the pickleball court's length.

Study these examples.

63 in. = ? ft ? in.

63 in. = (63 ÷ 12) ft   12 in. = 1 ft

$= 5\frac{3}{12}$ ft = 5 ft 3 in.

3.5 mi = ? yd

3.5 mi = (3.5 × 1760) yd   1760 yd = 1 mi

= 6160 yd

PRACTICE

Convert the measurement.

1. 60 in. = ? ft

2. 4 yd = ? ft

3. 2 mi = ? ft

4. 4 mi = ? yd

5. 3 mi = ? yd

6. 54 ft = ? yd

7. 3.5 ft = ? in.

8. 2 mi = ? yd

9. 2.7 yd = ? ft

10. 25 ft = ? yd ? ft

11. 8 ft 2 in. = ? in.

12. 58 yd = ? ft

Compare. Write <, =, or >.

13. 17 yd __?__ 50 ft

14. 8 mi __?__ 15,000 yd

15. 2700 ft __?__ 0.5 mi

16. $4\frac{1}{2}$ mi __?__ 25,000 ft

17. 0.6 yd __?__ 20 in.

18. 501 ft __?__ 167 yd

Select the appropriate unit for each measurement. Use inches, feet, yards, or miles.

19. the height of a door

20. the distance from your house to the nearest grocery store

21. the diagonal of a television screen

22. the length of a football field

Problem Solving

23. Henry measures the length of a kitchen floor in feet and then measures again in inches. Which will be greater—the number of inches or the number of feet? Explain.

The Mona Lisa is a painting by Leonardo DaVinci. It is located at the Louvre Museum in Paris, France. Use this information for Exercises 24–25.

1 ft 9 in.

2 ft 6 in.

24. What are the dimensions of the painting, in inches?

25. Harold buys a print of the painting. The print is 18 inches by 12 inches. He tells his friends that the dimensions of the actual painting are $1\frac{2}{3}$ times the dimensions of his print. Do you agree with Harold? Explain your reasoning and show any calculations.

26. Jake is $5\frac{3}{4}$ ft tall and his father is 6 ft tall. How many inches taller is Jake's father?

Write About It

27. Jayne wants to write an equation that relates inches to yards. Explain how she can do this. What is the equation?

14-2 Relate Customary Units of Capacity

Objective
- Convert customary units of capacity.

Math Words
fluid ounce
cup
pint
quart
gallon
convert

An elephant's trunk can hold as much as 10 quarts of water. What is this amount in pints? What is this amount in gallons?

◆ When converting from quarts to pints, which is a smaller unit, multiply.

10 qt = _?_ pt

10 qt = (10 × 2) pt | 2 pints = 1 quart

10 qt = 20 pt

◆ When converting from quarts to gallons, which is a larger unit, divide.

10 qt = _?_ gal

10 qt = (10 ÷ 4) gal | 4 quarts = 1 gallon

10 qt = 2.5 gal

Units of Capacity

8 fluid ounces (fl oz) = 1 cup (c)

2 cups = 1 pint (pt)

2 pints = 1 quart (qt)

4 quarts = 1 gallon (gal)

▷ An elephant's trunk can hold 20 pints or 2.5 gallons of water.

Study these examples.

2 gal 1 qt = _?_ qt

4 qt = 1 gal

2 gal = (2 × 4) qt = 8 qt

8 qt + 1 qt = 9 qt

21 c = _?_ pt = _?_ pt _?_ c

2 c = 1 pt

21 c = (21 ÷ 2) pt =

10½ pt = 10 pt 1 c

remaining cups →

```
        1 0 R 1
    2)2 1
    - 2
      0 1
      - 0
        1
```

PRACTICE

Convert the measurement.

1. 32 fl oz = _?_ c

2. 12 qt = _?_ gal

3. 5 pt = _?_ c

4. 12 c = _?_ pt

5. 22 pt = _?_ qt

6. 2.5 c = _?_ fl oz

Compare. Write <, =, or >.

7. 39 fl oz _?_ 5 c

8. 8 qt _?_ 8 pt

9. 10 qt _?_ 2.5 gal

Convert the measurement.

10. 16 c = _?_ pt

11. 10 fl oz = _?_ c

12. $\frac{3}{4}$ gal = _?_ qt

13. 16 c = _?_ fl oz

14. 15 qt = _?_ gal

15. $1\frac{1}{2}$ pt = _?_ c

16. 100 fl oz = _?_ c = _?_ c _?_ fl oz

17. _?_ qt = 64 pt = _?_ c

18. 8 pt = _?_ qt = _?_ gal

19. _?_ fl oz = 4 c = _?_ pt

Compare. Write <, =, or >.

20. 5 c _?_ 30 fl oz

21. 7 pt _?_ 4 qt

22. 75 fl oz _?_ 4 pt

23. 2 gal _?_ 16 pt

24. 3 qt _?_ 0.5 gal

25. 2 c _?_ 0.5 qt

Select the appropriate unit to measure each object. Use fluid ounces, cups, pints, quarts, or gallons.

26. a glass of juice

27. a solution in a test tube

28. a fuel truck

Problem Solving

29. Kathryn makes a smoothie. She blends 10 fluid ounces of mashed banana with $\frac{1}{2}$ cup of yogurt and 1 cup of mashed strawberries. How many fluid ounces is the smoothie?

Write About It

30. Derek wants to measure $2\frac{1}{2}$ quarts of water to make lemonade. He can't find a measuring cup, but he does have an empty 12-fl-oz can. Describe how he can use the can to approximate the amount water he needs.

Relate Customary Units of Weight

Objective
- Convert customary units of weight.

Math Words

ounce
pound
ton
convert

The curator of a museum is making plans to have a statue moved to a different display. The statue weighs one fourth of a ton, and $\frac{1}{200}$ of the weight comes from the gold plating on the statue. How many ounces of gold are in the statue?

- Convert tons to ounces.

$$\frac{1}{4} T = \underline{\ ?\ } lb$$

$$\frac{1}{4} T = \left(\frac{1}{4} \times 2000 \right) lb$$

2000 lb = 1 T

$$\frac{1}{4} T = 500 \ lb$$

$$500 \ lb = \underline{\ ?\ } oz$$

$$500 \ lb = (500 \times 16) \ oz$$

16 oz = 1 lb

$$500 \ lb = 8000 \ oz$$

- Find $\frac{1}{200}$ of 8000 oz.

$$\frac{1}{200} \times 8000 \ oz = \underline{\ ?\ }$$

$$\frac{1}{200} \times 8000 \ oz = 40 \ oz$$

Units of Weight

16 ounces (oz) = 1 pound (lb)

2000 pounds = 1 ton (T)

When you divide 52 oz by 16, the quotient is the number of pounds and the remainder is the number of ounces.

There are 40 oz of gold in the statue.

Study these examples.

$$3000 \ lb = \underline{\ ?\ } T$$

2000 lb = 1 T

$$3000 \ lb = (3000 \div 2000) \ T$$

$$= 1\frac{1}{2} \ T$$

$$52 \ oz = \underline{\ ?\ } lb = \underline{\ ?\ } lb \ \underline{\ ?\ } oz$$

16 oz = 1 lb

$$52 \ oz = (52 \div 16) \ lb$$

$$= 3\frac{1}{4} \ lb$$

$$= 3 \ lb \ 4 \ oz$$

$$\begin{array}{r} 3 \ R4 \\ 16\overline{)52} \\ -48 \\ \hline 4 \end{array}$$

PRACTICE

Convert the measurement.

1. 32 oz = $\underline{\ ?\ }$ lb

2. 12 T = $\underline{\ ?\ }$ lb

3. 10,000 lb = $\underline{\ ?\ }$ T

4. 5000 lb = $\underline{\ ?\ }$ T

5. 5 lb = $\underline{\ ?\ }$ oz

6. 24 oz = $\underline{\ ?\ }$ lb

7. Explain the difference between a fluid ounce and an ounce.

Convert the measurement.

8. 6 T = _?_ lb

9. 64 oz = _?_ lb

10. 4000 lb = _?_ T

11. 3.5 lb = _?_ oz

12. 9000 lb = _?_ T

13. 100 oz = _?_ lb

14. _?_ oz = 1000 lb = _?_ T

15. _?_ T = 2000 lb = _?_ oz

16. 7000 lb = _?_ T = _?_ T _?_ lb

17. 120 oz = _?_ lb = _?_ lb _?_ oz

Compare. Write <, =, or >.

18. 48 oz _?_ 3 lb

19. 5 T _?_ 4950 lb

20. 2 lb _?_ 40 oz

21. 6500 lb _?_ 3 T

22. 70 oz _?_ 4.5 lb

23. 5.5 T _?_ 11,000 lb

Select the appropriate unit to measure each object.
Use tons, pounds, or ounces.

24. the weight of a tractor

25. the weight of a kitten

26. the weight of a microscope

27. the weight of a cell phone

28. Why would it be better to express the weight of a kitchen table in pounds, rather than in ounces or tons?

Problem Solving

29. The table shows various weights and prices of cameras. Charlotte wants to purchase the lightest camera under $300. Which camera should she buy?

30. A baby penguin weighs $2\frac{1}{4}$ pounds. How many ounces does it have to gain to reach a weight of 3 pounds?

Weight	Price
22 ounces	$275
2.1 pounds	$210
20 ounces	$325
1.5 pounds	$250

31. A truck has a capacity of 2 tons. Tim loads the truck with crates that weigh 350 pounds each. How many crates can he load? Explain.

Write About It

32. Explain how you can use mental math and properties to convert from tons to pounds.

Compute with Customary Units

Objective
- Use computation skills to solve problems involving customary units.

Math Words
rename
regroup

A chef makes the 2 pots of soup shown. How much soup does she make in all? She is going to put the soup into six 3-quart jars. How much soup will she have left over?

- Start by finding how much soup the chef makes in all.

Add like units.	Rename units if needed.	Regroup.
3 gal 2 qt	3 gal 2 qt	4 gal 5 qt
+ 1 gal 3 qt	+ 1 gal 3 qt	= 4 gal + 1 gal 1 qt
4 gal 5 qt	4 gal 5 qt	= 5 gal 1 qt

4 qt = 1 gal

1 gal 1 qt

3 gal 2 qt

➤ The chef makes 5 gallons and 1 quart of soup in all.

- Now find how much soup can fit into six jars.

Multiply.	Rename units if needed.
3 qt	3 qt
× 6	× 6
1 8 qt	1 8 qt → 4 gal 2 qt

1 gal 3 qt

The jars can hold 4 gallons and 2 quarts of soup in all.

- Finally, subtract to find how much soup is left over.

Regroup.	Subtract like units.
5 gal 1 qt = 4 gal 5 qt	4 gal 5 qt
− 4 gal 2 qt = 4 gal 2 qt	− 4 gal 2 qt
	3 qt

➤ The chef will have 3 quarts of soup left over after she fills the jars.

PRACTICE

Find the sum or difference.

	1.	2.	3.	4.
	8 yd 5 in.	6 c 5 fl oz	3 qt 1 pt	4 lb 1 2 oz
	+ 3 yd 4 in.	+ 3 c 2 fl oz	− 2 qt 1 pt	− 2 lb 1 4 oz

Find the sum or difference.

5.   1 0 yd 2 2 in.
     + 9 yd 1 9 in.

6.   6 qt 6 pt
   − 2 qt 2 pt

7.   1 2 mi 2 2 0 yd
   +1 1 mi 3 6 0 yd

8.   3 5 lb 5 oz
   − 2 3 lb 1 2 oz

9.   1 5 ft 9 in.
   +1 7 ft 3 in.

10.   1 0 pt 1 c
    − 6 pt 2 c

11.   3 gal 3 qt
   +4 gal 4 qt

12.   1 7 ft 3 in.
   −1 5 ft 9 in.

Compare. Write <, >, or =.

13. 3 ft _?_ 30 in.

14. 5 qt _?_ 12 pt

15. 35 oz _?_ 2 lb

16. 3 mi 1230 yd _?_ 6090 ft

17. 8 gal 6 qt _?_ 42 qt 2 pt

Problem Solving

18. Laura has a new 60-foot roll of ribbon. She wraps 12 packages using 54 inches of ribbon for each package. How much ribbon is left?

19. Last week, a bunny weighed 15 oz. This week the bunny weighed 1 lb 2 oz. Describe the change in weight.

Sergio buys 4 pieces of pine. Two are 1 yd 2 ft long, and two are 4 ft long. Use the information for Exercises 20–21.

20. What is the cost of the 4 pieces of pine?

21. What is Sergio's change from $20 if there is no tax?

A farmer makes 42 gallons of maple syrup. He wants to fill the same number of pint bottles and quart bottles with the syrup. Use this information for Exercises 22–23.

22. How many of each size bottle does he need?

23. He sells the pints for $9 and the quarts for $16. If he sells all the syrup, how much money will he make?

CLEARANCE

2 × 2 Pine
$1.10
per foot

Write About It

24. To convert from a smaller unit to a larger unit, you divide. To convert from a larger unit to a smaller unit, you multiply. Explain with examples why this is so.

Convert each measurement of length.

| 12 in. = 1 ft | | 3 ft = 1 yd | | 5280 ft = 1760 yd = 1 mi |

1. 48 in. = _?_ ft   **2.** 15 ft = _?_ yd   **3.** 3 mi = _?_ yd

4. 2 mi = _?_ yd   **5.** 10 mi = _?_ ft   **6.** 9 yd = _?_ ft

7. 210 in. = _?_ ft   **8.** 1.5 mi = _?_ yd   **9.** 3.25 mi = _?_ ft

10. 198 in. = _?_ yd   **11.** 1 mi = _?_ in.   **12.** 8.3 ft = _?_ in.

13. 7.5 yd = _?_ ft = _?_ ft _?_ in.   **14.** 18 in. = _?_ ft = _?_ yd

15. 0.75 mi = _?_ ft = _?_ in.   **16.** 9540 in. = _?_ ft = _?_ yd

Convert each measurement of capacity.

| 8 fl oz = 1 c | | 2 c = 1 pt | | 2 pt = 1 qt | | 4 qt = 1 gal |

17. 40 fl oz = _?_ c   **18.** 44 qt = _?_ gal   **19.** 15 pt = _?_ c

20. 45 qt = _?_ pt   **21.** 12 c = _?_ fl oz   **22.** 18 gal = _?_ qt

23. 19 pt = _?_ qt   **24.** 21 c = _?_ pt   **25.** 50 fl oz = _?_ c

26. 48 fl oz = _?_ pt   **27.** 3.5 qt = _?_ c   **28.** 10 pt = _?_ gal

29. 0.375 gal = _?_ qt = _?_ qt _?_ pt   **30.** 210 fl oz = _?_ c = _?_ c _?_ fl oz

31. 14 c = _?_ pt = _?_ qt   **32.** 13 pt = _?_ qt = _?_ gal

Convert each measurement of weight.

| 16 oz = 1 lb | | 2000 lb = 1 T |

33. 12,000 lb = _?_ T   **34.** 4 lb = _?_ oz   **35.** 128 oz = _?_ lb

36. 9 T = _?_ lb   **37.** 20 oz = _?_ lb   **38.** 3500 lb = _?_ T

39. 52 oz = _?_ lb = _?_ lb _?_ oz   **40.** 3.8 T = _?_ lb = _?_ oz

Compare. Write <, >, or =.

41. 10 lb _?_ 160 oz

42. 15,000 ft _?_ 3 mi

43. 7 qt _?_ 1.5 gal

44. 10 oz _?_ 0.5 lb

45. 0.25 T _?_ 400 lb

46. 2640 yd _?_ 1.5 mi

47. 2000 lb _?_ 2 T

48. 11 pt _?_ 6 qt

49. 20 fl oz _?_ 1 pt

50. 4 gal _?_ 32 pt

51. 12 yd _?_ 4 ft

52. 20 c _?_ 10 qt

53. 45 yd _?_ 135 ft

54. 2.5 T _?_ 500 lb

55. 100 in. _?_ 10 ft

56. 8 c _?_ 1 fl oz

57. 15 oz _?_ 0.8 lb

58. 1 mi _?_ 63,000 in.

Find the sum or difference. Regroup as needed.

59.
```
  8 yd 1 5 in.
+ 4 yd 2 0 in.
```

60.
```
  4 ft   8 in.
+ 9 ft 1 0 in.
```

61.
```
  1 0 qt 5 pt
−   6 qt 1 pt
```

62.
```
  1 2 pt 1 c
−   8 pt 3 c
```

63.
```
  6 gal 5 qt
+ 3 gal 8 qt
```

64.
```
  1 5 lb 2 0 oz
− 1 6 lb   2 oz
```

65.
```
  1 0 ft 3 0 in.
− 1 2 ft   3 in.
```

66.
```
  4 mi 9 0 0 yd
+ 4 mi 9 0 0 yd
```

Problem Solving

67. A pair of twins are born. One baby is a girl weighing 6 lb 7 oz. The other baby is a boy weighing 5 lb 15 oz. How many more pounds does the baby girl weigh than the baby boy?

The rectangle represents a picture frame. Use the rectangle for Exercises 68–69.

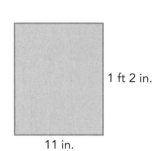

1 ft 2 in.

11 in.

68. What is the perimeter of the rectangle in inches?

69. What is the perimeter of the rectangle in feet and leftover inches?

70. For a science experiment, Lilly is filling a gallon milk jug with cups of water. How many cups of water will she need to pour in order to completely fill the jug?

71. A certain brand of cereal is sold in large and small boxes. Which box of cereal is cheaper by the ounce?

1 lb 8 oz

$4.25

1 lb 2 oz

$3.50

Relate Metric Units of Length

Objective
- Convert metric units of length.

Math Words
millimeter
centimeter
decimeter
meter
kilometer
convert

The height of a bamboo plant is 6.4 decimeters. How tall is the plant in centimeters? How tall is the plant in meters?

The millimeter (mm), centimeter (cm), decimeter (dm), meter (m), and kilometer (km) are metric units of length.

Sometimes it makes more sense to use one unit than another. When measuring a short distance, smaller units such as millimeters or centimeters are used. When measuring longer distances, meters or kilometers are used.

Units of Length
1 m = 1000 mm
1 m = 100 cm
1 m = 10 dm
1 dm = 10 cm
1 km = 1000 m

◆ To convert larger units to smaller units, multiply.

6.4 dm = __?__ cm

6.4 dm = (6.4 × 10) cm | 1 dm = 10 cm |

= 64 cm

▷ The height of the bamboo plant is 64 cm.

◆ To convert smaller units to larger units, divide.

6.4 dm = __?__ m

6.4 dm = (6.4 ÷ 10) m | 1 m = 10 dm |

= 0.64 m

▷ The height of the bamboo plant is 0.64 m.

Study these examples.

520 mm = __?__ m

| 1000 mm = 1 m |

520 mm = (520 ÷ 1000) m

= 0.52 m

3.2 km = __?__ m

| 1 km = 1000 m |

3.2 km = (3.2 × 1000) m

= 3200 m

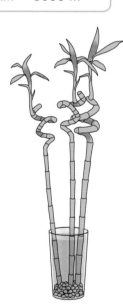

PRACTICE

Convert the measurement.

1. 1 dm = __?__ cm

2. 10 mm = __?__ cm

3. 1 dm = __?__ mm

4. 30 cm = __?__ dm

5. 41 cm = __?__ mm

6. 2500 m = __?__ km

Write the appropriate unit to measure each object. Use mm, cm, dm, m, or km.

7. the length of a dolphin

8. the thickness of a book

9. the height of a skyscraper

10. the width of a pencil lead

Convert the measurement.

11. 89 dm = _?_ m

12. 3.4 km = _?_ m

13. 6.1 m = _?_ dm

14. 670 mm = _?_ cm = _?_ m

15. 9 m = _?_ dm = _?_ cm

16. 17 dm = _?_ cm = _?_ mm

17. 940 dm = _?_ m = _?_ km

Compare. Write <, =, or >.

18. 0.7 dm _?_ 7 cm

19. 600 mm _?_ 6 cm

20. 45 m _?_ 450 dm

21. 1800 cm _?_ 180 m

22. 15 dm _?_ 15,000 mm

23. 100 m _?_ 1 km

Find the missing unit.

24. 9.5 dm = 950 _?_

25. 4 cm = 0.04 _?_

26. 2.5 mm = 0.25 _?_

Problem Solving

Cassandra makes pottery using a wheel. She makes a jug that is 3.1 dm tall and a mug that is 12.4 cm tall. Use the information for Exercises 27–29.

27. How much taller is the jug than the mug?

28. How many millimeters tall is the mug?

29. Tamika makes a bowl half the height of the jug. How many centimeters tall is Tamika's bowl?

Write About It

30. Complete the statement.

50,000 mm = _?_ cm = _?_ dm = _?_ m = _?_ km
Explain the pattern in the answers to the conversion between mm and m.
Explain why the pattern breaks when converting to km.

Relate Metric Units of Capacity

Objective
▪ Convert metric units of capacity.

Math Words
milliliter
centiliter
deciliter
liter
kiloliter
convert

Willis mixes several drops of peppermint oil with 0.75 liter of water to make a natural cleaning solution. What is the equivalent amount of milliliters of water? What is the equivalent amount of kiloliters of water?

The milliliter (mL), centiliter (cL), deciliter (dL), liter (L), and kiloliter (kL) are metric units of capacity.

◆ To convert larger units to smaller units, multiply.

0.75 L = _?_ mL

0.75 L = (0.75 × 1000) mL $\boxed{1 \text{ L} = 1000 \text{ mL}}$

= 750 mL

Units of Capacity
1 L = 1000 mL
1 L = 100 cL
1 L = 10 dL
1 kL = 1000 L

▷ 750 mL of water are used to make the cleaning solution.

◆ To convert smaller units to larger units, divide.

0.75 L = _?_ kL

0.75 L = (0.75 ÷ 1000) kL $\boxed{1 \text{ kL} = 1000 \text{ L}}$

= 0.00075 kL

▷ 0.00075 kL of water are used to make the cleaning solution.

It makes more sense to use milliliters or liters to describe the amount of water in the cleaning solution, since the number of kiloliters is so small.

Study these examples.

800 dL = _?_ L

800 dL = (800 ÷ 10) L

= 80 L

6.7 L = _?_ cL

6.7 L = (6.7 × 100) cL

= 670 cL

$\boxed{\begin{array}{l} 1 \text{ L} = 10 \text{ dL} \\ 1 \text{ L} = 100 \text{ cL} \end{array}}$

PRACTICE

Convert the measurement.

1. 1 cL = _?_ mL

2. 10 cL = _?_ dL

3. 100 mL = _?_ dL

4. 2 L = _?_ dL

5. 60 cL = _?_ mL

6. 700 L = _?_ kL

7. 1.5 dL = _?_ cL

8. 23 mL = _?_ cL

9. 40 cL = _?_ dL

Write the appropriate unit to measure each object. Use mL, cL, dL, L, or kL.

10. the liquid in a medicine dropper

11. the water in a swimming pool

12. the juice in a cup

13. the capacity of a cooler

Convert the measurement.

14. 120 dL = _?_ cL

15. 650 mL = _?_ cL

16. 204 dL = _?_ L

17. 735 mL = _?_ cL = _?_ dL

18. 8.2 kL = _?_ L = _?_ dL

19. 11.5 L = _?_ dL = _?_ cL

20. 2450 mL = _?_ cL = _?_ dL = _?_ L

Compare. Write <, =, or >.

21. 0.7 dL _?_ 7 cL

22. 600 mL _?_ 6 cL

23. 45 L _?_ 450 dL

24. 1800 cL _?_ 180 L

25. 15 dL _?_ 15000 mL

26. 100 L _?_ 1 kL

Problem Solving

To make tomato soup, Mike combines 1 can of soup with 1 can of water. Use this information and the picture for Exercises 27–29.

27. How many deciliters of soup does Mike make?

28. Beth prefers to use half a can of water and half a can of milk. How many kiloliters of milk does she use to make a can of soup?

29. Curt makes 3 cans of soup using 3 cans of water for his family. They eat $\frac{3}{4}$ of the soup. How many centiliters of soup are left over?

30. Mr. Martinez is making punch for a class event. He mixes 2 L of orange juice, 0.5 L of seltzer, and 150 cL of cranberry juice. How many deciliters of punch does he make?

284 mL (9.6 fl oz)

Write About It

31. Would you prefer to use customary or metric units to measure capacity? Explain.

Objective
- Convert metric units of mass.

Math Words
milligram
centigram
decigram
gram
kilogram
metric ton
mass

The nutritional information for one serving (180 grams) of an orange is shown. How many milligrams of fiber does one serving contain? How many grams of calcium does one serving contain?

The milligram (mg), centigram (cg), decigram (dg), gram (g), kilogram (kg), and metric ton (t) are metric units of mass.

Nutrition Facts	
Serving Size	180 g
Amount Per Serving	1 c
Calories	85
Dietary Fiber	4 g
Calcium	72 mg

◆ To convert larger units to smaller units, multiply.

$$4 \text{ g} = \underline{\ ?\ } \text{ mg}$$
$$4 \text{ g} = (4 \times 1000) \text{ mg} \quad \boxed{1 \text{ g} = 1000 \text{ mg}}$$
$$= 4000 \text{ mg}$$

◆ To convert smaller units to larger units, divide.

$$72 \text{ mg} = \underline{\ ?\ } \text{ g}$$
$$72 \text{ mg} = (72 \div 1000) \text{ g} \quad \boxed{1 \text{ g} = 1000 \text{ mg}}$$
$$= 0.072 \text{ g}$$

Units of Mass

1 g = 1000 mg

1 g = 100 cg

1 g = 10 dg

1 kg = 1000 g

1 t = 1000 kg

▷ A serving of an orange contains 4000 mg of fiber and 0.072 g of calcium.

Study these examples.

$$48 \text{ dg} = \underline{\ ?\ } \text{ g}$$
$$48 \text{ dg} = (48 \div 10) \text{ g} \quad \boxed{1 \text{ g} = 10 \text{ dg}}$$
$$= 4.8 \text{ g}$$

$$2.3 \text{ kg} = \underline{\ ?\ } \text{ g}$$
$$2.3 \text{ kg} = (2.3 \times 1000) \text{ g} \quad \boxed{1 \text{ kg} = 1000 \text{ g}}$$
$$= 2300 \text{ g}$$

PRACTICE

Convert the measurement.

1. 1 dg = $\underline{\ ?\ }$ cg

2. 100 mg = $\underline{\ ?\ }$ dg

3. 10 mg = $\underline{\ ?\ }$ cg

4. 3.2 g = $\underline{\ ?\ }$ dg

5. 50 cg = $\underline{\ ?\ }$ g

6. 37 kg = $\underline{\ ?\ }$ g

7. 7.2 g = $\underline{\ ?\ }$ mg

8. 9 mg = $\underline{\ ?\ }$ g

9. 500 g = $\underline{\ ?\ }$ kg

Write the appropriate unit to measure each object. Use mg, cg, dg, g, kg, or t.

10. the mass of a cell phone

11. the mass of a car

12. the mass of an adult

13. the mass of a housefly

Convert the measurement.

14. 3000 mg = $\underline{\;?\;}$ g

15. 52 g = $\underline{\;?\;}$ cg

16. 6800 kg = $\underline{\;?\;}$ t

17. 5.1 dg = $\underline{\;?\;}$ cg = $\underline{\;?\;}$ mg

18. 560,000 g = $\underline{\;?\;}$ kg = $\underline{\;?\;}$ t

Compare. Write <, =, or >.

19. 300 mg $\underline{\;?\;}$ 30 cg

20. 0.4 kg $\underline{\;?\;}$ 40 g

21. 2.5 g $\underline{\;?\;}$ 250 cg

22. 6400 mg $\underline{\;?\;}$ 64 g

23. 2 g $\underline{\;?\;}$ 200 dg

24. 100 kg $\underline{\;?\;}$ 1 t

Find the missing unit.

25. 31 mg = 3.1 $\underline{\;?\;}$

26. 0.034 kg = 340 $\underline{\;?\;}$

27. 908.2 mg = 9.082 $\underline{\;?\;}$

Problem Solving

28. Janice says 35 dg is 10 times the mass of 350 mg. Do you agree with Janice? Explain.

29. The mass of the rabbit shown was 830 grams on the day of its adoption. The scale shows the mass of the rabbit now. How many grams has it gained since then?

30. A case of 8 cartons of milk has a mass of 7.2 kilograms. How many decigrams is each carton?

31. Three packages are loaded into an elevator. The packages have masses of 65 kg, 90 kg, and 4500 grams. Do the packages exceed the 200-kg load limit of the elevator? Explain.

Write About It

32. Is a metric ton the same as a customary ton? Explain.

Wyatt is testing rubber bands to see how much they stretch when different weights are attached to them. He has two 50-gram weights, two 0.1-kilogram weights, and one 200-gram weight. Can Wyatt extend his table by testing how much a rubber band stretches when 500 grams of weights are attached?

- First convert 0.1 kg to grams.

$$0.1 \text{ kg} = \underline{?} \text{ g}$$
$$= 0.1 \times 1000 \text{ g}$$
$$= 100 \text{ g}$$

Rubber Band Stretch	
Mass (g)	Length (cm)
0	7.7
100	8.5
200	10.2
300	11.0

Each 0.1-kg weight equals 100 g.

- Then add all of the weights.

$$50 \text{ g} + 50 \text{ g} + 100 \text{ g} + 100 \text{ g} + 200 \text{ g} = 500 \text{ g}$$

▷ The weights add up to 500 g. Wyatt can extend his table.

Study these examples.

$$3.5 \text{ m} + 89 \text{ cm} = \underline{?} \text{ cm}$$
$$3.5 \text{ m} = \underline{?} \text{ cm}$$
$$= (3.5 \times 100) \text{ cm}$$
$$= 350 \text{ cm}$$
$$350 \text{ cm} + 89 \text{ cm} = 439 \text{ cm}$$

$$4.04 \text{ L} - 202 \text{ mL} = \underline{?} \text{ L}$$
$$202 \text{ mL} = \underline{?} \text{ L}$$
$$= (202 \div 1000) \text{ L}$$
$$= 0.202 \text{ L}$$
$$4.04 \text{ L} - 0.202 \text{ L} = 3.838 \text{ L}$$

The last two examples show that you can either convert first and then perform the operation, or operate first and then convert.

$$48 \text{ dm} \times 4 = \underline{?} \text{ m}$$
$$48 \text{ dm} = \underline{?} \text{ m}$$
$$= (48 \div 10) \text{ m}$$
$$= 4.8 \text{ m}$$
$$4.8 \text{ m} \times 4 = 19.2 \text{ m}$$

$$1500 \text{ L} \div 5 = \underline{?} \text{ kL}$$
$$1500 \text{ L} \div 5 = 300 \text{ L}$$
$$300 \text{ L} = \underline{?} \text{ kL}$$
$$= (300 \div 1000) \text{ kL}$$
$$= 0.3 \text{ kL}$$

PRACTICE

Complete the statement.

1. $0.025 \text{ g} + 253 \text{ mg} = \underline{?} \text{ mg}$

2. $175,000 \text{ mm} - 230 \text{ dm} = \underline{?} \text{ dm}$

3. $5.8 \text{ g} \times 2 = \underline{?} \text{ mg}$

4. $2.55 \text{ cL} \div 5 = \underline{?} \text{ L}$

5. $31 \text{ cm} \times 3 + 2.5 \text{ m} = \underline{?} \text{ m}$

6. $7.3 \text{ dL} - 85 \text{ mL} + 0.05 \text{ cL} = \underline{?} \text{ mL}$

Add or subtract. Complete the statement.

7. 11.25 m + 908.5 cm = __?__ cm

8. 15,235 mL + 9.885 L = __?__ mL

9. 6.06 cg − 4.08 cg = __?__ g

10. 105.5 cm + 5 mm = __?__ m

11. $42\frac{4}{5}$ dg + 165 cg = __?__ mg

12. 0.92 g − 63.072 mg = __?__ cg

Multiply or divide. Complete the statement.

13. 0.402 g × 80 = __?__ dg

14. 890,000 mm ÷ 25 = __?__ m

15. 500 m ÷ 4 = __?__ dm

16. 62 dl × 100 = __?__ kL

Compare. Write <, >, or =.

17. 4.3 m + 85 cm __?__ 5.2 m + 79 cm

18. $4\frac{9}{10}$ m __?__ $700 × \frac{7}{10}$ cm

19. 63.02 mg + 12.16 cg __?__ 24.9 cg − 18.4 mg

Problem Solving

Sierra uses a 1-L beaker in her yard to collect and measure rainfall. At the end of each day, she empties the beaker if needed. The table shows the amounts of rain she collects in November. Use the information for Exercises 20–23.

Date	Amount
11/3	190 mL
11/4	215 mL
11/8	195 mL
11/9	230 mL
11/20	225 mL
11/21	185 mL

20. Use clustering to estimate the total rainfall in November.

21. Does Sierra collect more or less than 1 L of rainwater in November? How much more or less?

22. In liters, what is the greatest difference between the amounts of rainfall for any two consecutive days in November?

23. Without calculating, in which consecutive two-day period did the most rain fall? Explain your reasoning.

┌─ **Write About It** ◇

24. You have worked with two different systems of measurement—customary and metric. Which do you prefer to work with? Explain your reasoning.

Problem Solving
Use a Picture

Objective
- Use information in a picture and apply the four-step problem-solving process.

Math Word
convert

Liam drives a dump truck that weighs 12,500 lb when empty. He has to deliver a load of gravel that weighs 3.5 T. His shortest route to the customer is $10\frac{5}{8}$ mi long. Is it safe for Liam, who weighs 200 lb, to use the shortest route?

Read and Understand

The key information is the weight of the empty truck, the weight of the load, Liam's weight, and the weight limit of the bridge, shown in the picture. The length of the route is not needed to solve the problem.

Represent the Situation

The weight of the truck, its load, and its driver cannot be greater than the weight limit of the bridge.

Make and Use a Plan

- Use the same units for all the weights. Convert the weight of the truck and Liam's weight to tons. Remember that 2000 lb = 1 T.

Weight of the Truck	Weight of the Driver
12,500 lb = __?__ T	200 lb = __?__ T
12,500 lb ÷ 2000 T	200 lb ÷ 2000 T
= 6.25 T	= 0.1 T

- Find the total weight of the truck, the load, and the driver.

  6.25 T + 3.5 T + 0.1 T = 9.85 T

- Compare the total weight to the weight limit.

  9.85 T < 10 T

> The total weight is less than the weight limit, so it is safe for Liam to use the bridge.

Look Back

Is there another way to solve this problem?

Would it be easier to express all the weights in pounds instead of tons?

Would it make sense to start with the weight limit and subtract the weights of the truck, the load, and the driver?

The sign shows the prices for items at a local grocery store. Use the information in the picture for Exercises 1–4.

Grapes $2.79 for 1-lb bag	**Cider** $4.12 for 1-gal jug
Cider $0.59 for 8-fl oz bottle	**Avocados** $1.98 each
Blueberries $2.49 for 6 oz carton	**Cherries** $3.35 for 12 oz bag

1. Molly needs 2 pounds of blueberries to make some jam. How many cartons of blueberries does she need to buy? How much will the blueberries cost?

2. Marco has a recipe that uses equal weights of grapes and cherries. He buys 3 pounds of grapes. How many bags of cherries does he need to buy? How much will the fruit cost?

3. Karen buys cider for a class party. She knows that 28 people will attend. Should she buy jugs of cider or bottles of cider? Explain your reasoning.

4. Julia buys 3 bags of grapes, a carton of blueberries, and 3 avocados. How many times as heavy are the grapes than the blueberries? How much change does Julia receive when she pays with a $20 bill?

5. Three large packages have the same mass, and a small package has a mass of 750 g. The total mass of the four packages is 10.5 kg. What is the mass of two large packages?

6. Mrs. Dean is making pancakes and oatmeal. She opens a new $\frac{1}{2}$-gallon container of milk. She uses the amounts of milk shown in the table. How much milk is left in the container? Is the container more than half full? Explain.

Amount of Milk Used	
Item	Amount (cups)
Pancakes	$1\frac{3}{4}$
Oatmeal	$3\frac{5}{8}$

7. A stick that is 1.6 meters long is cut into 2 pieces. One piece is $\frac{3}{5}$ as long as the other piece. How long is the shorter piece in centimeters?

8. Mr. Shaker mixes 2 quarts, 3 pints, and 1 gallon of the same paint. He needs $4\frac{1}{2}$ gallons of paint in all. How much paint does Mr. Shaker need?

Write About It

9. Which step in the 4-step problem-solving process do you think is most important? Why?

CHAPTER 14

Review

Convert each customary measurement.

| 12 in. = 1 ft |
| 3 ft = 1 yd |
| 5280 ft = 1760 yd = 1 mi |

| 8 fl oz = 1 c |
| 2 c = 1 pt |
| 2 pt = 1 qt |
| 4 qt = 1 gal |

| 16 oz = 1 lb |
| 2000 lb = 1 T |

1. 72 fl oz = _?_ c

2. 33 ft = _?_ yd

3. 2.5 lb = _?_ oz

4. 7 gal = _?_ qt

5. 0.25 T = _?_ lb

6. 0.25 yd = _?_ ft

7. 7.25 qt = _?_ pt

8. 900 lb = _?_ T

9. 5 mi = _?_ yd

10. 35,000 lb = _?_ T

11. 17.5 mi = _?_ ft

12. 56 oz = _?_ lb

13. 7 mi = _?_ yd

14. 8 pt = _?_ c

15. 100 c = _?_ fl oz

16. 4.25 yd = _?_ ft = _?_ ft _?_ in.

17. 45 in. = _?_ ft = _?_ yd

18. 1.625 gal = _?_ qt = _?_ qt _?_ pt

19. 20 fl oz = _?_ c = _?_ pt = _?_ qt

20. 76 oz = _?_ lb = _?_ lb _?_ oz

21. 0.2 T = _?_ lb = _?_ oz

Convert each metric measurement.

| 1 m = 1000 mm |
| 1 m = 100 cm |
| 1 m = 10 dm |
| 1 km = 1000 m |

| 1 L =1000 mL |
| 1 L = 100 cL |
| 1 L = 10 dL |
| 1 kL = 1000 L |

| 1 g = 1000 mg |
| 1 g = 100 cg |
| 1 g = 10 dg |
| 1 kg = 1000 g |
| 1 t = 1000 kg |

22. 3 dL = _?_ cL

23. 2700 cg = _?_ kg

24. 5 dg = _?_ cg

25. 300 m = _?_ km

26. 80 dm = _?_ cm

27. 35 mL = _?_ cL

28. 150 cL = _?_ dL

29. 480 kg = _?_ t

30. 18 cm = _?_ mm

31. 14 mm = _?_ cm

32. 9.8 g = _?_ mg

33. 742 cm = _?_ dm

34. 150 mL = _?_ dL

35. 24 kg = _?_ g

36. 11 dL = _?_ L

Compare. Write >, <, or =.

37. 10 qt _?_ 20 pt

38. 1000 m _?_ 10 km

39. 15 qt _?_ 4 gal

40. 45 oz _?_ 11.25 lb

41. 390 mL _?_ 3.9 cL

42. 0.2 dm _?_ 20 cm

43. 9600 mg _?_ 9.6 g

44. 30 pt _?_ 15 c

45. 120 fl oz _?_ 4 qt

46. 2 T _?_ 64,000 oz

47. 36 g _?_ 360 cg

48. 1760 ft _?_ 1 mi

49. 6000 yd _?_ 3 mi

50. 0.25 ft _?_ 4 in.

51. 28 dL _?_ 0.028 mL

Find the sum or difference.

52.
```
  9 pt 2 c
+ 4 pt 3 c
```

53.
```
  4 mi 6 0 0 0 ft
- 2 mi   5 0 0 ft
```

54.
```
  1 4 ft 2 0 in.
-   2 ft   8 in.
```

55.
```
        1 3 oz
+ 2 lb 1 5 oz
```

56.
```
  5 ft 2 3 in.
+ 3 ft   1 in.
```

57.
```
  6 yd 3 7 in.
+ 2 yd 1 5 in.
```

58.
```
  2 qt 8 pt
- 3 qt 3 pt
```

59.
```
  1 7 gal 9 qt
-   4 gal 5 qt
```

Complete the statement.

60. 8.241 L + 7109 cL = _?_ L

61. 75.4 cm − 500.3 mm = _?_ mm

62. 9.2 dg − 65 cg = _?_ cg

63. 4.09 L + 38 dL = _?_ L

64. 894 mg + 0.7 g = _?_ g

65. 1.8 km − 670 dm = _?_ m

Problem Solving

Mr. Boyd is building a playhouse for his pets. The design for the frame of the house is shown. Use this information and the drawing for Exercises 66–68.

66. How many centimeters long is the longer side of the house?

67. Find the perimeter of the house in centimeters, decimeters, and meters.

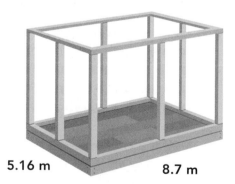

5.16 m   8.7 m

68. The wood Mr. Boyd plans to use to frame the perimeter of the base is sold in pieces that are 3 meters long. How many pieces of wood does he need? How much will he have left over?

Early humans developed systems of measurement before they could even write or count. Some of these early units of measurement are listed below.

- inch: the width of the thumb
- digit: the width of the middle finger (about $\frac{3}{4}$ inch)
- palm: the width of four fingers (about 3 inches)
- span: the distance covered by the spread hand (about 9 inches)
- foot: the length of the foot
- cubit: the distance from the elbow to the tip of the middle finger (about 18 inches)
- yard: the distance from the center of the body to the fingertips of the outstretched arm (about 36 inches)
- fathom: the distance spanned by the outstretched arms (about 72 inches)
- mile: one thousand paces (pace = two steps)

Hypostyle Hall, Temple of Hathor, Dendera, Egypt

1. Do these measurements describe length, capacity, or weight?

2. Which units of measurement listed above have you used before? Which units have you not used?

3. You have used equations such as 12 in. = 1 ft and 3 ft = 1 yd to convert between units. Copy the table onto your own paper and complete the statements using the information given above.

Ancient Measurement Conversion Equations	
1 palm = _?_ digits	1 yard = _?_ spans
1 span = _?_ palms	1 yard = _?_ cubits
1 cubit = _?_ spans	1 fathom = _?_ feet
1 fathom = _?_ cubits	1 fathom = _?_ yards

4. Name an appropriate unit from the list above that could be used to measure each of the following.

- distance from one village to another
- width of a doorway in a hut
- width of a small rock
- length of a spoon
- distance from one hut in a small village to another

5. These measurements varied from person to person. As a result, measurements were not always precise. With the help of a partner, measure each of the following in inches. Compare your measurements with those on the previous page. For instance, is the width of four of your fingers more than, less than, or exactly 3 inches?

- width of your thumb
- width of your middle finger
- width of your four fingers (pressed together)
- width of your hand (fingers spread, from thumb to pinky)
- length of your foot
- distance from your elbow to the tip of your middle finger
- distance between your outstretched arms

6. Convert the given measurement of each ancient artifact into two other units of measure (not including inches).

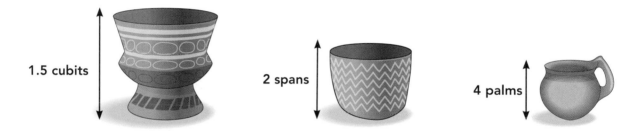

1.5 cubits

2 spans

4 palms

7. Suppose the distance between some ancient villages was described as follows. Find each distance in miles.
- five thousand paces
- seven hundred fifty paces
- fifteen hundred paces
- one hundred paces

8. Collect some common objects such as those listed below. Measure the length of each object in inches. Then convert the measurement into at least one ancient unit of measurement. An example has been provided.
- textbook (Example: 15 inches = 5 palms or 20 digits)
- deck
- pencil
- piece of paper

Determine the best answer for each problem.

1. A large water bottle has twice as much water as a small water bottle. If the small bottle has 8 fluid ounces of water, how much water is in the large bottle? (8 fl oz = 1 c, 2 c = 1 pt, 2 pt = 1 qt)

A. 1 c   **B.** 1 pt
C. 2 pt   **D.** 1 qt

2. A single serving of granola contains 3 grams of fiber. How many milligrams are in 5 servings of granola?

3. Which measurements are equal to 57 liters? Select all that apply. (1 L = 1000 mL = 100 cL = 10 dL; 1 kL = 1000 L)

A. 570,000 mL
B. 5700 cL
C. 570 dL
D. 0.57 kL
E. 0.057 kL

4. What is the perimeter of the triangle in inches?

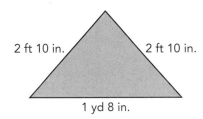

2 ft 10 in.   2 ft 10 in.

1 yd 8 in.

5. There are 10 dm in 1 m and 100 cm in 1 m. How many cm are in 1 dm?

A. 0.1   **B.** 10
C. 100   **D.** 1000

6. A pickup truck can hold up to 4 tons of cargo. The truck carries pallets of stone that weigh 750 pounds each. What is the maximum number of pallets the truck can hold? (1 ton = 2000 lb)

A. 8 pallets   **B.** 9 pallets
C. 10 pallets   **D.** 11 pallets

7. How many inches are in 8.5 yards?

8. The distance between two towns is 4.75 miles. Which of the following are equivalent to this distance? Select all that apply. (5280 ft = 1760 yd = 1 mi)

A. 0.003 yd
B. 25,080 ft
C. 27,645 ft
D. 7932.5 yd
E. 8360 yd

9. Complete:

2345 mL + 367 cL = _?_ dL

10. Select the greatest mass.

A. 10 g   **B.** 100 mg
C. 0.001 kg   **D.** 1 cg

Geometry

A polygon is a closed shape with line segments for sides. In this chapter, you will learn the names of polygons. For example, a 3-sided polygon is a triangle. Squares and rectangles are examples of polygons with 4 sides, called *quadrilaterals*.

Maximizing Areas of Quadrilaterals

Suppose you are designing a 4-sided horse pen. You have a certain amount of fencing available. Your goal is to enclose the greatest amount of space possible. Quadrilaterals with the same perimeter do not necessarily have the same area.

Consider the following:

◆ What shapes have four sides?

◆ What are the possible dimensions of each shape?

◆ What is the area of each shape?

◆ Do the side lengths and areas show a pattern?

At the end of this chapter, you will use the formulas for area and perimeter of squares and rectangles, as well as grid paper, to determine the greatest area that can be fenced in under these conditions.

Polygons

Objective
- Understand and use attributes of polygons.

Math Words
plane figure
polygon
vertex (vertices)
triangle
quadrilateral
regular polygon

Some geometric figures are plane figures. A plane figure is composed of points that lie in the same plane.

These plane figures are open figures:

These plane figures are closed figures:

Some closed figures are polygons. A polygon is a closed plane figure with line segments for sides. A point on a polygon where two sides meet is a vertex of the polygon. A polygon is named and classified by its number of sides.

Polygon	triangle	quadrilateral	pentagon	hexagon
Number of Sides	3	4	5	6
Example				

Polygon	heptagon	octagon	nonagon	decagon
Number of Sides	7	8	9	10
Example				

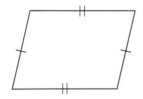

Identical marks on the quadrilateral mean equal side lengths. Identical arcs in the triangle mean equal angle measures.

A regular polygon has all equal side lengths and equal angle measures.

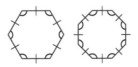

Classify each figure.

1.

2.

3.

4.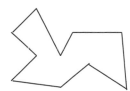

5.

6.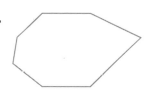

Tell whether each polygon is *regular* or *not regular*.

7.

8.

9.

10.

11. Is it possible to draw a polygon that has equal angle measures, but does not have equal side lengths? If so, give an example.

12. Is a closed plane figure always a polygon? Explain with an example.

Problem Solving

13. A square is a regular quadrilateral. The area of a square is 144 square inches. What is the length of one of its sides in feet? Hint: 1 square foot is not the same as 12 square inches.

Gwen forms a polygon by joining two regular triangles like the one shown along one side. Use this information for Exercises 14–15.

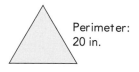

Perimeter: 20 in.

14. What is the perimeter of the new polygon?

15. What type of polygon is the new polygon? Is it a regular polygon? Explain.

Write About It

16. Define what a polygon is by explaining how one can be drawn. Compare your definition with those of classmates.

Triangles

Objective
▪ Understand and use attributes of triangles.

Math Words
triangle
equilateral triangle
isosceles triangle
scalene triangle
acute triangle
right triangle
obtuse triangle

◆ One way to classify triangles is by the lengths of their sides.

 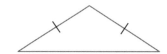 

equilateral triangle:
3 equal side lengths

isosceles triangle:
at least 2 equal side lengths

scalene triangle:
no equal side lengths

◆ Another way to classify triangles is by the measures of their angles. These triangle names are related to the angle names.

  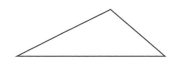

acute triangle:
3 acute angles

right triangle:
1 right angle
2 acute angles

obtuse triangle:
1 obtuse angle
2 acute angles

Angle Name	acute	right	obtuse
Angle Measure	between 0° and 90°	90°	between 90° and 180°
Example			

PRACTICE

Classify the triangle as *scalene*, *isosceles*, or *equilateral*.

1.

2.

3.

Classify the triangle as *acute*, *right*, or *obtuse*.

4.

5.

6.

Try to draw a triangle for the given description. If it is not possible, write *not possible*.

7. equilateral and acute

8. scalene and right

9. isosceles and obtuse

10. equilateral and obtuse

11. scalene and acute

12. equilateral and right

Classify the triangle in two ways.

13.

14.

15.

16. Is it possible for a triangle to have 2 right angles? Why or why not?

17. Is it possible to draw a right triangle that is scalene, isosceles, or equilateral?

Problem Solving

18. Gage says that all triangles have at least 2 acute angles. Do you agree? Explain why or why not.

19. The perimeter of an equilateral triangle is 27 feet. What is the length of a side in yards? In inches?

20. A triangle is isosceles and acute. Exactly one side has a length of 16 centimeters. Its perimeter is 0.5 meter. What are the lengths of the other sides of this triangle?

21. A triangle is isosceles and obtuse. Exactly one side has a length of 2 feet. Its perimeter is 50 inches. What are the lengths of the other sides of the triangle?

22. The perimeter of a right triangle is 12 inches. The longest side is 2 inches longer than the shortest side. The other side is 1 inch shorter than the longest side. What are the side lengths?

23. Cut out two identical right triangles. Put the triangles together on matching sides in different ways. What polygons can you form?

Write About It

24. Explain the reasoning you use when classifying triangles.

Match the name of the figure with its number of sides.

1. heptagon   **2.** triangle   **A.** 3   **E.** 7
                                                  B. 4   **F.** 8
3. quadrilateral   **4.** pentagon   **C.** 5   **G.** 9
                                                  D. 6   **H.** 10
5. decagon   **6.** nonagon

7. octagon   **8.** hexagon

Match the description with the correct term.

9. a two-dimensional figure that has straight or   **A.** regular polygon
curved sides   **B.** open figure
                                                             C. plane figure

10. a polygon with all equal side and angle measures

11. a shape in which two line segments aren't
connected to anything at their endpoints

Tell whether the figure is *open* or *closed*.

12.   **13.**   **14.**

Tell whether the polygon is *regular* or *not regular*.

15. 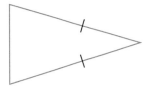   **16.** 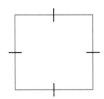   **17.**

Classify the polygon based on its number of sides.

18.    **19.**   **20.**

Match the type of triangle with its description.

21. equilateral   **22.** isosceles

23. acute   **24.** obtuse

25. scalene   **26.** right

A. 1 right angle and 2 acute angles
B. 0 equal side lengths
C. 3 equal side lengths
D. 1 obtuse angle and 2 acute angles
E. 2 equal side lengths
F. 3 acute angles

Classify the triangle based on angle measures and side lengths.

27.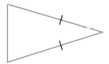

28.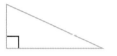

29.

30.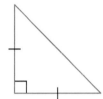

31.

32.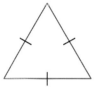

Problem Solving

33. The perimeter of a regular octagon is 2 feet. What is the length of each side, in inches?

34. A map of Julie's neighborhood consists of square blocks that are all the same size. A path on the map starts at Julie's house, and then goes 3 blocks north, 2 blocks east, 1 block south, and 1 block west. Describe the shape formed by the path.

35. The square shown is divided in half to form two identical triangles. Classify each triangle according to its side lengths and angle measures.

36. The rectangle shown is divided in half to form two identical triangles. Classify each triangle according to its side lengths and angle measures.

37. Matthew says this figure is a regular hexagon. Is Matthew correct? Explain why or why not.

38. The perimeter of a regular hexagon is 72 inches. Diagonals are drawn through the center of the hexagon to divide it into 6 regular triangles. What is the perimeter of one of the triangles?

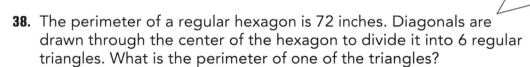

Quadrilaterals

Objective
■ Understand and use attributes of quadrilaterals.

Math Words
quadrilateral
trapezoid
parallelogram
rhombus
rectangle
square

Audrey is designing a stained glass window. She wants to be sure to include quadrilaterals with special names. What quadrilaterals does Audrey's design include?

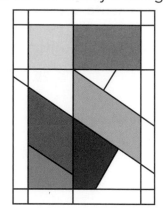

Look for the most specific name for each quadrilateral.

Some quadrilaterals have special names that are used to classify them.

- A trapezoid is a quadrilateral with exactly 1 pair of parallel sides (blue shape).

- A parallelogram is a quadrilateral with 2 pairs of parallel sides. Each pair of parallel sides is also equal in length (green, purple, orange, and yellow shapes).

- A rhombus is a parallelogram with 4 equal side lengths (purple and yellow shapes).

- A rectangle is a parallelogram with 4 right angles (orange and yellow shapes).

- A square is a parallelogram with 4 equal side lengths and 4 right angles (yellow shape).

- The red shape has no parallel sides, so it cannot be described by one of the special names listed. It is simply called a quadrilateral.

Audrey's design includes a trapezoid, a parallelogram, a rhombus, a rectangle, a square, and a quadrilateral.

PRACTICE

1. Which figures are trapezoids?

A.
B.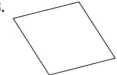
C.
D.

2. Which figures are rhombuses?

A.    B.    C.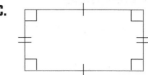

3. Which figures are squares?

A.   B.   C.

Complete the sentence or answer the question.

4. A quadrilateral has exactly _?_ angles.

5. What is special about a quadrilateral that is also a parallelogram?

6. Are all rhombuses also parallelograms? squares?

7. A square is a rhombus with four _?_ angles.

Problem Solving

8. The perimeter of a rectangle is 22 inches. Its area is 24 square inches. What are the dimensions of the rectangle?

9. A parallelogram with an area of 256 square inches has 4 equal side lengths and 4 right angles. What is another name for this figure? What are its dimensions in feet?

10. Samir draws a line segment from one vertex of a quadrilateral to the opposite vertex. Two right isosceles triangles are formed. Write the best name for the shape.

Write About It

11. The flag of Kuwait is shown. Write a brief paragraph that describes the flag. Be sure to use vocabulary from this lesson.

Classify Quadrilaterals

Objective
- Classify quadrilaterals in a hierarchy based on their properties.

Math Words
Venn diagram
quadrilateral
trapezoid
parallelogram
rhombus
rectangle
square

The Venn diagram illustrates the relationships among different types of quadrilaterals. How are rectangles and rhombuses related? Are all rectangles also rhombuses?

Everything inside this diagram is a quadrilateral, and anything outside the diagram is not.

This oval is separate from the other types of quadrilaterals.

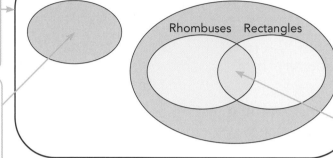

All figures in this oval are parallelograms.

Figures in the region where the green and yellow ovals overlap represent rhombuses and rectangles.

The Venn diagram shows that some figures are both rhombuses and rectangles. These figures are squares.

Pay close attention to ovals inside of ovals, overlapping ovals, and ovals that have no overlap.

The oval for rectangles is not completely inside the oval for rhombuses. So not all rectangles are rhombuses.

Study these examples.

This figure is a quadrilateral, a parallelogram, and a rectangle.

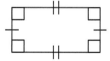

This figure is a quadrilateral and a trapezoid.

PRACTICE

Classify the quadrilateral in as many additional ways as possible.

1.

2.

3.

4.

Compare. Explain how the quadrilaterals are alike and different.

5. trapezoid and parallelogram

6. rectangle and square

7. rectangle and rhombus

8. parallelogram and rhombus

9. rectangle, rhombus, and square

10. parallelogram, rectangle, and square

Decide if each statement is *true* or *false*.

11. All rhombuses are squares.

12. All rectangles are parallelograms.

13. Some parallelograms are trapezoids.

14. All parallelograms with 4 equal side lengths are squares.

Problem Solving

15. Describe how you might use the drawing shown to remember the differences in quadrilaterals.

16. Daisy says the only difference between a trapezoid and a rhombus is that a rhombus has one more pair of parallel sides. Do you agree with Daisy? Why or why not?

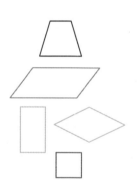

17. Devon says a rectangle with 4 equal side lengths and a rhombus with 4 right angles have the same name. Do you agree with Devon? Why or why not?

The photo shows a special V-shaped guitar. The dimensions of its body are labeled. Use the photo for Exercises 18–20.

18. What shape best represents the body of the guitar?

19. What is the perimeter of the body of the guitar in meters?

20. There are about 2.5 centimeters in an inch. Estimate the perimeter of the body to the nearest inch? Explain.

48.26 cm   48.26 cm

27.94 cm

—Write About It

21. In the Venn diagram for quadrilaterals, what does it mean when one section is completely inside another? Give an example.

Problem Solving
Use a Model

Objective
- Use models to represent and organize information while solving problems.

Math Word
Venn diagram

Twenty-four students take part in an after-school program. Today 12 students work on science fair projects and 15 play board games. Seven students do both, and the rest spend all the time reading.

How many students choose only to read today?

You can use a Venn diagram to help solve this problem.

- Organize the given information in a Venn diagram.

- Complete the Venn diagram.

- 12 students work on science fair projects. So, $12 - 7 = 5$ students only work on science fair projects.

- 15 students play board games. So, $15 - 7 = 8$ students only play games.

- Subtract to find the number of students who only read:
  $24 - (5 + 7 + 8) = 24 - 20 = 4$

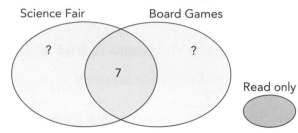

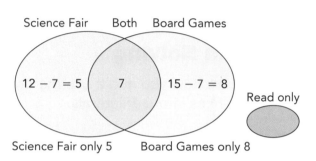

> In the after-school program today, 4 students choose only to read.

Study these examples.

Number of Pizzas: 42

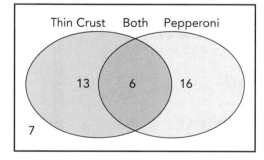

How many pizzas have thin crust?
$13 + 6 = 19$

How many pizzas have pepperoni but not thin crust? 16

How many pizzas do not have thin crust or pepperoni? 7

Sally has 12 heart stickers and 22 red stickers. She has 4 stickers that are neither hearts nor red. How many red heart stickers does Sally have?

Number of Stickers: 30

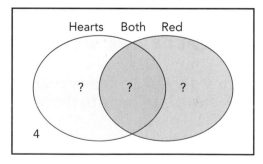

- There are $30 - 4 = 26$ stickers that are hearts, red, or both.

- There are $(12 + 22) - 26 = 8$ red heart stickers.

1. Kylie asks 24 students whether they like apples, oranges, both, or neither. She finds that 16 like apples and 12 like oranges. These numbers include 10 who like both. Draw a Venn diagram to organize the information. How many students like neither apples nor oranges?

2. The perimeter of a rectangle is 48 cm. Describe the dimensions of 3 different rectangles with this perimeter. Find their areas.

Max is making a poster using 75 shape stickers. He uses acute triangles, scalene triangles, and squares. In all, there are 45 acute triangles, 49 scalene triangles, and 10 squares. Use this information and the Venn diagram for Exercises 3–4.

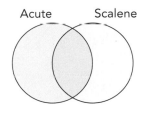

3. How many triangles are both acute and scalene?

4. The circles for acute and scalene triangles overlap, but the circle for squares is separate. Explain why.

5. A school's colors are green and yellow. On Pep Day, the 420 students are encouraged to wear something with both colors or at least with one of the colors. Some students wear only green, 315 wear something yellow, 250 wear only yellow, and 10 wear neither color. Draw a Venn diagram to organize the information. How many students wear only green?

6. Copy and complete the table of the perimeters and areas of squares with side lengths of 1, 2, 3, 4, 5, 6, and 7 units. Describe the relationship between the numerical values of the perimeter and area of these squares and any pattern you notice.

Side Length (units)	1	2	3	4	5	6	7
Perimeter (units)	?	?	?	?	?	?	?
Area (sq units)	?	?	?	?	?	?	?

7. An equilateral triangle and a square are different because one has 3 sides and the other has 4 sides. In what way are the two kinds of figures alike?

Write About It

8. Why is a Venn diagram helpful when you are solving problems that involve either, both, or none of two responses or situations?

Tell whether the polygon is *regular* or *not regular*.

1.

2.

3.

4.

5.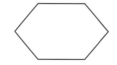

6.

Classify the polygon based on its number of sides.

7.

8.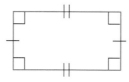

9.

Classify the triangle based on angle measure and side length.

10.

11.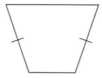

12.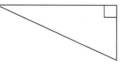

Write the most specific name for the polygon.

13.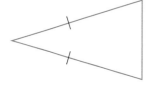

14.

15.

16.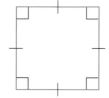

17.

18.

Determine if the statement is *true* or *false*.

19. All squares are rectangles.

20. All rhombuses are rectangles.

21. All trapezoids are parallelograms.

22. All rhombuses are parallelograms.

23. If a rectangle is also a rhombus, then it must be a square.

Classify the quadrilateral in as many ways as possible.

24.

25.

26.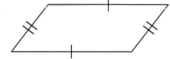

The Venn diagram shows the salads sold by a deli in one day. Use the Venn diagram for Exercises 27–31.

Number of Salads: 44

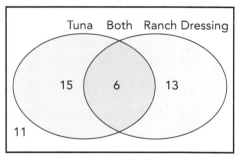

27. How many salads had tuna?

28. How many salads had ranch dressing?

29. How many salads had tuna but not ranch dressing?

30. How many salads had both tuna and ranch dressing?

31. How many salads did not have tuna or ranch dressing?

The Venn diagram summarizes the weather for January. Use the diagram for Exercises 32–33.

Number of Days: 31

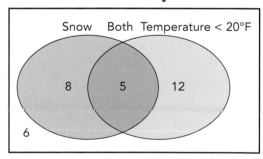

32. On how many days was the temperature 20°F or above, and it did not snow?

33. Madison says the diagram indicates there were a total of 12 days when the temperature dropped below 20°F. Describe Madison's error.

Suppose you are designing a small horse corral. The corral must have 4 sides, and you have 52 yards of fencing available. You want to enclose the greatest amount of space possible under these conditions. What shape will form the largest corral?

Think about the first condition: *The corral must have 4 sides.*

1. Name the possible shapes of the corral.

2. Draw a sketch of each possible shape of the corral.

3. Beside each sketch, list the key characteristics of that shape.

Think about the second condition: *There are 52 yards of fencing available.*

For each possible shape, determine the dimensions that will result in a shape with a perimeter of 52 yards. For some shapes, there is more than one set of possible dimensions.

Squares and Rectangles

To find the perimeters and areas of possible squares and rectangles, use a formula.

4. For a square with side length s, the expression for its perimeter is __?__ and the expression for its area is __?__ .

5. Find the side length s for a square with a perimeter of 52 yards.

6. Find the area of this square. Show your work.

7. For a rectangle with length ℓ and width w, the expression for its perimeter is __?__ and the expression for its area is __?__ .

8. Find the dimensions of at least 3 different rectangles with a perimeter of 52 yards. Show your work.

9. Find the area of each of these rectangles. Show your work.

10. Compare the area of each rectangle with the area of the square. Which shape produces the largest area?

11. Do you notice a pattern between the dimensions of a rectangle and the corresponding area? Explain.

Trapezoids, Rhombuses, and Parallelograms

Now, find the perimeters and areas of possible rhombuses, parallelograms, and trapezoids, through experimentation using a grid. For Exercises 12–13:

- Use graph paper to sketch a figure. Think of each grid square as 1 square yard (1 yard × 1 yard).

- To estimate perimeter, think of the diagonal that passes through opposite corners of a grid square as about 1.5 yards.

12. Draw various trapezoids that have a perimeter of no more than 52 yards. Estimate the area of each. Compare results with others.

13. Repeat the previous exercise for parallelograms.

The figure shows a red rhombus over a black square. Use the figure for Exercises 14–15.

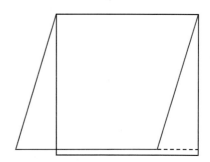

14. Explain why the figures have the same perimeter.

15. Explain why the square has a greater area than the rhombus. Hint: Look for two identical triangles.

Determine the best answer for each problem.

1. Which words can be used to describe this figure? Select all that apply.

A. closed plane figure
B. quadrilateral
C. pentagon
D. regular polygon

2. Which describes this triangle?

A. scalene, right   B. acute, isosceles
C. isosceles, right   D. scalene, acute

3. If this triangle is isosceles and has a perimeter of 24 inches, what is the length of each unknown side?

6 in.

4. What is the perimeter of the stop sign? Assume the shape is regular.

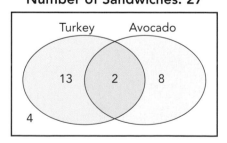

10 in.

A. 56 in.   B. 64 in.
C. 80 in.   D. 96 in.

5. What type of polygon comes next in the pattern?

A. hexagon   B. octagon
C. nonagon   D. decagon

6. Which of the following is NOT a quadrilateral?

A. square
B. circle
C. rectangle
D. parallelogram

7. Which of the following statements are true? Select all that apply.

A. All triangles have one obtuse angle.
B. All rectangles are parallelograms.
C. A right triangle can be equilateral.
D. All squares are rhombuses.
E. An obtuse triangle can be equilateral.

8. How many sandwiches have turkey?

Number of Sandwiches: 27

Turkey   Avocado

13   2   8

4

A. 2   B. 13
C. 15   D. 23

Volume

Skyscrapers are often large geometric figures. Many skyscrapers are rectangular prisms. Look around you. There are geometric figures everywhere.

Real-World Three-Dimensional Figures

♦ A box is shaped like a rectangular prism.

♦ A soup can is shaped like a cylinder.

♦ A ball is shaped like a sphere.

♦ A party hat is shaped like a cone.

♦ Number cubes are shaped like cubes.

A three-dimensional figure occupies space. The amount of space it occupies is its *volume*. The volume of an object is determined by its dimensions. The volume of a skyscraper is much greater than the volume of a box because it is longer, wider, and taller than a box.

Solid Figures

Objective
- Identify solid figures and their attributes.
- Relate plane and solid figures to identify nets for solid figures.

Solid figures are three-dimensional. Not all parts are in the same plane.

Polyhedrons are solid figures whose faces are all polygons.

A prism is a polyhedron with two parallel and identical bases. The shape of a base names the prism. The other faces of the prism are rectangles.

Math Words
solid figures
polyhedrons
prism
cube
face
edge
vertex
pyramid
cone
cylinder
sphere
net

triangular prism

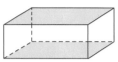
rectangular prism

pentagonal prism

hexagonal prism

A cube is a rectangular prism with 6 identical square faces.

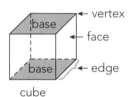
cube

← vertex
← face
← edge

A face is a flat, polygon-shaped surface of a solid figure. An edge is a line segment where 2 faces meet. A vertex is a point where 2 or more edges meet.

A pyramid is a polyhedron with one base. The shape of the base names the pyramid. The other faces are triangles that meet at a common vertex.

square pyramid

rectangular pyramid

triangular pyramid

pentagonal pyramid

hexagonal pyramid

Some solid figures have curved surfaces. Cones and cylinders have flat, circular bases. A sphere has no base.

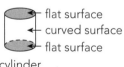
← flat surface
← curved surface
← flat surface
cylinder

cone

sphere

Some solid figures, such as a cube or a cylinder, can be unfolded to make a two-dimensional pattern, called a net.

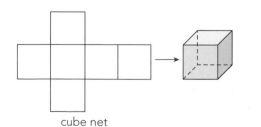
cube net

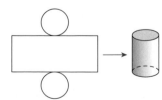
cylinder net

Which solid figure best represents the picture?

1.

2.

3.

4.

Write the number of faces, vertices, and edges for each solid figure.

	Solid Figure	Faces	Vertices	Edges
5.	triangular prism	?	?	?
6.	pentagonal prism	?	?	?
7.	hexagonal prism	?	?	?
8.	triangular pyramid	?	?	?
9.	pentagonal pyramid	?	?	?
10.	hexagonal pyramid	?	?	?

Write the solid figure that can be made from the net.

11.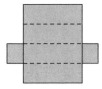

12.

13.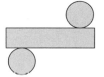

14.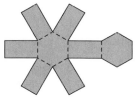

15. Which solid figure has 4 triangular faces and a square base?

16. Which solid figure has 3 rectangular faces and 2 identical triangular bases?

Problem Solving

Write *True* or *False* for each statement. Justify your answer.

17. Cylinders have no edges or vertices.

18. A cone has more than one base.

19. The bases of a prism are regular polygons. Claire says the other faces are identical, regular rectangles. Do you agree? Explain.

Write About It

20. Refer to Exercises 5–10. What is the relationship between the number of vertices and the number of faces of any pyramid? Provide at least two examples to support your answer.

LESSON

16-2 Cubic Measure

Objective
- Describe and use cubic measures.

Math Words
- volume
- unit cube
- cubic centimeter
- cubic inch
- cubic measure
- cubic millimeter
- cubic meter
- cubic foot
- cubic yard

The volume of a solid figure is a measure of the amount of space it contains. Volume is measured in cubic units.

One cubic unit is the volume of a cube with an edge length of 1 unit, called a unit cube. The number of unit cubes that fills a solid figure, without any gaps or overlaps, is the volume of the figure in cubic units.

This figure represents a cube that measures 1 cm on each edge. Its volume is 1 cubic centimeter (cm³).

This figure represents a cube that measures 1 in. on each edge. Its volume is 1 cubic inch (in.³).

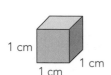

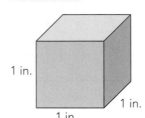

To find the cubic measure or volume of a figure, count the unit cubes.

The volume of this figure is 4 mm³.

The volume of this figure is 4 cm³.

One cubic centimeter, or 1 cm³, holds 1 milliliter (mL) of water, which has a mass of 1 gram (g).

Similarly, one cubic decimeter, or 1 dm³, holds 1 liter of water, which has a mass of 1 kilogram.

Other metric cubic measures include cubic millimeters (mm³) and cubic meters (m³). Other customary cubic measures include cubic feet (ft³) and cubic yards (yd³).

PRACTICE

Find the cubic measure of the solid figure.

1.  ← cm³

___?___ cm³

2.  ← mm³

___?___ mm³

3. 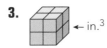 ← in.³

___?___ in.³

4. 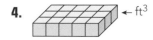 ← ft³

___?___ ft³

362 ■ LESSON 16-2

Find the cubic measure of the solid figure.

5. ← ft³

 ? ft³

6. ← dm³

 ? dm³

7. ← ft³

 ? ft³

8. ← m³

 ? m³

9. ← yd³

 ? yd³

10. ← cm³

 ? cm³

Copy and complete the table. Write the equivalent measure.

	Cubic Measure	Capacity of Water	Mass of Water
11.	5 dm³	?	5 kg
12.	?	5 mL	?
13.	?	?	8.4 kg
14.	4000 cm³	? L	? kg

Problem Solving

Find the cubic measure.

15.

Capacity: 20 L

16.

Capacity: 5 mL

17.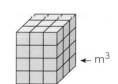

Capacity: 1893 L

18. Wendy imagines packing a cubic foot with cubic inches. How many cubic inches are in a cubic foot? Explain your reasoning.

Write About It

19. Think about this solid figure from Exercise 8. How did you find the cubic measure without being able to see all the cubes?

 ← m³

Volumes of Rectangular Prisms

Objective
▪ Find volume by packing with unit cubes.

Math Words
volume
cubic measure

A part for a computer is built to fit in a casing that is a rectangular prism with the dimensions shown in the diagram. Find the volume of the casing.

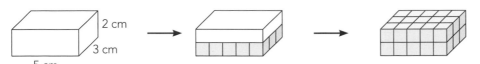

◆ Count the unit cubes.

You can find the volume of the prism by counting the cubes it contains in each layer, and then add.

• Find the number of cubes in the bottom layer: 15.

• Count the cubes in the remaining layers. Remember that each layer will have the same number of cubes.

There are 15 cubes in the top layer.

• Add the cubes found in all the layers: 15 + 15 = 30.

There are 30 cubes in all. The volume of the prism is 30 cm³.

◆ Multiply edge lengths.

You can find the volume of the rectangular prism by multiplying its three dimensions.

• Multiply the length times the width times the height.

Volume = 5 × 3 × 2

• Simplify: 5 × 3 × 2 = 30.

The volume of the casing is 30 cubic centimeters, or 30 cm³.

PRACTICE

Find the volume of each figure.

1.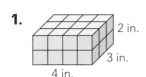

Use counting to find the volume.
Total: _?_ + _?_ = _?_

2.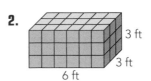

Use multiplication to find the volume.
Volume: _?_ × _?_ × _?_ = _?_

Find the volume of the figure.

3.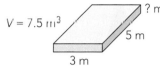
3 ft
2 ft
8 ft

4.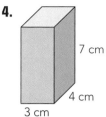
7 cm
4 cm
3 cm

5.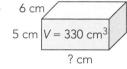
12 in.
8 in.
15 in.

Find the missing dimension in the figure.

6. $V = 7.5 \text{ m}^3$
? m
5 m
3 m

7.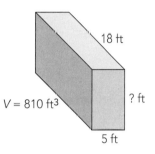
18 ft
? ft
$V = 810 \text{ ft}^3$
5 ft

8. 6 cm
5 cm $V = 330 \text{ cm}^3$
? cm

Problem Solving

A part for a computer measures 2 cm by 3 cm by 5 cm. It is packed into the box shown. Use this information for Exercises 9–10.

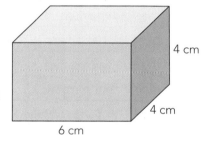
4 cm
4 cm
6 cm

9. What is the volume of the empty space in the box after the computer part is packed in it?

10. Packing material comes in 1 cm by 2 cm by 3 cm rectangular prisms. Can the part be centered in the box with 11 pieces of packing prisms around it? Explain.

Write About It

11. Two students find the volume of the prism. Analyze their work and use the Associative and Commutative properties to explain how the multiplication gave the same answer.

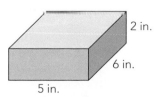
2 in.
6 in.
5 in.

Maria:
bottom layer:
$6 \times 5 = 30$
height: 2
$30 \times 2 = 60 \text{ in.}^3$

Camila:
side layer:
$6 \times 2 = 12$
length: 5
$12 \times 5 = 60 \text{ in.}^3$

Match the solid figure with its name.

A. cone
B. pentagonal pyramid
C. square pyramid
D. hexagonal prism
E. rectangular prism
F. sphere

1.

2.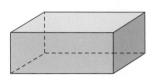

3.

4.

5.

6.

Write the number of faces, vertices, and edges for the solid figure.

	Solid Figure	Faces	Vertices	Edges
7.	cube	?	?	?
8.	square pyramid	?	?	?
9.	triangular prism	?	?	?
10.	pentagonal prism	?	?	?
11.	triangular pyramid	?	?	?
12.	hexagonal pyramid	?	?	?

Match the net with the solid figure it forms.

A. pentagonal prism
B. triangular pyramid
C. cube
D. cone

13.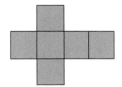

14.

15.

16.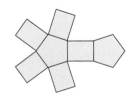

Find the cubic measure.

17.

Capacity: 15 L

18.

Capacity: 8 mL

19.

Capacity: 58 L

Find the missing equivalent measures.

	Cubic Measure	Capacity of Water	Mass of Water
20.	?	?	18 g
21.	?	32 L	32 kg
22.	?	75 mL	75 g
23.	20 dm³	?	?

Find the volume of the figure.

24.
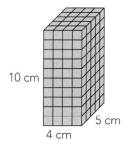
10 cm
5 cm
4 cm

25.
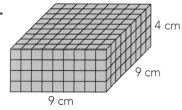
4 cm
9 cm
9 cm

26.
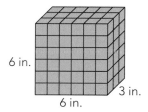
6 in.
6 in.
6 in.
3 in.

27.
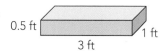
0.5 ft
1 ft
3 ft

28.
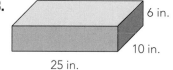
6 in.
10 in.
25 in.

29.
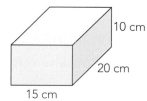
10 cm
20 cm
15 cm

Problem Solving

30. Name two real-world objects that have the shape of a cylinder.

31. Name two real-world objects that have the shape of a rectangular prism.

32. How many more liters does the large water cooler hold than the small water cooler?

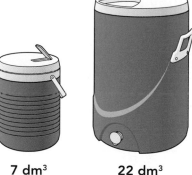

7 dm³   22 dm³

A medicine cabinet has the dimensions 20 in. by 15 in. by 3 in. It is packed into a box with the dimensions shown. Use the image for Exercises 33–35.

33. What is the volume of the medicine cabinet?

34. What is the volume of the box?

35. What is the volume of the packing material between the cabinet and the box?

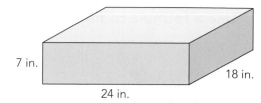
7 in.
18 in.
24 in.

Objective
- Use formulas to find the volumes of rectangular prisms.

Math Words
formula
rectangular prism

A stage prop is created for a production at a local theater. What is the volume of the stage prop?

You can use a formula to find the volume of a rectangular prism.

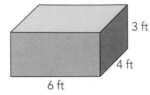

3 ft

4 ft

6 ft

$V = \ell \times w \times h$ The Associative Property can be used to group $\ell \times w$.

$V = (\ell \times w) \times h$

$V = B \times h$ Replace $\ell \times w$ with B, since $\ell \times w$ is the area of the base of the prism.

◆ Use the formula $V = \ell \times w \times h$.

- Use $\ell = 6$ ft for length, $w = 4$ ft for width, and $h = 3$ ft for height.

- $V = 6$ ft $\times$ 4 ft $\times$ 3 ft $= 72$ ft³

◆ Use the formula $V = B \times h$.

- $B = \ell \times w = 6$ ft $\times$ 4 ft $= 24$ ft²

- $V = B \times h = 24$ ft² $\times$ 3 ft $= 72$ ft³

▷ The volume of the stage prop is 72 ft³.

Study these examples.

The base of a rectangular prism has an area of 21 cm². Its height is 5 cm. What is the volume?

$V = B \times h$

$= 21 \times 5$

$= 105$ cm³

Find the length.

$V = \ell \times w \times h$

$80 = \ell \times 2 \times 10$

$80 = \ell \times 20$

$4 \times 20 = 80$, so:

$\ell = 4$ in.

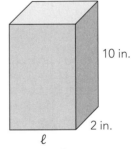

10 in.

2 in.

ℓ

$V = 80$ in.³

PRACTICE

Use a formula to find the volume of the rectangular prism.

1.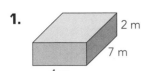

2 m

7 m

4 m

2.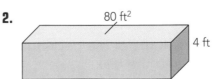

80 ft²

4 ft

Find the volume of the figure.

3.

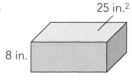

25 in.²

8 in.

4.

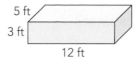

5 ft

3 ft

12 ft

5.

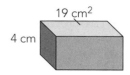

19 cm²

4 cm

6.

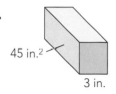

45 in.²

3 in.

7.

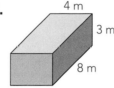

4 m

3 m

8 m

8.

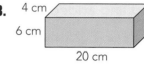

4 cm

6 cm

20 cm

9. $\ell = 1.5$ cm, $w = 6$ cm, $h = 12$ cm

10. $B = 38$ m², $h = 5$ m

11. $\ell = 30$ in., $w = 4$ in., $h = 3$ ft

12. $B = 44$ ft², $h = 24$ in.

Problem Solving

Find the missing dimension for the rectangular prism.

13. $\ell = 2$ m, $w = 15$ m, $V = 60$ m³, $h = \underline{\ ?\ }$

14. $B = 96$ ft², $V = 1152$ ft³, $h = \underline{\ ?\ }$

Use the toy chest shown for Exercises 15–17.

15. Jed builds a toy chest that is 4 in. taller than the one shown. How much greater is the volume of Jed's toy chest?

16. Sam builds a chest that has the same volume as the one shown. Its base area is 432 in.². How tall is Sam's toy chest?

18 in.

3 ft

20 in.

17. Nathan builds a mini toy chest that has half the volume of the one shown. What could be the dimensions of the mini toy chest?

Write About It

18. Two square prisms each have a volume of 125 yd³. Is it certain that the prisms have the exact same shape? Would your answer be the same for any two rectangular prisms? Explain.

Volume of Composite Figures

Objective
■ Find the volume of a solid figure composed of rectangular prisms.

Math Words
volume
rectangular prism
composite figure

What is the volume of the storage cabinet?

When a solid figure is not a rectangular prism, its volume can still be found by separating the figure into simple, common shapes. A composite figure is a figure made from several simpler shapes. The individual volumes of the shapes can be found and added together to find the volume of the entire figure.

Separate the solid into two rectangular prisms.

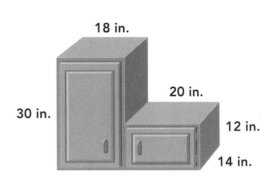

- Find the volume of the larger prism.

    $V = \ell \times w \times h$

    $V = 18 \text{ in.} \times 14 \text{ in.} \times 30 \text{ in.} = 7560 \text{ in.}^3$

- Find the volume of the smaller prism.

    $V = \ell \times w \times h$

    $V = 20 \text{ in.} \times 14 \text{ in.} \times 12 \text{ in.} = 3360 \text{ in.}^3$

- Add the two volumes.

    $7560 \text{ in.}^3 + 3360 \text{ in.}^3 = 10{,}920 \text{ in.}^3$

▷ The volume of the cabinet is 10,920 in.³.

What is the volume of the figure?

Whole:
$V = \ell \times w \times h$

$= 5 \text{ ft} \times 9 \text{ ft} \times 4 \text{ ft}$

$= 180 \text{ ft}^3$

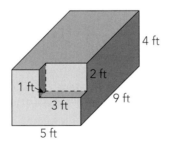

Cutout:
$V = \ell \times w \times h$

$= 3 \text{ ft} \times 1 \text{ ft} \times 2 \text{ ft}$

$= 6 \text{ ft}^3$

The volume of the cutout can be subtracted from the volume of the whole prism.

Total:
$V = 180 \text{ ft}^3 - 6 \text{ ft}^3$

$= 174 \text{ ft}^3$

▷ The volume of the figure is 174 ft³.

Find the volume of the composite figure.

1.

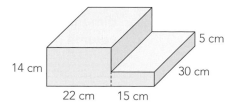

Total volume: ?

2.

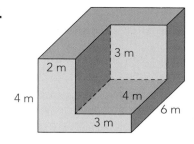

Total volume: ?

3.

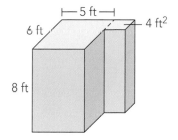

Total volume: ?

4.

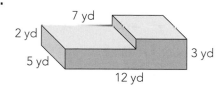

Total volume: ?

Problem Solving

Becky builds a multi-section flower box as shown. Use the flower box for Exercises 5–6.

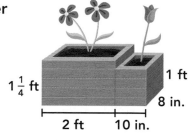

5. Becky wants to fill each section with soil. Use the exterior dimensions to estimate the cubic inches of soil needed.

6. A store sells potting soil in bags of 2 cubic feet. How many bags should she buy to fill the boxes?

7. For his woodshop class, Joel makes the paperweight shown for his final project. What is the volume of the paperweight?

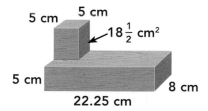

Write About It

8. Two students are finding the volume of the figure shown. Jen wants to split the figure using the red line and Kari wants to split the figure using the blue line. Which will give the correct answer? Explain.

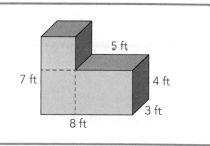

Problem Solving
Act It Out

A consumer group is collecting data about tissues. The box of tissues shown contains 200 tissues. What is the volume of one tissue in the box?

Measure each dimension in inches or centimeters.

- Align the ruler so that the edge of the box is aligned with the 0 on the ruler.

- Read the value at the other end of the ruler. Repeat for each of the three dimensions.

The smaller the unit you use to measure, the more accurate your calculations will be. Some tissue boxes have the dimensions written on the box.

Length = 9.5 in. Width = 5 in. Height = 4 in.

Find the volume of the tissue box.

$V = \ell \times w \times h = 9.5 \text{ in.} \times 5 \text{ in.} \times 4 \text{ in.} = 190 \text{ in.}^3$

Divide to find the volume of one tissue.

$V = 190 \text{ in.}^3 \div 200 \text{ tissues} = 0.95 \text{ in.}^3 \text{ per tissue}$

A single tissue has a volume of 0.95 cubic inch.

PRACTICE

1. Explain in your own words why the last step of the example gives the volume of a single piece of tissue.

2. Janet says that rather than finding the volume of each unfolded tissue, the thickness of each tissue could be calculated. Which measure can be divided by the number of tissues to give the thickness of a single tissue? Find this thickness.

3. If each tissue is considered to be a rectangular prism, what are its dimensions?

4. Use the Act It Out strategy and measure a box of tissues or ream of paper. Determine the volume of a single tissue or sheet of paper. If the packaging includes its dimensions, use them to check your measurements and answer.

5. If you measured the dimensions of the tissue box in centimeters instead of inches, how would your numbers look different?

Find a whiteboard or a bulletin board in the classroom. Use this board for Exercises 6–7.

6. Measure each dimension and find the area of the board.

7. What unit did you use for the dimensions of the board? What unit would be too large or too small to use?

Use a bookcase or storage cabinet in your classroom for Exercises 8–9.

8. Measure each dimension and find the volume of the available storage space.

9. Design a box that has the same storage space but has different dimensions. Draw a net and label each dimension.

10. Measure the top of your desk and find its area. If 20 desks that are the same size as your desk are placed together to create one large space, what is the total area of all of the desks?

11. The volume of the rectangular prism shown is 96 cubic inches. Work backward to find the length of one side of the base.

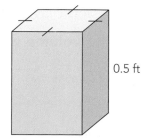

0.5 ft

12. Eddy used Act it Out to multiply 3 by 7 using tiles. Explain why this strategy is not as useful for finding 34 × 172.

13. Christian is taller than Joshua, but not as tall as Tony. Aaron is taller than Christian, but not as tall as Tony. What is the order of the boys from tallest to shortest? Act it Out to find the answer.

Write About It

14. Describe how the Act it Out strategy can be a benefit when solving volume problems. Explain.

Name the solid figure.

1.

2.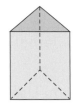

3.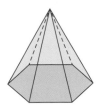

4.

Find the cubic measure.

5.  ← ft³

_?_ ft³

6.  ← cm³

_?_ cm³

7. 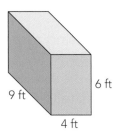 ← in.³

_?_ in.³

8. 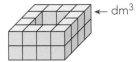 ← dm³

_?_ dm³

9.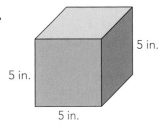

Capacity: 9 L

10.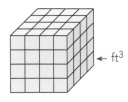

Capacity: 11.5 mL

11.

Capacity: 20 L

12.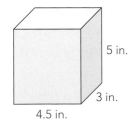

Capacity: 35 mL

Find the volume of each figure.

13.

5 in.
5 in.
5 in.

14.

6 ft
9 ft
4 ft

15.

5 in.
3 in.
4.5 in.

16.

17 cm
4 cm
10 cm

17.

4 m
1.5 m
1.5 m

18.

16 cm
8 cm
20 cm

Find the volume of the prism that the net would form.

19.

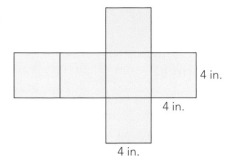

4 in.

4 in.

4 in.

20.

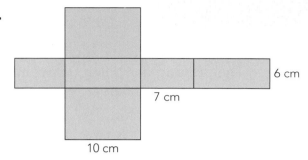

6 cm

7 cm

10 cm

Find the volume of the figure.

21.

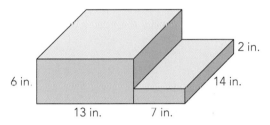

2 in.

6 in.

14 in.

13 in.

7 in.

22.

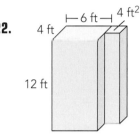

6 ft — 4 ft²

4 ft

12 ft

23.

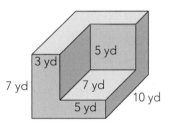

5 yd

3 yd

7 yd

7 yd

10 yd

5 yd

24.

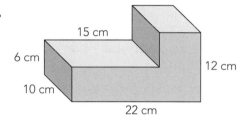

15 cm

6 cm

12 cm

10 cm

22 cm

Problem Solving

An architect draws a sketch of a master bedroom addition to the front of an existing home. She also draws a sunroom addition on the side of the home. Use the sketch for Exercises 25–27.

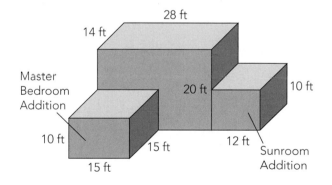

28 ft

14 ft

Master Bedroom Addition

20 ft

10 ft

10 ft

15 ft

12 ft

Sunroom Addition

15 ft

25. What is the existing volume of the home before the additions?

26. What will be the volume of the renovated home after the additions are complete?

27. Suppose the architect raises the ceiling height of the master bedroom and sunroom by 2 feet. What will be the volume of the renovated home?

The rectangular prism below has been unfolded to form a two-dimensional net.

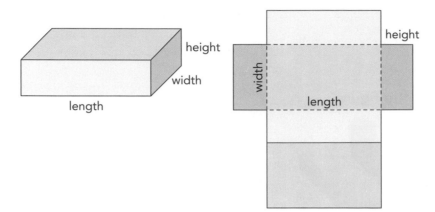

Build Rectangular Prisms

1. On a large piece of paper, draw a medium-sized net similar to the one above. Note which rectangles are identical. Use a ruler to make each side a whole-number length in inches. What is the volume of the rectangular prism formed by the net?

2. Use scissors to cut out the net. Fold the net along the edges to form a rectangular prism. Compare your rectangular prism with a classmate's rectangular prism. How do the prisms look alike? Different? Which prism has a greater volume? How do you know?

You want to make a new prism that has either twice or half the volume of the original prism.

3. Determine the volume of the new prism:

   _?_ in.³ × _?_ = _?_ in.³

4. Determine the dimensions of the new prism:

   _?_ in.³ = _?_ in. × _?_ in. × _?_ in.

5. Draw a net of the new prism using these dimensions. Then cut and fold the net to form the rectangular prism. Compare your prisms. Does one look twice as big as the other? Explain.

Design Rectangular Prisms

6. Many real-world objects are shaped like rectangular prisms. Suppose you are an engineer designing the objects listed below. Copy and complete the table by determining a set of dimensions that give the desired volume of each object. Make sure the dimensions are reasonable for each object and be sure to consider the special properties of a cube.

Object	Desired Volume	Length	Width	Height
Shed	384 ft³	?	?	?
Cereal box	960 in.³	?	?	?
Number cube	6859 mm³	?	?	?
Skyscraper	93,750 m³	?	?	?

7. Are there more than one set of possible dimensions for each object? Explain.

8. Nesting blocks are cube-shaped blocks of various sizes that can be easily stacked. One face of each block is missing so that smaller blocks fit inside larger blocks, similar to those shown. You want to design a set of 5 nesting blocks. Each block should be 1 inch wider than the next largest block. Design a set of nesting blocks that meets these requirements. What is the total volume of these blocks when they are stacked on top of each other?

Copy the table below onto your own paper. Then enter the dimensions of each block.

Object	Length	Width	Height	Volume
Block A (smallest)	?	?	?	?
Block B	?	?	?	?
Block C	?	?	?	?
Block D	?	?	?	?
Block E (largest)	?	?	?	?
			Total	?

9. A building has an atrium in its center that is open to the outdoors. The blueprint of the building shows the atrium, which has the shape of a square prism. What is the volume of the office building without the atrium? Explain how you found your answer.

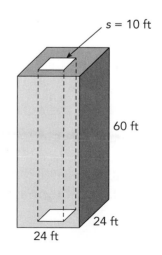

s = 10 ft

60 ft

24 ft

24 ft

Determine the best answer for each problem.

1. A watering can holds 3 liters of water. What is the cubic measure of the watering can?

A. 3 kg   **C.** 3 dm³

B. 3 g   **D.** 3 cm³

5. What is the volume of the figure?

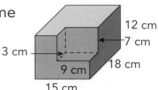

A. 189 cm³

B. 3051 cm³

C. 3240 cm³

D. 3429 cm³

2. Name the solid figure that can be made from the net.

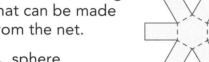

A. sphere

B. hexagonal prism

C. pentagonal prism

D. hexagonal pyramid

6. A kitchen island is shaped like a rectangular prism. The island is 4 feet wide. The length of the island is double its width. The height of the island is 1 foot less than its width. What is the volume of the kitchen island?

A. 48 cubic feet   **C.** 96 cubic feet

B. 72 cubic feet   **D.** 128 cubic feet

3. Which expressions give the cubic measure of the solid figure? Select all that apply.

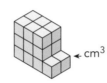

A. 8 cm³ + 6 cm³ + 6 cm³

B. 6 cm³ + 6 cm³ + 6 cm³

C. 6 cm³ + 4 cm³ + 4 cm³ + 4 cm³

D. 6 cm³ + 6 cm³ + 6 cm³ + 2 cm³

7. Which statements describe the prism? Choose all that apply.

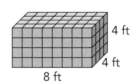

A. There are 32 small cubes in the bottom layer.

B. Each small cube has a volume of 16 ft³.

C. Its shape is a cube.

D. Its total volume is 128 ft³.

E. It has 4 layers of 32 cubes.

4. Name the solid figure.

A. cylinder

B. sphere

C. cone

D. pentagonal pyramid

8. What is the volume of the prism formed by the net?

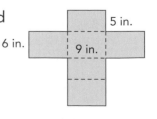

A. 54 in.³

B. 125 in.³

C. 232 in.³

D. 270 in.³

Graphs and Data

What is your favorite game? Chances are you have played games on a board, computer, or gaming system. But did you know that game designers use math concepts to determine the positions of elements in a game?

Game Space as a Grid

♦ Imagine a grid that works like a map, overlaid on a gameboard or video game screen. The entire area could be divided into grid squares. Think of each grid square as 1 square unit.

You Can Do Research

♦ Look for information regarding a classic board game or video game. See what background is available about the dimensions of the game area, any objects or designs that are shown on the board or screen, and where objects or other elements appear.

Line Plots with Whole Numbers and Decimals

Jenna's gymnastics class is selling candles for a fundraiser. She is keeping track of the number of candles sold by each student. Her data set is shown in the frequency table, which shows how many times each value occurs in the data set.

Number of Candles	14	15	16	17	20
Tally	|||	||	||||	||		
Frequency	3	2	4	2	1

Use a line plot to display the data. A line plot is a number line that uses Xs to represent data values.

◆ Choose a scale and a title.

Use the data from the table to choose an appropriate scale and title.

14 is the least number of candles in the table and 20 is the greatest number.

• The scale is from 14 to 20.

• The interval on the scale is 1.

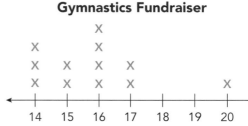

◆ Draw a number line.

Use the scale and label the intervals.

• Start with 14 and end with 20.

• Use equally-spaced intervals.

◆ Complete the line plot.

Use an X to represent each data value.

• Vertically stack the correct number of Xs above each tick mark.

• There should be the same number of Xs as data values.

PRACTICE

1. How many students are in the gymnastics class?

2. How many candles were sold in all?

3. What does it mean when there are no Xs above a number?

4. How many candles were sold by the person who sold the most?

The table shows the weights of baby rabbits that have been rescued.
Use the data for Exercises 5–8.

Weight (ounces)	3.3	3.4	3.5	3.6	3.9
Tally	IIII I	II	IIII I	IIII I II	I
Frequency	5	2	5	7	1

5. What is the scale for the data in the table?

6. What is an appropriate interval for the data?

7. Which weight occurred most frequently?

8. Copy the number line and use it to create a line plot for the data.
   Include a title and a label.

3.3   3.4   3.5   3.6   3.7   3.8   3.9

Problem Solving

The line plot shows students' scores on a vocabulary
quiz. Use the line plot for Exercises 9–11.

9. How many more points was the highest score than
   the lowest score?

10. What is the interval of the line plot?

11. How many scores are recorded in the line plot? How can you tell?

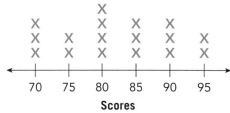

Vocabulary Quiz Scores

Write About It

12. The table shows the amout a manager spent on office supplies each
    month over the last 18 months. Explain the errors in the line plot.

Order Amount ($)	55	57	58	62	65	66
Tally	IIII	II	II	I	IIII	II
Frequency	4	2	2	1	4	2

```
X
X                      X
X   X   X          X   X
X   X   X   X   X   X
55  57  58  62  65  66
```

Line Plots with Fractions and Mixed Numbers

Objective
- Make and use line plots with fractions and mixed numbers.

Math Words
line plot
scale
interval

An art supply store sells sheets of canvas. The lengths of some sheets, in inches, are shown in the list.

$$8\frac{1}{2}, 10, 9\frac{1}{2}, 11, 8\frac{1}{2}, 8\frac{1}{2}, 11, 10, 9\frac{1}{2}, 11, 9, 9, 8\frac{1}{2}, 8\frac{1}{2}$$

How can an employee make a line plot to analyze the sheet lengths?

- Make a line plot to display the data.

  Draw a number line. The scale should go from $8\frac{1}{2}$ to 11.

  Use evenly-spaced intervals of $\frac{1}{2}$.

  Include a title. Label the number line data.

- Analyze the line plot.

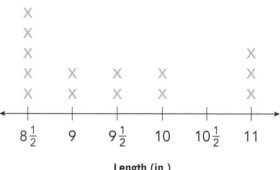

Inventory of Small Canvas Sheets

Length (in.)

  Since there are 14 sheets of canvas, there are 14 Xs in the line plot.

  The most frequent length is $8\frac{1}{2}$ inches, since this length has the tallest stack of Xs on the line plot.

  There are 3 sheets that are 11 inches long, since there are 3 Xs above 11.

  There are the same number of 9, $9\frac{1}{2}$, and 10-inch sheets of canvas, since each of these lengths has the same number of Xs.

PRACTICE

The list shows the number of cups of spinach needed for different juices available on a menu at a juice bar. Use the data for Exercises 1–4.

$$\frac{3}{4}, \frac{1}{2}, 1, 1\frac{1}{4}, 1, \frac{1}{2}, \frac{3}{4}, 1\frac{1}{4}, \frac{1}{2}, \frac{3}{4}, 1\frac{1}{2}, \frac{3}{4}$$

1. Copy the number line. Use a line plot to display the data in the table. Include a title.

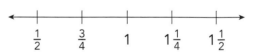

Cups of Spinach

2. How many cups of spinach are needed if one of each type of juice was made?

3. Would the interval $\frac{1}{2}$ be sufficient for this line plot? Explain.

4. What is the most common number of cups needed? Explain how you know.

Use the data to answer Exercises 5–9. The list shows the number of miles students traveled to get to school.

$$5, 3\frac{1}{2}, 5\frac{1}{2}, 4\frac{1}{2}, 7, 3\frac{1}{2}, 4\frac{1}{2}, 8, 4, 5\frac{1}{2}, 5\frac{1}{2}, 7, 6\frac{1}{2}, 5\frac{1}{2}, 5$$

5. What are the least and greatest values?

6. What is an appropriate interval for the data?

7. Use a line plot to display the data.

8. How many students travel more than 6 miles to school? Explain how you know.

Make a line plot to display the data.

9. The weights, in pounds, of guinea pigs at a pet store:

$$1\frac{1}{5}, 1, \frac{4}{5}, \frac{3}{5}, 1, \frac{4}{5}, \frac{4}{5}, 1\frac{1}{5}, 1, 1$$

10. The weights, in pounds, of ferrets at a pet store:

$$\frac{1}{3}, \frac{1}{3}, \frac{2}{3}, 1, 1, \frac{2}{3}, 1, \frac{1}{3}, \frac{1}{3}, 1$$

Problem Solving

Use the line plot for Exercises 11–15.

11. How many plants does the line plot represent? Explain.

12. Which height is the most common? Explain.

13. What is the difference in height between the tallest and the shortest plant?

14. How many plants are shorter than 9 inches?

15. Suppose all the plants are cut and set end-to-end. What is the total length of all the plants in feet?

Heights of Plants

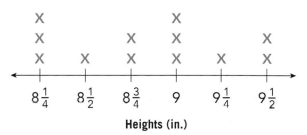

Heights (in.)

Write About It

16. Explain how to determine the interval when creating a line plot.

The table shows students' scores on a 5-question math quiz.
Use the data for Exercises 1–4.

Score	0	1	2	3	4	5
Tally	I			IIII	IIII	ⅣⅡ
Frequency	1	0	0	4	4	5

Find the indicated value.

1. scale   **2.** interval   **3.** number of scores

4. Use a line plot to display the data.

The table shows how many cups of diced onion are used at a
restaurant each day. Use the data for Exercises 5–8.

Cups of Onion	$6\frac{1}{2}$	$6\frac{3}{4}$	7	$7\frac{1}{4}$	$7\frac{1}{2}$	$7\frac{3}{4}$	8	$8\frac{1}{4}$
Tally	II	I	II	IIII	ⅣⅡ	III	II	I
Frequency	2	1	2	4	5	3	2	1

Find the indicated value.

5. scale   **6.** interval   **7.** number of days

8. Use a line plot to display the data.

The table shows how many hours fifth graders spend studying
each week. Use the table for Exercises 9–10.

Hours Studying	0	1	2	3	4	5	6	7
Tally	I	II	IIII	ⅣⅡ	III			I
Frequency	1	2	4	5	3	0	0	1

9. How many more hours are spent studying by the student who studies
the most than the student who studies the least?

10. In a line plot of this data, which numbers would have no Xs
above them?

A 5-pound bag of apples usually weighs slightly less or slightly more than 5 pounds. The table shows the actual weights of some 5-pound bags of apples. Use the data for Exercises 11–13.

Actual Weight (lb)	4.7	4.8	4.9	5.0	5.1	5.2	5.3
Tally	III	II	II	III	IIII	II	I
Frequency	3	2	2	3	4	2	1

11. What is the most frequent weight?

12. What are the least and greatest weights?

13. What is an appropriate interval for a line plot of this data?

Students rode skateboards around a quarter-mile track. The line plot shows the distances they traveled on the track. Use the line plot for Exercises 14–17.

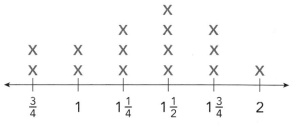

Number of Students who Traveled Various Distances

Miles

14. What was the greatest distance traveled?

15. What is the interval of the line plot?

16. How many more students skateboarded $1\frac{1}{2}$ mile than 1 mile?

17. Which distances were each traveled by exactly 2 students?

Problem Solving

An employee of Jim's Gym records the number of new members who sign up each day. He collects this data for a month. Use the data in the table for Exercises 18–19.

New Members	8	10	11	12	13	20
Tally	ЖII	ЖI	ЖIII	Ж	IIII	I
Frequency	7	6	8	5	4	1

18. Use a line plot to display the data.

19. Which statements about the data are true? Select all that apply.

    A. The greatest number of members signed up in one day is 8.
    B. On four days, 13 new members signed up each day.
    C. A total of 30 new members signed up at the gym this month.
    D. The most frequent number of members signed up in one day is 11.

The Coordinate Plane

Objective
- Plot and name ordered pairs on the coordinate plane.

Math Words
coordinate plane
axes
x-axis
y-axis
origin
ordered pair
coordinates
x-coordinate
y-coordinate

Cheyenne draws a map of her local nature center. The otter exhibit is located at point B. Find the coordinates of the otter exhibit. What is the ordered pair that represents the exhibit?

Nature Center Map

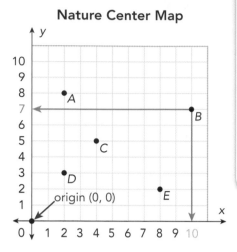

To determine the location of the otter exhibit, think about a coordinate plane. A coordinate plane (or grid) is formed by a pair of perpendicular number lines, called axes.

The horizontal number line is the x-axis, and the vertical number line is the y-axis. The point where the two number lines intersect is the origin.

An ordered pair locates a point on a coordinate plane. The numbers that represent a point are called its coordinates. An ordered pair shows the x-coordinate first and the y-coordinate second: (x, y).

To name the location of the otter exhibit:

- Find the position of point B along the x-axis. The number on the x-axis is 10, so the x-coordinate of B is 10.

- Find the position of point B along the y-axis. The number on the y-axis is 7, so the y-coordinate of B is 7.

> The ordered pair for the otter exhibit is (10, 7), or B(10, 7).

Study these examples.

- Plot A at $\left(1\frac{1}{2}, 2\frac{1}{4}\right)$.

  Start at (0, 0).
  Move right $1\frac{1}{2}$ units.
  Then move up $2\frac{1}{4}$ units.

- Plot D $\left(0, \frac{1}{2}\right)$.

  Start at (0, 0).
  Move right 0 units.
  Then move up $\frac{1}{2}$ unit.

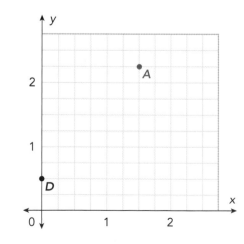

There are 4 squares between whole numbers on each axis. So, one grid space represents $\frac{1}{4}$ unit.

Name the point represented by the ordered pair.

1. (4, 2)

2. (2, 3)

3. $\left(4\frac{1}{2}, 0\right)$

4. $\left(\frac{1}{2}, 1\right)$

5. (0, 2.5)

6. (1.5, 4.5)

7. $\left(2\frac{1}{2}, 3\right)$

8. $\left(4\frac{1}{2}, 5\right)$

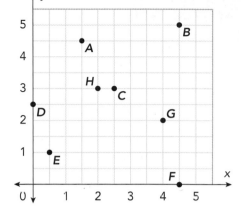

Write an ordered pair for the point.

9. A

10. B

11. C

12. D

13. E

14. F

15. G

16. H

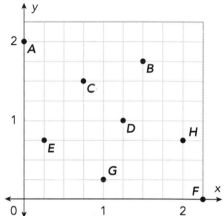

Plot and label each point on a coordinate grid.

17. A (1, 4)

18. $B\left(\frac{3}{4}, 1\right)$

19. $C\left(0, \frac{1}{2}\right)$

20. $D\left(2\frac{1}{4}, 1\frac{1}{2}\right)$

21. $E\left(2, 2\frac{1}{4}\right)$

22. $F\left(1\frac{3}{4}, 0\right)$

23. Suppose a point is on the y-axis. What can you say about the coordinates of the ordered pair that represents the point?

Problem Solving

24. Gwen plots (0, 4) and (6, 4). Find two more points so that the 4 points are the vertices of a square.

25. Stephen plots the points (0, 3), (1, 0), and (5, 3). Find another point so that the 4 points are the vertices of a parallelogram.

Write About It

26. Describe in your own words how to plot a point in a coordinate plane. Use vocabulary from the lesson.

Using Coordinate Graphs

Objective
- Interpret coordinate graphs.

Math Words
coordinate graph
x-coordinate
y-coordinate

The coordinate graph shows the weights and fuel efficiencies of different cars. How can you interpret the ordered pair (35, 28)?

In the ordered pair (35, 28), 35 is the x-coordinate: weight, in hundreds of pounds. 28 is the y-coordinate: efficiency, in miles per gallon.

> So, (35, 28) means that there is a car with a weight of 3500 pounds that gets 28 miles per gallon.

You can also use a coordinate graph to show distances between locations.

Mark's house is located at (3, 5). From home, he walks 3 blocks south and 5 blocks east to the lecture hall for class. Then he walks 3 blocks north and 1 block east to the chemistry lab. How many blocks does he walk in all?

- Find Mark's house at (3, 5).

- Count the blocks from Mark's house to the lecture hall: 3 + 5 = 8 blocks.

- Count the blocks from the lecture hall to the chemistry lab: 3 + 1 = 4 blocks.

- Add to find the total distance: 8 + 4 = 12 blocks.

> Mark walks 12 blocks in all.

Car Fuel Efficiency

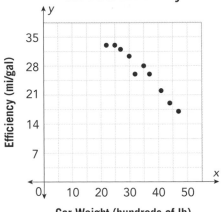

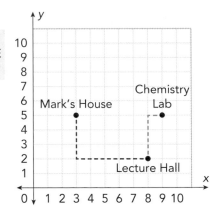

PRACTICE

The coordinate graph represents the exhibits students will visit. Each grid space is 10 yards. Use the graph for Exercises 1–3.

1. How far is it from the Science Lab to the Space Station?

2. Describe how to walk from the Weather Station to the Space Station.

3. A water fountain is 10 yards west of Mission Control. What are its coordinates?

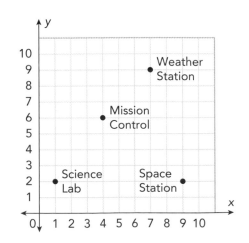

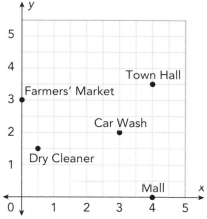

PRACTICE

On the map of a town, each grid space represents half a mile. Use the graph to answer Exercises 4–7. Assume Beth travels only north, south, east, or west.

4. Beth walks from the farmers' market to the dry cleaner. How many miles does she walk?

5. Beth drives from the car wash to the mall, then to the dry cleaner. How far does she drive?

6. Beth wants to go from the dry cleaner to the mall. Does it matter if she travels east and then south, rather than south and then east? Explain.

7. Jo says the mall is 7 miles from the town hall. Do you agree? Explain.

Problem Solving

The coordinate graph shows the number of games played and the number of games won for players in a tennis tournament. Use the graph for Exercises 8–13.

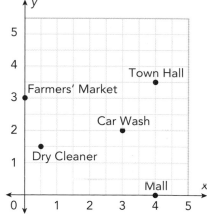

8. What do the points (8, 8) and (4, 0) mean in terms of the situation?

9. Henry won 2 games. Is this an *x*-value or a *y*-value?

10. Do the points (8, 5) and (5, 8) have the same meaning? Explain.

11. Two points have 4 as the *x*-coordinate, but they have different *y*-coordinates. Explain why.

12. Suppose a player plays 10 games. What are the possible *y*-coordinates for this ordered pair? Explain.

13. If players played up to 20 games, how would the *x*- and *y*-axes need to be changed?

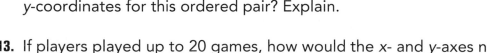

Write About It

14. When you use a coordinate graph to represent a map, when is it possible to find distances between points along one straight line?

Write Number Patterns

Objective
- Use pattern rules to generate patterns; find rules for given patterns.

Math Words
pattern rule
term

In cell biology, a cell can split into two daughter cells. These daughter cells can grow and then divide again in the same way. How many cells form in the sixth division from one cell?

You can look for number patterns and write a pattern rule that describes this process.

A pattern rule for the number of divisions is: Begin with 0; add 1.

In each cell division, 2 cells are formed. The pattern rule for the number of cells is: Begin with 1; multiply by 2.

Use the rules to make a table of the two patterns.

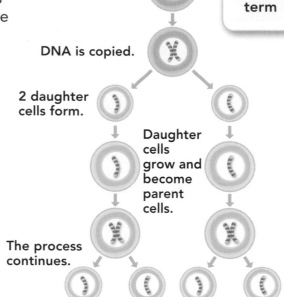

Parent cell

DNA is copied.

2 daughter cells form.

Daughter cells grow and become parent cells.

The process continues.

	+1	+1	+1	+1	+1	+1
Number of Divisions	0	1	2	3	4	5	6
Number of Cells	1	2	4	8	16	32	64

×2 ×2 ×2 ×2 ×2 ×2

Each number is a term of the pattern. The number of divisions starts with 0, so 0 is the first term of that pattern.

Find the term in the cells pattern that corresponds to the term 6 in the divisions pattern. That term is 64.

▷ In the sixth division from one cell, 64 cells form.

Study these examples.

Use the pattern rule to write the first 4 terms.

Rule: Begin with 54; subtract 6.

−6 −6 −6
54 48 42 36

Find the pattern rule:
128, 64, 32, 16, …

The terms are decreasing, so try subtraction or division.

−64 −32 −16
128 64 32 16
÷2 ÷2 ÷2

Begin with 128; divide by 2.

Use the pattern rule to write the next 3 terms.

1. Begin with 6; add $3\frac{1}{2}$.
   6, $9\frac{1}{2}$, 13, …

2. Begin with 108;
   subtract 12.
   108, 96, 84, …

3. Begin with 11;
   multiply by 3.
   11, 33, 99, …

4. Begin with 128;
   multiply by 0.25.
   128, 32, 8, …

5. Begin with 108;
   divide by 3.
   108, 36, 12, …

6. Begin with 64;
   divide by 8.
   64, 8, 1, …

Find the pattern rule.

7. 63, 72, 81, 90, …

8. 80.1, 67.1, 54.1, 41.1, …

9. 200, 20, 2, 0.2, …

10. 16.8, 8.4, 4.2, 2.1, …

11. 384, 96, 24, 6, …

12. 41.6, 10.4, 2.6, 0.65, …

Find the sixth term of both patterns.

13. Begin with 1; add 1.
    Begin with 3; add 3.

14. Begin with 0; add 1.
    Begin with 1;
    multiply by 3.

15. Begin with 35; subtract 4.
    Begin with 243;
    divide by 3.

Problem Solving

The table shows the cost of eggs. Use the table for Exercises 16–18.

Eggs	12	24	36	48
Cost ($)	2.4	4.8	7.2	9.6

16. Write a rule for both patterns in the table.

17. What is the relationship between the corresponding terms?

18. Suppose the first row of the table was labeled Eggs (dozen). How would the rules or the relationship between the terms of the patterns change?

19. Gianna receives $75 as her prize for winning an essay contest. Each week she spends $5 of the money for an e-book. Find the pattern rule for the amount of money she has left. How much money does Gianna have left after 6 weeks?

Write About It

20. When you look at a number pattern, how do you begin to try to find a rule for the pattern? Explain.

Graph Number Patterns

Objectives
- Graph ordered pairs from number patterns.
- Identify relationships between corresponding terms of two patterns.

Math Words
term
ordered pair

A store owner donates two cans of food to a food bank for every $100 in sales each week. How does the number of cans relate to the weekly sales? Graph the relationship on the coordinate plane.

- Make a table.

Weekly Sales ($)	0	100	200	300	400	500	← Rule: Begin with 0; add 100.
Number of Cans	0	2	4	6	8	10	← Rule: Begin with 0; add 2.

The number of cans is equal to the weekly sales divided by 50.

- Form ordered pairs. Use weekly sales terms as the *x*-coordinates.

Use number of cans terms as the *y*-coordinates.

(0, 0), (100, 2), (200, 4), (300, 6), (400, 8), (500, 10)

- Graph the ordered pairs. Choose appropriate scales.

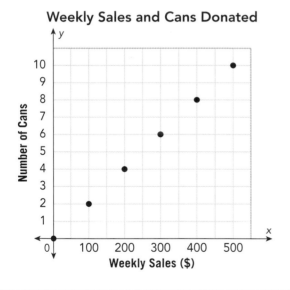

Weekly Sales and Cans Donated

The weekly sales numbers are greater than the numbers of cans, so the *x*-axis scale has greater intervals than the *y*-axis scale.

PRACTICE

Use the table for Exercises 1–2.

Pattern A	0	2	4	6	8
Pattern B	0	5	10	15	20

1. Write the rule for each pattern. What is the 6th term in each pattern?

2. Use the corresponding terms to form ordered pairs. Then graph the ordered pairs.

Use the table for Exercises 3–6.

Pattern A	0	3	6	9	12
Pattern B	0	2	4	6	8

3. Write each pattern rule. What is the 9th term in each pattern?

4. Use the corresponding terms to form ordered pairs.

5. Use grid paper. Plot the ordered pairs.

6. How are corresponding terms of the patterns related?

7. Each x-coordinate of a set of ordered pairs is 3 less than its corresponding y-coordinate. Write three possible ordered pairs. Use grid paper to plot the points.

Problem Solving

The table shows the number of laps two students run this week. Use the table for Exercises 8–11.

	Number of Laps				
Avonlea	2	3	4	5	6
Anika	0	1	2	3	4

8. Write each pattern rule.

9. Form ordered pairs from the corresponding terms. Then plot the ordered pairs on grid paper.

10. Write a sentence that describes the relationship between the x- and y-coordinates of the ordered pairs in terms of the situation.

11. Ben runs 2 fewer laps each day than the day before. He runs the same total number of laps this week as Avonlea. Write the pattern rule for Ben.

12. Two patterns are shown on the coordinate plane. Write rules for the x- and y-coordinates for each pattern. If each pattern is extended by one term, what is the ordered pair for each pattern?

13. Anna and Samantha each need to save $30 for a class trip. Anna has $12 to start and saves $3 each week. Samantha has no money to start and saves $5 each week. Who saves $30 first? How long does it take her to save $30?

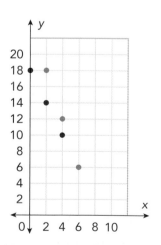

Write About It

14. How can a pattern, table, and graph show the same information?

Problem Solving
Find and Use a Pattern

Objective
- Find and use patterns to analyze information while solving problems.

Math Words

pattern
ordered pair

The graph shows the cost for purchasing various numbers of pens. How much do 3 pens cost?

- Connect the points with a straight line. Find $x = 3$ on the x-axis. The corresponding y-value on the line is about 2.25.

- Check your answer.

  (2, 1.5) means two pens cost $1.50.

  $1.50 ÷ 2 = $0.75 ← ⎰ Divide to find the cost of 1 pen.

  3 pens × $0.75 = $2.25

Cost of Pens

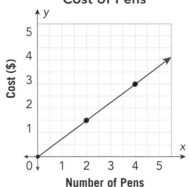

> The cost of 3 pens is $2.25.

Study these examples.

An oyster festival charges an admission fee plus a cost per oyster.

Oysters	2	4	6
Cost ($)	14	16	18

Steve attends the festival and buys 0 oysters. How much does he spend?

- Extend the table to the left, to include 0 for the number of oysters. Follow the pattern to find the cost.

Oysters	0	2	4	6
Cost ($)	12	14	16	18

Subtract 2 from 14. Steve spends $12.

Liam attends the festival and buys 10 oysters. How much does he spend?

- Extend the table to the right. Extend each pattern. They both increase by 2 from left to right.

Oysters	2	4	6	8	10
Cost ($)	14	16	18	20	22

Liam spends $22 for 10 oysters.

PRACTICE

Use the above data for Exercises 1–4.

1. How many pens could you buy for $3.75?

2. What ordered pair represents the cost of one pen?

3. Steve did not buy any oysters. Why must he pay $12?

4. To find the cost for 12 oysters, Bob doubles the cost for 6 oysters. Explain Bob's error.

5. Dominic makes bread by using 5 cups of flour for every 2 cups of water. Copy and extend the table to find the amount of flour he needs for 12 cups of water.

Flour (cups)	5	10	15
Water (cups)	2	4	6

The graph shows the height of a candle after a certain number of hours. Use the graph for Exercises 6–9.

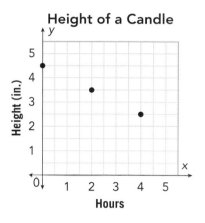

Height of a Candle

6. About how tall is the candle after 1 hour?

7. About how tall is the candle after 6 hours?

8. How long has the candle been burning if its height is 2 in.?

9. Estimate the height of the candle after 2.5 hours. Explain what you did.

10. Ellen swims every 4 days, runs every 2 days, and has a music lesson every 7 days. She does all three activities today. When will she next do all three activities on the same day?

11. Hope visits her cousins at their farm. Her cousins raise goats and chickens. Hope counts 49 animals with a total of 142 legs. How many goats and how many chickens does she count?

12. Ed invents two plans to save $100 for summer camp. The first is to save $10 each week. The second is to save $50 the first week, and then $5 each week after that. With which plan will Edward save $100 sooner? Explain.

Two shops at a lake offer canoe rentals. Their rates are shown in the table. Use the table for Exercises 13–15.

Rental Time (hours)	1	2	3	4
Water Way ($)	9	13	17	21
Lake Land ($)	13	16	19	22

13. At which shop does it cost less to rent a canoe for 4 hours? How much less?

14. At which shop does it cost less to rent a canoe for 8 hours? How much less?

15. For what rental time do both shops charge the same amount?

Write About It

16. What method do you prefer to use to represent and analyze two number patterns?

The frequency table shows the volumes of different blocks in a toy set. Use the data in the table for Exercises 1–3.

Volume (cubic inches)	8.5	9	10	10.5	15
Tally	|||	||	|||	|||		
Frequency	3	2	3	3	1

1. What are the least and greatest volumes in the table?

2. Copy the number line and use it to create a line plot for the data. Include a title and a label.

3. What is the total volume of the largest 3 blocks?

Each number in the table represents the time in hours it takes a train to travel from one station to another. Use the data in the table for Exercises 4–9.

$\frac{3}{4}$	1	$\frac{1}{2}$	$\frac{1}{4}$
$\frac{1}{2}$	$\frac{1}{2}$	$\frac{3}{4}$	$1\frac{1}{4}$
$\frac{1}{2}$	$\frac{3}{4}$	$\frac{1}{4}$	$\frac{1}{4}$

4. Display the data in a line plot. Include a title and label.

5. Why can't the intervals be $\frac{1}{2}$ unit long?

6. What is the most frequent time between stations?

7. Which of the given times are the least frequent?

8. How many data values are recorded in your line plot? How can you tell?

9. Suppose the train travels to each stop today. How many hours will the train travel in all?

10. A store is going out of business and the owner is trying to sell everything in the store. Every week, the prices of all items are cut in half. Jacqueline wants a coat that costs $256 but she has saved only $20. In how many weeks will she be able to buy the coat if it is still in the store?

Use the grid for Exercises 11–21. Name the point represented by the ordered pair.

11. (3, 3)   **12.** (4, 0)   **13.** (4, 5)

14. (5, 1)   **15.** (1, 4)   **16.** (0, 6)

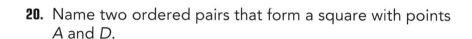

Write the coordinates of the point.

17. D   **18.** E   **19.** G

20. Name two ordered pairs that form a square with points A and D.

21. Jeff starts at point H. He walks north and west to point A. How many units does he walk?

Use the pattern rule. Write the next 3 terms.

22. Begin with 6; add 4.
6, 10, 14, …

23. Begin with 28; subtract 5.
28, 23, 18, …

24. Begin with 1; multiply by 3.
1, 3, 9, …

Use the graph for Exercises 25–27.

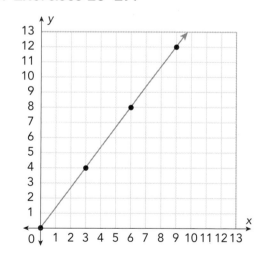

25. The x-coordinates of the plotted points increase by ? . The rule for the x-coordinates is ? .

26. The y-coordinates of the plotted points increase by ? . The rule for the y-coordinates is ? .

27. If this pattern continues, what is the next point that would be plotted on the graph?

Computer programmers use coordinates to code the positions of elements in a video game. Think of the screen of a video game as part of a coordinate plane.

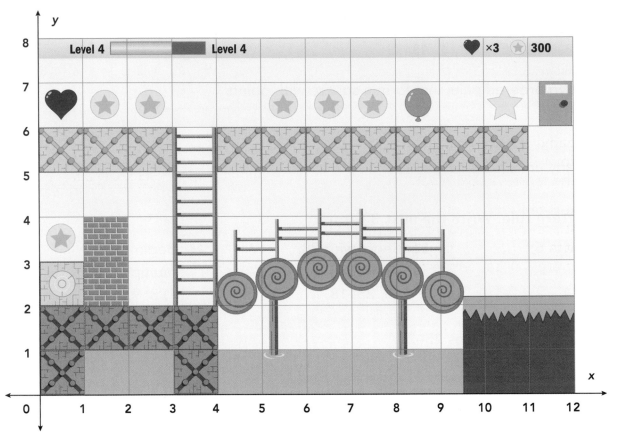

A computer programmer is coding the video game scene shown above. She lays a coordinate grid on top of the video game design. Help the computer programmer identify the coordinates that represent elements and movements of the game.

1. To code the exact position of an element, identify the position of each corner. Copy the table below onto your own paper and then enter the missing information.

	Coordinate Positions			
	Top Left	Top Right	Bottom Left	Bottom Right
Ladder	(3, 6)	(4, 6)	(3, 2)	?
Brick Chimney	(1, 4)	?	?	(2, 2)
Door	(11.25, 7)	(12, 7)	?	?
Water Under Bridge	?	?	?	$\left(\frac{91}{2}, 0\right)$

2. To code a movement on screen, identify the beginning and ending positions of the movement. Each movement begins and ends in the center of a grid square. Copy the table below onto your own paper and then enter the missing information.

	Coordinate Positions	
	Beginning	Ending
Climbing Ladder	(3.5, 2.5)	(3.5, 5.5)
Running from Top of Ladder to Door	(3.5, 6.5)	?
Falling from Door to Grass Below	?	?
Running Across Bridge from Grass	?	?

3. In this game, a player can also move by jumping. The following coordinates represent jumping from the top of the ladder to the door.

x	3.5	5.5	7.5	?	?
y	6.5	6.5	6.5	?	?

   A. What is the rule for the x-coordinates?
   B. What are the last two x-terms in this pattern?
   C. What is the rule for the y-coordinates?
   D. What are the last two y-terms in this pattern?

4. Create your own video game on grid paper. Use a grid with the scales shown.

   A. Draw various elements in grid squares. Your game can have any theme you want but elements may include roads, trees, stars, jewels, and buildings, for example.

   B. Identify the positions of the elements for the computer programmer. Use the four corners of each element to indicate its exact position. Use a table similar to the first table on the previous page to organize your work.

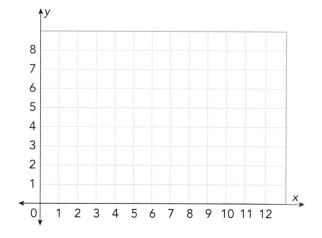

   C. Identify at least three movements for the computer programmer. You will need to indicate each movement's beginning and ending positions. Think of each movement beginning and ending in the center of a grid square. Use a table similar to the first table on this page to organize your work.

5. Think of some video games you've played or research different video games. Describe how coordinate grids and number patterns may have been used to create these video games.

Determine the best answer for each problem.

1. What is the next term in each pattern?

A	1	1.5	2	2.5	?
B	2	6	18	54	?

A. 3 and 54.5
B. 3.5 and 162
C. 3.5 and 108
D. 3 and 162

2. What are the coordinates of point A?

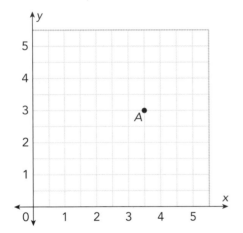

A. (3, 3.5)   **C.** (3.5, 3)
B. (3, 3)   **D.** (3.5, 3.5)

3. A line plot of a data set has 10 Xs. What does this tell about the data set?

A. There are 10 values in the set of data.
B. Each value in the set occurs 10 times.
C. The difference between the greatest and least value in the data set is 10.
D. The greatest value in the data set is 10.

4. What is the 5th term in the pattern?

Rule: Begin with 3; multiply by 2.

3, 6, 12, …

5. Each space on the grid represents $\frac{1}{2}$ mile. Lisa bikes from her house to Kim's house and then back home. How many miles does she bike?

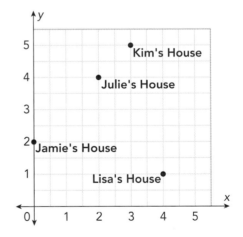

6. How many flowers are 6 inches tall?

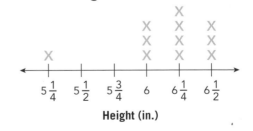

A. 1   **C.** 3
B. 2   **D.** 4

A

acute triangle A triangle with
3 acute angles.

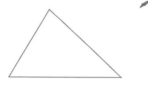

addend A number that is added to
another number or numbers.

algorithm A set of steps used to
perform a mathematical calculation.

analyze To evaluate the details and
make sense of a situation.

area model A way to show
multiplication using a rectangle
where the length and width
represent the factors.

$$\begin{array}{cc} 10 \;+\; 1 \;=\; 11 \\ 12 \begin{array}{|cc|} \hline 132 & 12 \\ -120 & -12 \\ \hline 12 & 0 \\ \hline \end{array} \end{array}$$

array A set of objects arranged in rows
and columns.

Associative Property of Addition
Changing the grouping of the addends
does not change the sum.
$(5 + 6) + 7 = 5 + (6 + 7)$

Associative Property of Multiplication
Changing the grouping of the factors
does not change the product.
$(6 \times 5) \times 2 = 6 \times (5 \times 2)$

axes The horizontal and vertical
number lines that define a coordinate
plane or graph.

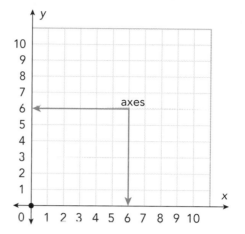

B

bar model A diagram that uses a series
of rectangles to represent the parts and
the whole of a problem.

base The number used as the factor in
an expression with an exponent.

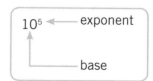

benchmark A value used to help
estimate a calculation for
reasonableness.

benchmark fraction A common
fraction, such as $\frac{1}{4}$, $\frac{1}{2}$, or $\frac{3}{4}$, that you can
use to help compare two fractions.

billion One thousand million.
1 billion = 1,000,000,000

cent An amount equal to $\frac{1}{100}$ of a dollar.

centigram (cg) A unit of metric measure to describe mass that equals $\frac{1}{100}$ gram. 100 cg = 1 g

centiliter (cL) A unit of metric measure to describe capacity that equals $\frac{1}{100}$ liter. 100 cL = 1 L

centimeter (cm) A unit of metric measure to describe length that equals $\frac{1}{100}$ meter. 100 cm = 1 m

cluster A place in a data set where several data points are closer together.

common denominators A shared multiple of the denominators of two or more fractions.

common factor Any number that is a shared factor of two or more numbers.

common multiple A shared nonzero multiple of two or more numbers.
3, 6, 9, 12, 15, 18, …
5, 10, 15, 20, 25, …
15 is a common multiple of 3 and 5.

Commutative Property of Addition Changing the order of addends does not change the sum.
40 + 27 = 27 + 40

Commutative Property of Multiplication Changing the order of factors does not change the product.
3 × 12 = 12 × 3

compare To describe a number as greater than (>), less than (<), or equal to (=) another number.
90 < 900
$2.5 = 2\frac{1}{2}$
7 > 6.9

compatible numbers Numbers that are easy to compute with mentally. For example, you can estimate the quotient 593 ÷ 19 with the compatible numbers 600 and 20. 593 ÷ 19 is about 600 ÷ 20 = 30.

composite figure A shape that can be broken down into smaller shapes.

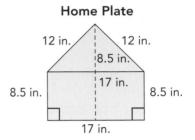

Home Plate

composite number A whole number greater than 1 that has more than two factors.
Examples: 6, 42, 100

cone A solid shape with one curved surface and one flat surface shaped like a circle.

cone

convert To change the units of a measurement without changing its size.

coordinate graph A graph shown on a coordinate plane.

coordinate plane A grid made of two number lines: a horizontal *x*-axis and a vertical *y*-axis.

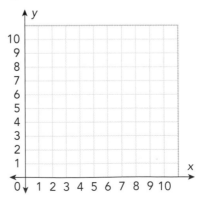

coordinates A pair of numbers used to locate a point on a coordinate plane; the first number tells how far to move horizontally and the second number tells how far to move vertically.

cube A solid shape with 6 flat surfaces all shaped like squares.

cubic centimeter A cube that measures 1 cm on each edge.

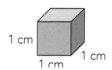

cubic inch A cube that measures 1 inch on each edge.

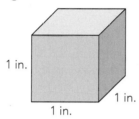

cubic measure The amount of space inside a three-dimensional figure.

cup A unit of measure to describe capacity that equals 8 fluid ounces.

cylinder A solid shape with one curved surface and two flat surfaces shaped like circles.

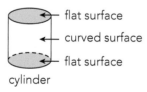
flat surface
curved surface
flat surface
cylinder

decigram (dg) A unit of metric measure to describe mass that equals $\frac{1}{10}$ gram. 10 dg = 1 g

deciliter (dL) A unit of metric measure to describe capacity that equals $\frac{1}{10}$ liter. 10 dL = 1 L

decimal A number in base ten that is written with a decimal point.

decimal point A point used to separate a whole-number part from a decimal part.

decimeter (dm) A unit of metric measure to describe length that equals $\frac{1}{10}$ meter. 10 dm = 1 m

denominator The numeral below the bar in a fraction; it names the total number of equal parts.

$$\frac{1}{3} \longleftarrow \text{denominator}$$

diagram A visual model of a problem or solution.

difference The result of subtracting.

dimension A measure of an object involving distance, such as length, width, or height.

Distributive Property A multiplication fact can be broken apart into the sum of two other multiplication facts.
$3(4 + 5) = (3 \times 4) + (3 \times 5)$

divide To share or separate into equal parts.

dividend The number being divided in a division expression.

divisibility rules Rules that help you decide if one number is divisible by another number.

divisible One number is divisible by another if it can be divided by that number and yield no remainder.

divisor The number by which the dividend is divided.

dollar An amount equal to 100 cents.

dollar sign A symbol ($) used to show an amount in dollars.

E

edge The line segment where two faces of a three-dimensional figure meet.

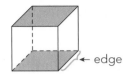

cube (square prism)

equal parts Parts of a whole that are exactly the same size.

equation A number sentence with an equal sign (=) that shows the value on the left side is the same as the value on the right side.
$12.7 + 1.05 = 13.75$

equilateral triangle A triangle with 3 sides that have the same length.

equivalent fractions Fractions that name the same number.
$$\frac{2}{3} = \frac{4}{6} = \frac{10}{15}$$

estimate An approximate answer; to find an answer that is close to the exact answer.

expanded form A form that shows a number written as the sum of the place values of each digit.

exponent A number that tells how many times another number, called the base, is used as a factor.

10^5 ← exponent
└ base

expression A mathematical phrase with operators, variables, and/or numbers.

F

face A flat surface with straight sides on a three-dimensional figure.

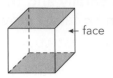

cube (square prism)

factors Two or more numbers that are multiplied to give a product.

factor tree A diagram that breaks down a number into its prime factors.

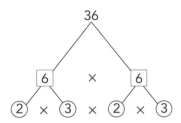

fluid ounce A customary unit of measure to describe capacity that equals $\frac{1}{8}$ of a cup.

foot A customary unit of measure to describe length that equals 12 inches.
1 ft = 12 in.

formula A rule that describes a mathematical relationship between two or more quantities.
$A = \ell \times w$

frequency table A table that lists the number of times each item in a data set appears.

Number of Candles	14	15	16	17	20
Tally	|||	||	||||	||	|
Frequency	3	2	4	2	1

front-end estimation A way of estimating that uses the first digit in each number in a calculation. $456 + 225$ is about equal to $400 + 200$, or 600.

G

gallon A customary unit of measure to describe capacity that equals 4 quarts.

gram (g) A unit of metric measure to describe mass that equals $\frac{1}{1000}$ kilogram.

graph A model of values or data.

greatest common factor (GCF) The greatest number that is a factor of two or more numbers. The GCF of 12 and 8 is 4.

greatest place The place of the first digit of a number.

grouping symbols Symbols that show which parts of an expression to simplify before applying the normal order of operations.

H

hexagon A polygon with 6 sides and 6 angles.

hundredth One part of a whole that is divided into 100 equal parts.
0.03 = 3 hundredths

I

Identity Property of Addition The sum of 0 and a number is the same as that number.
8 + 0 = 8

Identity Property of Multiplication The product of 1 and a number is the same as that number.
5 × 1 = 5

improper fraction A fraction with a numerator that is greater than or equal to its denominator.
Examples: $\frac{5}{5}, \frac{13}{4}$

inch (in.) A customary unit of measure to describe length. 12 in. = 1 ft

interpret To determine the meaning of.

interval The distance between each tick mark on a number line.

isosceles triangle A triangle with two or more sides that are equal in length.

K

kilogram (kg) A unit of metric measure to describe mass that equals 1000 grams. 1 kg = 1000 g

kiloliter (kL) A unit of metric measure to describe capacity that equals 1000 liters. 1 kL = 1000 L

kilometer (km) A unit of metric measure to describe length that equals 1000 meters. 1 km = 1000 m

L

least common denominator (LCD) The least common multiple of the denominators of two or more fractions.

least common multiple (LCM) The least number, except 0, that is a common multiple of two or more numbers. 30 is the LCM of 10 and 15.

line plot A graph that uses X marks on a number line to represent data.

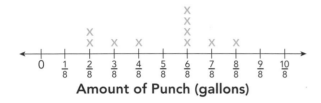
Amount of Punch (gallons)

liter (L) A metric unit of capacity that is about the amount in 4 juice glasses.
1 L = 1000 mL

logical reasoning Using correct thought processes and steps to solve a problem.

M

mass The measure of the amount of matter an object contains.

meter (m) A metric unit of measure that is equal to 100 centimeters.
1 m = 100 cm

metric ton (t) A unit of metric measure to describe mass that equals 1000 kilograms. 1 t = 1000 kg

mile A customary unit of distance;
5280 ft = 1 mi; 1760 yd = 1 mi.

milligram (mg) A unit of metric measure to describe mass that equals $\frac{1}{1000}$ gram. 1000 mg = 1 g

milliliter (mL) A unit of metric measure to describe capacity that equals $\frac{1}{1000}$ liter. 1000 mL = 1 L

millimeter (mm) A unit of metric measure to describe length that equals $\frac{1}{1000}$ meter. 1000 mm = 1 m

minuend A number from which another number is subtracted.

mixed number A number made up of a whole-number part and a fraction part.
Example: $4\frac{1}{2}$

model A diagram or picture that represents a problem or helps to solve a problem.

multiple The product of a given number and any nonzero whole number.

multiplicand A number to be multiplied by another number (the multiplier).

multiplier A number that multiplies another number (the multiplicand).

multiply To calculate a product.

N

net A two-dimensional pattern that folds into a three-dimensional figure.

nonzero digit Any digit from 1 to 9.

number line A line that shows numbers in order using a scale.

numerator The numeral above the bar in a fraction; it names the number of parts being considered.

$$\frac{1}{3} \longleftarrow \text{numerator}$$

O

obtuse triangle A triangle with one obtuse angle.

octagon A polygon with 8 sides and 8 angles.

order of operations The order in which operations in an expression must be performed when more than one operation is involved.

ordered pair A pair of numbers used to locate a point on a coordinate plane; the first number tells how to move horizontally and the second number tells how to move vertically. Example: (3, 7)

organized list A list of all the possible ways to do something, ordered so that you know all possibilities have been listed.

origin The point (0, 0) in a coordinate plane where the axes intersect.

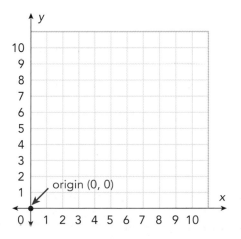

ounce A customary unit of measure to describe weight that equals $\frac{1}{16}$ of a pound.

P

parallelogram A quadrilateral with two pairs of parallel sides.

partial product When multiplying numbers with two or more digits, the product of one factor and a single digit of the other factor; the partial products are added to find the answer.

partial quotient A quotient in which a number less than the dividend is divided by the divisor; the partial quotients are added together to find the answer.

pattern An arrangement of objects or values that follows a rule.

pentagon A polygon with 5 sides and 5 angles.

period A group of three digits set off by commas in a whole number.

pint A customary unit of measure to describe capacity that equals 2 cups.

place value The value of a digit depending on its position, or place, in a number.

plane figure A two-dimensional figure.

polygon A closed plane figure made up of line segments that meet at vertices but do not cross.

polyhedron A solid figure whose faces are polygons.

triangular prism

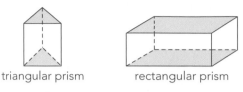
rectangular prism

pentagonal prism

hexagonal prism

square pyramid

rectangular pyramid

triangular pyramid

pentagonal pyramid

hexagonal pyramid

pound A customary unit of measure to describe weight that equals 16 ounces. 1 lb = 16 oz

power of 10 The result of using 10 as a base, or factor, a given number of times.

prime factor Any factor of a number that is also a prime number.

prime factorization A number written as the product of its prime factors.

prime number A whole number greater than 1 that has exactly two factors, itself and 1.

prism A three-dimensional figure that has two polygons as identical parallel bases joined by rectangular faces.

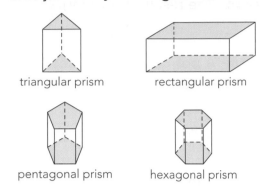
triangular prism

rectangular prism

pentagonal prism

hexagonal prism

product The result of multiplying.

proper fraction A fraction with a numerator that is less than its denominator.

pyramid A solid figure whose base is a polygon and whose faces are triangles with a common vertex.

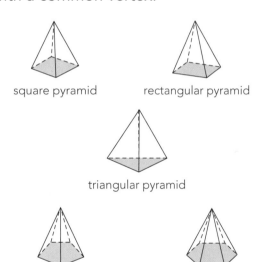
square pyramid

rectangular pyramid

triangular pyramid

pentagonal pyramid

hexagonal pyramid

Q

quadrilateral A polygon with 4 sides and 4 angles.

quart A customary unit of measure to describe capacity that equals 2 pints.

quotient The result of dividing.

R

reasonable An answer that makes logical sense.

reciprocals Two numbers whose product is 1.
Example: $\frac{3}{5}$ and $\frac{5}{3}$

rectangle A parallelogram with 4 right angles.

rectangular prism A prism with identical, rectangular bases.

regroup To rename ten in a place as one in the next greater place, or one in a place as ten in the next lesser place, in order to add or subtract.

regular polygon A polygon with sides of equal length and angles of equal measure.

remainder The number left over after dividing.

rename To write the same value in more than one way.

repeated addition Adding the same value more than once.

represent A way to show the meaning of something by using another expression or symbol.

rhombus A parallelogram with four sides of equal length.

right triangle A triangle with one right angle.

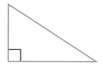

rounding A process that determines which multiple of 10, 100, 1000, and so on a number is closest to.

S

scale (of a graph) A series of numbers at equal intervals along an axis of a graph; also, the relationship between each picture in a picture graph and the number of actual items represented.

scalene triangle A triangle in which no two sides have the same length.

simplest form The form of a fraction where the numerator and denominator have no common factor other than 1.

simplify To replace an expression with its simplest name or form.

solid figure A figure that is three-dimensional.

sphere A curved solid figure made up of points that are all the same distance from a point called the center.

sphere

square A parallelogram with four right angles and four sides of equal length.

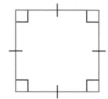

standard form of a number The numeral form of a number.

strategy A plan or method for solving a problem.

subtrahend A number that is being subtracted from another number.

sum The result of adding.

T

table An organized chart of rows and columns.

tenth One part of a whole that is divided into 10 equal parts.

term A particular value in a pattern of numbers.

thousandth One part of a whole that is divided into 1000 equal parts. 0.006 = 6 thousandths

tile To cover a shape using unit squares.

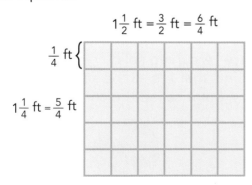

ton (T) A customary unit of measure to describe weight that equals 2000 pounds. 1 T = 2000 lb

trapezoid A quadrilateral with exactly one pair of parallel sides.

triangle A polygon with 3 sides and 3 angles.

U

unit cube A cube that measures 1 unit on each edge.

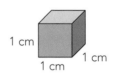

unit fraction A fraction with a numerator of 1.

Example: $\frac{1}{8}$

unit square A square with a side length of 1 unit.

unlike denominators Denominators that are not the same in two or more fractions.

V

Venn diagram A diagram that shows how two or more groups of data are related.

Number of Pizzas: 42

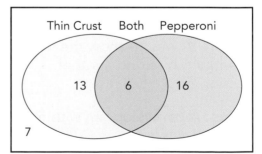

vertex (plural vertices) The common endpoint of two rays in an angle, of two line segments in a polygon, or of three or more edges in a solid figure.

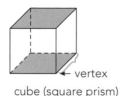

← vertex

cube (square prism)

volume The number of cubic units that a solid figure contains.

W

whole number Any of the numbers 0, 1, 2, 3, 4, ...

work backward A strategy where the answer is known and the unknown is found by reversing the operations or steps in the problem.

X

***x*-axis** The horizontal axis of a coordinate plane.

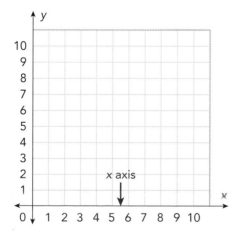

x axis

***x*-coordinate** The first number in an ordered pair that gives the horizontal location of a point on a coordinate plane.

Y

***y*-axis** The vertical axis of a coordinate plane.

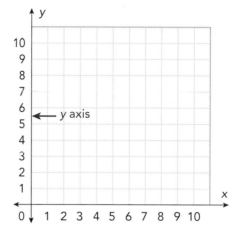

← y axis

***y*-coordinate** The second number in an ordered pair that gives the vertical location of a point on a coordinate plane.

yard (yd) A customary unit of measure to describe length that equals 3 feet. 1 yd = 3 ft

Z

Zero Property of Multiplication The product of 0 and a number is 0.